SAN FRANCISCO

WALKS AND TOURS IN THE GOLDEN GATE CITY

SAN FRANCISCO

RANDOLPH DELEHANTY

Drawings by William Walters

The Foundation for San Francisco's Architectural Heritage

THE DIAL PRESS *NEW YORK*

For Candace Allgaier

Published by
The Dial Press
1 Dag Hammarskjold Plaza
New York, New York 10017

A portion of this book first appeared in *A Victorian Sampler,* published by the Foundation for San Francisco's Architectural Heritage. The opinions expressed herein are those of the author and not necessarily those of Heritage.

The bird's-eye views that illustrate the Financial District, Nob Hill, Chinatown, and Russian Hill tours are details from "A Bird's-Eye Panoramic Map of San Francisco," field-compiled and hand-drawn by John Tomlinson. The full map is available from The Picture Map Company, P.O. Box 141, San Francisco, Calif. 94101.

Design by Paul Chevannes

Manufactured in the United States of America

First printing

Library of Congress Cataloging in Publication Data

Delehanty, Randolph.
San Francisco: walks and tours in the Golden Gate city.

1. San Francisco—Description—Tours. I. Title.
F869.S33D44   917.94'610453   80–14286
ISBN 0–8037–7651–9

Contents

Author's Note

I wish to thank the Bancroft Library at the University of California at Berkeley, the California Historical Society Library, and, especially, the San Francisco History Room of the San Francisco Public Library. Their courteous assistance made my work a pleasure. So many others have been so helpful with this book that I must limit my public thanks to a few individuals and one institution. William M. Roth, Charles Hall Page, and Candace Allgaier were the three indispensable people behind this project. I sincerely thank them. I also wish to thank James Chafee for permission to use four bird's-eye views, the San Francisco Department of City Planning, David R. Simmons, John Schmiedel, Bruce Judd, Jon Nix, and especially William Walters. Heritage—the Foundation for San Francisco's Architectural Heritage: its board, staff, volunteers, and membership, and in particular Linda Jo Fitz—was the fourth essential ingredient in this book. My five years as Heritage's historian in its formative days saw me meet and guide more encouraging people than I can remember and name. This book is my valentine to them all.

San Francisco   Randolph Delehanty
The Feast of St. Francis
October 4, 1979

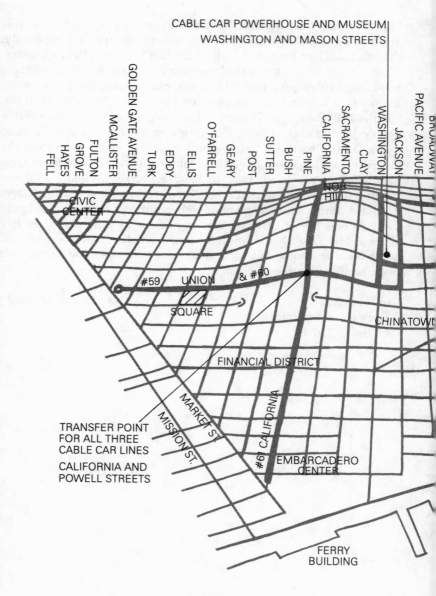

CABLE CAR POWERHOUSE AND MUSEUM
WASHINGTON AND MASON STREETS

GOLDEN GATE AVENUE
MCALLISTER
FULTON
GROVE
HAYES
FELL
TURK
EDDY
ELLIS
O'FARRELL
GEARY
POST
SUTTER
BUSH
PINE
CALIFORNIA
SACRAMENTO
CLAY
WASHINGTON
JACKSON
PACIFIC AVENUE
BROADWAY

CIVIC
CENTER

NOB
HILL

#59   UNION   & #60

SQUARE

CHINATOWN

FINANCIAL DISTRICT

MARKET ST.

MISSION ST.

#6 CALIFORNIA

CALIFORNIA

TRANSFER POINT
FOR ALL THREE
CABLE CAR LINES

CALIFORNIA AND
POWELL STREETS

EMBARCADERO
CENTER

FERRY
BUILDING

Note: Map does not show freeways.

→ⓩ

DOWNTOWN SAN FRANCISCO AND CABLE CAR LINES

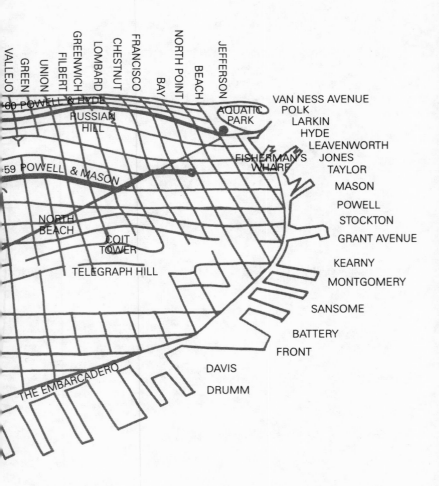

VALLEJO
GREEN
UNION
FILBERT
GREENWICH
LOMBARD
CHESTNUT
FRANCISCO
BAY
NORTH POINT
BEACH
JEFFERSON

60 POWELL & HYDE

RUSSIAN
HILL

AQUATIC
PARK

VAN NESS AVENUE
POLK
LARKIN
HYDE
LEAVENWORTH

FISHERMAN'S
WHARF

JONES
TAYLOR

59 POWELL & MASON

MASON

POWELL

STOCKTON

NORTH
BEACH

GRANT AVENUE

COIT
TOWER

KEARNY

TELEGRAPH HILL

MONTGOMERY

SANSOME

BATTERY

FRONT

THE EMBARCADERO

DAVIS

DRUMM

Randolph Delehanty

Introduction

This guide to San Francisco's historical and architectural treasures includes all the places most people come here to see, plus areas usually overlooked by visitors—and all too often by San Franciscans as well. It serves the needs both of the visitor with only a few days in San Francisco and of the resident interested in thoroughly exploring the past and present of this unique, ever more fascinating city. While it concentrates on the architecture of the city, this book weaves into its narrative something of the history of the people of San Francisco as well. As everyone knows, it is a colorful and dramatic history that has produced one of the world's great cities—a richly varied, compact city of countless hills and valleys, varied microclimates, many cultures, all classes, divergent histories, a city with a distinctive "look" and living architectural tradition.

The best way to use this guide is to read the entire tour before the walk (and, ideally, "San Francisco's Architectural Evolution" before your first walk). You may wish to select only the features of greatest interest. These walks each take about two-and-a-half hours, except for the Mission, all of Fisherman's Wharf, and all of Golden Gate Park, which take about four hours each, or half a day. In addition to well-known places, the visitor ought to explore at least one San Francisco neighborhood. My advice is to choose carefully and to see a few places well rather than too many places too quickly. Take time to savor the still-humane pace of San Francisco. Most important, find the time to sit on a windy hilltop (best at dawn and sunset) and simply gaze on San Francisco and let *it* come to you.

Each tour has a map (some, bird's-eye views) with a number key that is repeated in the heading for each entry. The pen-and-ink drawings were selected to present not just random, individual buildings but important building types characteristic of San Francisco. Taking all or most of the tours presents a mosaiclike picture of the important architectural styles and historical periods in San Francisco's development. Each tour is prefaced by practical information on the best time for the walk, public transit, parking, and a short list of good restaurants. Museums and important publicly accessible interiors are included in the tours. Tour 11 includes great interiors from each of the important surviving architectural periods in the city's history since the late 1890s. The practical information given in the following section should answer most of the travelers' questions.

AREAS OF TOURS

San Francisco Department of City Planning

Practicalities

1. PLANNING WHAT TO SEE

The visitor with only a short time in San Francisco has difficult choices to make in this city of rich variety. Most visitors, unfortunately, don't get beyond the obvious; they (1) ride the cable car, (2) view the city from Coit Tower on Telegraph Hill, (3) poke down Grant Avenue in Chinatown, and (4) eat and shop on Fisherman's Wharf or in Ghirardelli Square. Many also visit the Japanese Tea Garden in Golden Gate Park and historic Mission Dolores.

But there is so much more to San Francisco! The table on page 4 suggests how to get the most out of a three-day visit. The visitor with only a little extra time should visit at least one San Francisco neighborhood—perhaps North Beach, Russian Hill, the Mission district, or the Haight-Ashbury—to see the natives' city.

Included among the walks in this guide are all the places most people come here to see, plus areas usually overlooked by visitors— and all too often by San Franciscans as well. This guide serves the needs both of the visitor with only a few days here and of the San Franciscan interested in thoroughly exploring the past and present of this unique, ever more fascinating city.

2. BEST TIMES FOR THE WALKS

Downtown. The Downtown is best explored on business days during banking hours—from 10:00 A.M. to 3:00 P.M. All commercial buildings are open then. And after three you can ride to the top of the (second) tallest tower in the city for a comprehensive overview. Lunchtime is the best time to people-watch downtown. All the vest-pocket parks and other sitting places fill up with office workers slowly eating their brown-bag lunches. Impeccably dressed businessmen march by on their way to expense-account lunches in dim restaurants. Financial District exterior architecture pure and simple, without the people, is most easily seen on weekends and holidays when the district is deserted and parking is possible anywhere.

Neighborhoods. Sunday from midmorning to midafternoon is the most relaxed yet active time to see residential areas. The neighborhoods are at their stillest and most serene weekdays during school hours. Then the residential streets are only their silent rows of endlessly varied, light-colored, bay-windowed houses climbing up and down the precipitous hills or marching along the relentlessly straight streets.

Special days. Most San Francisco neighborhoods have one weekend during the year, often in the summer, when the local shopping street

A THREE-DAY VISIT IN SAN FRANCISCO

	FIRST DAY	SECOND DAY	THIRD DAY
Morning	espresso in North Beach North Beach and Telegraph Hill (Coit Tower and Panorama)	Golden Gate Park, East Half (Conservatory, Tea Garden, Asian Art Museum)	Ferry to Sausalito *or* Alcatraz
lunch	lunch in North Beach, Chinatown, *or* Downtown	brown bag lunch *or* lunch on Haight Street	lunch in Sausalito, Fisherman's Wharf, *or* Downtown
	Cable Car Powerhouse		
Afternoon	Eastern Pacific Heights (Victorians) *or* Russian Hill	Shopping *or* Haight-Ashbury *or* The Castro and Noe Valley *or* The Mission District *or* Chinatown	Financial District *or* one or two Great Interiors *or* another neighborhood walk
cocktails		cocktails, top of Bank of America	dinner (Palace Garden Court for decor, Vanessi's for the San Franciscans' San Francisco)
dinner	dinner at Ghirardelli Square *or* Fisherman's Wharf	dinner Downtown *or* Chinatown	
Evening	Fisherman's Wharf and Aquatic Park at night *or* Walk the summit of Nob Hill	Theater (see "SF After Dark"), opera, symphony, *or* club *or* Union Street at night	Cable Car ride at night *or* Skyline Vantage Points at night
nightcap	Top of the Mark	Chinatown and North Beach *or* Polk and Castro Streets	Pub-crawling

is closed to automobiles for a festive, low-key street fair. These are always the best times to see the locals. The food sold is nearly always surprisingly good, often "organic," and the crafts, from artisans all over the West Coast, are offered at reasonable prices. But it is the constant parade of determinedly varied people that makes these neighborhood street fairs particularly San Franciscan. Each neighborhood happily celebrates its own special life on its particular day. Be it the drums and dancing lion of Chinatown at Chinese New Year, the Columbus Day carnival in North Beach, or the fantasies on Castro Street on Halloween, San Francisco has many expressive days. The annual Fall Arts Festival in the granitic Civic Center even succeeds in transforming that formidable bureaucratic stage set into a lively, human place. The San Francisco Convention and Visitors Bureau can tell you of such events (phone 391-2000; the area code for all San Francisco numbers is 415).

3. CLIMATE

In even-tempered San Francisco the weather forecast on the morning radio is always the same: "Fair through Wednesday except coastal low clouds extending locally inland night and morning hours. Highs today in the low sixties near the coast and in the seventies inland." People other than meteorologists call the "coastal low clouds" fog. But under the daily almost-sameness of San Francisco's technically Mediterranean climate (long dry summers, short rainy winters) is what turns out to be an always surprising daily experience, especially if one is sensitive to the quick-shifting moods of the changing skies. San Francisco's skies are always special.

San Francisco's climate is unique and usually benign, but only if one is appropriately equipped. Few areas on earth display as many varieties of weather simultaneously as the San Francisco Bay Area. Microclimates within the city itself vary greatly. The downtown, the Mission district, and the east face of Telegraph Hill enjoy more sunshine and good weather than the western (ocean) districts. The Haight-Ashbury and Golden Gate Park chill rapidly when the summer fog blows in from the Pacific after 3:00 P.M.

The irony in San Francisco is that most visitors come during the summer, the grayest time of the year, rather than the fall, winter, and early spring, when San Francisco's skies are their brightest, bluest, and most dramatic, with huge mountain ranges of pure white clouds standing over the bay and unforgettable sunsets. But then each season here has its agreeable atmospheric effects, the all-dissolving summer fogs included.

All first-time visitors are surprised at how chilly San Francisco is, especially in the late afternoon. Most visitors expect all of California to be subtropical, a land of tanned surfers and stringy palm trees. But Northern California is another world; it is decidedly cool. Bright, sunny, but cool; unprepared visitors say cold. A warm, wind-breaking jacket is essential equipment here. (It often warms up considerably around midnight.) The light can also be implacable; sunglasses are useful here the year round. And sensible walking shoes, it goes without saying, are as necessary as snowshoes in the Arctic.

4. MANNERS AND MONEY

Manners. This is, and has been for most of its history, a city with no monolithic majority, but rather, a constantly shifting arrangement of visible and assertive minorities. In San Francisco a long tradition of social diversity has resulted in a widely practiced and genuinely relished tolerance toward—and vast enjoyment in—nearly all the possible permutations of human behavior. San Franciscans have already seen everything. Their silent and cool collaboration as bemused, sophisticated observers makes possible a flourishing variety of peoples and ways on this cramped, sandy peninsula. Though the city's physical space is small, her "social space" is virtually limitless and constantly expanding. San Franciscans are united only in their cherishing of the exotic, the eccentric, the amusing, and the human.

San Franciscans are determinedly non-aggressive, and, while not especially outgoing, are generally civil to one another and are especially understanding of, and kind to, bewildered outlanders lost in their irrigated paradise. The density of population is high but generally agreeable, and tempers are not strained by inhumane congestion or degrading pollution. San Franciscans do not push ahead in queues. Many shops, bars, restaurants, and parks are remarkably calm oases. Salespeople are slow and deliberate. If rushed they will only slow down more. Hard as it is for non-Californians to believe, the often-heard "Have a nice day" is usually sincerely uttered.

Perhaps the even climate soothes people's moods. Casualness and informality characterize Californians in general, and this is to some extent true of San Franciscans, though other Californians see San Franciscans as excessively formal. Manners are increasingly egalitarian in the treatment of men and women; as of 1960 women can stand on the running boards of cable cars.

Money. San Francisco is, and always has been, a rich and expensive city. In the nineteenth century mere pennies did not circulate in gold-and-silver-rich San Francisco. Today San Francisco still has money. It is a financial power on the West Coast and, increasingly, throughout the Pacific basin. It is the home of the largest privately owned bank in the world. It has a great number of very rich people still living inside it, not in the suburbs.

Land is extremely scarce; the buildings are continually appreciating in value; rents are high. Most San Franciscans spend a larger portion of their income on housing than the national average. But then this is only right. One must *choose* to stay in San Francisco; other places are always cheaper. But with his or her high rent the San

Franciscan is inhabiting not just certain rooms but the richly varied city in which they are set.

For the difference between San Francisco and all other large American cities boils down to the fact that in other cities success is invariably defined as moving up and out, while in San Francisco success—no matter how poor one remains—is simply staying here forever. There are other cities, and a very few are almost as beautiful as this one. But there are many who breathe a sigh of relief when they cross those long bridges spanning the majestic bay and come back to their hilly, gleaming city. These are San Franciscans. They have chosen to live here and they invest their city with their proud love. Even the most casual visitor will feel the pervasiveness of this special affection for what everyone here calls "The City."

5. THE APPROACH TO SAN FRANCISCO: PAST AND PRESENT

In the nineteenth century, the transcontinental railroad had its terminus in Oakland, across the bay from San Francisco. Rail passengers transferred to large, white, well-appointed ferries which connected the Oakland mole with the Ferry Building on the Embarcadero at the foot of Market Street. The peninsular city was approached from the water, its low horizon of undulating hills densely covered by the neat cubes of the city. The streets north of Market Street appeared as straight lines that cut from the docks over the hills. Those who arrived by sea debarked in the city along the Embarcadero as well. In those days San Francisco was a major seaport crowded by ships from all nations. Like a small island, San Francisco developed a compact core. Reinforced by the streetcar network, that tight core still flourishes.

Today most visitors reach San Francisco by air. Travelers coming from the east enjoy a quick California geography lesson. After passing over the majestic and forbiddingly high Sierras, the traveler's plane quickly crosses the narrow waist of the enormous Central Valley of California, one of the most productive agricultural regions in the world. The low mountains of the coastal range encircling San Francisco Bay are hardly noticed before the sudden appearance of the multi-colored salt evaporation pans at the shallow south end of the bay. Their brilliant mosaic of unbelievably vivid colors, caused by algae, is quickly followed by the panorama of the hilly, white city with its tight cluster of skyscrapers at the edge of the blue bay. Taking the freeway from the airport south of the city into downtown, the visitor is impressed again with the clean whiteness of San Francisco. Bright green shrubbery bordering the highway waves in welcome, the first appearance of the Californians' and the State of California's love of plants and landscaping. As one passes through the hilly, built-up southern residential areas, a panorama of countless small stucco cubes unfolds. Passing around Potrero Hill the visitor has a sudden view of the contemporary downtown high-rises across the low foreground of the warehouse and light industrial South of Market district. The freeway is elevated over the "backstage" South of Market and connects with the city's streets there. A few long blocks along Sixth Street harbor skid row, then, crossing wide Market Street, one is all at once downtown. The airline bus terminal is in the sleazy and lasciviously named Tenderloin district immediately southwest of Union Square. Most of the city's reasonably priced hotels are in this area. Average hotel costs are between $25 and $45 per day. The Visitors Bureau notes that the average visitor stays for three days and spends at least $75 per day.

6. WHERE TO STAY
Grand Hotels
San Francisco has always been famous for its great hotels. Many are more than hotels; they are civic institutions. The tradition began during the Gold Rush when miners came down from the hills seeking all the earthly comforts absent at the diggings. The historic Palace, the elegant St. Francis, the Fairmont, the Mark Hopkins, and the Huntington are both social and architectural landmarks. The Stanford Court, the Hyatt-Regency with its interior space, and the fine tower of the Hyatt Union Square are recent and worthy additions to the ranks of great hotels.

Years ago, the St. Francis had its own silver dollar polishing machine so that even the mere money it dispensed had a certain éclat. Today the St. Francis dispenses nothing but stiff, fresh banknotes to its patrons. At the Huntington, regular patrons are greeted in the morning with their accustomed newspaper. Tariffs are, of course, commensurate with service.

Downtown:
Clift Hotel, Geary and Taylor, 775-4700
Sir Francis Drake Hotel, Powell and Sutter, 392-7755
Hyatt Union Square, Post and Stockton, 398-1234
Hyatt-Regency, 5 Embarcadero Center, 788-1234
Palace Hotel, Market and New Montgomery, 392-8600
St. Francis Hotel, Powell and Geary, 397-7000

Nob Hill:
Fairmont, Mason and California, 772-5000
Mark Hopkins Hotel, California and Mason, 392-3434
Huntington Hotel, 1075 California Street, 474-5400
Stanford Court, 905 California Street, 989-3500

Good Small Hotels
Somewhere in between luxury and penance there are, or should be, good small hotels for those seeking comfortable accommodations, convenient locations, and careful service. These are, of

course, the hardest kind to find, but San Francisco even has some of these.

Bedford Hotel, 761 Post Street, 673-6040
Bellevue Hotel, 505 Geary, 474-3600
Beresford Hotel, 635 Sutter, 673-9900
Carlton Hotel, 1075 Sutter, 673-0242
El Cortez Hotel, 550 Geary, 775-5000
Elks San Francisco Hotel, 465 Post, 392-6600
Gaylord Hotel, 620 Jones, 673-8445
Lombard Hotel, 1015 Geary, 673-5232
Manx Hotel, Powell and O'Farrell, 421-7070
Hotel Mark Twain, 345 Taylor, 673-2332
Raphael Hotel, 386 Geary, 986-2000
York Hotel, 940 Sutter, 885-6800

Motels
Most San Francisco motels are clustered along "motel row" on Lombard Street and on Van Ness Avenue.

Bed-and-Breakfast Inns
The most welcome recent development in San Francisco accommodations are the bed-and-breakfast inns. Most are very small and lodged in older buildings in the city's neighborhoods. You must book well in advance. All are delightful and get the visitor closer to the residential city than the large downtown hotels or faceless anywhere motels.

Bed and Breakfast Inn, 4 Charlton Court (Union Street), SF 94123, 921-9784
Jackson Court, 2198 Jackson at Buchanan (Pacific Heights), SF 94115, 931-6406
The Mansion, 2220 Sacramento (Pacific Heights), SF 94109, 929-9444
Obrero Hotel, 1208 Stockton (Chinatown), SF 94133, 986-9850
The Red Victorian, 1665 Haight Street (Haight-Ashbury), SF 94117, 864-1978
Union Street Inn, 2229 Union Street, SF 94123, 346-0424
Washington Square Inn, 1660 Stockton (North Beach), SF 94133, 981-4220

Recreational Vehicles
The San Francisco Recreational Vehicle Park has 200 sites. It is south of Market Street near the Southern Pacific Depot, between Third and Fourth Streets, Townsend and King. Advance reservations advised: 250 King Street, SF 94107, 986-8730.

Campgrounds and Hostels

There are no campgrounds inside San Francisco. The American Youth Hostel is in Building 240 at Fort Mason, two blocks inside the Franklin and Bay Street entrance. Mailing address: American Youth Hostel, Fort Mason, Building 240, SF 94123, 771-4646

7. GETTING AROUND

San Francisco is crisscrossed by streetcar, bus, trolley-bus, and cable-car lines. For information in the city, phone 763-MUNI. The city publishes a free map of the municipal railway system, but it is not widely available. Try the information desk at City Hall or the Cable Car Barn at Washington and Mason for a copy. There is also a commercial transit system map of San Francisco for sale at some newsstands. The tours in this book have suggestions for getting from the Union Square–downtown area to the starting point of the tour, and back from the end.

BART (Bay Area Rapid Transit)

BART is a seventy-one-mile-long rail system with tunnel, elevated, surface, and transbay tube routes. It links downtown San Francisco with Alameda (Oakland) and Contra Costa Counties. The system cost $2.3 billion to build and opened in 1974. An extra half-percent sales tax in three counties helps pay for the system. San Mateo County, south of the city, where the airport is located, refused to join BART, making it of much less use to the traveler than it might have been. The system has thirty-four stations and serves some 135,000 passengers a day.

Fares on BART vary according to the distance between the start and end of your ride. You can ride the entire system for the cost of the fare between two successive stations. Consult the fare map at the station where you enter and buy a ticket for the next station at the automatic vending machine. Once inside the electronic gate you can ride the entire system, stopping at as many stations as you wish. Just be sure to exit from the station for which you bought the ticket. Most of the stations across the bay are above ground and have interesting panoramic views. Ask the attendant in the glass booth at any station for a BART map, and, if they have it, a Regional Transit Guide. For BART information phone 788-BART.

Ferries

Ferry service was resumed on the bay in 1969. The Golden Gate Ferry operates from the Ferry Building at the foot of Market Street to Sausalito and Larkspur in Marin County, north of the Golden Gate. The view of the city from the bay is memorable. This was the way the city was approached by most visitors before the completion of the two great bridges in the late 1930s. The ferries operate from about 6:00 A.M. to 8:00 P.M. daily. There is a third ferry line to Tiburon, also in Marin. During peak commute periods the Tiburon ferry departs from the Ferry Building; at other times the Tiburon ferry departs from Pier 43½ at Fisherman's Wharf. Free transfers obtainable aboard the boat allow Sausalito ferry patrons to go by the #10 bus from Sausalito, around Richardson Bay, to Tiburon. From there the Tiburon ferry provides transportation back to San Francisco. For Golden Gate Ferry information phone 332-6600. For the Tiburon ferry (Red and White Fleet) phone 398-1141. The Red and White Fleet also operates between Fisherman's Wharf and Angel Island during the summer, and on weekends and holidays during the winter. The Metropolitan Transportation Commission (mailing address: Hotel Claremont, Berkeley, Calif. 94705) publishes an excellent free regional transit guide to the Bay Area sometimes available at the Trans-Bay Terminal at Mission and First Street, or at BART stations.

Cable Cars

Every visitor will want to see and ride the cable cars. The turntables at Powell and Market, and at Victorian Park and Fisherman's Wharf are often swamped with people. The California Street line is the least congested, if not as scenic as the Hyde Street lines. The best place both to catch a cable car and understand how they run is to take a taxi to the Cable Car Powerhouse and Museum at Washington and Mason Streets (see Tour 7). Cable-car stops are indicated by yellow bars painted across the tracks and white boxes painted near the tracks, not always easy to find.

The first Baedeker to the United States described San Francisco's famous cable cars in 1893 as "crawling up the steep inclines like flies on a window-pane." Today, ten and a half miles of cable railroads survive in San Francisco; some forty cars serve three lines with a central powerhouse. The three lines are:

#59 Powell and Mason Line: Market and Powell turntable, to Union Square, over Nob and Russian Hills, then to Bay Street near Fisherman's Wharf.

#60 Powell and Hyde Line: Market and Powell turntable, to Union Square, over Nob and Russian Hills, then to the turntable in Victorian Park near Ghirardelli Square

#61 California Street Line: California and Market (at Hyatt Regency Hotel), via California Street through the Financial District, over Nob Hill, and down to Polk Street and Van Ness Avenue.

All lines cross at Powell and California, where free transfers can be made if you're continuing in one general direction.

Remember, the way to win a San Franciscan's heart is never to call them "trolleys."

Taxis

The visitor with only a short stay in the city should plan to use taxis to get the most out of his time. With pay telephones and radio-dispatched taxis the city can be very efficiently explored. And, although San Francisco has perhaps the highest taxi fares in the country, the compactness of the city and the relative lack of auto congestion means that two or three dollars will take you to most of the frequented parts of the city.

De Soto Cab Co.: 673-1414
Luxor Cab Co.: 552-4040
Veteran's Taxicab Co.: 552-1300
Yellow Cab Co.: 626-2345

8. PARKING ON HILLS

It is unlawful to park any vehicle on any grade exceeding 3 percent (a rise of 3 feet in 100 feet) without setting the brakes and blocking the wheels by turning them against the curb. When parking downhill the front wheels must be "toed" or turned in so that a tire is against the curb. When parking uphill the front wheels must be "heeled" or turned out so that a tire is resting against the curb. The emergency brake must always be set. It is also recommended that the gear shift lever be placed in low gear when headed uphill and in reverse when headed downhill.

9. SHOPPING

San Francisco has historically been a great shopper's city, particularly for luxury goods. In addition to American and European goods, foods, and wines, San Francisco has traditionally been the port of entry for teas, silks, spices, and art goods from China and Japan. And, ever since the late 1890s and the influence of the arts-and-crafts movement, California has had a strong artist-craftsman tradition in pottery, metal, glass, wood, and jewelry. Photography is also an art with important Northern California traditions, because of the fine light here.

Generally speaking, San Francisco's best shopping is on east-west streets along old streetcar routes. The shops are usually on the ground floor of two- to six-story buildings with apartments above. The shops are usually uninterrupted; parks, churches, schools, and other noncommercial uses—and today, parking facilities—rarely break the continuous rows of plate-glass shop windows. Shops are often only 25 feet wide and 100 feet deep, the size of the old Victorian house lots that were assembled at the turn of the century for the larger commercial-residential buildings that replaced them. Many shops have indented vestibules and canvas awnings that "absorb" the shopper walking past. There is a happy absence of steel shutters and grates. Boxed trees along the sidewalk complete this ideal browser's environment.

Each shopping street in San Francisco, while generally similar in configuration, is distinct and often has its own specialization. The best way to shop in San Francisco is to pick a street with what you want, and, starting anywhere on one side, walk its full length to where shops abruptly stop, cross the street, walk back up the other side to the other end, cross again, and return to where you started. This circular route is surprisingly agreeable and is the automatic way the crowds move. Along the way, everyone is bound to find something that will arouse intense covetousness and probable purchase.

A Few Special Shops

Asian Art Goods:
G.T. Marsh and Company, 522 Sutter Street, the oldest Asian art gallery in San Francisco.
Gump's, 250 Post, near Union Square, top floor.

California Arts and Crafts:
Contemporary Artisans, 530 Bush Street, near Grant.
Family and Friends, Ghirardelli Square, corner of Polk and North Point.

Photography:
Focus Gallery, 2146 Union Street, an institution in San Francisco, on the top floor of a typical turn-of-the-century Edwardian shops-and-flats building.

Art Galleries:
See the *Guide to Exhibitions of Art,* a monthly free pamphlet available in most art galleries that lists the exhibitions in fine arts galleries and regional art museums.

Shopping Streets

In descending order of expense, but by no means of interest, here is a select list of San Francisco shopping streets briefly characterized:

Union Square area:
The best department stores in the city cluster around Union Square; Magnin's and Saks are here as well as Macy's, a local favorite.

Union Square itself, 2 3/5 acres, one full city block, both is and is not the center of San Francisco. As an area of department stores, specialty shops, and hotels, the streets around the square are the center of both the visitors' and the residents' city. Smartly dressed San Franciscans march by the square, or park underneath it, every day. For an hour at lunchtime the square is a lively, social place filled with young workers from the surrounding stores. But except for that hour, San Franciscans rarely enter the square. In fact, most white-gloved ladies shopping downtown will use the sidewalks across the street from the square, walking a two-block "L" rather than cutting diagonally through the square. The center of the square is left to poorer San Franciscans, many old and alone, who sun themselves there in the late morning and early afternoon. West of the square is the most densely populated, and one of the poorest, parts of San Francisco.

The present park is in reality the slanted and landscaped roof of a four-level underground parking garage designed by Timothy Pflueger and built in 1942. It was the first such garage in the United States and has been important in keeping San Francisco's retail core alive. When it first opened, it offered valet parking; shoppers could call for their cars at the entrances to smart shops.

The 1847 O'Farrell plan for San Francisco provided only the stingiest number of small parks in its grid. Union Square, the principal downtown park, was a donation of Mayor John White Geary (pronounced "GEER-y"), the first American mayor and postmaster in San Francisco. Geary Street on the square's south side is named for him. He subsequently became governor of Kansas, and later of Pennsylvania. He was a real estate speculator and expected his enlightened donation to increase the attractiveness and value of land he owned in what was then an area well south of the Downtown. The name Union Square is said to come from the 1860s when this park was the scene of mass rallies organized in support of the Union cause. The square today, with an almost invisible stage at its west end, is still the favorite site for downtown political rallies and civic demonstrations.

To the west and north of the square is the downtown luxury hotel district. To the north, along Post and Sutter Streets, on the southern slope of Nob Hill, cluster San Francisco's famous private clubs, all housed in imposing structures. On Geary Street, in the block between Mason and Taylor Streets, is San Francisco's legitimate theater district. To the east of the square, along the 200 block of Post Street, is the heart of the luxury shopping district. Maiden Lane, with Frank Lloyd Wright's former V.C. Morris Store (see Great Interiors), is the narrow alley that leads from the east side of the square. The buildings on that side are capped by airline billboards that blink the names of the world's principal cities. The south side of the square is the focal point for the city's major department stores.

Commanding the west side of the square, and its architectural center of gravity, is the grand Hotel St. Francis built in 1904 before the fire and designed by Bliss and Faville. It was rebuilt in 1907 and expanded in 1913. The gray-green Colusa sandstone façade and green copper cornice, one of the most elaborate in the city, have an assured dignity. The lobby, carpeted internal "street" of shops, Borgia Room, and English Grill survive in all their restrained Edwardian splendor. In 1972, a 32-story tower addition was built behind the hotel. It was designed by William Pereira Associates and features the fastest—much too fast—exterior elevators in the city. The top of the tower is finished with a wide, bronze-colored cornice echoing that of the old building. When foreign dignitaries are staying at the St. Francis the appropriate flag is displayed over the Powell Street entrance.

In the late nineteenth century Union Square was surrounded by the churches of several of the city's principal Protestant congregations, and, on Sutter Street, the oldest Jewish temple. The park then was simply landscaped with a circle of benches at the center. In 1902, as the United States entered her expansionist age, an imperial trophy was erected in the center of the square commemorating Admiral Dewey's victory at Manila Bay in the Philippines in 1898. The granite Corinthian column, designed by Newton Tharp, supports a bronze figure of Victory bearing a trident and a wreath, sculpted by Robert Aitken. The monument was built by public subscription and epitomizes the confidence of the dawn of America's Pacific empire. But alas, Victory seems to be heading for the raffish Tenderloin. The column did not topple in the earthquake of 1906.

The southwest corner of the square, where Geary and Powell Streets cross, is the city's vortex. To this one crossroad is drawn a wider variety of humanity than to any other spot in the city. Geary is the principal corridor connecting the western, middle-class districts with the Downtown. At Union Square—a sharp frontier between the very rich and the very poor—native and visitor, shopper, tourist, and transient, the complete parade of human conditions passes by.

The three blocks of Powell Street, from Union Square to Market Street and the cable-car turntable, slope gently downhill. It is a lively, democratic street all built about 1907–1915 and designed to entice the pedestrian with wares, mostly souvenirs. With its cable cars, old neon signs, hotel marquees, and continuous distractions it is a perfect piece of the Edwardian downtown. The Powell Street cable-car turntable is a frantic spot. News vendors, street musicians, and soapbox preachers appeal to the indifferent flood of passersby. Patient visitors wait to board the cable cars to Fisherman's Wharf. In the lower level of nearby sunken Hallidie Plaza is the Visitors Information Center where a good free map of the city can be obtained. This not-too-useful open space was designed by Mario Ciampi, Lawrence Halprin and Associates, and John Carl Warnecke and Associates as part of the Market Street Beautification Project of 1971–78. An entrance to BART and the city streetcar lines is located here.

200 Block of Post Street:
This is ground zero for luxury shopping. Surrounding venerable Gump's, with its fine Asian art on the top floor, is a string of shops with internationally known names, from Dunhill's to Gucci. Fine

household goods, china, linen, glass, jewelry, and well-tailored women's fashions cluster here, on the nearby block of Grant, and around into Maiden Lane.

300 Block of Sutter:
Here, between the Financial District and the private men's clubs, are the finest men's stores in this city of well-dressed lawyers and bankers. Shop interiors are often striking examples of the latest architectural trends. There are both shrines to traditional American business attire, and, increasingly, modish European, especially Italian styles. Here the priests of the bureaucratic mysteries acquire their robes.

Jackson Square:
Roughly the blocks bounded by Washington and Battery Streets and Pacific and Columbus Avenues, embracing the red-brick, prefire Jackson Square Historic District. Fine antique shops, art galleries, and to-the-trade-only fabric and furniture wholesalers. Pleasant, tree-lined nineteenth-century streets with windows full of treasures, especially antique English furniture, fine American fabrics, and Asian art. A veritable sidewalk museum of furnishings and design; especially attractive at night when the lights in the shops give a domestic glow to the costly treasures.

Upper Sacramento Street, Fillmore to Presidio Avenue:
Without doubt the most genteel shopping street in San Francisco. Small specialty shops and many antique stores with distinct characters. A delight at Christmastime with strings of tiny white lights outlining each window. The once-a-year Christmas Store with its milky way of shiny Christmas ornaments from all over the world makes everyone a child again.

Union Street, from Gough to Steiner:
Perhaps the most phenomenal transformation in San Francisco retailing of the recent past. This formerly ordinary neighborhood shopping strip sandwiched between wealthy Pacific Heights and the well-to-do Marina district has become one of the poshest boutique and restaurant-bar streets in the nation. Thriving business has sprouted tiny shops in alleys, backyards, and basements, creating a street of satisfying adventure and complexity. Old and new architecture blend with the continual reworking of older buildings to make a collage of styles never quite the same twice. Quality shops, excellent neighborhood stores, many restaurants, and several of the city's most popular singles bars keep the street alive from about 11:00 A.M. to 2:00 A.M.

Ghirardelli Square and The Cannery:
See Tour 12.

Castro Street and 2300 Block of Market Street:
Along the south side of this block of upper Market Street is a string of shops displaying the latest in revivals—furniture and accessories

of a determinedly modern persuasion. Sleek objects from the 1930s to the 1950s provide a history of futuristic design. On Castro and the two flanking blocks of Eighteenth Street are men's clothing stores that continue the tradition of consciously masculine dress that began when Eastern-born miners of the Gold Rush eagerly adopted Western duds. No need to be reminded here that San Francisco is the birthplace of the denim jean.

Polk Street:
Polk Street is one of San Francisco's few north-south shopping streets, and began by serving the carriage trade of Nob and Russian Hills and the mansions that once lined Van Ness Avenue. Stretching from Geary to about Lombard Street, Polk's shopping district is divided into two distinct parts by Broadway. Lower Polk near Russian Hill is quiet and low-key. Upper Polk, from Broadway to Geary, is as notable for its sidewalk parade as for its trendy shops. Freed, Teller, and Freed's coffee, tea, and spice shop is a veritable museum of legal addictions. Swan's Oyster Depot serves the finest cold seafood in San Francisco. Chicken Little's Museum of Modern Retail is always au courant and amusing.

Columbus Avenue and Vallejo Street:
Columbus Avenue in North Beach, from about Washington Square to Vallejo, and Vallejo Street, from Columbus to Powell, shelter several old-time Italian-American businesses and more and more new Chinese-American stores. The specialties here are food, both imported delicacies and the freshest fish and vegetables. Not a fashionable area, but one with unmistakably San Franciscan cultural crosscurrents.

Haight Street, Masonic Avenue to Stanyan Street:
After a disastrous interlude following the hippie period, the Haight Street strip has blossomed into an amalgam of the hip and the artistic. The near-to-antique stores of the cheap-rent early 1970s have been steadily replaced with specialty shops, particularly a few fine shops selling hand-made and costly arts and crafts, including furniture. Somewhat scruffy at the edges, but well worth exploring.

Grant Avenue/Chinatown:
Grant Avenue, from California to Columbus, is an unbroken string of trinket shops and restaurants. Do not expect quality, only a bewildering variety in souvenirs of San Francisco made everywhere but here. Along with rubber snakes and other items best called "curios" are flashy Japanese space toys that marry science fiction with toy racing cars.

Jefferson Street and Fisherman's Wharf:
Postcards, T-shirts, and similar essentials fill the high-volume shops along this visitor-favored strip.

10. MUSEUMS
Art Museums
Asian Art Museum/Avery Brundage Collection
(See De Young Museum)

California Palace of the Legion of Honor
Lincoln Park
George A. Applegarth, 1924
Modeled after the Palais de la Legion d'Honneur in Paris and set on a dramatic site with views of the Golden Gate and the city. An all-French collection with some fine period rooms and a large Rodin collection.
(Fee) 10–5 daily. 558-2881

M.H. De Young Memorial Museum
Music Concourse, Golden Gate Park. See Tour 9.
The city's most diversified art museum. The fine Asian Art Museum is in the west wing.
(Fee) 10–5 daily. 558-2887

San Francisco Museum of Modern Art
Van Ness Avenue, Civic Center
Brown and Landsburg, 1932; interior remodeled by Robinson and Mills, 1972.
(Fee) Tuesday–Friday, 10–10; Saturday–Sunday, 10–5.

Historical and House Museums
African-American Historical Society
680 McAllister, near Van Ness
Phone for hours. 864-1010

Alcatraz Island
See Tour 12.
Pier 43. 546-2805

American Indian Historical Society
1451 Masonic Avenue, near Frederick
Phone for hours. 626-5235

Balclutha (1886 square-rigger)
See Tour 12.
Pier 43. 982-1886

Cable Car Barn and Museum
Washington and Mason Streets. See Tour 7.
(Free) 10–6 daily except major holidays. 474-1887

California Historical Society/Whittier Mansion
2090 Jackson, at Laguna. See Tour 3.
($1) Wednesday, Saturday, and Sunday, 1–5. 567-1848

Chinese Historical Society of America
17 Adler Place, between Grant and Columbus. See Tour 6. 391-1188

Fort Point National Historic Site
Presidio of San Francisco, under the Golden Gate Bridge, reached by
Lincoln Boulevard and Long Avenue.
A rare, red-brick coastal fort built between 1853 and 1861 to accom-
modate 120 cannon mounts.
(Free) 10–5 daily except Christmas. 556-1693

Haas-Lilienthal House/Heritage
2007 Franklin, near Jackson. See Tour 3.
441-3004

Hyde Street Pier Historic Ships
Foot of Hyde Street, at Jefferson
See Tour 12. 556-6435

The Mexican Museum
1855 Folsom Street (at 15th Street)
Phone for hours. 621-1224

Mission Dolores and Museum
Dolores Street at Sixteenth Street. See Tour 4.
(25¢) May–October, 9–5; November–April, 10–4.

Museo Italo-Americano
512 Union Street
Phone for hours. 788-9266

Museum of Russian Culture
2450 Sutter Street
Phone for hours. 921-7631

Museum of the Money of the American West
400 California Street, at Sansome. See Tour 2.

National Maritime Museum
Foot of Polk Street. See Tour 12.
556-8177

North Beach Museum
1453 Stockton Street, near Columbus. See Tour 1.
Open banking hours. 391-6210

Oakland Museum
1000 Oak Street, near Lake Merritt, Oakland
Kevin Roche, John Dinkeloo and Associates, 1969
Perhaps the finest history museum in the state; also California art and
natural history. Housed in what looks like a hanging garden; one of
the finest modern buildings in the region. Easily reached by Bay Area
Rapid Transit; exit at the Lake Merritt station. Until San Francisco

builds its own much-needed city history museum, this is the best place to get an historical introduction to the Bay Area.
(Free) Tuesday–Sunday, 10–5. 273-3000

Octagon House / Colonial Dames of America
2645 Gough Street, at Union. See Tour 3.
885-9796

Old Mint
Fifth and Mission Streets
Alfred B. Mullett, 1870–73
The "Granite Lady" survived the earthquake and fire and was restored as a monetary museum in 1973. Much of the silver from the Comstock Lode was coined here. Fine monumental interiors and interesting exhibits.
(Free) Tuesday–Saturday, 10–5 except major holidays. 556-3630

Palace of Fine Arts
(See Exploratorium p. 21)

Presidio Army Museum
Presidio of San Francisco, Lincoln Boulevard and Funston Avenue
The old Station Hospital, built in 1857, now a unique historical building type in San Francisco, converted into a fascinating military museum.
(Free) Tuesday–Sunday, 10–4 except major holidays. 561-4115

San Francisco Fire Department Museum
655 Presidio Avenue, at Bush Street
A collection of equipment and memorabilia. If closed, ring the bell of the firehouse next door.
(Free) Thursday–Sunday, 1–5. 861-8000 ext. 210

San Francisco History Room
Main Library, Civic Center, third floor
George Kelham, 1917.
A research library with fascinating changing exhibits of choice San Franciscana.
(Free) Tuesday–Saturday, 9–6; except Wednesday, 1–6.

Society of California Pioneers
456 McAllister, near Polk Street, Civic Center
Across from City Hall is this collection concentrating on California history before 1869.
(Free) Monday–Friday, 10–4. Closed holidays and July and August.
861-5278

Wells Fargo History Room
420 Montgomery, near California. See Tour 2.
Open banking hours. 396-2649

Wine Museum
633 Beach Street, near Columbus Avenue. See Tour 12.
673-6990

Scientific Museums
California Academy of Sciences
Music Concourse, Golden Gate Park
Exhibits on natural history, an aquarium, and a planetarium.
See Tour 9. 221-4214

Exploratorium/Palace of Fine Arts
Marina Boulevard and Lyon Street
Installed in the semicircular hall that is part of Maybeck's 1915 Palace
of Fine Arts, built for the Panama-Pacific International Exposition,
this is a museum concerned with perception. See Tour 3.
(Fee) Wednesday–Sunday, 1–5 except major holidays. 563-3200

Fleishhacker Zoological Gardens
Foot of Great Highway, at Sloat and Skyline Boulevards
A zoological garden begun in 1929.
(Fee) 9–5:30 daily. 661-4844

State Mineral Exhibit
Ferry Building, foot of Market Street, second floor
An old-fashioned mineral museum established by the California Di-
vision of Mines and Geology in 1880.
(Free) Monday–Friday, 8–5. 557-0633

11. SAN FRANCISCO AFTER DARK
The Sunday newspaper's "pink section" has the best listing of
entertainment in the city. Opera, dance, and music find appreciative
audiences in San Francisco, as does the resident American Conservatory Theater. There are also clubs and cabarets to suit all tastes. The
Great American Music Hall at 859 O'Farrell, near Larkin, often has
fine popular singers and musicians in a congenial setting.
Broadway in North Beach introduced the topless bar in 1964 but
has seen better days. Union Street, between the Marina and Pacific
Heights, has the best-known singles bars. Castro, Polk, and Folsom
Streets attract gay men. Women's bars are scattered and not clustered.
The best theater in San Francisco is the sidewalks just about any
time you pay attention.

12. MAPS, GUIDES, AND VISITORS BUREAUS
There are two good map stores in downtown San Francisco: Rand
McNally on Market Street at Third, and Thomas Brothers Maps at
550 Jackson Street, near Columbus Avenue. What maps and bird's-
eye views are available can be found here.

Recommended guides for walks in San Francisco are:
Heritage Walks, conducted by the Foundation for San Francisco's
Architectural Heritage. 441-3046
City Guides, conducted by the San Francisco Library History Room.
558-3981

The San Francisco Visitor Information Center is located in the
lower level of Hallidie Plaza, on Market Street at the foot of Powell
Street, near the cable-car turntable. A daily-events information tape
can be heard by phoning 391-2000. The mailing address of the San
Francisco Convention and Visitors Bureau for specific information is
1390 Market Street, San Francisco 94102.

13. SKYLINE VANTAGE POINTS
Before the mid-1960s, San Francisco's skyline was dominated by
its undulating hills. The Downtown skyscrapers clustered along
Montgomery Street; the Fairmont Hotel and the Telephone Building
on New Montgomery were the only major accents on the landscape.
But the high-rise boom that began in the 1960s and has continued
to the present has created a totally new dimension in Bay Area
landforms: the man-made "hill" of tightly clustered high-rises is
almost as high as Twin Peaks.

View from Treasure Island
On a November or December day, when sunset comes early and
end-of-the-year work keeps office lights burning, San Francisco's
new Downtown appears as a gigantic, multifaceted light sculpture set
against a blue-black velvet sky. The Transamerica Pyramid accents
the skyline like a giant Christmas tree. The front-row seat from
which to enjoy this billion-dollar twentieth-century, quintessen-
tially American show is the west side of Treasure Island in the middle
of the bay. From there the honeycomb of light stands reflected in the
water. As the sky darkens behind the city, the lights become more
intense and the glass boxes glitter like jewels.

View from Twin Peaks
Many visitors drive to the top of Twin Peaks (South peak, 910
feet; North peak, 904 feet) to look down on the city at night. This
view from the west looks straight down Jasper O'Farrell's Market
Street boulevard, recently relighted with harsh orange streetlights.

View from Sausalito
The most attractive daytime view of San Francisco is from Bridge-
way in Sausalito north of the city. From there the old, low-rise,
fine-scale pattern of San Francisco's white stucco buildings and the
rigid street grid cast over the ridge of Pacific Heights and Russian and
Telegraph Hills screen most of the Downtown buildings. But the

tallest high-rises pop up over the old city, emphasizing the radical change of scale of twentieth-century buildings.

View from Berkeley

The Northside Berkeley hills are set like box seats in the amphitheater of the Bay Area, directly across from the Golden Gate. The views from the Berkeley Municipal Rose Garden and from the road leading up the canyon behind the University of California campus provide unforgettable panoramas of San Francisco across the blue bay. Also fine on a clear night.

Timeline of office building types in San Francisco from 1850 to the present.

William Walters

San Francisco's Architectural Evolution

EARLY HISTORY

San Francisco is the successor of three points of settlement: a battery, the Presidio, set up on the Golden Gate by the Spanish army in 1776; a Franciscan mission founded in a sheltered valley on October 8, 1776; and a trading post established by a secure anchorage at Yerba Buena Cove in 1835. The fort and Mission were Spanish establishments; the trading post was British and American in population, though founded under Mexican sovereignty.

When Mexico declared her independence from Spain, Alta California became part of the new nation. In 1835 Mexico secularized the missions, and parceled out huge ranches. The settlement around the mission church quickly vanished. The Presidio continued as a rudimentary military installation, more a legal claim than a potent fortress. But the trading settlement took root at the cove.

Yerba Buena Cove—named after a wild mint *(Micromeria douglasii)* that grew here—was the anchorage closest to the Presidio, the commanding center of governmental authority. The cove's sandy bottom provided a secure anchorage, and it gave shelter from the swift bay currents. It began to attract merchant ships that came to the great bay to buy the hides and tallow produced on the sprawling cattle ranches around the bay. The thriving hide trade attracted the first permanent settlers to Yerba Buena Cove, the traders who acted as brokers between the merchant ships from New England and the local Mexican ranches.

The tiny seaport was, from the very first, an international settlement. In 1835 a trader named Richardson scratched out the *calle de la fundación* (present-day Grant Avenue, between Clay and Washington, now in Chinatown) one block from the cove. The rude path connected the trails of the Presidio in the north and the Mission in the south.

In 1837 the settlement along the cove was platted out as a small town, using the plaza-and-gridiron pattern traditional in Spanish and Mexican colonial towns. A Swiss navigator named Jean Vioget, the only man who had the necessary surveying instruments, was officially commissioned by the Mexican governor at Monterey to lay out the town. This earliest grid was peculiar in that the blocks were not square, but rather 2½ degrees off. (This was later corrected.)

In July 1846, the United States occupied California and the American flag was raised over the sandy Plaza in the village of Yerba Buena. The great bay became the base of the U.S. Navy and the point from which America penetrated the Pacific. In July 1847, the settlement of Yerba Buena renamed itself San Francisco after the great bay familiar to mariners around the globe.

When "manifest destiny" drew the young United States from the Atlantic to the Pacific, great changes were in store. The American drive for a Pacific empire was both vigorous and thorough. Not all the works of the Native Americans, Spaniards, and Mexicans put together would equal in impact a single decade of American expansion.

In the decade before the Gold Rush in 1849, Yerba Buena was a sleepy little settlement of some five hundred very assorted souls. After the Gold Rush the *Annals of San Francisco* exclaimed,

> to see nations, come to San Francisco! You meet a Spaniard in a wide hat, an Italian with ink in his hair, a correlative of frogs and *soupe-maigre,* all in a minute. A California Indian in still shoes, a moon-faced Mexican in partial eclipse and a sort of African by brevet, a Russian with a square chin and a furry look, all in three squares. You elbow South Americans, Australians, New Zealanders. You accost a man who was born in Brazil, who hails from Good Hope, who trades in Honolulu. One of the great Chinese merchants with an easy gait, an erect head and a boyish face, is coming around the corner. A man from Calcutta is behind you. "An Israelite in whom is no guile" is before you. The Scotchman is here with the high cheek bones, the blue eyes, and the cutty-pipe and a word from Bobby Burns in his mouth. The Dutch have taken us, and the Irish, do they not "thravel the round wurrld"? Of course, New-England is here, and New York and the South. They are *every*where, but show us your Colombians and Peruvians and Sea-Islanders, and all sorts of people from the outer edges of geographies and the far borders of atlases, as here. Japanese and Chinese signs grow familiar to you in a week. Sclavonians and Mongolians are as thick as red pepper in East India curry. It is a tremendous Polyglot. . . .

The real beginnings of modern San Francisco can be dated precisely from March 1, 1847. On that day the United States military governor, who had no formal authority to do so, abolished the communal landholding system fostered by Mexican law and ushered in unrestrained land speculation. The town commons and the waterfront were sold off at a series of hasty auctions.

A civil engineer named Jasper O'Farrell was hired by the new American town government to carve up the land surrounding the original Mexican grid in order to sell it off. O'Farrell corrected the

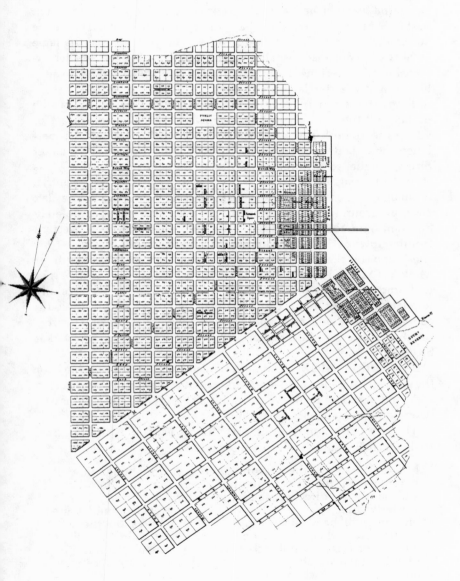

O'FARRELL SURVEY OF 1847

casual survey made by Vioget, giving the new blocks, and the old ones, right angles. But O'Farrell added his own peculiarities to the plan, with long-lasting results. To the north and northwest of the original settlement, O'Farrell repeated the inherited block size and their east-west orientation. Most of the streets here were the same width (68 feet 9 inches) as in the Mexican-era plat of 1837 and later. East of Sansome Street, on the bay-fill between the original shoreline and the wharves, O'Farrell produced a second grid: he used the same street width but made smaller square blocks, using the smaller dimension of the rectangular blocks. These square blocks housed warehouses and wharf-related businesses.

From the southern edge of Yerba Buena Cove, south of the harbor and the city's main hills, O'Farrell sighted Twin Peaks (for which the Spanish had had a more vivid female anatomical appellation) and laid out a grand, 120-foot-wide boulevard, Market Street, parallel to the well-worn dirt trail out to the Mission. This street cuts diagonally across the original grid, creating eccentric, triangular or gore-shaped lots just north of Market. On the flat, swampy ground south of Market, O'Farrell laid out a completely different grid. Like Salt Lake City and the wide-open western frontier towns, the new addition had wide streets (82 feet 9 inches) and blocks about four times bigger than those north of Market. O'Farrell's fateful survey established a permanent barrier to traffic across town, since the old and new grids were totally unrelated. Almost none of the streets allowed easy north-south communication; one geographer has quipped that no other street can have as many intersections and as few crossings as Market Street.

The north-of-Market grid is European in scale and designed for the pedestrian. The south-of-Market grid is vast and American in scale and designed for wheeled traffic. The difference was to have a strong effect on the city's development, as we shall see.

The city's street-numbering system uses Market as its base line. As Disturnell's guidebook of 1885 explained:

Market Street is the starting point for the numbering of buildings on the streets running therefrom in a northerly and southerly direction, and the waterfront for more in a westerly direction. . . . On all streets the even numbers are on the right-hand side, and the odd numbers on the left, starting from the point of beginning. One hundred numbers are allowed for each block between principal streets. . . . One hundred numbers, or as many thereof as are necessary, are allotted to each block bounded by main streets, for instance, Montgomery Street commences at Market, and the main streets crossing as you proceed north are Sutter, Bush, Pine, etc.; therefore any numbers between 1 and 100 will be found on the right- or left-hand side of the street between Market and Sutter, between 100 and 200 from Sutter to

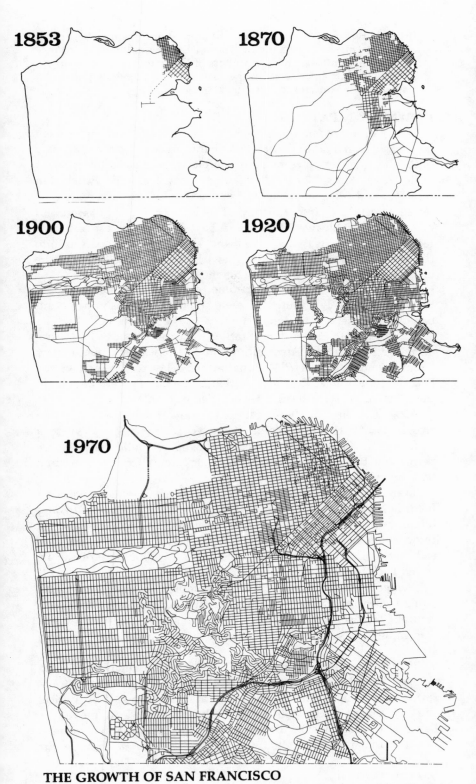

1853

1870

1900

1920

1970

THE GROWTH OF SAN FRANCISCO
San Francisco Department of City Planning

Bush, between 200 and 300 from Bush to Pine. The numbers on all streets not commencing at Market Street or the waterfront run in conformity with the numbers of the main streets running parallel with them, except in the case of a few streets which are numbered in an irregular manner.

DOWNTOWN PATTERNS

Under the sudden impact of the Gold Rush and subsequent land rush, San Francisco blossomed into a boom town. It was a hastily thrown-up place made of simple wood shacks interspersed with canvas tents. The shallow, sandy cove was quickly laid out into lots and filled in. Wharves were extended east over the projected street lines into the bay. The hills to the west were cut down and carted away to fill the bay. In this process the protected anchorage was destroyed and ships were forced out into the treacherous currents. As it grew, San Francisco destroyed its original *raison d'être*—its safe anchorage.

San Francisco became the epitome of the mercantile city. Clustered in central San Francisco were all the stores, shippers, and bankers that served the gold country in the Sierra foothills. The streets leading to the wharves, rather than the Mexican Plaza, became the heart of the American town. The block on Dupont (now Grant Avenue) between Washington and Clay to the west of the Plaza, where Richardson first settled in 1835, was left behind in the Chinatown slum by the 1850s. (See page 205)

After the fire of June 14, 1850, downtown San Francisco crossed two critical thresholds: it passed from being a town to a city, and it changed from temporary wooden buildings to more permanent brick ones. These two developments froze the existing patterns of use.

Its architecture and building scale have changed tremendously, the focus of the Downtown has migrated to the east and then south, and buildings have shot up many more stories, but the most remarkable thing about San Francisco's central business district has been the stability of its basic pattern of uses, or "set." This pattern can be traced back to the summer of 1850. One geographer has described it this way: "The hotel-entertainment complex around Portsmouth Square was to the west of the apparel-shopping nucleus focused on central Clay, Washington, and Sacramento streets, and this nucleus was, in turn, west of the financial-office district centered on Sansome street."

In the three years between 1866 and 1869 the Financial District skipped from Montgomery between Sacramento and Clay to California Street between Montgomery and Sansome. This critical shift occurred when William C. Ralston decided to move the Bank of California from Battery Street to California at Sansome, where it remains today. By 1866 the *San Francisco Real Estate Circular* was referring to California Street as "our Wall Street." In June, 1867, the Bank of California opened its new business palace on California at Sansome. The San Francisco Stock and Exchange Board moved three blocks south to be next door to the Bank of California. Stockbrokers followed the Exchange, completing the transition.

Appropriately enough, considering San Francisco's historic character as a financial center, the only book ever written in San Francisco that swept the literate world was a work of political economy, Henry George's *Progress and Poverty,* published in 1879. Faced with the coexistence of opulence and squalor in mid-nineteenth-century San Francisco and New York, George set out to explain the phenomenon of deepening poverty amid advancing wealth. He found his single answer in the monopoly of land by a few corporations, and he proposed his solution, the "single tax" on land.

In 1906, D.L. Tilden observed,

If one carefully studies the manner in which San Francisco has grown, he will note that its business quarter had always flown in the direction of the hills, and that, striking the foot of the hills, was invariably turned aside. Thus that quarter originally spread [from Portsmouth Square east and north] to the foot of Telegraph Hill and its vicinity [the Jackson Square Historic District], and turning around [south] went up Montgomery and Kearny Streets—always skirting the foot of the hills. Swinging around westward [toward Union Square] as soon as it was clear of obstructions, it began to crawl up Market Street.

At the end of the nineteenth century, headquarter banks moved as far south as Market Street, but this southward shift was stopped by Market Street, a man-made design, not a hill. Location north of Market Street was associated with prestige business or office space, luxury shopping, and wealthy residential districts. South of Market was first an industrial and working-class district, mostly Irish, and later a warehousing district with many newly arrived ethnic families.

From the Ferry Building at the foot of Market Street, the hub of the Bay Area in the nineteenth century, streetcar lines radiated west out California Street to upper-class districts, or southwest to working-class districts. Some investors tried to induce the Downtown to move farther south, past Market Street. William Ralston made New Montgomery Street in 1867 and built the Palace Hotel, one of the largest hotels in the world in its day, in an attempt to draw the Downtown south of Market Street into an area owned by a syndicate of which he was part. But Ralston's enormous bay-windowed pile of a hotel did not draw development south; instead it acted as a wall and effectively stopped prestige businesses from moving down New Montgomery.

By 1890 Market Street was the southern edge of the Downtown

and it was clear that the scale of the blocks south of Market, and their orientation, would keep prestige developments from crossing this great divide. The gore lots on the north side of Market attracted better buildings because of their high visibility and high accessibility by streetcar. The intersection of Montgomery and Market attracted a cluster of fine steel-frame, Beaux-Arts bank buildings. But the banks, the heart and engine of the Downtown's "set," never moved farther south and in fact regrouped north along the 400 block of California Street after about 1912.

The ten to twelve-story office blocks of the 1900s and the twenty to thirty-story skyscrapers of the 1920s allowed the Financial District to expand vertically at central sites. The high-rise boom of the late 1960s to about 1974 added millions of square feet of office space to the Downtown, mostly in a rough ring around the earlier office-building cluster. This ring has an abrupt flat edge where the office district meets Market Street.

The area between Battery Street and the Embarcadero's wharves, which housed industry and warehousing in the nineteenth century, was redeveloped with high-rise structures as investors and engineers acquired more confidence in their abilities to build on the man-made land east of Sansome and First Streets. Expansion by the office core west into Chinatown or north into North Beach has been contained by the hills and the residential areas on their slopes. Nineteenth-century industrial and warehousing areas near the waterfront were assimilated into the Downtown fringe service area of galleries, show-rooms, restaurants, and bars.

The prime office area has expanded eastward, to Embarcadero Center, and upward. The density of offices and people per block exploded, and auto traffic has increased dramatically. To deal with this increased congestion, the city began widening the Downtown streets. Blocks have been continually shaved and this has reduced the square footage of land available for Downtown development. At Clay and Leidesdorff Streets, south of the Pyramid, this street-widening is most apparent.

DOWNTOWN OFFICE-BUILDING TYPES

Ever since the Gold Rush in 1849 with its high-technology, prefabricated temporary structures—some entirely of iron—downtown San Francisco has eagerly adopted the latest construction methods and architectural designs. By the first decades of the twentieth century San Francisco ranked third in the United States —after New York and Chicago—in number of tall buildings. Introduced in the 1890s, the steel-frame office blocks survived the earthquake of 1906. The new Downtown built between 1906 and about 1930 was architecturally cohesive and was one of the greatest achievements of the City Beautiful Movement in America. The 1890s, 1910s, 1920s, and 1930s are all represented by fine examples of luxury office buildings in downtown San Francisco. After the hiatus of World War II and the 1950s, San Francisco participated with relish in the high-rise construction booms of the late 1960s and 1970s, producing one of the period's most striking designs in the silhouette of the Transamerica Pyramid. Not only are many of San Francisco's tall buildings well designed, they are also well placed. San Francisco has perhaps the most practical, compact, and pleasant downtown core of any American city. Following is an historical outline of San Francisco's principal office-building types.

1. 1850 to 1890 (continuing less prominently to about 1910)
Low-Rise Brick-and-Timber Commercial Buildings (Cast-Iron Pilasters)
One- to five-story walk-ups.
Small, narrow lots, often 25 feet by 100 feet, completely built over.
Service entrance on back alleys that subdivide the blocks.
Brick bearing-wall construction with timber posts, floors, and roofs. Some cast-iron pilasters used to frame large sidewalk shop windows.
Sidewalk frontage often treated with an arcade motif.
Rooflines usually straight, but with ornamented cornice.
Best examples:
The east side of the 700 block of Montgomery Street between Washington and Jackson, 1850s.
The south side of the 400 block of Jackson Street between Montgomery and Sansome, 1860s.

2. 1870 to late 1890s
Large Brick, Timber, and Cast-Iron Commercial Blocks with Cage Elevators
Five- to eight-story cage-elevator buildings.
Sites usually the consolidation of several lots. Preference for corner locations and gore lots. Site completely covered.
Brick bearing-wall construction with heavy timber posts, floors, and roofs. Cast iron and plate glass used for ornate sidewalk arcade. Shop windows often surmounted by a mezzanine with large windows.
Rooflines emphatically picturesque, with cupolas, corner towers, high dormers, mansard roofs, and other ornament. Façades often completely covered with vertical rows of bay windows.
Best examples: None extant; all lost in 1906.

3. Late 1890s to 1910
Steel-Frame Beaux-Arts Office Blocks
Ten- to twelve-story cab-elevator buildings.
Sites usually the consolidation of several lots. Preference for corner locations. Parcels often roughly square in shape. Blocks often had back or side doors and ground-floor corridors leading to alleys or other large (separately owned) office buildings.

First use of steel-frame construction. Masonry curtain wall of brick or brick with a stone veneer.

Tripartite design, with a two- or three-story *base,* a six- to eight-story *shaft,* and a two- or three-story *top.* The base, with its shops, entrance, and mezzanine, carried the cornice line of the old low-rise brick buildings across the façade of the Beaux-Arts blocks. The masonry curtain walls of the shaft were usually smooth, with cleanly punched-out, emphatically framed windows (usually double-hung sashes; bay windows were not used).

The top two or three stories were treated as a whole, often with an arcade, a denticulated cornice, and a flat roofline.

Buildings had a maximum of natural light and ventilation, openable windows, and transoms. Blocks either had a hollow core with a white lightwell, or were E-, H-, or F-shaped.

Interior finish, glass, mosaics, metalwork, etc., usually custom-made in San Francisco.

All were deluxe buildings, very well built. All survived the earthquake of 1906, though the fire gutted their interiors.

All were carefully restored with the finest interior finish.

Best examples:

Kohl Building, 400 Montgomery, northeast corner of California Street, Percy and Polk, 1901.

Rialto Building, 116 New Montgomery, southwest corner of Mission Street, Meyer and O'Brien, 1902.

  Steel-Frame Beaux-Arts Commercial Buildings with "Chicago Windows"

Four- to twelve-story cab-elevator, post-fire buildings.

Same as 3 above except that (1) the metal-and-glass sidewalk window and mezzanine base was usually emphasized with larger mezzanine windows, and (2) the brick or reinforced-concrete curtain wall was covered with off-white, glazed terra-cotta tiles.

Buildings had very large window areas set as horizontal bands.

Three windows per structural bay arranged "Chicago style"—that is, one large horizontal window flanked by two narrow, vertical windows often double-hung. Center window often set on vertical pivots. Wood or metal sash.

The basic post-1906 reconstruction commercial block. Best seen in the architecturally coherent retail district between the Financial District and Union Square.

Best example:

W. & J. Sloane (Rose Building), 216 Sutter, Reid Bros., 1908.

Because the rare reinforced-concrete structures survived the 1906 earthquake, San Francisco adopted reinforced concrete as a basic building material (by itself or in combination with a steel frame) for the reconstruction. San Francisco's commercial and industrial districts had more reinforced-concrete buildings earlier than any other city in the world.

4. 1920s and 1930s

Skyscrapers

Twenty- to thirty-story elevator buildings. Most are commercial but a few are residential.

Preference for corner sites, usually not more than one-eighth of a block. Below-grade parking garages, with automobile entrance placed unobtrusively to the side.

Steel-frame, brick and reinforced-concrete curtain walls clad with glazed terra-cotta tiles in a light color. Standard-sized sash windows; large wall areas.

Building covered all of its site and was often designed as a blocklike base continuous with the surrounding streetscape, rising to a thin, soaring tower with a fanciful top. The terra-cotta tile exterior was usually styled to emphasize the building's verticality.

The skyscrapers had two principal entrances—the side garage entrance and a two-story-high, embellished central pedestrian entrance leading to the lobby and elevator banks.

Lobby spaces were often small and narrow, but lavishly finished in stone or metal. Most of the sidewalk level was given over to small personal-service shops. These shops tended to preserve the old scale, 25-foot-wide lots devoted to continuous ground-level shopfronts. Large skyscrapers had internal shops and services principally for tenants.

The top of the building was often highly ornamented with towers and spires. Part of the roof was used for glass-walled sundecks.

Best Examples:

Russ Building, 235 Montgomery, George Kelham, 1927.

Pacific Telephone, 134–140 New Montgomery, Miller and Pfleuger, 1925.

Medical-Dental Building, 450 Sutter, Miller and Pfleuger, 1929.

1930 to 1960

Penthouse Additions

There was little large-scale construction in San Francisco from the Depression to 1960. Many office buildings expanded by adding penthouse stories.

5. 1960 to the Present

High-Rise Box on a Plaza

Twenty- to fifty-story, high-speed-elevator tower. Parking garage beneath, sometimes incorporated within a two-story podium.

Quarter-, full-, or multiblock parcels. Complexes designed as distinct entities composed of (1) an open plaza, sometimes atop a two-story podium, (2) a rectangular, high-rise tower with a flat top, and (3) sometimes an eccentrically shaped satellite building for a branch bank. The whole is composed as an interplay of sculptural forms. Tower often set back from the building line.

Steel frame with curtain walls of glass, metal, concrete, or sometimes stone. Curtain wall usually styled vertically, sometimes horizontally. Internal shops and services for tenants.

Open space around tower ornamented with large abstract sculpture.

Best Examples:

Crown Zellerbach Building, 1 Bush, Skidmore, Owings and Merrill, 1959.

Bank of America World Headquarters, 555 California, Wurster, Bernardi, and Emmons, 1968.

Embarcadero Center complex, The Embarcadero, John Portman and Associates, 1970.

EARLY RESIDENTIAL PATTERNS

The residential areas that encircled the port and the Downtown, filling the blocks of O'Farrell's survey with wooden houses, immediately developed distinct enclaves based on class and ethnicity. North of the core, at the foot of Telegraph Hill where the passenger docks were located, a lower-class transient district sprang up named Sydneytown, after the many ex-convicts from the penal colonies in Australia who inhabited its cheap lodgings. Later this became the infamous Barbary Coast. To the west of Sydneytown was Little Chili, the Latin district in the early days. South of Little Chili was Portsmouth Square, the original plaza of the village of Yerba Buena, which soon became, and still is, the focus of Chinatown.

West of Portsmouth Square, especially along Stockton and Powell Streets, an upper-class, mostly white Anglo-Saxon Protestant neighborhood developed. This sector of the population continued its northwestward migration to Nob and Russian Hills, and later to Pacific and Presidio Heights, with the advent of the hill-conquering cable cars in the 1870s.

South of the plaza was an important French community engaged in trade, which eventually left San Francisco for other Pacific ports. Southeast of the French was German Town, and east of them, near the docks, was Boston Row, favored by New Englanders.

As the Downtown expanded, it displaced the latter neighborhoods. The early horse-car lines—and later cable cars and streetcars—drew the middle classes away from the congested core to new areas like the Western Addition. It was in these new neighborhoods of the 1870s and later that San Francisco's distinctive bay-windowed row houses evolved.

Each house and plot was a separate unit facing the sidewalk and street. People often knew only a few of their neighbors. Religious, class, ethnic, and other differences separated families into many small societies interacting among themselves, and with the larger city, in complex patterns not confined to their own neighborhoods. Then too, people moved a lot. Two years was a long time for anyone, rich or poor, to stay in one place. Neighborhoods were constantly changing. Anonymity, movement, and variety have always been characteristic of San Francisco neighborhoods, even those with clear ethnic identities.

VICTORIAN AND EDWARDIAN DOMESTIC ARCHITECTURE IN SAN FRANCISCO

In the 1870s and 1880s valentines were assembled using blank rectangular cards and layers of die-stamped paper filigrees, gilded cupids, hearts, flowers, and arabesques. The boxlike wooden houses of the period were decorated with machine-sawn redwood ornament in just the same way.

The exuberant prosperity of late-nineteenth-century San Francisco was expressed in her architecture, which borrowed styles from Europe and the East Coast but used them in her own way. The plain houses of the pioneer period gave way in the 1870s and 1880s to what one observer called "the remarkable passion for architectural adornment which did so much to convert San Francisco into a place of pinnacles and steeples which . . . gave the town its . . . picturesque appearance." By 1888 Hittell's guidebook explained, "The superior facility for shaping wood, and the abundance of machinery for planing and molding, had led to the adoption of more architectural ornamentation here than in any other city." He dryly added: "The visitor from the East is at once impressed by the rarity of plain exteriors in the dwellings of the wealthy."

And not just the wealthy. The real achievement of Victorian San Francisco was the construction of thousands of modest homes for skilled mechanics, craftsmen, and office workers. Visitors from the East constantly commented on the noticeably higher standard of living enjoyed by San Francisco mechanics and artisans. The wealth of Victorian San Francisco rested on the seemingly limitless agricultural abundance of California's great Central Valley. In the 1880s it was the endless stream of wheat that flowed through this port to the mushrooming cities of Europe that began the sustained growth and prosperity of California in general, and San Francisco in particular.

The story of the Victorian house begins with the land and the way it was divided and graded. After an initial "land rush" in the late 1840s and early 1850s, San Francisco seems to have developed a pattern of very small lots originally claimed by squatters and large blocks of land held by investors. It was a common pattern for large fortunes made in mining or other natural resource development to be invested in large blocks of land on the edge of the growing city.

Would-be homeowners had to secure a lot. They did so by form-

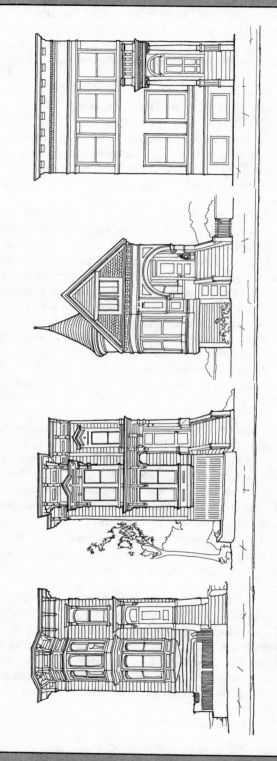

VICTORIAN AND EDWARDIAN DOMESTIC
ARCHITECTURE IN SAN FRANCISCO 1860 to 1915

Italianate
1860 to 1880

Stick-Eastlake
1880 to 1890

Queen Anne
1890 to 1900

Edwardian
1900 to 1915

William Walters

ing homestead associations, whereby members pooled their savings to buy large tracts for subdivision into house lots, generally 25 feet by 100 feet. By 1868 there were no less than thirty of these homestead associations in San Francisco. Members borrowed from them to build their houses, usually at 7 percent interest. In an age before the government regulation of the stock market, and at a time when ordinary people mistrusted banks, building-and-loan and homestead associations were attractive places for small investors to put their money even if they had no intention of building. As the many surviving rows of Victorian houses testify, relatively large pools of capital were amassed by these associations. As in many nineteenth-century American institutions, there was often an ethnic base to these associations.

Other whole rows of frame houses were constructed by speculative builders who, like those today, built small batches of houses to sell to the public. This resulted in standard floor plans and exuberant redwood exterior decoration. Gingerbread trim was a low-cost way to customize a standardized house or string of houses.

These houses are essentially simple wood boxes. But because of the interaction between the hilly terrain and the rigid gridiron street pattern, a pleasing steplike profile was created in many parts of the city. Many of the long, narrow lots were tilted at steep angles to the street, and the grading of the streets accentuated this condition. The common result was a steep embankment between the sidewalk and the house. The striking vertical effect of San Francisco's Victorians is often dramatically reinforced by their high bases.

Retaining walls and house footings (most houses did not have basements) were usually brick covered with cement plaster scored and painted to look like granite blocks. The Victorian houses have fir frames and redwood siding. Most were built according to the system of Western plate framing, whereby each floor is built as a separate layer, one on top of the other.

The long, narrow lots dictated the floor plan. The common row-house plan consisted of a long windowless hall on one side of the house, from which branch three interconnected principal rooms: a rarely used formal front parlor with a bay window, a second, or family, parlor, and a dining room. Behind the dining room were the kitchen and pantry. Ten-foot-high sliding doors connected the three ornamented front rooms. As one architect noted: "The lower floor of such a house can be made into one large room—admirably suited for receptions." The second, or bedroom floor, repeated the plan of the first floor without the interconnecting sliding doors. The master bedroom was usually in the front and had a bay window. The children's bedrooms were next back, and servants were housed in the rear rooms or in the attic. The bathroom was placed over the kitchen to minimize plumbing. Water closets were usually separate from wash-rooms to maximize accessibility.

In the Victorian period, houses began to be equipped with a variety of mechanical conveniences, which invariably became the building's chief selling points. By 1890 Newsom's *Picturesque Homes* reported,

> Almost all have modern improvements such as electric bells, electric lighters for the gas fixtures, hardwood mantels, art tiles, bronze hardware, open work plumbing, tiled vestibule, spindle arches, swell shelves, and a tasty staircase lighted with domed skylight. These residences are generally finished interiorly with fine hardwoods and redwood, interspersed with dados of Lincrusta-Walton [a textured wall-covering]. Throughout, the interior is full of novel features, and well planned for furniture.

The Bay Window

The basic box was embellished with ornament and bay windows. These "building adjuncts" were bought from woodworking mills south of Market Street. Builders picked out ornamental elements from catalogues. These house parts were machine-carved on newly invented machinery. Redwood—soft, knot-free, inexpensive, and easily worked—was ideal for this.

Bay windows are an ancient idea, but in San Francisco they were rare in the 1850s and 1860s. In the 1870s they started to become popular, and in the 1880s and 1890s they became nearly universal. "One can tell the age of any dwelling in San Francisco within five years by the amount and quality of glass in it," wrote one observer. Another wrote, "The unparalleled abundance of bay-windows, constructed to catch the sunlight, makes this pre-eminently the Bay-Window City." Bay windows were equated with gentility. One guidebook, anxious to tell visitors inspecting hotel rooms what natives thought, advised that "One bay window at least, with a sunny aspect, is considered important in rooms occupied by ladies."

The popularity of the bay window led to problems as builders sought to extend buildings out over the public spaces of streets and alleys. It became necessary for the city to regulate how far into public space bays could go. In 1886, as part of the fire ordinances of the city, the maximum allowable projection of the bays was defined. The ordinance read:

> No person shall build a bay or oriel window which shall project over the line of any street more than three feet, or more than nine feet in width, nor shall the bottom of said bay or oriel window be less than thirteen feet from the sidewalk. No bay or oriel window shall be constructed upon any street, lane, alley or place which is less than thirty-five feet in width. . . . [N]o bay or oriel window shall be more than four stories in height above the sidewalk.

Amendments in the same year allowed corner bays at the intersection of streets over the sidewalks, provided they were at least 14 feet from the ground. This ordinance and its successors proved to be the chief instruments through which San Francisco achieved its unique urban-architectural form as "the Bay-Window City."

Additions to the Box
As families grew, or after middle-class neighborhoods became rooming-house districts, most frame houses acquired extra bedrooms, baths, bays, back sleeping porches, or glassed-in sun porches. These "add-ons" create a picturesque jumble behind nearly every house. Each lot was protected by a high board fence. The backs of houses and insides of the block acquired an indescribable complexity of small gardens with fruit trees (pears and figs in particular), sheds, extensions of the house, and sometimes even another small house moved into or built on the back of the lot.

Landscape and House Color
In the Victorian period gray was one of the favorite house colors in San Francisco. The base was often dark gray or white (to look like stone), the body of the building and all its ornament were gray or white, the window sash (the narrow wood frame around the glass) was glossy black, and vestibules were painted to look like brown mahogany. Multicolor paint schemes became the fashion only in the late 1960s.

The landscaping in San Francisco was generally just as plain. Front embankments were planted with grass and decorated with desert plants such as yucca, palms, or century plants. There were only a few large lawns, and shade trees were rare. Simple lawns, spiky, geometric, exotic plants, black wrought-iron fences, and gilded or stained-glass numerals in the transom over the front door were the rule. Water was precious on these sandy wastes; San Francisco landscaping became lush only in the present century. An abundance of plants was reserved for glass conservatories attached to the houses of the wealthy or to the parks, especially Golden Gate Park, enjoyed by all. Just like the hilly site, which was rigorously subjected to a geometrical gridiron street pattern, plants were also subjected to a formal attitude. In the Victorian period, the hardy Monterey cypress was imported from the California coast, but it was rarely allowed to grow naturally into a random shape. Instead it was trained into high, wide hedges for windbreaks and into columns, urns, cones, spheres, or hollow squares set like abstract sculptures on plain lawns.

VICTORIAN STYLES AND THE EDWARDIAN REACTION: 1860 to 1915

The kind and degree of ornament on San Francisco's houses followed a clear pattern, even if many individual houses combined more than one style. Between 1860 and 1915 the movement was from plain (Greek Revival) to fancy (Italianate) to fancier (Stick-Eastlake, Queen Anne), then back to plain (Edwardian period designs). To simplify a complex history, Victorian and Edwardian San Francisco architectural taste went through these phases:

1. 1850 to 1860
Greek Revival

The houses built in post–Gold Rush San Francisco were often copies of Greek Revival building types common back East or in the South. Pioneers built house types evolved in other climates. Steep-pitched roofs for shedding snow and heavy rain and open porches for hot summer afternoons are both unnecessary in San Francisco. Bay windows appeared occasionally, usually on the sides of houses.

2. 1860 to 1880
Italianate

More elaborate houses, many with slant-sided bay windows, rapidly became increasingly common. They are named after their classically derived ornament. In their own day they were often called "London Roman" after the Italianate men's clubs along Pall Mall in London. The real importance of what happened in the Italianate period lies not in its style of redwood ornament but rather in its adaptation of the basic box of the house to San Francisco's long, narrow lots and peculiar climate. Cheaper flat roofs succeeded gable roofs. Open porches gave way to more and more bay windows, which admitted light and views while protecting from the cool breeze, expanded interior floor space, and created interesting patterns from the outside and opportunities for adornment. During this period in San Francisco, bay windows went from being rare to nearly universal. A local row-house type evolved: a long, narrow frame box, one or two stories high, with windows and a "slot" along one side, a blank wall on the other side, bay windows in front, a flat tar-and-gravel roof, and utilitarian, adaptable backs. This house type had a long life in San Francisco, lasting from the 1860s to the 1900s. Changes in architectural fashion were limited to how the front was adorned.

3. 1880 to 1890
Stick-Eastlake

In this booming period, house ornament became increasingly elaborate. The style was marked by flat, angular, incised-redwood ornament. Right-angled, three-sided bay windows became the vogue. The label "Stick style" refers to the simpler designs of the 1880s, which usually relied on relatively plain vertical board decorations applied to the corners of the façade and the edges of the right-angled bay windows. When completely drenched with sawn redwood ornament they are called Eastlake or Stick-Eastlake; Sir Charles Eastlake was an influential London furniture designer—not an architect—whose flat, angular designs, often enlivened with incised trefoliate decorations, swept the English-speaking world. Pullman-car interiors and San Francisco houses took the style to its farthest extreme. In the late 1880s, the search for variety and novelty resulted in some fascinating, agitated designs, where not just surface ornament but room shapes and floor plans as well sought the widest possible variety. Some late Eastlake houses incorporated almost every conceivable geometric form: cubes, rectangles, hexagons, octagons, cylinders, and shapes that have no simple name. These forms were chopped apart and set in tense combinations, creating complex designs. San Francisco investors and architects scattered examples of the San Francisco Eastlake from the Canadian to the Mexican borders, and from the Rockies to Hawaii. It was especially these restless, agitated, manipulated storybook castles that were considered monstrous during the first two-thirds of the twentieth century. Now we look back at them (in particular the front façade of the Haas-Lilienthal House at 2007 Franklin) as bold, inventive, amusing, and worth puzzling out. (What *is* that bracket doing?) The wild courage of these uninhibited designs, as well as what clients could afford and craftsmen could build, amazes and pleases us today as much as these houses amazed and pleased the "making it" generation that built them.

The 1880s are important also for the sheer number of residential buildings that were built then, and that survive, in San Francisco. They were go-go years and seem to have been a time when standards of accommodation rose for many.

When Sir Charles Eastlake was apprised of what was being built in San Francisco and given his name he cried, "I now find, to my amazement, that there exists on the other side of the Atlantic an 'Eastlake style' of architecture, which, judging from the specimens I have seen illustrated, may be said to burlesque such doctrines of art as I have ventured to maintain." To Eastlake the design of these proliferating houses was "extravagant and *bizarre.*"

4. 1890 to 1900
Queen Anne

In the late 1880s the angular lines of the Stick-Eastlake style gave way to the rounded shapes of the Queen Annes. The name was taken from architect Norman Shaw's designs in England and has no relation to the eighteenth-century British monarch. In San Francisco the new style meant rounded corner towers, convex bay windows with curved sheets of glass, and classically derived cast-plaster ornament, including wreaths, flowing ribbons and garlands, torches, and beaded moldings. As the style evolved, house silhouettes gradually became increasingly symmetrical and balanced in their organization. In some grand examples, great central halls became the dominant element in the floor plan. Designs began to deviate from the standard row-house floor plan. In the most assured examples, such as 1701 Franklin Street, smooth curves were effected where round turrets met flat walls. Porches were often recessed into the body of the structure and framed by broad, round arches supported by squat pillars. Hints of the Richardsonian Romanesque were also absorbed.

Most buildings are rectangular and employ right angles for the simple reason that milled lumber, bricks, and pieces of glass are flat or straight. During the 1890s the art of carpentry in San Francisco reached such a degree of sophistication that architects and carpenters literally bent their recalcitrant materials to their will. Swelling forms and soft curves became a demonstration of the builder's mastery over his materials. Wood was bent, brick cut and molded, glass bowed out in convex sheets, and shingles were trimmed in delicate scallops and fine saw-tooth edges.

San Francisco Queen Annes, seeking picturesque effects, brought back gable roofs. By this time the valleys had been built up and houses, especially workingmen's cottages, began to climb up the city's hills. Rows of charming, low-budget Queen Anne cottages created saw-tooth patterns on the city's horizon. The profile of the hills around Eureka Valley looks as if it were cut with pinking shears. This style led San Francisco editor Gilette Burgess to comment that the ideal Queen Anne

> should have the conical corner-tower, it should be built of at least three incongruous materials, or better, imitations thereof; it should have its window-openings absolutely haphazard; it should represent parts of every known and unknown order of architecture; it should be so plastered with ornament as to conceal the theory of its construction; it should be a restless, uncertain, frightful collection of details, giving the effect of a nightmare about to explode.

The continual elaboration of ornament and room shapes reached its height about 1888. After that there was a gradual move toward simplicity in two stages. First there was increasing control in the disposition of the variety of geometric volumes such as bays and turrets in the Queen Anne style. In its second phase this movement away from "excess" and toward order culminated in dry, correct Neoclassical designs of great sobriety during the Edwardian reaction at the turn of the century. (Edward VII succeeded Victoria and reigned from 1901 to 1910.)

5. 1900 to 1915
Edwardian Period Styles

At the close of the nineteenth century, and into the first decade of the twentieth, a willful self-control and deep conservatism overtook the tastes of the wealthy and the designs they patronized. The brash individuality of the late Victorians subsided into studied reticence and deliberate good manners. This change is best seen in house design and in men's formal evening dress. Eccentricity gave way to strict convention, quiet lines, and understated but high-quality materials. Money now made understatement its chief method of display. Flat planes and refined, historically correct ornament in quiet colors ruled. Style was no longer measured in pounds of gingerbread ornament per square foot but in elegant proportions and an air of restfulness. The two Flood mansions, at 2120 and 2222 Broadway, neatly bracket the evolutionary process in this era of studied understatement. At the same time massive, dark, American-made furniture was replaced with light, imported French pieces or copies. The internationalization of the American rich culminated in the marriage of the children of great magnates to European aristocratic families. One can easily imagine the granddaughter of a Nevada silver magnate feeling embarrassed and oppressed in the dark, heavy, old-fashioned business office of her moneybags grandfather.

The perfect symbol of this process of refinement was the fate of Victorian San Francisco's much-loved bay window. The new Period palaces built in Pacific Heights after 1900 seemed embarrassed by these ubiquitous "building adjuncts." They were therefore banished from "modern" façades. Bay windows did survive, but they were used only occasionally and were hidden in the back or on the sides of houses. Occasionally the perfect stuffy, repressed compromise was achieved; bay windows were built but they were recessed into the wall plane, thereby negating their purpose and effect. One is impressed by the virtuosity but not by the idea.

Interiors

Victorian interiors followed the same evolution as house exteriors and became increasingly elaborate before a reaction set in with plainer surfaces in the Edwardian age. Rooms were heavily draped and decorated. Bay windows were often shuttered from within, draped, and filled with furniture. As one guide described it: "Interiors were resplendent with horsehair divans, marble-topped tables, and bronze statuary. Gaslight flickered in dim vestibules and up redwood staircases."

One detail of Victorian interiors that has survived is the love of plants. Another distinctive San Franciscan characteristic is a love of Asian art. In addition to the standard embellishments found in every middle-class Victorian parlor from London to Buenos Aires to Singapore, San Franciscans developed a passion for two things: large oils depicting mountain scenery; and small, delicately embellished metal, wood, lacquer, ivory, and porcelain objets d'art from China and Japan. As the chief western port on the Pacific, San Francisco felt the influence of Asia.

Victorians Today

Today the word "Victorian" in a real estate agent's description has as irresistible an attraction as "Modern Gothic" or "London Roman" had in the day these buildings were brand new. Well-built, well-located, redolent of the city's rich past, Victorian houses are among the most sought-after buildings. A happy combination is achieved when their façades are restored, interiors are remodeled to create more open spaces, and decks and sun porches are added in the rear. Where dramatic views are available from the backs of buildings, or where auto traffic makes the front rooms unpleasant, old floor plans are reversed and the principal rooms are placed in the back of the house rather than facing the street.

TWENTIETH-CENTURY RESIDENTIAL PATTERNS

Until the turn of the century, single- and two-family houses proliferated from the slopes of Twin Peaks to the bay. In the middle- and upper-class districts in the central and northern parts of the city the houses were usually two stories high. On the western and southern fringes many one-story "mechanics' cottages" were built. At the turn of the century, when the city had built over most of the easily accessible areas east of Twin Peaks, a denser building type, three- or four-story Edwardian flats and apartment houses, replaced earlier Victorian houses and shops along the streetcar-served shopping streets. These frame buildings adopted the bay window in all its many shapes as a way of making apartments seem larger from within—and also to make large buildings look domestic in the eyes of San Franciscans. In San Francisco usage a flat is a living unit with its own separate entrance, even if that entrance shares a vestibule with other entrances. An apartment building has one principal entrance and a hallway from which separate units are entered. Real-estate listings in the newspapers make a sharp distinction between the two. Flats, of course, are more desirable.

The fire of 1906 spurred growth on the city's fringes. Both wealthy areas like Presidio Heights and working-class neighborhoods like the Outer Mission saw much new building. The burned-over central districts were rebuilt to a much higher density with the bay-win-

MAP OF SAN FRANCISCO IN 1906 SHOWING AREA BURNED AND SURVIVING VICTORIAN ARCHITECTURAL ZONES TODAY

The area within the black border burned in 1906 when the city's two water mains broke south of the cemeteries. The numbered areas are present-day Victorian architectural zones. The gap in the Victorian ring is due to demolition during the "urban renewal" of 1950–1970.

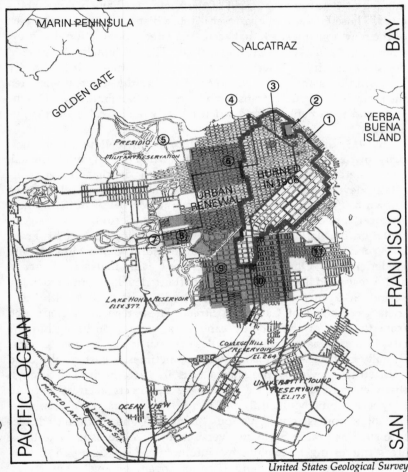

United States Geological Survey

1. **Jackson Square Historic District / Tour 2**
2. **Telegraph Hill (East Slope) / Tour 1**
3. **Russian Hill (Summit) / Tour 7**
4. **Fort Mason (Franklin Street) / Tour 12**
5. **Presidio Military Reservation (Funston and O'Reilly Avenues)**
6. **Pacific Heights / Tour 3**
7. **Golden Gate Park (East Half) / Tour 9**
8. **Haight-Ashbury / Tour 8**
9. **The Castro and Noe Valley / Tour 10**
10. **Inner Mission District / Tour 4**
11. **Potrero Hill**

dowed flats and apartments that still blanket North Beach, Russian and Nob Hills, and parts of the Inner Mission. It is these buildings, not Victorian houses, that the visitor sees from the surviving cable routes. The size of their units makes them ideal for couples and single people. They embody a livable city density for San Francisco and will probably be the next building type to be discovered by restoration-minded owners now that most of the Victorians have been rehabilitated. These Edwardian apartment-house districts were a major part of the new housing stock that accommodated a population that grew from 342,782 in 1900 to 416,912 in 1910. The earthquake and fire did not slow the city's growth. The geographic confinement of the city by Twin Peaks and the bay, and the fact that the streetcar was then the main form of public transit, made the new San Francisco's Downtown and apartment-house districts dense, even in scale, and energy-efficient.

In 1918, under Mayor James Rolph, a firm believer in municipally owned transit and utilities, the Twin Peaks Tunnel opened, and streetcar lines penetrated the western districts. Large real-estate developers opened new tracts in what had once been known as "the great sand waste" or "the fog belt." Both the new streetcar tunnel and a newly improved road, Portola Drive (a continuation of Market Street), spurred the development of St. Francis Wood, a garden district laid out by John Galen Howard and Frederick Law Olmsted in 1912. Forest Hill, Ingleside Terraces, and Westwood Park are other important developments from the period. St. Francis Wood broke the tradition that all wealthy districts were north of California Street. These new areas, separated from the rest of the city by sand hills, were suburbs within the city designed as separate capsules for particular income groups. Racially restrictive covenants were sometimes a part of the deed until struck down by the state courts in 1948. Sprinkled through these western districts are houses by architects such as Bernard Maybeck, Louis Mullgardt, and Henry H. Gutterson. A wide mixture of historicist styles, various "revivals," and modern architecture such as Prairie Style and versions of Secessionism make these areas interesting to explore by automobile. Neo-Georgian, Stockbroker Tudor, Mission, and Mediterranean, among other styles, show a catholicity of taste. The most interesting houses were built before 1917 and are in the Craftsman or Secessionist style.

Michael M. O'Shaughnessy, the city's Chief Engineer under Mayor Rolph for a generation, designed and constructed a net of boulevards in the undeveloped western half of the city. The 1920s were good years for San Francisco, and the population grew from 506,676 to 634,394 by 1930. Prosperity also turned the automobile into an important shaper of the new sections of the city. In 1914 there were only 12,000 autos in the city; by 1937 there were 160,000. It became the rule for semidetached stucco houses to have a garage on the first floor, and a living space with a shallow bay window above. San Francisco very quickly adapted to the automobile. Vast areas of houses, the Marina District for example, all have parking at their ground level. (In the Downtown the 1920s saw the construction of garages—as a matter of fact, the most attractive parking garages the city was ever to see. See, for example, the Palace Garage at 111–127 Stevenson Street, off New Montgomery across from the main entrance to the Palace Hotel, designed by the O'Brien Brothers in 1921.)

In 1917, Mayor Rolph appointed the first City Planning Commission. In 1921, zoning laws were enacted which essentially confirmed existing uses in the various areas of the city. Although the boom of the 1920s began the automotive era, the early zoning laws continued the development of the new parts of the city essentially along the lines of the old. This meant areas of residential blocks, with one local (generally) east-west street devoted to shops (often with apartments above) served by a streetcar line. Churches, schools, libraries, and parks were placed anywhere except along the high-rent commercial strip.

In the 1920s the variants of the Mission, Mediterranean, or Spanish style emerged as the dominant style. Movie palaces in California were the style's cathedrals, and stucco houses its innumerable progeny. The blocks around the Sunset Reservoir, and the nearby Parkside District, are rich in such houses; the Castro Theater and its interior are also worth mentioning.

The depressed 1930s were a decade of stagnation; the population expanded by only 142 during the period. Except for some early—and still the most handsome—high-rise reinforced-concrete apartment buildings, there was little residential construction. The construction industry was kept alive by federal WPA and PWA projects including such outstanding structures as the San Francisco–Oakland Bay Bridge and Coit Tower. (The Golden Gate Bridge of 1937 and the Bay Bridge finally broke the geographic isolation of San Francisco. They are also among the finest works of art in the region. While the Golden Gate Bridge is popularly acclaimed, and is, indeed, among the finest Moderne works in the nation, the San Francisco half of the Streamline Bay Bridge awaits the sophisticated connoisseur of the art of bridge design. The Golden Gate Bridge uses ornament to persuade us of its stability in its precarious situation. The Bay Bridge's twinned suspension spans add nothing to themselves for ornament; they make an ornament of the stripped-down necessity of themselves. Here bridgebuilding in America reached an utter perfection of simplicity and beauty. The rational disposition of the rivets in the X-braces become the only "ornament" the bridge needs. And it is a kinetic sculpture; as one drives toward San Francisco the X-braces make a flowing pattern of diamonds as they overlap in moving perspective.)

Only with the war-related industrial boom of the 1940s did the city grow again in population. But little housebuilding went on during the war except for housing projects near the Hunters Point shipyards, which were intended to be temporary. More important, existing buildings were subdivided to provide housing for the workers who built the vast fleet required for the struggle with Japan. The city saw its population peak sometime in the late 1940s, right before the 1950 census counted 775,357 resident San Franciscans. After the deferred maintenance of the depressed 1930s, the sudden bloating of the city during the 1940s was very hard on the housing stock and the public transit system. With postwar G.I. loans came rapid suburban growth and the gradual decline of the city's population. By 1970 the population had fallen to 715,674. The composition of the population also changed; there was a notable increase in the number of single people, and a peaking of the school-age population. This reflected a national pattern. Age segregation seems to be increasing in America. The inner city serves the old and the young single people, while the suburban belt has most of the middle-aged adults and school-age children.

Some old, inner-city neighborhoods became sinks of dire poverty by 1960, something San Francisco was not used to. In the nineteenth century and the early twentieth, poverty in California was invisibly dispersed in rural areas; the cities were generally prosperous places for the middle classes and the blue-collar workers, who were generally better paid than industrial workers back East. While there always were down-and-out areas in the city near its docks and industry, and squatter shacks on the sandy fringes, large areas of slums in the center were a new development. What was also new was that many of these new San Franciscans were black.

In 1948 the city declared the run-down Victorian Western Addition a redevelopment area and began wholesale demolition and block clearance. Block-sized subsidized housing projects were built. Some early ones were high-rise, but later development conformed to the low-rise profile of the district. There was large-scale displacement, and only a fraction of the number of units destroyed was replaced. Virtually all the buildings demolished were Victorian and Edwardian frame buildings with elaborate gingerbread façades.

In the 1950s the State began the construction of a partially elevated freeway system through the city. The working-class districts in the south of the city were sliced through, and the Downtown was walled off from the Embarcadero. But when it was proposed to pave the Golden Gate Park Panhandle, and to cut through the upper-class residential areas in the northern tier of the city, the famous "Freeway Revolt" erupted. It successfully blocked the completion of the hideous (if serviceable) freeway through the northern districts of San Francisco.

In the 1950s, as in the early 1900s, the bay window disappeared from new designs. Flat façades, inspired by the International style, and "picture-frame" windows became the modern thing. The stucco box utterly devoid of ornament came into its own as the California vernacular. When perched atop poles with exposed parking underneath, the so-called "ding-bat" was born. Apartment-building design reached its nadir. Views of gaping garages and exposed gas meters assaulted the passerby. The coherence of vintage blocks was shattered when these "higher and better uses" invaded the city's neighborhoods. When built in uninterrupted strings, such as in the area above Market Street on the east side of Twin Peaks, the monotony and ugliness of these modern buildings from the street is overwhelming.

In 1952 the Stonestown Shopping Center opened in the extreme southwest corner of the city and the last large parcels of open space were built up with stucco houses in a modern style. Some of these otherwise spartan buildings were decorated with thin slats of wood at the eaves or porch that looked like airplane struts—an odd last gasp for wooden ornament.

In the 1960s the population continued to fall, but the size of new buildings increased dramatically. Large concrete apartment houses sprouted here and there around the city center. In the neighborhoods, bulky, unattractive apartment houses were built. The threat of encroaching ugliness led the city to reexamine its building regulations in the 1970s. While particular styles are not imposed, other design criteria are now better defined. Bay windows, for example, which some developers had corrupted into continuous overhangs from the second floor of their buildings, or which were sometimes built with three sides but only one window, were redefined and must now be real bay windows, not just one-window extensions of the building. Lot coverage was also redefined to preserve backyards and to prevent the disruption of the private open spaces traditionally at the heart of so many San Francisco residential blocks.

Now that the city is almost completely built up, the lots that remain are often rugged sites in the central hills. Simply preparing a foundation and providing the mandatory parking garage can now cost as much as an entire house used to. Some houses continue to be built in the city, often very fine contemporary wood, glass, and stucco designs, but they are very few and very expensive.

The greatest change in the recent past has been the sudden turnaround in the appreciation of older, particularly Victorian, houses. Now instead of knocking down what were considered "monstrosities" in the 1940s and 1950s, even houses in the very worst condition and in the least attractive locations are thoroughly and beautifully restored. Stucco and asbestos-shingle "improvements" of the last generation are one by one being removed. Specialist craftsmen now design and install completely new Victorian gingerbread façades. Now, with each passing year, the city has more complete Victorian houses!

House prices in San Francisco are now among the very highest in the nation. Few derelict buildings remain to be restored, and the competition among buyers for vintage houses seems to know no end. While this is good for the housing stock, it works hardship on the many San Franciscans who are being priced out of their city. The trend toward condominiums, if not controlled, could wipe out rental housing in San Francisco and fundamentally alter the composition and character of the population. San Francisco's problems are the problems of success.

Tour 1

North Beach, Coit Tower, and Telegraph Hill

The Essential San Francisco Cityscape

TOUR 1 □ NORTH BEACH, COIT TOWER, AND TELEGRAPH HILL

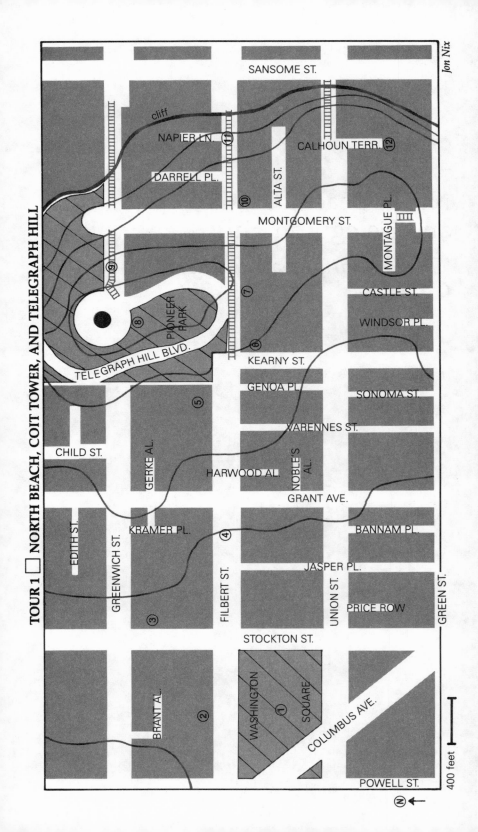

Jon Nix

400 feet

WHAT THIS WALK COVERS

This climb from Washington Square in the heart of North Beach proceeds up Filbert Street to Coit Tower atop Telegraph Hill. After a tour of the fine 1930s frescoes inside Coit Tower depicting the working life of California, and a view of the sweeping panorama of the city and bay, the walk descends Filbert Steps to Napier Lane, a delightfully landscaped cul-de-sac in the heart of the city. Return to Washington Square by bus.

PRACTICALITIES

Best time for this walk: The frescoes in Coit Tower are open every afternoon from 2:00 P.M. to 4:00 P.M. Start an hour ahead in Washington Square. The small but fine North Beach Museum in the Eureka Federal Savings office at 1435 Stockton Street is open only during banker's hours (Phone: 391-6210) and gives an overview of the area before starting the walk.

Getting there by public transit: The northbound #30 Stockton trolley-bus at Sutter and Stockton connects Downtown with Washington Square via the Stockton Street Tunnel and Chinatown.

Parking: The best place to park for this walk is the city garage over the police station on Vallejo Street, between Stockton and Powell. The #39 Coit bus at Montgomery and Union, at the end of the climb, will bring you back downhill to Washington Square, about two short blocks north of the garage on Vallejo Street.

Cafés and restaurants: The espresso in all of North Beach is excellent. Much of it comes from the Graffeo Coffee Roasting Company at 733 Columbus Avenue. The delicious aroma of roasting coffee is a distinctive North Beach smell. There are cafés for every taste in North Beach. The fanciest is Enrico's Sidewalk Café at 504 Broadway, near Kearny. The best neighborhood cafés are the Caffè Trieste (at Grant and Vallejo) and the Caffè Roma (414 Columbus, near Vallejo). Either would be a good place for an invigoratingly strong coffee before you start the tour; the Trieste even offers impromptu guitar and mandolin music and operatic singing every Saturday morning. The best Italian pastries are at Victoria Pastry Company at 1362 Stockton, corner of Vallejo.

The best restaurant in North Beach is Vanessi's at 498 Broadway. They make their own pasta; sit at the counter for the best floor show in town. Another institution is La Pantera at 1234 Grant, one of the last family-style restaurants. Mama's on Washington Square (1701 Stockton) is inexpensive and good for breakfast and lunch. Take-out sandwiches at Molinari's Delicatessen (373 Columbus, at Vallejo) and Panelli Brothers Delicatessen (1419 Stockton) are very good.

Jasper Street looking south from Filbert Street. Typical post-1906 alley flats and apartments. Fire codes prohibited bay windows on narrow streets.

INTRODUCTION

North Beach, Telegraph Hill, and Coit Tower are full of surprises for natives and visitors alike. North Beach now has no beach, and Telegraph Hill no telegraph. Coit Tower was not modeled on a fire-hose nozzle; a statue of Benjamin Franklin stands in the middle of Washington Square.

North Beach got its name from a long-vanished beach at Francisco Street, four blocks north of Washington Square. Bayfill very soon extended the city several blocks north, eliminating the beach but leaving the name. Much of the city's industry in the Civil War years was clustered on that landfill, extending to the smelting works near the present-day Cannery.

All of North Beach burned in 1906 but was rapidly rebuilt with three-story frame flats and apartment buildings. Landownership patterns and, most important, the long, narrow old lot shapes remained the same after reconstruction. Many Irish, and some Italians, moved out of North Beach to the Mission district after 1906, but both absentee and resident lot owners rebuilt to the highest density permitted by the fire codes and the economics of wood building. A fortunate legal interpretation held that the fire destroyed the city, not the earthquake. By April, 1908, insurance companies had paid out $150,000,000, with which San Franciscans very rapidly rebuilt a denser, more uniform, up-to-date city.

In the many narrow alleys, no overhanging bays were allowed. North Beach blocks therefore have a clearly differentiated "outside" of bay-windowed streets and an "inside" of alleys with flat façades; the cheaper housing was built along the alleys. Fire codes also required leaving a minimum backyard as a firebreak between the buildings. Sheds and extensions have been built over some, but a surprising number shelter small gardens or potted plants.

The streets lined with standard three-story apartment houses, while very dense, are nonetheless agreeable. The buildings on the main streets are about as high as the streets are wide, and a generous amount of sunlight reaches many rooms. The airshafts between the tightly packed buildings allow some reflected light to filter into many rooms.

In 1873 a diagonal street, originally named Montgomery Avenue, was cut across the city's grid along the bottom of the valley between Telegraph and Russian Hills, just nipping off the southwest corner of Washington Square. It was one of the few concessions—and, at that, a later adjustment—to the shape of the land in laying out nineteenth-century San Francisco's streets. Its name was changed to Columbus Avenue in deference to the sizable Italian-American colony that settled in the valley starting in the 1880s.

North Beach has never become run-down. Its walking-distance proximity to the Financial District has kept real-estate values high. The fact that this has never been a very poor neighborhood is evident in the continual modernization of the buildings. Many of the façades of the *circa* 1910 Edwardian apartments in North Beach were stuccoed in the 1930s and 1940s in an attempt to bring the buildings up to date. This was particularly true around Washington Square, where the buildings are highly visible. Some of the stucco has Art Deco designs.

Virtually every San Francisco neighborhood or district has its own commercial strip of shops and services. They are all linear and usually continuous. By "reading" the mix of shops and services, especially grocery stores, one can tell much about the locals. Commerce changes as the people change, and a good San Francisco shopping strip, of which there are many, will have "layers" of businesses that mark the waxing and waning of groups and subcultures in their area.

Upper Grant Avenue—from Broadway to Lombard—was an Italian-American commercial enclave in the early twentieth century. A few old-time businesses still stud the street, among them La Pantera Café (est. 1907, 1234 Grant at Vallejo), Caffè Trieste (est. 1956, 601 Vallejo, at Grant), Figoni Hardware (1351 Grant, an old-style hardware store with wooden floors, cabinets, and racks and racks of shelves stacked with small boxes; outside is an old enameled-metal-and-neon Sherwin-Williams paint "Cover the Earth" sign!), Panama Canal Ravioli and Tagliarini Factory (1358 Grant), and the Italian & French Baking Company (1501–03 Grant, at Union; excellent sourdough bread and panettone, a specialty fruit bread). North Beach Italian-Americans continue the old European and nineteenth-century American custom of hanging a black wreath with a purple ribbon when the owner of a shop dies. One by one, old Italian-American businesses have followed this last old-world custom.

A striking example of the geographic and climatological uniqueness of San Francisco is the case of the Italian salamis. Because of its unusual weather with constant mild temperatures, the San Francisco Bay Area is the only place in the United States where Italian dry salami can be made without air conditioning and other artificial environmental controls. In fact, such is the special character of certain sub-areas that some old-time salami manufacturers say that different areas of the city produce different-tasting salami! Old-time, small-scale salami manufacturers are, as one would expect, a vanishing breed. But here and there in North Beach there are traditional makers who cure their pungent pork and bull-meat sausage the full forty-five days in North Beach's uniquely congenial climate.

North Beach achieved worldwide fame in the 1950s when, along with Greenwich Village in New York, a new generation of bohemians emerged here called "beats." The then relatively low rents in North Beach, the European air of a quarter dotted with coffeehouses and inexpensive restaurants, and the tolerant acceptance of all kinds of behavior made this district a mecca for artists and writers, as well as would-be artists and writers. In 1955 Allen Ginsberg came to San Francisco and that December, at a celebrated Six Gallery reading, read *Howl* publicly for the first time. The "angel-headed hipsters" had found a haven in this café-studded old Italian neighborhood.

In August of 1958, North Beach's beatniks, tired of being the object of visitors' curiosity, organized "The Squaresville Tour." One hundred beats in Bermuda shorts and beards, or black slacks and sandals, marched—if that's the word—across Downtown's Union Square to I. Magnin. A bongo drummer led the incursion on a busy Monday shopping night. One marcher brandished a good-natured sign that read, "Hi Squares! The citizens of North Beach are on tour!" Newspaper accounts reported that after touring several fashionable hotels and Downtown stores, the beats withdrew across Columbus Avenue to the Co-Existence Bagel Shop in North Beach.

Today, only poet Lawrence Ferlinghetti's City Lights Books (361 Columbus, below Broadway) and the Vesuvio bar next door survive from the days of the beats. In the late 1960s, upper Grant attracted a swarm of trendy boutiques and art galleries. At the end of the 1970s, North Beach emerged as the refuge of San Francisco's minuscule punk scene. Occasional heads of screaming red or green hair and revived 1950s fashions appeared on Broadway. The Mabuhay Gardens, once a Filipino restaurant, became the city's "punk palace" and the stage for "new wave" rock-and-roll bands. The latest change on Grant is the appearance of more and more Chinese-American businesses, particularly grocery stores, real-estate agencies, and anonymous-looking storefront garment factories. Like its neighborhood, the mix of shops is a complex mosaic of cultures, subcultures, and waves of population.

Today Vallejo Street, from Columbus to Stockton, has the greatest concentration of Italian specialty groceries, pastry shops, Italian magazines, etc.

THE TOUR

1 Washington Square: The Park
· Reserved, 1847; redesigned, 1955

Washington Square was one of only three parks reserved in the city plan of 1847. The present landscaping was designed in 1955. Washington Square is the ideal vantage point from which to see what is best about San Francisco: the extraordinary collective effect of "ordinary" nineteenth- and twentieth-century frame buildings that march up and down her hills. From Washington Square, San Francisco appears as a cubist composition, a city of countless light-colored facets that reflect the changing light of day. Like a whitewashed village clustered on a steep Aegean island, San Francisco's memorable effects are achieved by simple, relatively uniform buildings perched on a dramatic site, all under a Mediterranean-blue sky.

Washington Square is also an ideal place to experience the social essence of San Francisco, the great variety of her population and the relative civility with which different people treat one another. Worlds overlap in the park; vastly different city people all enjoy coming here. Watching the parade of humanity—a parade of all races, ages, and conditions—is what this cosmopolitan seaport has always enjoyed most.

Illogically enough, Washington Square's centerpiece is a statue of Benjamin Franklin presented to the city in 1879 by H.D. Cogswell, a philanthropic dentist and prohibitionist. The long dry taps at the base of the monument are labeled "Cal Seltzer," "Vichy," and "Congress," though they provided only ordinary water. Cogswell gave similar propagandistic monuments to American cities coast to coast. The grim inscription on the pedestal reads: "Presented by H.D. Cogswell to our boys and girls who will soon take our places and pass on." This odd monument is the oldest piece of public sculpture in San Francisco.

A block of stone on the east edge of the park is inscribed,

U.S. Coast & Geodetic Survey
Astronomical & Telegraphic Longitude
Station Washington Square, 1869–1880
Latitude: 37.47'57" N
Longitude: 122.24'37" W

The low, even ring of buildings surrounding the square is echoed in the ring of low trees that enclose the park. The trees are kept trimmed and confined to the edges in order to flood the park with sunlight. An amazing variety of small trees form the green screen that defines the park. Each tree has its distinct profile; some look like enormous bonsai. The paths go around the lawn and do not cut across the center of the square. This preserves the lawn as an island away from traffic. The benches look into the square and face the sun. Each is a donation in memory of some civic-minded San Franciscan. The center of the square is punctuated by three tall poplars whose soaring shapes converse with the twin spires of Saints Peter and Paul Church.

2 East Side of Park
Dante Building
· 1606 Stockton Street
San Francisco Athletic Club
· 1630 Stockton Street
North Beach Post Office
· 1640 Stockton Street, 1930s

On the east, or Stockton Street side of the square, are two interesting buildings. The corner Dante Building with its Gothic portal is a stucco-covered San Francisco interpretation of Venetian Gothic architecture. Seagulls often alight on its cornice. Next door to it at 1630

Stockton is the pleasing two-story, horizontal Moderne building that houses the San Francisco Athletic Club, an Italian-American club. The two buildings are reminders of the relative prosperity of this district in the 1930s, when many new buildings were built and when Edwardian buildings were refaced in Art Deco or Moderne style. The next building is the North Beach Post Office, a simpler but similarly pleasing Moderne building.

3 Saints Peter and Paul Roman Catholic Church and School
· 666 Filbert Street on Washington Square
· Steel-frame and concrete, Romanesque Revival, Charles Fantoni, 1922

This church building, with a school tucked in above and alongside the church, is visually most effective when illuminated at night, its twin towers seeming to float over the city. In 1923, while the reinforced-concrete church was still under construction, Cecil B. DeMille filmed part of *The Ten Commandments* here. In 1926 and 1927 the church was the scene of a series of anarchist bombings.

The church is dedicated to Saints Peter and Paul, he of the earthly keys and he of the sword of truth. Symbols of all four evangelists and two rondels of wheat and grapes decorate the façade, with a Romanesque corbel above. The inscription that runs across the façade reads: LA GLORIA DI COLUI CHE TUTTO MUOVE PER L'UNIVERSO PENETRA E RISPLENDE, "The glory of him who moves all things penetrates and shines throughout the universe"—the opening of the first canto of Dante's *Paradiso.* The original plans for the façade included two large mosaics, one of Columbus landing in America, and another of Dante writing his *Divine Comedy.*

The church is still the spiritual home of San Francisco's Italian-Americans. Until recently, a sign in the church vestibule read: *Tutti gli Italiani e figli d'Italiani residenti in San Francisco possono venire a questa chiesa e in essa avere ogni servizio religioso compresi battesimi, matrimoni, funerali senza bisogno di chiedere altri permessi.* "All Italians and children of Italians who reside in San Francisco can come to this church for every religious service including baptisms, weddings, and funerals without need of other permission." The other permission is that of the archbishop.

Italian immigration to San Francisco was rather different from that to East Coast cities. Here many of the Italians came from the north of Italy, from Liguria (Genoa) and Tuscany. Fishermen, shopkeepers, and traders came as well as unskilled laborers. It was not essentially a peasant migration but was, to a great extent, a movement of town people. Their gift for town living gave North Beach's Little Italy its village feeling. Many of these immigrants were fiercely anticlerical, and a Masonic lodge, "Speranza Italiana Loggia," flourished. In 1881 St. Peter's Church, a church of simple fishermen, enlisted the patronage of the intellectual and argumentative Saint Paul to help church the diverse Italian colony. In 1890 there were only 5,000 Italians in San Francisco, but by 1939 that number had swollen to more than 60,000.

The district has two festive days, the blessing of the fishing fleet in the spring, and Columbus Day on October 12. On Columbus Day, a long parade, traditionally attended by the city's politicians, marches down Columbus Avenue. A temporary fair with rides and food is set up in Washington Square.

As the second generation prospered, many young couples moved to the adjoining Marina district to the northwest. Today, North Beach is a varied neighborhood; but the once-strong Italian colony is still evident. As Chinatown has expanded, many of the alleys in North Beach, where the less expensive housing is, have become largely Chinese-American. Mixed in with the Italians and Chinese is a great variety of other nationalities and life-styles. Only the uninformed would dare to generalize about North Beach's population; it is indescribably varied. The only safe generalization is that the cheaper apartments are in the valley, and the more expensive ones are on the slopes with marine views.

4 Maybeck Building
· 1736 Stockton Street
· Bernard Maybeck, 1909–28

Walk to the intersection of Filbert and Stockton, the northeast corner of the square. The prospect up Filbert Street toward Russian Hill to the west includes a view of the steepest paved street in San Francisco, the 1100 block of Filbert Street, between Leavenworth and Hyde, which has a 31½ percent grade (a rise of 31½ feet in 100 horizontal feet).

At the corner of Stockton and Filbert, 1700 Stockton Street, is the Liguria Bakery, housed in a post-earthquake Edwardian building with rounded corner bay windows built about 1912. The interior of the bakery remains unchanged. Photographs in the windows show the making of panettone, an Italian fruit bread and a specialty in North Beach.

Walk north on the east side of Stockton Street, to the charcoal-gray wood Maybeck Building built in 1909—designed, added onto, and remodeled by famed Bay Area architect Bernard Maybeck, and later by others. Horizontal grooved boards cover the first story, and rustic board-and-batten siding sheathes the second and third. The porches, painted window boxes, and eaves-detailing recall a Swiss chalet. The building originally housed the Telegraph Hill Neighborhood Association, the oldest neighborhood group in San Francisco, but has since been remodeled into offices and apartments. Climb the stairs and peek into the intimate courtyard surrounded by staircases, balconies, and roof decks. An interestingly shaped tree twists its way out of one corner and lightly roofs half the space with its branches. The building has been continually reworked but retains the intention and flavor of Maybeck's design.

5 300 and 400 Blocks of Filbert Street
· Post-1906 Edwardian apartments

Retrace your steps to the corner of Stockton and Filbert. Slowly climb Filbert Street on the righthand sidewalk (south). Stop now and then to look back. What begins as a constricted city street view soon opens up to a magnificent panorama of the bay and Marin County. These blocks were all burned in 1906. In the decade that followed, the lots were built up with frame, bay-windowed apartment houses, all the same yet individualistic. From the southwest corner of Filbert and Kearny Streets there is a majestic view of the bay and Mt. Tamalpais.

6 Garfield Elementary School
· 420 Filbert Street
· Esherick Homsey Dodge and Davis, 1979

San Francisco makes an effort to place parks and schools at the tops of hills, and this school is one of the best-sited and best-designed contemporary buildings in the city. The grammar school previously on this site was monumental and free standing. It was replaced in 1979 because it no longer met seismic safety standards. The bulk of this fine, mildly "post-modern" building has been broken up so as to fit in with the neighboring apartment houses. The two "parts" of the school are even painted differently—one in a dark tan color, the other in a faded terra-cotta. A pergola links the building to the sidewalk. The building is placed so as to protect the schoolyard from the wind. Interestingly designed windows look out to the Golden Gate. The exaggerated false "keystone" design surrounding the Filbert Street door pays witty tribute to the classicized building that the new school replaced and says much about theater in architecture. No doubt children will remember this portal, an excellent symbol for a school. It is a cheery building. Here is the very best of contemporary Northern California architecture. The building is learned and rich with references to the region's architectural traditions, but still light, alive, happy to be where it is doing what it's doing.

7 1454–56 Kearny Street
· c. 1910 Edwardian flats; penthouse by Bond and Brown, 1978

From the southwest corner of Filbert and Kearny Street is a good view of 1454–56 Kearny Street, typical postfire flats but with a modern, streamlined, nearly-all-glass penthouse added in 1978. Sleek, simple, very modern, it is a beautiful design speaking in the design idiom of today. Now that the city is almost entirely built up and most of the view lots have been developed, penthouses become the solution to housing with a view.

8 Filbert Steps West
- 351 Filbert
- Modern flats, Gardner Dailey, 1941

Walk up the shrub-lined staircase that begins where Filbert Street stops. This was approximately the edge of the fire in 1906. Part of the hill escaped the flames, and some prefire cottages survive here and there. Walk up to where the sidewalk meets Telegraph Hill Boulevard. Near that point is 351 Filbert (101 Telegraph Hill Boulevard), modern flats designed by Gardner Dailey in 1941. The windows are angled to catch the view. Do not continue down the steps; instead take the path bordered by stone walls that parallels Telegraph Hill Boulevard. The path leads to the turn-around in front of Coit Tower at the summit of Telegraph Hill.

Pioneer Park
- Donated 1876

Telegraph Hill got its name from a wooden semaphore tower built on its summit in the Gold Rush period that signaled merchants down in Yerba Buena Cove (the present-day Financial District) of the ships entering the Golden Gate. Though this semaphore signal system was in operation for only a few years, the name Telegraph Hill stuck to the spot. In the mid-nineteenth century, 274-foot-high Telegraph Hill was a barren, rocky peak devoid of landscaping. Every two weeks, on steamer day, people would climb to the top of the hill to watch the approach of the steamers that brought the mail from back East. In 1876 a group of businessmen purchased the lots at the top of the hill and donated them to the city; their gift was given the name Pioneer Park. In 1883 Gustave Sutro opened a "high-class pleasure resort" at the top of the hill. A funicular railroad to the Gothic Revival restaurant-bar was opened in 1884, but closed in 1887; it was called the steepest railroad in the world.

9 Coit Tower
- Arthur Brown, Jr., 1934
- Open daily, 9:30–4; 1930s frescoes open daily, 2–4

In 1934 Arthur Brown, Jr., the architect of City Hall and other noted structures, designed Coit Tower. It was built with funds from a bequest to the city by Lillie Hitchcock Coit. Popular legend notwithstanding, the building was not designed to look like a firehouse nozzle, but is a single free-standing column. Its style could be dubbed stripped Classical or Mussolini Modern. Coit Tower is 210 feet high and is constructed of reinforced concrete throughout; expensive materials were not permitted by the $125,000 budget. The tower was designed as a handsomely fluted shaft resting on a base and capped by three levels of arched loggias. Its base is encircled by terraces with fine views of the city. Over the entrance is a bas-relief of the city's emblem, a phoenix rising from its ashes.

Lillie Hitchcock was born in 1843 at West Point, the daughter of an army surgeon. In 1851 she and her family came to San Francisco. Here she became a celebrity as a teenager for her constant attendance at fires, particularly those fought by Knickerbocker Engine Company No. 5. At fifteen she became the mascot of the company and later was made an honorary member. In 1903 a deranged man attempted to shoot Lillie Coit, and the Coits moved to France, where Lillie stayed until she suffered a stroke in 1925. She then returned to San Francisco, where she spent the last four years of her life, speechless, at Dante Sanitarium. An Engine Company No. 5 pin accompanied her to the grave. Lillie Hitchcock Coit left one-third of her estate to the City and County of San Francisco "to be expended in an appropriate manner for the purpose of adding to the beauty of the city which I have always loved." In 1931 the Coit Advisory Committee was formed and commissioned two monuments, one a bronze statuary group on Columbus Avenue in Washington Square by Haig Patigan in memory of the original volunteer fire department in San Francisco, and the other an observatory tower on Telegraph Hill. After the construction of the Art Deco apartment house on the north side of the hill on Telegraph Hill Boulevard in the 1930s, the Coit Advisory Committee called for the rezoning of Telegraph Hill "so that skyscrapers would not interfere with the view from or detract from the beauty of the Coit Memorial." Consequently, a forty-foot (fourstory) height limit was placed on buildings on the hill.

The Coit Tower Murals

The Coit Tower murals are among the finest 1930s murals in the country and were commissioned by the "New Deal" Public Works of Art Project in 1934, shortly after the completion of the tower. Twenty-five master artists and nineteen assistants worked for six months to cover some 3691 square feet of wall space with a well-thought-out cycle of frescoes. True fresco, *buon fresco,* is the art of painting on freshly spread plaster before it dries. The pigments are applied with water as a vehicle, and the lime of the ground, which penetrates the painting, is converted by exposure to the air into calcium carbonate, which acts as a binding material. It takes years for frescoes to cure and reach their peak of brilliance.

The cycle, on the working life of California in the 1930s, is unified in narrative conception, but each section was done by a different group of painters and some vary markedly in style. Some are straightforwardly documentary, while a few are militantly political. The chief artistic influence on the mural painters was the famed Mexican artist Diego Rivera, who was in San Francisco for a brief time in the 1930s. The intense colors and rounded forms in the murals clearly show Rivera's influence on Ralph Stackpole and the other artists. Left-wing political views permeate parts of the cycle and caused much consternation in San Francisco when the completed murals were seen in June, 1934. That was the summer of the great Maritime and General Strike in San Francisco, the only general strike in American history. The city Art Commission decided to close the Tower for four months until some minor revisions were made in the murals and while public opinion quieted down. Finally, after some bad press and much wrangling, the murals were opened to the public in October, 1934.

A *American Eagle.* Enter the Tower and look straight ahead over the inner archway that leads to the elevators. A pair of awesome, penetrating eyes surrounded by clouds, thunder, lightning, rain, the sun, and the moon stare at the entrant like the eyes of God the Creator in a Byzantine apse. An American eagle, like the one on the back of a twenty-five-cent piece, adorns the arch itself. Step left and follow the murals in a clockwise direction.

B *Animal Force and Machine Force* (inner north wall, both sides of the inner doorway), by Ray Boynton, a 36-foot-long, 10-foot-high fresco panel flanking both sides of the inner doorway. Ancient society is differentiated from modern by the motive forces underlying them. On the left is the traditional source of power: human and animal muscle. The fishermen pulling their heavy nets from the sea repeat an ancient fresco theme. In a small niche is a young boy curled up reading the dedication book for Coit Tower. To the right of the central doorway a hydroelectric dam harnesses elemental forces for modern man's work.

C *California Industry: Timber and Dairying* (outer wall, northeast corner), by Gordon Langdon. To the left, a sawmill transforms Northern California redwood trees into milled lumber. Look carefully in the mill to find the primitive and communicative roots of all art in a worker's graffito on a pillar. This fresco is 10 feet high and 27 feet wide. (The same primitive need to record one's presence in the material world forced the closing of the frescoes for many years; scratched initials, dates, and messages are a constant menace to this splendid piece of public art. Please do not even touch the painted surfaces, for the oil of even the cleanest hand will damage the fresco.)

D *Farmer and Cowboy* (flanking the large east window), by Clifford Wright, two frescoes each 10 feet high and 4 feet wide of single figures with implements of their trade. The two figures represent the classic struggle in every cowboy movie, the contest between the cattlemen's desire for open range and the farmers' need for fenced-in fields.

E *California* (inner east wall), by Maxine Albro, a fresco 42 feet long and 10 feet high, depicting a synthesis of California agricultural scenes in an abundant valley. From left to right are wheat farming (California's first important agricultural commodity in the 1880s and the basis of some of the wealth that built Victorian San Francisco), flower-raising (note the romantic garb of the workers), and viticulture and wine-making. It is a prettified picture of farmworkers in California. This has never been a state of small family farms such as the one shown on the horizon. Enormous grain fields in the nineteenth century and huge corporate agribusiness holdings in this century, both worked by migrant labor, have been the hallmarks of California agriculture. California remains one of the most productive agricultural regions on earth and exports its produce to the rest of the nation and the world.

F *Department Store* (outer wall, left southeast corner), by Frede Vidar, a fresco 10 by 10 feet showing a soda fountain, a wine shop (around the small window), and a department store with customers, merchandise, and attendants. Fear and melancholy pervade the café; one woman shyly hides behind another as if afraid of a photographer. In the background a woman reads a paper with news of Hitler and of the destruction of the Diego Rivera murals in New York's Rockefeller Center. Anguish and foreboding are present everywhere.

G *Banking* (outer wall, right southeast corner), by George Harris, a fresco 10 by 10 feet showing lawyers reading in a law library, armed guards protecting a bank vault, and the grain-exchange board. The themes are money, law, and force. The downward sloping line on the graph of the grain exchange tells the economic history of the Depression era. Some of the titles of the "law books" are amusing and include a volume on the *Law of Averages* and the *Laws of Seduction*.

H *Stockbroker and Scientist* (outer wall, flanking the large south window), by Mallette Dean, two frescoes each 10 feet high and 4 feet wide, of single figures with symbolic tools of their professions. The man who has ideas, the scientist and inventor; and the man who makes ideas social realities, the businessman and investor, flank the window that faces the Financial District. A light switch on the wall is incorporated into the scientist's observatory.

I *City Life* (inner south wall), by Victor Arnautoff, a fresco 36 feet long and 10 feet high synthesizing various street scenes, crowds, and buildings. A newsstand occupies the center of the composition. A holdup is in progress as the crowd hurries by. A car crash has taken place in front of the Stock Exchange. This complex scene is the heart of the mural cycle and shows various parts of San Francisco as they looked in the 1930s. Silk-hatted men and sailors, workers and shoppers, policemen and thieves crowd the city streets. Note the newspapers that surround the prosperous businessman in the brown homburg. A woman's legs peek out from an ad in the paper he clutches under his arm. He is reading the New York stock tables; and he stands on a cheap tabloid depicting a gangster slaying. The papers epitomize money, sex, and death. At the center of all this activity is a stock ticker and quotation symbolizing society's preoccupation with the economic collapse of the 1930s.

J *Library* (outer wall, left southwest corner), by Bernard Zakheim, a fresco 10 by 10 feet depicting a library reading room with patrons reading a variety of things. Most of the newspapers are communist and socialist periodicals with headlines recording the political crises of the day. One of the most prominent figures is taking Marx's *Capital* from the shelf. A happy hedonist amidst this politically passionate group of readers is relishing a girlie newspaper.

K *News Gathering* (outer wall, right southwest corner), by Suzanne Scheuer, a fresco 10 by 10 feet showing the editorial office, linotyping, composing, printing, and selling of the *San Francisco Chronicle.* A reporter with his back to the viewer hands his story in to his editor on the right. The production process dominates the scene; the frame around the small window shows the printing of the separate colors for the Sunday comics. A newsboy stands to the left with the finished product. On the windowsill is a copy of the *Chronicle* with the headline, ARTISTS FINISH COIT TOWER MURALS.

L *Surveyor and Steelworker* (outer wall, flanking the large west window), by Clifford Wright, two frescoes 10 feet high and 4 feet wide showing single figures with the tools of their work. They represent mental and physical labor.

M *Industries of California* (inner west wall), by Ralph Stackpole, a fresco 36 feet long and 10 feet high depicting in realistic detail a synthesis of California industries from canning to steel to chemicals. This is the third major passage in the cycle (the others were agriculture and city life) and clearly shows the influence of Rivera on the artist. Note the NRA blue eagle on the sacks.

N *Railroad and Shipping* (outer wall, northwest corner), by William Hesthal, a fresco 10 by 10 feet depicting another pairing, here land transport and sea transport. The small window is treated like the underside of a trestle.

O *California Industrial Scenes* (outer north wall), by John Langley Howard, a fresco 24 feet long and 10 feet high showing construction, oil drilling, mining, and panning for gold. This is another politically charged passage, with striking miners massed menacingly before the viewer. Panning for gold in already worked-over streambeds was revived in California during the Depression and brought the state back to its beginnings. Here an impoverished migrant family camped in the open is the object of the curiosity of the idle rich, who have arrived in their yellow limousine to view the poor. The hungry mongrel and the pampered poodle eye each other and sum up the conflict. Looming above the squalor of the migrants' camp is a monumental hydroelectric dam and a sleek streamlined train. The theme of technological progress and social catastrophe reflects the somber insights of the Depression era.

P *Social Revolution* (over the inner lintel of the door leading outside), by John Langley Howard, the last, most direct, and least-noticed passage in the cycle, is a powerful image. In the cramped space over the door is a vast wheatfield moving under a stormy sky. Thunder and lightning echo and flash across the ominous black sky. The wheatfield below is ablaze; out of the flames rises a clenched fist. This symbol of social revolution closes this cycle on the history of California workers in a way that satisfied the artists, but was not borne out by time.

To the left of the front door is a scrap of paper with a quote from President Franklin Roosevelt, "I'm a tough guy. I learned a lot from the barracudas and the sharks."

The View from Coit Tower

Take the elevator to the open-roofed observation deck. Visible to the northwest is the Golden Gate Bridge spanning the entrance to the bay. The name "Golden Gate" was given to the entrance to San Francisco Bay by Captain John C. Frémont in 1848; on his map of California and Oregon published in that year he used the Greek equivalent *Chrysopylae*. The title was not suggested by the discovery of gold but by the name of the harbor of Constantinople, *Chrysoceros,* or Golden Horn. The great bridge designed by Joseph Strauss, chief engineer, and Irving Morrow, architect, opened in 1937, financed by a $35 million bond issue. Eleven workers had lost their lives during its construction. It is painted international orange—not the gold so many expect. Its emphatic Moderne piers support a 4200-foot clear span (the longest in the world until 1959). From this vantage point the massive bridge piers reveal Gothic buttress profiles. When the fog pours in through the gate, the bridge seems suspended in the clouds.

The Marin headlands on the opposite shore, set aside as military reservations in the 1840s, are now part of the Golden Gate National Recreation Area. Their untreed slopes give an idea of what the entire Bay Area looked like before irrigation and extensive forestation with imported plants changed the ecology of the region and the state. The posh village of Sausalito ("little willow") nestles on the man-forested hillside east of the bridge.

The highest peak visible to the north is Mt. Tamalpais, which, according to Indian legend, is a sleeping maiden lying with her feet toward the sea. A small rocky island in the middle of the bay is Alcatraz, now abandoned but once a military and then a federal penitentiary. Appearing as a dark, wooded island, visible to the left beyond Alcatraz, is Belvedere—one of the most sensitively designed turn-of-the-century and contemporary residential enclaves in the Bay Area. The large wooded island to the right of Alcatraz is Angel Island, a state game refuge that once served as San Francisco's Ellis Island, a quarantine point for Asian immigrants. This northern part of the bay is a favorite area for sailors, and countless sails dot the blue waters of the bay on weekends. The silver bridge to the right of Angel Island is the Richmond Bridge. Beyond it is San Pablo Bay, where California's rivers flow into the bay. Across the bay, due north, is an enormous natural-gas storage tank and the smaller oil storage tanks of the Point Richmond refinery that serve the Bay Area. Bulk shipping is dispersed along the Carquinez Straits—the Silver Gate—farther to the northeast.

In the foreground, between the piers and the circular parking lot, is the one-time warehouse district now being redeveloped for offices and condominiums. The low red-brick buildings with the black-and-red roof patterns were designed in 1975 by Robinson and Mills, and house the Telegraph Landing Office Park. The modern white buildings with the intricate roof gardens were designed in 1976 by Bull, Field, Volkman, and Stockwell as a luxury condominium, Telegraph Landing.

The flat, man-made island in the middle of the bay is Treasure Island, built with WPA funds for the 1939 Golden Gate International Exposition to celebrate the completion of the two great bridges. Its enormous concave-fronted hangar was built for the Manila Clippers, used on the first trans-Pacific air route. A sloping causeway connects it to Yerba Buena Island, a rocky, man-forested island used by the Navy and Coast Guard. The San Francisco–Oakland Bay Bridge connects Yerba Buena Island to the east and west shores of the bay. It was begun in 1933 and completed in 1936. The $70 million cost was financed by the New Deal Reconstruction Finance Corporation and the State of California and created needed employment during the

Depression. This bridge is a complex of two joined suspension bridges on the San Francisco side, a tunnel that bores through Yerba Buena Island, and a truss bridge on the Oakland side. The simple X-brace design of the two suspension bridges is the work of Charles H. Purcell, chief engineer, and Timothy Pfleuger, who streamlined what was once proposed to be a Gothic design. The Bay Bridge was built with two decks: the lower deck originally carried an electric commuter train, which provided excellent service and should never have been removed. The great engineering feat of the bridge is the center pier joining the two 2310-foot suspension spans. This pier reaches 220 feet below the surface of the water to bedrock.

Visible in the foreground is the old warehouse district and the east slope of Telegraph Hill, where this tour is headed.

To the south is the dense cluster of San Francisco's high-rise district, built on landfill on the site of Yerba Buena Cove. The clock tower on the waterfront tops the 1895 Ferry Building. The contemporary skyline is mostly the result of the building boom of the 1960s. The tall white pyramid is the Transamerica Building. Its dark neighbor to the right with the zigzag façade is the headquarters of the Bank of America, the world's largest private bank.

Partially visible to the southwest, but almost completely surrounded by tall apartment houses, is Grace Cathedral atop Nob Hill, replacing the Charles and W.H. Crocker houses, which burned in 1906. In the valley between Nob and Telegraph Hills are the even, steplike streets of bay-windowed postfire flats built between 1906 and 1915. Virtually everything visible in this direction burned after the earthquake and was reconstructed almost entirely with three- and four-story frame apartment buildings of remarkably even texture. Note the great number of roof gardens and sun decks on the slope of Telegraph Hill. Between the downtown high-rises and the Nob Hill high-rises is a district of lower, red-brick buildings capped by white flagpoles. This is Chinatown, totally reconstructed in 1906, but re-creating the scale of the red-brick commercial city of the 1880s.

The park in the valley to the southwest is Washington Square, where the tour began. In the valley is North Beach, cut through by the diagonal of Columbus Avenue. The hill beyond Washington Square with the aggressive mixture of residential high-rises and brown-shingled houses nestled in dense greenery is Russian Hill, one of San Francisco's finest apartment districts.

Visible on the southwestern horizon, atop forested Mt. Sutro, is the three-pronged, empire-waisted Sutro television tower, built in 1972. The densely forested area on the western horizon south of the Golden Gate Bridge is the Presidio Military Reservation with its man-made forests designed by Major Jones in the 1880s.

Before leaving the observation deck, take a moment to appreciate the de Chirico-like stripped Classical arcade with which architect Arthur Brown, Jr., capped his tower. The small windows, closely

spaced arcades, and tall, well-like, sky-roofed observation area create
a sense of security for the viewer.

10 Greenwich Steps

Leave the tower, go down the front steps, turn right, cross the road
to the light pole, and descend red-brick Greenwich Steps, which
cascade down the east face of the hill. The almost-hidden stairs are
flanked by a profusion of flowers and greenery. Most of this landscaping dates from the early twentieth century. In the nineteenth
century, Telegraph Hill was barren and goat-infested. In 1888, one
woman described how hard it was to locate a particular shanty on the
east slope of the hill:

> It requires some physical exertion to mount a Telegraph Hill
> stairway, but that is nothing in comparison with the mental
> effort necessary in finding one's way after reaching the top. We
> jump a ditch that serves as an open channel for sewage, make
> a detour around a pile of tomato cans, bring up in a blind alley
> that purports to be a street leading directly to the house we
> seek, try a path that ends abruptly on the edge of the cliff, and
> narrowly escape a landslide that goes careening down the bluff,
> and which has lost its precarious hold just a moment too soon
> to give us a free toboggan ride. . . .

Many of the earliest residents of this east slope were Irish stevedores
who worked on the docks below. As local poet Wallace Irwin wrote
in 1904:

TELYGRAFT HILL

O Telygraft Hill she sits mighty fine,
    Like a praty that's planted on ind,
And she's bannered wid washin's from manny a line,
    Which flutter and dance in the wind.
O th' goats and th' chickens av Telygraft Hill
    They prosper all grand and serene,
For when there's short pickin' on Telygraft Hill
    They feed their swate sowls on the scene.
For the Irish they live on the top av it,
And the Dagos they live on the base av it,
And every tin can in the knowledge av man,
    Is scattered all over the face av it.
Av Telygraft Hill, Telygraft Hill,
Nobby owld, slobby owld Telygraft Hill!

By the late nineteenth century, Telegraph Hill was also sprinkled
with the residences of artists and theater people. The area became one
of San Francisco's bohemias. Maguire's Opera House and the Metropolitan Theater were within walking distance. Lola Montez, the
sweetheart of the gold-mining camps, was once a resident of the hill.
So were the Booths, a famous family of actors. Like many other

bohemias, Telegraph Hill began to attract the attention of more comfortable classes. By the late 1930s, the writers, painters, and sculptors happily ensconced in their small wooden shacks were joined by office workers and others who appreciated the hill's visual and romantic qualities and its immediate accessibility to the Downtown. By 1939 this low-rent island in the sky began to be taken over by those with "the longing for bohemia . . . whose incomes permit them to be comfortably daring." And, as the same commentator noted, "It is well on the way to becoming smart." Robert Louis Stevenson's "peak in the wind" went from low-rent bohemia to high-rent respectability.

At the landing, turn left and continue down the brick stairs. Note the Mediterranean-style stucco house off the landing at 356 Greenwich. Farther down the stairs on the left is Number 308, an unpretentious two-story shingled building reminiscent of the early shacks that once clung to the hill.

Julius Castle
· 1922

Continue down the stairs to the head of Montgomery Street. At the end of the street is Julius Castle, built in 1922, a crenellated, shingled fantasy perched on the cliff, which houses a well-known San Francisco restaurant. This end of Montgomery was improved in the 1930s. Before that, there was a narrow one-lane road here with a turntable for automobiles at its foot. When the street was redesigned it was split into two levels with a narrow space in between which has been most effectively landscaped. Walk up the lower, or left-hand, side of the street. Note how the pollarded pines and other clipped plants enhance what would otherwise be an unsightly retaining wall. The illusion of a large park is created in a cramped space, a typical San Francisco trick.

1 1 1360 Montgomery
· Moderne apartments, J.S. Malloch, 1937

Walk to the intersection of Montgomery and Filbert. The white, four-story streamline Moderne-style apartment house at 1360 Montgomery is one of San Francisco's best small designs of that engaging style. The sand-blasted glass window over the entryway is ornamented with the obligatory leaping gazelle and zigzag design. Glass blocks and a banister rail shaped like waves also ornament the entryway. The top of the building has streamlined corners and a rail reminiscent of a steamship. The three decorative panels on the exterior are good examples of 1930s artwork. On the west side of the building, a panel represents the port of San Francisco; here a muscular figure holds up a globe. Above him are three of the Manila Clippers, the earliest air link across the Pacific, inaugurated in October, 1936.

At the figure's feet is the Bay Bridge, opened in November, 1936, and beneath the bridge a silhouette of Telegraph Hill with Coit Tower, another public improvement of the period. The companion panel on the north side of the building represents California, a goddess at the end of the rainbow. Behind her is the outline of the state with San Francisco Bay clearly visible. A sun sets in a zigzag landscape. A third panel on the south end of the building depicts a Spanish conquistador in the New World. At the corner of the apartment house is a typically pruned, streamlined shrub: a quintessential bit of San Francisco landscaping. The vegetation in the city has been subjected to a geometrical rigor equal to that imposed on the site by the gridiron street plan.

1400 Montgomery
· Brown shingle cottage

Facing this streamlined building is a reminder of Telegraph Hill's early period, the simple, shingled, tarpaper-roofed cottage at 1400 Montgomery Street, now a member of an endangered architectural species. Few buildings of this type survive on the hill; once this became a fashionable district, simple buildings such as these were cleared away and multistory apartment houses constructed in their place. Shingles were more luxurious than the earlier workers' clapboarded houses, shacks, and shanties. Visible beyond the cottage is the south wall of 1406 Montgomery Street, a simple and characteristic frame apartment building with a spiral staircase in the airshaft, ship railings surrounding the sundeck, and potted trees on the roof.

12 Filbert Steps and Napier Lane: An Island in the City

At the Montgomery and Filbert signpost, a staircase descends to Filbert Steps. Walk down the staircase and penetrate this delightful green island in the city. The parklike space is legally a city street but is too steep to pave. A sign was placed here by the residents of the steps to thank Grace Marchant on her eighty-sixth birthday for her efforts in landscaping this spot. Filbert Street Steps has simple buildings and rich landscaping. Many of the buildings are types inherited from the nineteenth century; the lush landscaping is all modern. Simple buildings dramatically sited and lovingly landscaped are the essence of San Francisco's cityscape. San Franciscans, aware that space is scarce in their city, are adept at turning the smallest, most ungainly nook into a garden. They all seem hopelessly involved with their plants. An astonishing number will tell you they communicate with their plants and play music for them! Everybody, it seems, has a potted plant in his quarters, and even public places are alive with greenery. Those with a back porch or fire escape will invariably crowd it with plants. Among other distinctions, San Francisco has the highest per capita consumption of cut flowers of any American city. Even very modest, homely buildings that would simply stand naked and unloved in other American cities will sport an improvised array of planters with a miniature forest of succulents.

The unthought-out grid plan rigidly clamped down over the undulating topography has had its happy accidental effects. In the nineteenth century this area was overrun by goats and was barren. Now it is a vertical garden of vines, roses, and flowering trees, all tended by the people who live along the steps. On the north side of the steps is a row of simple wooden buildings that escaped the fire in 1906 and whose architecture accurately reflects the unpretentious buildings of the nineteenth century.

228 Filbert
· Gothic Revival, 1873

Number 228 Filbert was built in 1873 by an Englishman from Jersey in the stevedoring business. The Gothic-style house replaced a simple shanty on the site.

224 Filbert
· Cottage, 1863

Number 224 Filbert, with its curious roof shape, was built in 1863 and thoroughly restored in 1978. The picturesque but decrepit cottage was jacked up and new concrete footings were inserted underneath it. All construction materials had to be carried down 128 steps from Montgomery Street or up 140 steps from Sansome Street.

222 Filbert
· Corner of Napier Lane
· Gothic Revival, 1875

This simple and picturesque frame building housed Michael Thornton's grocery store and home from the 1880s to about 1918. Some say the grocery store was only the legitimate front for a "blind pig"—an unlicensed saloon that once occupied the corner. According to one eminent American historian, Arthur Meyer Schlesinger, San Francisco had more saloons per capita than any other American city. An impossible distinction to prove, but one that San Franciscans would not vigorously deny.

Napier Lane Boardwalk

Off Filbert Street Steps is an even more intimate streetscape, Napier Lane, a wooden boardwalk garnished with pots of flowers. There always seems to be something in bloom along this lane, no matter what the month. San Francisco is a city of delightful, hidden-away cul-de-sacs. The ground here is carpeted with a small green plant called Baby Tears. Boardwalks were common in early San Francisco. They were inexpensive, but proved to be fire hazards and were gradually replaced. This is the last one left in the city.

Number 10 Napier Lane is a simple one-story false-fronted Italianate building typical of the earliest houses in the city and built in 1875. Number 21 Napier Lane, built in 1885, is a typical three-story frame apartment house with a precipitous exterior staircase that creates interesting patterns. At the end of Napier Lane is Number 30, a board-and-batten brown-stained building with a delightful country feeling. This kind of unpretentious siding was usually used for California farm buildings. Some of these shacks were reputedly used for shanghaiing sailors in the nineteenth century. Between the buildings on Napier Lane are fascinating glimpses of the backyards, roof decks, and porches that spill down the eastern face of the hill. An extraordinary number of sleek cats populate the steps. Flowerpots are informally scattered about.

View of the Ice House

Continue down Filbert Steps to the concrete staircase that replaced the old wood stairs in 1972, and stop at the first landing. A welcome park bench was a recent gift of one of the residents of the hill and has a plaque that reads: "I have the feeling we're not in Kansas anymore." To the left, on the northwest corner of Filbert and Sansome, is the H.G. Walters Warehouse with a Moderne-style house, garden, and guest house perched on its roof, another curious example of the San Franciscan's cleverness in utilizing random space. To the right is the abrupt cliff of the eastern face of the hill, the site of a quarry that continued to operate into the twentieth century. The rock quarried here was used as fill around the base of the hill to create land for the brick warehouse district. The undermining of the hill caused several houses at the crest to slide down the cliff to their destruction. There was even a proposal to quarry the hill away entirely for bay-fill, but the excavating was stopped at this point. Cement shoulders have been placed on the crest of the hill to prevent erosion. Fragrant wild anise, a tall weed with a crownlike head, thrives here, as in many of San Francisco's empty lots.

Visible beyond the quarried face of the hill is the red-brick bulk of Icehouses #1 and #2, large cold-storage facilities constructed in 1914 to serve the docks along The Embarcadero. When shipping moved to other more spacious sites around the bay, these old warehouses were remodeled as furniture showrooms by Wurster, Bernardi and Emmons in 1970. A glass-and-iron bridge, invisible from this angle, connects the two icehouses. This entire former warehouse district has been recently converted almost entirely to architects' and landscape designers' offices and furniture showrooms.

Walk back up Filbert Steps to Montgomery Street and turn left up Montgomery as far as Union Street. Those not too tired from the walk should explore two architectural jewels and the fine view on Calhoun Terrace, half a block east, toward the bay.

13 Calhoun Terrace

Calhoun Terrace is a quiet, split-level cul-de-sac perched on the edge of the Telegraph Hill cliff with a dramatic view of the bay and the downtown high-rises. The sidewalk ends abruptly at a cement wall and a view like that from a box in an opera house.

Gothic Revival House
· 9 Calhoun Terrace, c. 1855

This charming house with its light balconies and delicate gingerbread is one of the oldest houses in San Francisco and was built about 1855.

Kahn House
· 66 Calhoun Terrace
· Richard Neutra, 1939

In the twentieth century, Southern California was fertile ground for architectural genius. Richard Neutra, a Vienna-born architect based in Los Angeles, was among America's greatest. He designed in the International style. This classic, elegantly refined house perches on the edge of the cliff with its face to the view and its back to the street.

To end this tour where it began, retrace your route to Montgomery and Union. On the corner, at 301 Union, is Speedy's New Union Grocery, where you can buy refreshments. The bulletin board here serves as the local information post for the blocks at the summit of the hill. The #39 Coit bus stops here and returns to Washington Square.

Tour 2

The Financial District and Jackson Square

Gold Rush to Skyscraper

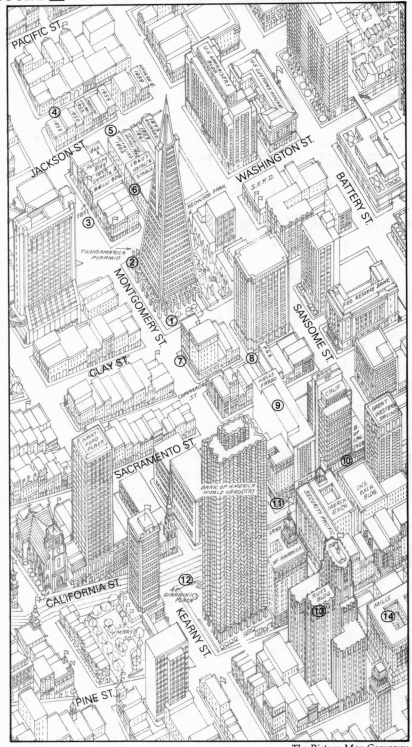

1 Transamerica Pyramid
2 Columbus Avenue
3 700 Block of Montgomery, 1850s
4 Gold Street to Balance Street
5 400 Block of Jackson
6 Hotaling Place
7 Old Bank of America Headquarters
8 Leidesdorff and Commercial Streets
9 Wells Fargo History Room
10 400 Block of California
11 Kohl Building
12 Bank of America World Headquarters
13 Russ Building
14 Mills Building and Tower

WHAT THIS WALK COVERS

San Francisco's Financial District is the banking and insurance center for the world's seventh richest "nation"—California. The world's largest privately owned bank (Bank of America), the world's largest construction firm (Bechtel), one of the largest private utilities in the country (Pacific Gas & Electric), and Standard Oil of California, to name but four leaders, have their headquarters within the blocks bounded by Washington, Kearny, and Mission Streets and the bay.

This walk from the Transamerica Pyramid to the Bank of America, the two dominant buildings on the city's skyline, charts the history of San Francisco from the Gold Rush of the 1850s, when the population of this sleepy port jumped from 500 to 10,000 overnight, to the high-rises of today. These blocks are dense with associations from every phase of California's phenomenal development. Decisions made here helped turn what was once a virtual desert into a flourishing, dynamic, globally important region.

The walk proceeds from north to south, the direction in which the Downtown shifted in the late nineteenth century, and from the intimate, low-scaled streets of the Jackson Square Historic District to the top of the tallest building in the city, the granite-clad, fifty-two-story Bank of America. In between are fascinating architectural works, including the finest banking halls of California's turn-of-the-century architects. Also on the route are a few outstanding small museums and paintings, heirlooms from the city's rich past. Along the way we cross the paths of the shades of flannel-shirted, gold-seeking Forty-Niners, as well as Mark Twain, William Tecumseh Sherman, Bret Harte, William Ralston, Black Bart, the madams of the Barbary Coast, Domingo Ghirardelli, Darius Ogden Mills, Daniel Burnham, William Randolph Hearst, and more recent titans such as A.P. Giannini.

PRACTICALITIES

Best time for this walk: A business day during banking hours (10:00 A.M. to 3:00 P.M.) is when the Financial District is liveliest and its grand interiors and small museums are open to the public. Lunchtime is the peak time to see the conservatively and fashionably dressed nine-to-five denizens of the district. On Sundays and bank holidays the district closes up; the buildings are easier to see then as pure sculptural forms.

Parking: The best place to park for this walk is the city-owned Portsmouth Square Garage on Kearny Street, between Clay and Washington. Portsmouth Square was the central plaza of the old Yerba Buena.

The Bank of California, old (1908) and new (1967), on the 400 Block of California Street, the heart of the banking district.

Getting there by public transit: This tour is downtown, just a short walk from Union Square.

Cafés and Restaurants: The Financial District has many fine restaurants, particularly seafood restaurants, whereas Fisherman's Wharf has only a few. A San Francisco institution is 115-year-old Jack's, at 615 Sacramento. The Tadich Grill (240 California) serves some of the finest seafood in San Francisco and is worth the wait in line. Hoffman's Grill (619 Market, at the head of New Montgomery) is like stepping back into the turn of the century. Sam's Grill (374 Bush) is unassuming but well known for its seafood. For the setting if nothing else, the Garden Court of the Palace Hotel on Market Street is memorable; good Sunday brunch. Financial District bars are innumerable. The one with the best view is the Carnelian Room atop the Bank of America (which, before 3:00 P.M., houses the Bankers' Club).

INTRODUCTION

In the 1880s Robert Louis Stevenson described San Francisco's stock exchange as a great pump continually forcing the savings of the city into concentrated fortunes. Today's high-rises and the great corporations they house can be seen in the same way, great pumps that draw capital and talent to the oldest commercial center on the West Coast and keep San Francisco economically vital.

Money is the ultimate commodity. Financial districts are among the most conservative of land developments. Banks and insurance companies can afford to stay on whatever property they choose because they finance their own structures. There is a practical reason why financial districts are always as dense as they are: the financial and legal world is one that depends on face-to-face transactions. Finance, though it all ends up being written down on paper and recorded on tape, is done face to face between people who need to meet each other. Finance—the distribution of human resources— needs to be highly centralized and densely arranged for maximum efficiency. Those concerned with finance must be able to see several different people in a day: a lawyer in the morning, a banker at lunch, an accountant or an investor or a printer in the afternoon. This concentration of services maximizes human choice. High concentration also drives up the value of real estate, and on expensive sites investors feel justified in erecting expensive, up-to-date structures. This, in turn, attracts talented architects.

The physical compactness and high density of its office core, plus a traditionally very high level of services and utilities, make San Francisco an expensive but highly efficient place to do financial business in. Within the Downtown, for example, there is overnight delivery of mail within the Downtown ZIP-code areas. In the business district, telephones can be ordered and installed in a couple of days. Young delivery-service workers pedaling bicycles and carrying walkie-talkies can hand-deliver a packet within minutes. A businessman can walk to any spot in the downtown office core during lunch hour. Such economies of time, convenience, and tempers more than justify the expense of doing business in the Downtown. San Francisco attracts and holds the headquarters of large, well-capitalized firms and the specialized human talents in law, finance, and information that these businesses need.

Time is the essence of the Financial District. Its product is measured not in tons, gallons, or square feet but in time, billable hours of human brains. These hours are ultimately spent deciding where society's present capital and future efforts will be invested.

San Francisco is both an accumulator and a gateway for capital. One of the earliest European habitations on Yerba Buena Cove was an unsuccessful branch of the London-based Hudson's Bay Company established in 1841. Immediately on the heels of the Gold Rush there was an agent of the Rothschild banks in San Francisco. The city instantly became the gateway to capital from New York and Europe seeking major investment in the resource-rich West. San Francisco's nineteenth-century directories are studded with the names of men proud to describe themselves simply as "Capitalists."

The New York orientation of San Francisco's financial industry is evident at 6:45 A.M., when young, on-the-go, smartly tailored stockbrokers quickly stride the sidewalks of the deserted district to be in their offices when the New York Stock Exchange opens at 10 A.M. New York time. This curious submission to time finds its release on the last business day in December. On that day the Financial District enacts its only spontaneous, traditional ritual: human ingenuity and determination find a way to dump one hundred cubic yards of loose desk-calendar pages from high-rise buildings where the windows won't open. In a celebration of seeming abandon, the days of the year are thrown to the four winds to carpet the city streets in a confetti of days, black for business and red for holidays. It seems like a most unbusinesslike thing to do, to throw one's appointment calendar with its daily record of meetings and tasks out the window. And so it would be, if office workers actually threw *their* calendars out to the streets. For when one inspects the countless pages one finds that almost all are blank.

Land-use patterns in San Francisco's Financial District have been very conservative. If Rip Van Winkle had been a San Francisco banker or lawyer, and he had fallen asleep in the 1870s and awakened in the 1970s, he would find bankers and lawyers still doing business on the same blocks, if often many stories higher up. Notably, the 400 block of California Street, between Sansome and Montgomery, is still the favored location for major banks; around them are grouped, in a predictable pattern, lawyers, insurance agents, accountants, publicists, and printers.

The Post-1906 Financial District

Most of today's Financial District is principally the result of three waves of building. The first was the post-1906 reconstruction, which in about a decade produced a coherent, even-scaled downtown whose buildings were all in a sober Beaux-Arts style. The city was well insured and, when the earthquake and fire cleared away the Victorian city, there was money with which to build a completely modern, up-to-date city. San Francisco rebuilt when her regional economic supremacy was secure: the rebuilding was done with the expectation that her commercial importance was assured. The high quality of San Francisco's 1906–1920 office blocks was the result of ample capital and high expectations. As the San Francisco *Call* observed in 1908: "Where once unsightly, three-story buildings cut the sky are now the classic lines of buildings modeled after one style of architecture only . . . the building plane is higher in more ways than one." The area between California and Market was filled in, visually creating what had been an economic fact since the Gold Rush—Wall Street West.

The second boom of the late twenties, epitomized in the Russ, Shell, and New Montgomery Street Telephone buildings, built the highest towers on the San Francisco skyline for thirty years. This boom filled in the gap between the 400 block of California Street (location of the Bank of California) and the Market-Montgomery intersection built up in the early 1900s. The 1920–1930 skyscrapers always met the sidewalk ingratiatingly, had fanciful tops, and were clad in light-colored terra-cotta tiles. These large-scale buildings harmonized with the city's traditional skyline despite their size.

World War II brought a construction boom to the San Francisco Bay Area, but the growth was in industrial facilities on the city's fringes and in war workers' housing projects nearby. The bureaucratic core of San Francisco did not grow in the startling way Washington, D.C., did. After the war the growth was once again principally on the fringes: suburban San Mateo County to the south, the Peninsula, in particular. Not until the late 1960s did San Francisco's Financial District see much change. But the change, when it did come, transformed the skyline completely. This next wave of large-scale construction adopted the internationally favored glass box. The first example of this new mode was the well-regarded Crown Zellerbach Building at Market and Bush, built in 1959. Constructed for a proud San Francisco-based paper company whose owners have long had an interest in fine architecture, the building introduced the notion of the tower in an open space, first proposed by Le Corbusier in the late teens, to San Francisco. The Bank of America later took this form of generous display to its ultimate limit, and devoted fully a quarter of a block to a plaza in front of the highest tower in the city, on California and Kearny. The new wave of construction washed around the Montgomery Street corridor. Large high-rises were built to the east, southeast, north, and west of the established old big building core.

THE "SET" OF SAN FRANCISCO'S FINANCIAL DISTRICT

The basic geographic arrangement of uses in the downtown core since about 1850. While the entire Financial District has shifted southward, and expanded vertically with steel-frame buildings, the overall pattern of the "set" has remained remarkably stable.

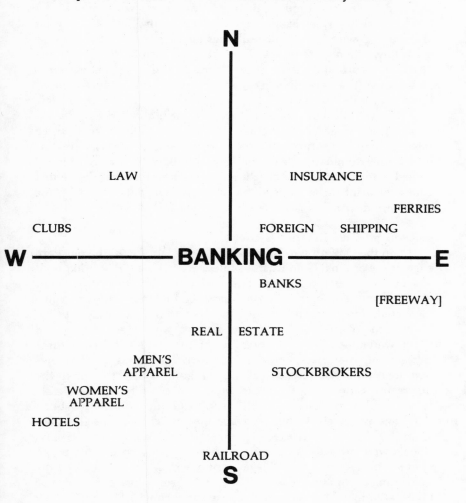

After the earthquake and fire of 1906, the subdistricts in the "set" became more discrete entities within the expanded Financial District. (Source: Martyn John Bowden, *The Dynamics of City Growth: An Historical Geography of the San Francisco Central District, 1850–1931* [1967].)

Today's Financial District has a clear core-ring pattern. The 1890–1930 cluster of office blocks and skyscrapers remains, while a recent ring of simple high-rise boxes in dark or light colors has sprung up around them. This has strengthened the centrality of the traditional core. This high-rise ring of the post-1965 period has completely replaced the former produce district of one-story warehouses.

The blocks between Market and Mission south of First Street were also built up with large-scale buildings on the site of simple low-rise brick Edwardian warehouses. Thus, it was possible to preserve the 1890–1930 core and also make a more radical jump between the Downtown (the new high-rises) and the residential fringes (Chinatown, North Beach, South of Market, the Tenderloin/North of Market). The Downtown was totally transformed: a low-rise, hill-hugging, white, cubist city punctuated by light, slender towers turned into a twentieth-century cluster of glass boxes set in plazas. A skyline of low hills dominated by the horizontal bulk of the Fairmont Hotel turned into a glittering nighttime panorama of randomly lighted cubes piled into a hill-like shape of their own punctuated by the graceful, fanciful Transamerica Pyramid.

Jackson Square Historic District

When the Downtown shifted south in the late 1860s, the northern edge of the original Gold Rush business district was "discarded" and abandoned to less prestigious uses. Like a receding tide, the flow of development left behind the 700 block of Montgomery. From banking, retail, and professional uses the district went to warehousing, liquor and tobacco dealers, cigar factories, and later printing and paper warehousing. The Depression of the 1930s weakened these subsequent enterprises, and artists and writers moved into the low-rent area; some had already called Montgomery Street home in the nineteenth century. In the 1950s interior decorators and wholesale furniture dealers discovered the area, and the vintage red-brick buildings were refurbished and became attractive properties once again. By the 1960s architects, planners, lawyers, and other professionals were attracted to the area. These higher-rent tenants began to push the decorators out. Elegant antique stores also succeeded the pioneering decorators. Now, as more high-rises displace the low-rise brick buildings downtown that house the Financial District's fancy bars and expense-account restaurants, these uses have increased in Jackson Square.

Many of the brick buildings in Jackson Square were built during the 1850s and 1860s. Their brick exteriors were demanded by new building codes passed after the disastrous fires of the early 1850s. Timber posts, beams, floors, and roofs complete the buildings' structure. A choice was made within the technology of the time between the hazards of fire and the hazards of earthquakes. Fire is the great destroyer in California; so, while frame buildings are safer in an earthquake, brick was mandated to retard fire in the Downtown, "the congested district."

The brick used before 1870 was made from inferior local clays and varied widely in color and hardness. This was disguised by stuccoing the façades with a material called mastic, often scoring lines in it and painting it gray, white, or brown to look like stone. The vogue for exposed brick is a modern one; nineteenth-century San Franciscans considered brick common and covered it. Only a few stuccoed-over façades survive. Stripping the covering off the brick is not always the best thing for the brick because it weathers faster.

The fire after the earthquake of 1906 damaged many of these buildings, but since it was no longer a fashionable area for business, owners simply patched up the gutted shells rather than build new structures. After the discovery of the area by interior decorators in the 1950s, the made-up name Jackson Square was given to the area from Washington to Pacific, and from Columbus to Sansome. There is, in reality, no square here; the name was taken from Jackson Street, which has the most elaborate surviving Victorian commercial buildings. In 1972 the area was made San Francisco's first historic district. Official City Landmark and Historic District designations, however, should not be misunderstood to mean much. Any owner can tear down a building, but there is a mandatory six-month delay that can be renewed once. The City Planning Commission, however, would certainly refuse to permit the construction of a larger building; and so a combination of public zoning and the economics of private ownership preserve these small-scale buildings.

THE TOUR

1 The Transamerica Pyramid
· 600 Montgomery Street
· William Pereira and Associates, 1972
· Observation Room, 27th Floor, open Monday–Friday, 9–5

The forty-eight-story, 853-foot-high Transamerica Pyramid (the top 212 feet is a hollow ornamental spire lighted from within) was designed by Los Angeles architect William Pereira and Associates in 1972 for a $4.2 billion San Francisco-based conglomerate. Founded by A.P. Giannini as a bank holding company, the corporation divested itself of its domestic bank stock in the late 1950s and moved into a wide variety of businesses, such as insurance, real estate, movies and records, rent-a-cars, moving and storage, charter airlines, mobile-home parks, computers, hotels, business services, and international banking.

The distinctive pyramid is a classic example of the use of architecture to create a clearly understood image for an otherwise hard-to-conceptualize institution. Pereira's easily perceived form is a prime example of architecture as corporate packaging. No San Franciscan or visitor can fail to note the slim white pyramid, but probably fewer than one person in a thousand could tell you what Transamerica does. One-third of the building is used by Transamerica and two-thirds are leased out, mostly to major law firms, banks, financial consultants, and other executive offices. The pyramid has become the signature of the San Francisco skyline as the Ferry Building tower once was.

The structure is remarkable for more than its unorthodox shape. The pyramid has only 530,000 square feet of office space, in contrast to the Bank of America's 1,600,000. In the pyramid, offices range from 180 feet square at the base to 45 feet square at the top. The tapered design makes it an extravagant building. (It is far more profitable, considering the cost of land and steel-frame construction, to build straight up in a box shape, maximizing the amount of office space.) Two factors justified the extravagant design: first, the pyramid is a corporate headquarters, where the display of power and wealth is as important as mere accommodation; second, the corporation, because of the building, enjoyed an unusual tax exemption. California-based insurance companies paid both state taxes on premiums and local property taxes on their headquarters' buildings. As an incentive to attract more insurance companies to California, they were allowed to deduct the amount of their local property tax on their principal office from the state tax on premiums. A report published in 1972 when the building was nearing completion noted that this exemption was expected to wipe out Transamerica's state-tax liability. This now-abolished special treatment explains why so many San Francisco high-rises were built by insurance companies.

The pyramid cost some $34 million, land included. It stands on the original shoreline of Yerba Buena Cove. The steel frame rests on a 9-foot-thick concrete-and-steel foundation mat 52 feet below the sidewalk. The precast quartz aggregate panels of the curtain wall each weigh three and a half tons. There are three thousand of them, each with two windows that pivot to wash from the inside.

As befits an insurance company, the building was equipped with a state-of-the-art fire protection and life-safety system controlled from a command post underground. The building is fully sprinklered independent of roof tanks, has smoke controls, an intercom for firemen, an audio system to direct occupants, and safeguards for the elevators. These "extras" cost some $340,000 but reduced insurance premiums by 40 percent.

The "wings" on the two sides of the tip house eighteen elevators on the east side, and emergency stairs and a smoke tower on the west side. Because of its unusual, and purely decorative, top, cooling equipment had to be placed on the sidewalk in two large cylinders on the Clay Street side of the building. Behind the building, on the east side, is a welcome and unexpected half-acre park of eighty coast redwood trees, open only during business hours. Also on the east side of the pyramid is the Bank Exchange Saloon, a modern bar that preserves the name of the famous San Francisco establishment that once was part of the Montgomery Block, which used to stand here.

The Montgomery Block was built in 1853 as San Francisco's first large-scale business and office block. The old building was the investment of a law firm with the amusing name of Peachy, Billings and Halleck. They were the best-known land lawyers in California in the 1850s and customarily charged half the land in any transaction as their fee. Since nearly all the land in California was contested as Yankees squatted on Mexican land grants, it was a prosperous firm. The building housed the city's first law library, the U.S. Army Corps of Engineers, the Adams Express Company's gold bullion vaults, the offices of the Pacific and Atlantic Railroad, and the offices of two early newspapers, the *Alta California* and the *Daily Herald,* as well as a bank, the very important Bank Exchange Saloon, and many other services, including a portion of Adolph Sutro's library. When the focus of the Downtown moved south, the Montgomery Block became the home of artists and writers, including muckraking novelist Frank Norris and local poet George Sterling. It acquired the nickname of the "Monkey Block." The historic structure, which escaped destruction in 1906, was demolished for a parking lot in 1959. The Montgomery Block's bronze plaque and a picture of the old building are displayed in the Transamerica lobby.

2 Columbus Avenue
· Cut in 1873

In 1873 the diagonal swath of Columbus Avenue, which we encountered at Washington Square in Tour One, was cut through the city's grid from Montgomery and Washington at the northern edge of the Downtown to Beach Street in what was then an industrial district (today The Cannery). It was the only major alteration of the city's relentless grid. It cuts through the valley between Telegraph and Russian Hills and was visually aligned on Mt. Tamalpais across the bay. Today the Downtown end is anchored by the Transamerica Pyramid and is now the northern frontier of the high-rise district: to the north are the two- and three-story brick buildings of old San Francisco, to the south are the steel-framed towers of the modern era.

Old Transamerica Building
· 701 Montgomery Street
· Salfield and Kohlberg, 1911

Number 701 Montgomery, on the gore of Columbus Avenue, is a white terra-cotta-clad flatiron building. This elegant little building was built as the home of the Banco Popolare Italiano Operaia Fugazi.

Its rounded corner was originally capped by a cupola. It preserves not only its carefully detailed Mannerist Revival terra-cotta exterior, but also the plasterwork of its grand, ground-floor interior. In 1928 the Fugazi Bank was merged into A.P. Giannini's Bank of Italy, now the Bank of America. In 1938 it became the headquarters of another Giannini financial entity, the Transamerica Corporation, the original holding company for Giannini's many banks. In 1972 Transamerica moved into its new pyramid across the street but retained this small landmark building for part of its operations.

Columbus Savings Bank, K101 Radio
· 700 Montgomery Street
· Meyer and O'Brien, 1905

The green-stone-faced, two-story structure on the corner to the east is the old Columbus Savings Bank. The location of this originally Italian-American financial institution reminds us that this intersection was once at the edge of North Beach. The building is a fine example of the Baroque Revival style of the early twentieth century. Its richly carved detail and finely executed stonework display the excellent craftsmanship of the period. Beside it at 708 Montgomery is the Canessa Building that housed the Black Cat Bar, a celebrated bohemian rendezvous of the 1930s, 1940s, and 1950s.

3 The 700 Block of Montgomery Street
· San Francisco after the Gold Rush (1850s)

The east side of the 700 block of Montgomery Street harbors one of the finest clusters of 1850s San Francisco buildings, which originally contained artists' studios. Though most of the buildings were gutted by fire in 1906, they were reconstructed shortly afterward much as they had been. The seven buildings on the east side of the street preserve the two- and three-story scale of the brick city of the pre-Civil War period, even though not all are that early. The only major interruption in the block is the former Playboy Club at 736 Montgomery, the southeast corner of Jackson and Montgomery, built in 1965. A sign of the importance of this block in the history of early California is the bronze plaque at 728 Montgomery, which reads: "This site marks the birthplace of Freemasonry in California. At this location on October 17, 1849, the first meeting of the Free and Accepted Masons in the Golden State was held by California Lodge No. 1 F. & A.M." Across the street is another plaque affixed to the base of the old Transamerica Building, which records that on that site the first Jewish religious service in San Francisco was held on Yom Kippur (5610), September 26, 1849.

Belli Building
· 722 Montgomery Street

The Belli Building was built as the Langerman tobacco warehouse, probably in the early 1850s. This historical relic now houses the offices of lawyer Melvin Belli, the flamboyant "King of Torts," whose knickknack-stuffed office can be seen through the first-floor windows. In 1857 an equally theatrical enterprise inhabited these walls, the Melodeon Theater, which boasted such celebrated entertainers as Lotta Crabtree. The building sits on soft bayfill. Engineer Henry W. Halleck devised a method of building on such treacherous sites. He dug a hole to the water line, not far below the surface, and laid down a raft of 6-inch-thick redwood planks, which sank into the soft ground. More planks were laid over those until the footing was pushed deep into the mud; an 8-foot-thick raft of redwood planks supports the brick walls. Halleck's construction methods were laughed at at the time, but they were actively used later in Chicago and Mexico City and his buildings have lasted in amazingly sound condition to the present. After an eventful history as a tobacco warehouse, a theater, an office for commission merchants and auctioneers, Turkish baths, medical offices, a paper warehouse, and garment factory, the building and its neighbor at 728 Montgomery were made into offices in 1958. Belli's two buildings have been much "improved" with added fancy ironwork, lamps, a French post box, landscaping, and a pleasant interior court. The mastic façades were removed, exposing the underlying red brick. Today the buildings are far more elaborate than they were originally.

Genella Building
· 728 Montgomery Street

The Genella Building was built in 1853–54 as a china-and-glassware shop with living quarters above. In the 1850s Bret Harte wrote "The Luck of Roaring Camp" here.

Golden Era Building, Knoll Showroom
· 732 Montgomery Street

At 732 Montgomery Street is the Knoll Building, originally the Golden Era Building, built in 1852 on the foundations of an 1849 building destroyed in the fire of 1851. This building goes through the lot to Hotaling Place, where the service entrance is located. A look through the window shows the timber interiors of these old structures. The building was altered slightly at various times but has preserved its mid-nineteenth-century appearance. The cast-iron pilasters on Hotaling Place are dated 1857; those on the Montgomery Street façade are dated 1892. This painted brick, mastic, and timber building once housed the literary weekly, the *Golden Era,* which published early works of Mark Twain and Bret Harte. Upstairs was Lafayette Hall, the meeting place of the Lafayette Guard, a pioneer militia company. Today the building houses the Knoll furniture showrooms, which carry a famous line of classic twentieth-century furniture including designs by Marcel Breuer and Mies van der Rohe. Florence Knoll designed the simple and pleasing modern black-metal-and-glass shopfront, which successfully blends old and new.

Redwood Bank
• 735 Montgomery Street

Across Montgomery Street, at 735, is the Redwood Bank. This three-story mustard-colored building was built in 1918 as a warehouse and totally rebuilt in 1976 as an office and bank building. An ordinary reinforced-concrete commercial building was adapted in a modern Northern California manner. Balconies with plants and a roof garden were introduced into what had been a somewhat dryly detailed warehouse.

Bank of Lucas, Turner and Co.
• 800 Montgomery Street
• Keyser and Brown, 1854

At 800 Montgomery, on the northeast corner of Jackson, was the San Francisco branch of the Bank of Lucas, Turner and Co. of St. Louis. This originally three-story building built for the then lavish sum of $82,000. The top story was removed after the 1906 earthquake. The building has a rusticated-granite first-floor façade facing Montgomery Street; the brick above that was originally covered in mastic and painted to look like stone. This beautifully detailed building is the only survivor of a type preferred by early San Francisco banks. Such simple architecture of the 1850s was succeeded after the Civil War by the more ornate architecture we associate with the later Victorian era; in the late 1890s and early 1900s architectural taste returned to simpler period designs.

This branch bank was managed by William Tecumseh Sherman, who resigned his army commission in 1853 to come to California; he later became the Union general who led the infamous march through Georgia during the Civil War. The Hibernia Savings and Loan Society and the Sacramento Rail Road Company, the West's first railroad, were later tenants. In the 1870s this building housed the Chambers of the Justices of the Peace. More recently, the National Trust for Historic Preservation had its offices upstairs. It was also the first home of the Foundation for San Francisco's Architectural Heritage.

View of Montgomery and Pacific: The International Settlement and the Barbary Coast

At the intersection of Montgomery and Pacific Avenue, half a block uphill, is a pair of black metal piers that announce the 500 block of Pacific Avenue. They once supported elaborate flag-decked arches that marked the International Settlement, a string of bars and dance halls that catered to fun-seekers and tourists, and later to the rivers of soldiers and sailors that passed through San Francisco during World War II.

Included originally in this area, but more active half a block east, was the infamous Barbary Coast of the 1850s. This notorious quarter near the docks was Gold Rush San Francisco's slum for transients, new arrivals, sailors, and the down-and-out. Among its denizens were ex-convicts released from Britain's penal colonies in Australia. Some of these ex-convicts—often deported Irishmen—formed gangs, the best-known of which was called the Sydney Ducks. Their quarter, only a few blocks from the Plaza, was described in the nineteenth century as "an assorted place of wildlife such as no naturalist has ever observed." It was also billed as "the region which is supposed to be under the direct supervision of the historical party with the cloven foot and tail." The name Barbary Coast was given to this vice-ridden slum because of its violence and danger. The real Barbary Coast was a pirate-infested stretch of the North African coast that the U.S. Navy cleaned up in the late eighteenth century. San Francisco's district of flophouses, brothels, gambling dens, and saloons acquired this nickname during the Gold Rush, and the name has lived in the city's memory ever since. Unwary sailors were fleeced and occasionally "shanghaied" here. Both that descriptive word and the term "hoodlum" originated in San Francisco. The latter word is said to be derived from the shout "huddle 'em," made by Barbary Coast gangs when they attacked their victim. These slang words are linguistic monuments to the violence endemic in the early city.

San Francisco's carefully cultivated reputation as a wild and bawdy town had its roots here. At the turn of the century, San Francisco saloonkeepers and cabaret owners discovered that this inherited notoriety made for good business. During the flood of visitors to the 1915 Fair, San Francisco learned to promote her scarlet past. An unsavory reality like "the Coast" was transformed into a remunerative myth. When the United States entered World War I, the military authorities closed down parts of the revived Barbary Coast, but its character continued in the International Settlement. Today San Francisco's oldest profession is centered in the aptly named Tenderloin area west of Union Square, while sanitized and literally plasticized "vice" flourishes along Broadway, a block north of Pacific.

"Terrific Pacific" itself is now a quiet and tasteful street of designers' showrooms, architects' offices, shops, restaurants, and advertising firms. In the 1950s and 1960s these then run-down buildings were one by one upgraded. Most preserve the scale, materials, and, though cleaner, the appearance of mid-nineteenth-century San Francisco.

814–22 Montgomery Street, Northeast Corner of Gold Street
· Former Four Monks Vinegar Warehouse

This lot was a gift of early San Francisco real-estate tycoon James Lick to the Society for California Pioneers in 1863. The society had its headquarters here until 1886. Later it became a livery stable. In 1906, after the earthquake, the present utilitarian structure was built. For many years it was the Four Monks wine vinegar warehouse and the pungent odor of vinegar permeated the alley. In 1978 rising real estate values drove this last warehouse out of Jackson Square and the plain brick structure was imaginatively converted for office and entertainment uses. A skylit interior court was introduced and the brick walls were reinforced with steel I-beams.

4 Gold Street to Balance Street

Walk down Gold Street—really an alley—and look around. The cupola-topped building visible to the west is Columbus Tower at 920 Kearny Street, built in 1907 by architects Salfield and Kohlberg. San Francisco's infamous turn-of-the-century political boss, Abe Ruef, had his offices there after he was released from San Quentin. The curious flatiron structure is a popular landmark. The buildings visible down Gold Street recapture the feeling of pre-earthquake San Francisco. This was originally a service alley for the unloading of goods. Today such intimate side streets often shelter cozy restaurants and bars. Executives on expense accounts retreat here at lunchtime from the massive high-rises to the south.

The Assay Office Restaurant and Bar
· 56 Gold Street

This simple brick building was built after the 1906 earthquake and fire. It was used as a vinegar warehouse, a cooperage, and a truck storage depot before its conversion into a bar.

The latest tenant is the Assay Office, never actually an assay office but, one hopes, nonetheless, a gold mine for its owners. Inside is a grand modern-old interior created with such props as a 32-foot-long bar from the Kansas City Hotel, a 15-foot-diameter art glass dome from an Ohio cathedral, and two circa-1865 panels from the Imperial Theater in Chicago. The pride of the establishment is a bronze 8-by-8-foot assay scale from the U.S. Mint in San Francisco, once used to weigh gold.

Balance Street to 408 Jackson Street

Walk down Gold to the narrow alley of Balance Street, so named because timbers from the sailing ship *Balance* were discovered here during excavations. In the nineteenth century Jackson Street was treeless, but today pruned sycamore trees line the street. A handsome effect is created by the pattern of light and shade that filters through the trees onto the mellow partially painted brick walls. This block now houses several of the finest antique shops in the city. At night, when the shops are lighted from within, the street becomes an outdoor museum of high-quality antique English and French furniture and objets d'art. Browsing in these shops during the day is one of San Francisco's most sophisticated pastimes. Through Balance Street and to the left is 408 Jackson, a simple, modern two-story building, designed in 1953 with a deeply recessed glass façade and a carefully trained wisteria vine reaching up to its balcony. While different in size, material, design, and treatment from the other buildings in this district, this small up-to-date building adapts quite sensitively to its setting. It is an excellent example of an "infill" building, which respects its setting and lends a subtle counterpoint of modernity to this historic area.

5 400 Block of Jackson Street

- Antiques and showrooms, Commercial Italianate
  San Francisco in the 1860s
- Original Ghirardelli Chocolate Company

Across the street, at 407 Jackson, is the annex built for the Ghirardelli Chocolate Company in 1860. This three-story building and its immediate neighbor to the west continued to be used by this pioneer firm until it moved to the large red brick complex at Aquatic Park (now known as Ghirardelli Square; see Tour Twelve) in 1894. Number 415–431 Jackson was built in 1853 and became Domingo Ghirardelli's manufactory in 1855. Later it was a woodworking mill, a cigar factory, and a printing shop. After the revival of the area in the 1960s, the buildings housed wholesale fabric showrooms downstairs and architects upstairs.

Yeon Building

- 432 Jackson Street, Northwest Corner of Balance Street

This was the site of the Tremont Hotel in 1855 and the existing post-1906 building incorporates parts of that early structure.

Medico-Dental Building
· 441 Jackson Street

This two-story brick building with cast-iron pilasters and iron shutters was built in 1861 over the buried hulls of two ships abandoned by gold seekers in 1849. The building displays a caduceus, the Greek mythological and medical symbol of staff and serpents, placed over each cast-iron pilaster. The building was also a wine, tobacco, and coffee warehouse.

Presidio and Ferries Railroad Car Barn
· 440–444 Jackson Street

Built in 1891 and later reconstructed, this building stabled the horses that drew the cars on one of San Francisco's earliest public transit lines. When electric motors replaced horses, the building became a car barn and repair shop.

Moulinie Building
· 458–460 Jackson Street

This building was built in the early 1850s on a lot purchased by a French sea captain after the Gold Rush. The same family has owned it ever since. Wine and liquor merchants occupied it in the early days. A stone obelisk in the recessed vestibule echoes the shape of the Transamerica Pyramid to the south.

Larco's Building
· 470 Jackson Street

Nicholas Larco, an important Italian-American merchant in San Francisco, built this office building in 1852. The consulates of Spain and Chile were here in 1856, and in the first half of the 1860s the Consulate of France was an important tenant. There was an influential French colony in San Francisco in the early days, but many of the French refused to learn English or assimilate and soon departed for other places. Later in the 1860s the Italian newspaper *La Parola,* edited by Augustus Splivalo, was here, as well as the offices of the Italian Benevolent Society. San Francisco's cosmopolitan beginnings are thus epitomized in the early history of this building.

Solari Building, Old French Consulate
· 472 Jackson Street

Number 472 Jackson Street is one of the oldest commercial buildings in the city and dates from 1850–52. The second story still has its original wrought-iron shutters. Theft and fire were great problems for mid-nineteenth-century merchants, and buildings were built with maximum security in mind. Descriptions of the commercial district after business hours in the 1860s depicted a practical, well-protected downtown, with all windows and doors covered with iron shutters. There is a purity and beauty to the design of this building; it is similar to the Wells Fargo agencies that sprouted in the gold country of the Sierra foothills in the 1850s. The building was constructed for a wine merchant and also housed the French Consulate from 1865 to 1875. It is exceptionally well preserved and shows the original construction virtually unaltered. It had walls of fine, uniform dark-red brick, with granite sills.

The Hotaling Buildings
· 451, 445, and 463–73 Jackson Street

Anson Parsons Hotaling was a pioneer liquor merchant whose thriving business occupied these three Jackson Street Italianate buildings and a stable in the alley behind them. The two-story building at 445 was built in 1860, the three-story building at 451 in 1866, and the less elaborate three-story building at 463–473 circa 1860. A.P. Hotaling was engaged in wholesale liquor, real estate, and general trade; his business reached from Alaska to the South Seas. Number 451 Jackson is the most elaborate surviving Italianate commercial building in San Francisco. It is built of brick, covered in mastic, and has cast-iron pilasters and wrought-iron shutters. The corners are accentuated by quoins and the top is capped by a denticulated cornice with modillions, the whole supported by decorative brackets. The second- and third-floor windows have wrought-iron shutters and are capped by alternating triangular and segmental projecting pediments. It is the Downtown decorated masonry companion to the two-story, bay-windowed, painted redwood row houses so characteristic of San Francisco's domestic Victorian architecture.

These substantial buildings replaced the earlier wooden buildings of pioneer days. Hittell's guidebook of 1888 observed that, in the business district, "year by year the wooden buildings that form the landmarks of earlier days are being crowded out by substantial brick and iron edifices. . . . The leading business blocks are built up of brick, with the front on the ground-floor of iron, which allows nearly all the width to be occupied for windows and doors. The architecture is elegant and varied. The ceilings are high; the glass is large plate."

The offices of the Hotaling Whiskey Co. survived the earthquake in 1906. A doggerel verse penned immediately after the quake asked, "If as they say God spanked the town for being over frisky, / Why did he burn the churches down and save Hotaling's whiskey?" Number 463–73 Jackson, the Hotaling Annex West, was the headquarters of the Federal Artists and Federal Writers Projects during the Depression of the 1930s. A number of famous San Francisco artists had their studios in this historic building.

Before turning into Hotaling Place, compare the plain red-brick buildings on the north side of Jackson Street built in the 1850s with the more elaborate, cast-iron-embellished Italianate buildings on the south side built in the 1860s. Architectural styles in San Francisco became more and more richly varied as the nineteenth century progressed. The Downtown buildings of the 1870s and 1880s, of which none survive, were covered with ornament and bay windows. A sharp reaction against this "excess" set in in the late 1890s to 1900 when commercial designs became plainer again. Except for these Jackson Square blocks, San Francisco's Downtown was totally destroyed in 1906 and rebuilt in the simpler "modern" styles of the Edwardian age.

6 Hotaling Place
· Backstreets then and now

This one-time service alley (pronounced HOTE-uh-ling) was originally called Jones Alley but was renamed and redesigned by famed San Francisco landscape architect Thomas D. Church. Pairs of old streetlights frame the entrance. A wavy design in the pavement draws the pedestrian through this enclave. There is a dramatic view of the Transamerica Pyramid beyond the alley. The two red-brick walls to the right, embellished with flower boxes ornamented with the scales of justice, are the backs of the Belli buildings.

A few steps down on the right is the Villa Taverna, a private luncheon club, its brick façade veneered with granite paving blocks salvaged from the produce district to the east, which was redeveloped in the 1960s. A large marble bas-relief of a woman holding wheat sheaves and poppies and serpents serves as a massive lintel over the front door; two spiky Florentine Renaissance-style lamps complete this interesting façade.

Immediately across from the Villa Taverna is 30 Hotaling Place, a three-story poured-concrete zigzag Moderne building of the 1930s tastefully remodeled into office space. Today's building codes forbid the use of brick as a structural material and limit its use to surface coverings. But as far back as 1906, reinforced concrete began to replace brick because of its greater resistance to earthquakes. Concrete buildings enjoyed lower insurance premiums, and this long-term cost differential encouraged wealthy commercial builders to use the new, more expensive material. While much of the city was quickly rebuilt in brick, many reinforced-concrete warehouses, garages, and other commercial structures also appeared. The building trades resisted the introduction of reinforced concrete in the early 1900s, fearing the loss of bricklayers' jobs. But concrete came in, nonetheless, and by 1910 one visiting engineer claimed that everything but the teaspoons in San Francisco was made of reinforced concrete!

7 Old Bank of America Headquarters
• 552 Montgomery Street
• Fine interior and photomurals, Shea and Lofquist, 1908

Walk back past the Transamerica Pyramid to the granite-clad branch of the Bank of America on the southeast corner of Montgomery and Clay at 552 Montgomery. This steel-frame Beaux-Arts office block was, at one time, the headquarters of Giannini's Bank of Italy. The decorative marble, plaster, and metalwork inside are superb examples of high-quality turn-of-the-century craftsmanship. The bronze tellers' cages and elaborate, custom-made wall fixtures were recently refurbished. Large sepia photomurals of San Francisco's downtown in the 1850s and of old Chinatown were installed against the back wall. These murals are visible through the side door on Clay Street when the bank is closed. A bronze plaque on the Montgomery Street corner marks the spot said to be where Captain John B. Montgomery of the U.S. sloop of war *Portsmouth* landed on July 9, 1846, to claim California as a military conquest for the United States during the Mexican-American War.

Nearby, at the southwest corner of Montgomery and Merchant, a plaque marks the spot where the first Pony Express rider arrived in San Francisco in April 1860. This famous overland courier service flourished for only a year and a half but left an indelible impression on the American imagination. The eastern terminus was at St. Joseph, Missouri, and the extended western one was at Montgomery Street. The first letters cost five dollars per half ounce to send in 1860.

8 Leidesdorff and Commercial Streets
• Edwardian San Francisco, 1906–15

From Clay Street, turn right into the narrow alley of Leidesdorff Street (pronounced LIE-des-dorf), named after an early merchant born in the West Indies of Danish and black parentage whose house was nearby. The small post-1906 buildings clustered here are charming survivors of the early-twentieth-century city. From the hidden-away intersection where Leidesdorff crosses Commerical Street, view corridors penetrate four distinct parts of San Francisco. Few places sum up so well the practical compactness and vivid variety that make San Francisco such a fascinating city.

Commercial Street was not part of the O'Farrell survey of 1847. It was cut through from the Central Wharf west to Kearny Street and the Plaza in July, 1850. Brick commercial buildings quickly lined it; the block between Montgomery and Kearny became the heart of the banking district.

Visible at the foot of Commercial Street on the Embarcadero are the towers of A. Page Brown's Union Ferry Depot, built by the State of California in 1895–1903. The 235-foot-high, 32-foot-square tower, modeled after the Giralda of the cathedral in Seville, was once San Francisco's premier landmark. It was to turn-of-the-century San Francisco what the Golden Gate Bridge is today. The tower caps a 659-foot-long terminal building whose supports were cast as a continuous structure, one of the early uses of reinforced concrete. It was the transit hub of the Bay Area, where ferries and streetcars met. Some 170 ferry crossings a day docked here. Over 50 million commuters a year passed through the Ferry Building, making it the world's second busiest passenger terminal; only Charing Cross Station in London was busier. Beyond the tower is one of the X-braced piers of the 1937 San Francisco–Oakland Bay Bridge, which rapidly made the ferries obsolete.

The light-colored high-rise slabs that frame the Ferry Building tower are part of the $300 million Embarcadero complex of offices, shops, and restaurants with a hotel designed by Atlanta architect John Portman. This 8.5-acre development is part of a redevelopment area designated by the city in 1955 and built in phases since 1970. The complex, sometimes called Rockefeller Center West after one of its principal investors, is notable for its superb contemporary art: sculptures, fountains, and large-scale weavings. The high-rise slabs present their thinner sides to the city, thus preserving views of the bay. From here you can look through the pedestrian mall that penetrates the Embarcadero complex, carrying street life back into the block itself, just as nineteenth-century alleys did. The Hyatt Regency Hotel, with its dramatic soaring interior court, in the extreme southeast corner of the development (not visible from here), is the best-known part of this contemporary complex.

The tall tower to the right is Embarcadero One, also known as the Security Pacific Bank. Behind it is Embarcadero Two, the Levi Strauss building, headquarters of one of San Francisco's most famous products: blue jeans. Levi Strauss, a Bavarian Jewish immigrant, came to San Francisco during the Gold Rush and made his fortune manufacturing canvas work pants. Jeans have become more than just a garment; they seem to symbolize a way of life and are nearly universal in casual California. The metal rivets on Levi's jeans have carried San Francisco's initials into the remotest corners of the world.

View West up Commercial Street

The view west up Commerical Street, past the old U.S. Sub-Treasury at 608, is terminated by the buildings on Chinatown's Grant Avenue. The brick at the hilly end of Commerical is one of the last bits of old street paving in the city. This is an exotic view; from here Chinatown really looks like an Oriental city nestled within an Occidental one. Beyond Chinatown are the high-rise hotels and apartments that crown Nob Hill. Where Commercial Street begins to slope was the original shoreline of Yerba Buena Cove; most of the flat ground on which the Downtown stands is bayfill. In the 1850s Commercial Street was the heart of the Gold Rush city; today its low-rise buildings house restaurants and other small businesses that service the high-rise core.

At 569 Commercial is Paoli's Restaurant, with an impressive stucco façade that looks like the frontispiece of a Renaissance tome. It was built as Pacific Gas & Electric Substation "J" and was designed in 1914 by architect Frederick H. Meyer. While the building was built simply as a utilitarian electrical substation, the façade is ornamented with an oversized door and elaborate frame, with a large central cartouche above. The interior was originally one large 48-foot-high room; it was converted into a nightclub in the 1950s.

At 222 Leidesdorff, at the southeast corner of Commerical, is the replacement PG&E Substation "J," designed in 1923 by Ivon C. Frickstad. This steel-frame, reinforced-concrete, stucco-faced structure stands on the spot where William Randolph Hearst, California's lord of the American press, began his career in journalism when his father, Senator George Hearst, bought him the *San Francisco Examiner.*

The most noticeable small building at this intersection is the checkerboard cream-and-red-orange brick building housing Zott's restaurant at 554 Commercial, built in 1908. A simple building, it is still one with a lot of flavor.

At 566 Commercial is another three-story brick building built in 1907 and distinguished by an oversized Gothic-arched and wood-molded window in the two upper stories. This is the location of Andrew Hoyem's Arion Press, one of the most distinguished hand-printing houses in the country. Fine, hand-set, limited-edition printing has had a long tradition in San Francisco; many of America's great names in printing are associated with the city. Businessmen-patrons have encouraged this art for over a century. Such diverse, fiercely individual activities tucked away in small buildings on narrow backstreets are part of the essence of downtown San Francisco.

The Leidesdorff Views

Looking north up Leidesdorff, beyond the side of the pyramid, is the east slope of Telegraph Hill, a picturesque residential area with sweeping views of the north bay (see Tour 1). Its houses cling to the shoulder of the hill like swallows' nests.

The view south down Leidesdorff looks into the heart of the Financial District. The block of California Street straight ahead is the center of the banking district. The vista is terminated by the low-rise, gray terra-cotta building at 333 Pine Street, built in 1917 and originally the San Francisco Chamber of Commerce. (Next door to it, but not visible from here, is the Pacific Coast Stock Exchange, designed in 1930 by Miller and Pfleuger with massive exterior sculptures by Ralph Stackpole.) Beyond 333 Pine is the red-tile roof of the late Medievalizing-style skyscraper designed in 1922 by George Kelham for Standard Oil of California. Its arcade-in-the-sky repeats the unifying architectural theme of the Downtown buildings built between 1900 and about 1930. Visible beyond the red-tile roof is the top of the forty-three-story, black-and-silver Wells Fargo Dillingham Building on the southeast corner of Montgomery and Sutter designed by Seattle architect John Graham in 1966. Here, like the layers of an onion, are three office buildings that epitomize the three building booms of post-1906 San Francisco.

9 Sutro Building to Wells Fargo History Room

If you wish, make a detour and walk a half block up Commercial Street to Montgomery Street to see the Sutro Building, the old Borel Bank, and the Wells Fargo History Room. Otherwise continue south on Leidesdorff Street to the 400 block of California.

Sutro Building (Italian-American Bank)
· 460 Montgomery Street
· Howard and Galloway, 1908

This little bank temple is in the center of a row of classically colonnaded bank buildings on the east side of Montgomery from Washington to California. The L-shaped, three-story, steel-frame headquarters bank was designed by the architect of the University of California's Berkeley campus and his engineer partner. Howard was a master California architect who founded and taught in U.C. Berkeley's School of Architecture. The front entrance is flanked by a pair of monolithic granite Doric columns standing before a recessed bronze-and-verd-antique marble façade; simple double-hung wood-sash windows are inset. The interior, now remodeled, was accented by more dark-green marble, so that the overall design was that of a light-gray granite exterior with a richly colored, dark interior. A concrete vault from the basement through the first story that had survived the earthquake was incorporated into the new building. Inside, costly steelwork, which spanned the whole room, permitted a column-free interior space.

Anton Borel and Co. Bank
· 440 Montgomery Street
· Albert Pissis, 1908

This little architectural gem was also a headquarters bank. It has a steel frame and monolithic granite Corinthian columns. The carved capitals are finely executed.

Wells Fargo Bank Headquarters
· History Room
· 420 Montgomery Street
· Ashley, Keyser, and Runge, 1959

The Wells Fargo Bank Headquarters is a conservative, unspectacular gray granite. This twelve-story, T-shaped building has its front door on California Street, the prestige address for bankers, a back door on Sacramento Street, and a smaller side entrance at 420 Montgomery Street for its History Room. This, the third largest bank in California and the eleventh in the nation, is the proud successor of an express and banking business launched on March 18, 1852, in New York City by Vermont-born Henry Wells and New Yorker William G. Fargo. The company was organized to transport gold from the Mother Lode back East and eventually had more than one hundred offices, agents, and correspondents in the California gold country.

Go to the Montgomery Street entrance to see the History Room. It is devoted to the saga of the gold country and proudly exhibits a fine red-and-yellow stagecoach made in Concord, New Hampshire. A large relief map on the back wall, showing California's rich hinterland, is the best visual explanation of why San Francisco developed into a great port. Gold nuggets and memorabilia record the life of the Forty-Niners. Perhaps the most amusing exhibit covers the life of Black Bart, the famous highwayman who robbed twenty-eight stages, single-handed, over eight years in the 1870s and 1880s. He often left mocking verses behind. He signed his literary work "the PO8"—the poet! The best example of his verse reads:

> I rob the rich to feed the poor
> Which hardly is a sin,
>
> A widow ne'er knocked at my door
> But what I let her in.
>
> So blame me not for what I've done
> I don't deserve your curses
>
> And if for any cause I'm hung
> Let it be for my verses.
>
> Black Bart
> The PO8

Unfortunately for Black Bart, he also dropped a handkerchief at the scene of one holdup, which a Wells Fargo detective traced to a laundry in San Francisco. The infamous highwayman turned out to be a mild-mannered runaway husband, Charles E. Boles, with an exciting second life. He served five years at San Quentin prison and then disappeared.

The Wells Fargo building occupies several historic sites including that of the What Cheer House, a temperance hotel that had such unlikely guests as Mark Twain and U.S. Grant, San Francisco's first free library, and its first museum. The original Wells Fargo headquarters of 1852 was only ten feet north of the present 420 Montgomery Street entrance.

The modern bank is the result of a long series of mergers and reorganizations effected by a Bavarian-born Jew, I.W. Hellman. Hellman came to America at sixteen to work as a clerk in his cousins' dry-goods store in the tiny village of Los Angeles. Since the store had one of the only iron safes in town, it became a place to deposit valuables. In the 1860s Isais put up a sign in a fenced-off corner of the store with the legend, "I.W. Hellman, Banker." Throughout his long career—he died in harness at seventy-seven—he proudly described himself as a "conservative banker." The promising young man made a fortunate match in 1870 when he married Esther Neugass, daughter of a New York and London banking family related to the Lehmans. I.W. moved from Los Angeles to San Francisco and bought out the interests of Nevada silver king James G. Fair in the Nevada Bank. In 1905 he merged his bank with Wells Fargo Bank. He had interests in some fifteen California banks, Los Angeles and San Francisco street railways, and Southern California real estate. In 1901, during the heyday of the trusts, Hellman obtained control of the California wine industry. His motto was, "Work is a very necessary and good habit." Another favorite phrase went: "Always build your foundation before you start the roof." He was a Republican, a Jew, a Mason, and a Regent of the University of California. I.W. was also part of the ecumenical and future-minded triumvirate of a Protestant, a Catholic, and a Jew that donated the land for the University of Southern California in Los Angeles.

When the earthquake devastated the city in 1906, I.W. Hellman quickly checked his deposits in eastern banks and declared to the press: "It will only take one-third of the Hellman resources to pay off the depositors of the Wells Fargo Nevada Bank and the Union Trust Company. The Hellman surplus will be $30,000,000. Every dollar of this will be used for the rebuilding of San Francisco."

10 The 400 Block of California Street: The Heart of the Banking District

Walk through Leidesdorff Street to California Street. The 400 block of California Street has been at the heart of San Francisco's Financial District since 1866, when the Bank of California moved to its present site. Today the Federal Reserve Bank is one block to the northeast, the Bank of America a block to the west, and the Pacific Coast Stock Exchange a block to the south. In the late 1890s several large steel-frame-and-masonry office buildings were constructed along Market Street and in the Financial District. These modern structures are from ten to twelve stories high, have light courts within, and period detailing without. Several survived the earthquake and fire and, rebuilt, continue to grace the district today. In the early twentieth century San Francisco had the third largest number of skyscrapers in the U.S., after New York and Chicago.

Along this block of California Street many of the major California banks have their headquarters—this despite the fact that Los Angeles has been the richest city in California since the 1920s. Such banks and their predecessors have been the major financial instruments—other than the federal government—in the growth of the American West. The decisions about investment made within these few blocks have shaped, and continue to shape, the development of the West Coast and, increasingly, of the Pacific basin.

Bank of California Headquarters
· Museum of the Money of the American West
· 400 and 420 California Street
· Bliss and Faville, 1908; Anshen and Allen, 1967

The Bank of California, the oldest incorporated commercial bank on the West Coast, with branches in California, Oregon, and Washington, has been a consistent patron of fine architecture in San Francisco for more than a century. The previous bank building on this corner, built in 1866–67, was a Renaissance-inspired design by David Farquharson. It was razed shortly before the earthquake to make way for Bliss and Faville's colossal granite-sheathed temple to finance, which opened for business in 1908. The bank was modeled after McKim, Mead, and White's long-gone Knickerbocker Trust Company on Fifth Avenue in New York. Corinthian columns carved from granite quarries at Raymond, California, surround the exterior on two sides. These column sections were carted through the city's streets by eighteen-horse teams. The colonnade frames generous windows that increase the psychological height of the banking hall within.

Enter through the great wood doors. The great hall within measures 112 feet by 80 feet, and has 60-foot-high ceilings. It is finished in Tennessee marble and ornamented at one end with two sculptures of mountain lions by Arthur Putnam, a well-known California artist. The basement shelters the Museum of the Money of the American West, a choice collection of California gold. Descend the staircase to the left. This was, and part of it still is, a safety-deposit vault. The collection includes gold nuggets, gold coins minted in San Francisco in the 1850s and 1860s, a collection of paper money, and memorabilia associated with the history of the Comstock silver mines in Virginia City, Nevada, once called "San Francisco's richest suburb." The museum includes the famous fiftydollar gold coin struck in 1915 for the Panama-Pacific International Exposition, and the exceptionally beautiful Saint-Gaudens double eagle. This last coin, like this steel-and-granite temple, was a product of the refined eye of the Edwardian era.

Californians in general, and San Franciscans in particular, had a taste for "hard money"—gold and silver—in preference to mere paper banknotes throughout the nineteenth century. San Franciscans disdained small change; pennies did not circulate generally in Civil War-era San Francisco. Small change was often left on counters uncollected. Not until the price of San Francisco newspapers dropped to one and two cents during the deflationary days of 1907–08 did the city adopt the penny. Silver dollars, a local product, manufactured at the Old Mint at Fifth and Mission Streets, held on in the West long after eastern states had changed to paper money. Only in 1917, with America's entry into the first World War, did San Franciscans give up their tenaciously loved "hard money."

The Bank of California was the bank of William Ralston, the financier behind San Francisco's first woolen mill, first iron mill, first dry dock, the grand Palace Hotel, the Kimball Carriage Factory, the Cornell Watch Factory, the West Coast Furniture Co., the San Francisco Sugar Refinery, the New Montgomery Street extension, the Sherman Island reclamations, and the California Theater. His partner William Sharon wrote: "In building the Palace Hotel he wanted to get some oak planks for it and he bought a ranch for a very large sum of money and never used a plank from it. . . . I said to him, 'If you are going to buy a factory for a nail, a ranch for a plank, and a manufactory to build furniture, where is this thing going to end?' "

Ralston had a vision of San Francisco as the manufacturing metropolis of the Pacific. Unfortunately, it turned out that he was doing many of these things with extended-credit funds. The afternoon that the shortage at the bank was discovered, Ralston went for his daily swim off what is now Aquatic Park; he never came back alive. His funeral was one of the biggest social events in the city at the time, and everyone turned out for it. San Franciscans were willing to forgive the financial problems of the man who so fervently believed in their city's destiny.

The Bank of California survived Ralston's one-way swim. By the 1960s the bank had offices scattered all over the financial district and decided to build a new headquarters. The chairman of the board, Charles de Bretteville, decided that the old bank should be saved. Anshen and Allen, a San Francisco firm, designed a twenty-one-story annex to the gray granite temple in 1967. The new tower was designed to incorporate the old bank as part of its design. Its cast-concrete skin echoes the fluting of the old granite columns. The sidewalk was paved with granite to link the two buildings together with a darker ground. The roof of the old temple was transformed into an outdoor garden entered from the tower. It is an outstanding example of the happy marriage of historic and contemporary architecture.

California and Sansome: View of Southern Pacific Building

To the east is a view of the red-brick Southern Pacific Building at the foot of Market Street, designed by Bliss and Faville and built in 1917. It is the headquarters of *the* railroad of the West, originally called the Central Pacific, and the first transcontinental railroad. In the late nineteenth century the Southern Pacific was the most powerful corporation in California. The building has a classical colonnade along its top so that if the eye scans the opposite side of the block, with its columns, and sweeps down to the Southern Pacific Building at the foot of California Street, and then comes back up to the Bank of California, one sees the way that the Beaux-Arts architecture of the post-1906 period sought to pull the city together visually. Modern high-rise towers tend to isolate themselves from the street. They want to stand apart from all the other buildings, and they create mere holes—not "plazas"—in the urban fabric. Turn-of-the-century design was different; the Beaux-Arts ideal was that every building was an element in a larger cityscape that someday would be complete.

California First Bank
· 370 California Street
· Skidmore, Owings and Merrill, 1970

On the northeast corner of California and Sansome is the twenty-two-story bank and office building designed originally for the Bank of Tokyo. Its enormous "columns" echo the architectural motif of the Bank of California's temple on a gargantuan scale. When it was sold in 1974 this was the costliest piece of real estate in California. The site was formerly occupied by the Alaska Commercial Building, built in 1908. Its ornament was a pictorial summation of San Francisco's place in northern Pacific trade: walruses, icicles, ropes, and nautical motifs of one sort or another covered the building. The cornice had seal heads sticking out of it because the fortune of the corporation was based on seal pelts from the Pribiloff Islands. Some of the sculptural ornaments were saved and used alongside the California Street entrance.

Great Western Building
· 425 California Street
· John Carl Warnecke, 1968

This jarring, black-glass-clad, twenty-six-story, bay-windowed high-rise is on the southeast corner of California and Sansome. The bay windows were a deliberate effort to reflect the city's architectural heritage, even though there are almost no bay windows Downtown. The black glass skin differs from the generally white or gray color of most Downtown office buildings.

Insurance Exchange
· 433 California Street
· Willis Polk, 1913

Next up California Street is the Insurance Exchange Building. This eleven-story, terra-cotta-clad building harmonizes with its neighbor across the alley, the Merchants Exchange.

Merchants Exchange
· 465 California Street
· D. H. Burnham and Company; Willis Polk
· 1905

The Merchants Exchange is at the very heart of San Francisco's business core. All the major transportation systems visually converge here. Standing immediately in front of the twin granite columns and looking all around, you can see reminders of all the major phases of California's transportation history. Straight ahead, inside the great Grain Exchange beyond the glass-roofed lobby, is a large painting of a Matson steamship leaving Honolulu harbor headed for San Francisco's Embarcadero. Looking east, toward the foot of California Street where it meets Market Street, is the end of the cable-car line, only one block from the Ferry Building, the hub of passenger traffic in the nineteenth century. Today the Embarcadero station of the Bay Area Rapid Transit (BART) subway system lies beneath the cable-car terminus. The red-brick bulk of the Southern Pacific Railroad headquarters closes the view down California Street. Beyond it looms the gray steel pier of the streamlined Bay Bridge, a graceful monument to the automotive age and to the electric interurban railway lines that are no more. Running down California Street itself is the famous cable-car line, a system of transportation invented here that once was adopted by cities as far away as New York. To the north, at Clay

Street, is the approach to the elevated Embarcadero Freeway, the essential contemporary link that connects the Downtown with the international airport south of the city.

For many years the Merchants Exchange was the tallest building in the Downtown, looming white and splendid above the brick city. The building opened in January, 1905, one of the earliest examples of the vertical expansion of the Downtown core. The massive steel-frame, courtyarded building survived the earthquake a year later but was gutted by the fire. Polk reconstructed it, and it resumed its place at the center of commerce in San Francisco.

The great Grain Exchange Hall was restored in 1976 by the Chartered Bank of London (now part of the Union Bank) for their banking hall. Inconceivable as it may seem, the 1947 tenants had dropped a false ceiling from the elegant vault. This splendid space with its four gigantic columns, skylight, and oversize marine paintings is one of the finest Edwardian interiors in San Francisco. Mayor Phelan called this great room "the Forum of San Francisco." Within its rebuilt splendor the business leaders of San Francisco raised more than $4 million within two hours on April 29, 1910, in a mass meeting called to fund the great Panama-Pacific International Exposition of 1915, which celebrated the reconstruction of the Pacific Coast metropolis. Today the building is still central to the business life of San Francisco; it houses the Merchants Exchange Club, the Commercial Club, and the San Francisco Chamber of Commerce, among others.

Private clubs, for which San Francisco is famous, serve as relaxed, neutral meeting grounds where businessmen can get to know one another as individuals rather than just business functionaries. If adherence to New York exchange hours means the young financial types have to get up early, it also means that by 1:00 P.M. San Francisco time, the money market in New York is closed. Perhaps this is an important factor in explaining the strong businessmen's-club tradition in San Francisco. Most of the clubs are to the west of the office core but, appropriately enough, the Commercial Club and Merchants Exchange Club are nestled right next to the big banks. (The exalted Pacific Union Club is most remote, up the California cable line atop Nob Hill. The Bankers' Club is ensconced atop the Bank of America; it becomes the Carnelian Room after 3:00 P.M. and is then open to the public.)

In plan the Grain Exchange is like the porch of a temple. Looking through the entrance, beyond the four columns, the eye is caught by a series of truly heroic marine paintings in the facing arches of the upper area of the room, which carry the view beyond the room to the great Pacific Ocean. These 1907 paintings are among the finest public art in San Francisco and are well worth slow examination. They depict, from left to right:

A *Port Costa,* by William A. Coulter. A view through the Silver Gate, where the American and Sacramento Rivers enter San Francisco Bay from the northeast. The abundant agricultural wealth of California's great Central Valley flowed down these river routes to the great bay and the port city of San Francisco on their way to burgeoning world markets. Sailing vessels ride at anchor, while a small hay scow and two barges towed by a stern-wheeler head for San Francisco. In the foreground fishermen in a dinghy haul in their nets.

B *Honolulu Harbor,* by William A. Coulter. Honolulu is the next port west of San Francisco and the only stepping-stone across the Pacific to Asia. This view shows Honolulu when it was a small seaport nestled at the base of green volcanoes with their heads in the clouds. A pristine Waikiki Beach and Diamond Head appear to the right. A Matson steamship carrying island sugar heads east for San Francisco, while an outrigger canoe returns to the island of Oahu.

C *Arrived, All Well,* by William A. Coulter. The sailing ship *W.F. Babcock* of the Dollar Line enters the Golden Gate at sunset as the sun burns through the late-afternoon fog. The Marin headlands to the right and red-brick Fort Point to the left guard the gate to the largest harbor on the West Coast.

D *Full and By,* by William A. Coulter. The ship *Dashing Wave* rides a stormy sea through the straits beyond Tatash Light, carrying a cargo of redwood destined for San Francisco. California redwood and Oregon pine and fir were the prime building materials for San Francisco's Victorian houses.

E *War Time,* by William A. Coulter. Shipbuilding at Hunter's Point in south San Francisco was important during World War I. Here the launching of the freighter *Cotati* is shown. Other vessels lie at anchor, painted in geometrical camouflage patterns. An early airplane flies overhead, an augury of future travel patterns.

F *Northwest Passage, 1903–06,* by Nils Hagerup. The first ship to make the long-sought-after Northwest Passage was the tiny one-masted schooner-rigged sloop *Gjøa,* commanded by Danish captain Roald Amundsen. Here the dauntless vessel plunges through Arctic swells off a bleak coast. Amundsen and his six companions explored the Arctic for three years, discovered the Passage, and also determined the location of the magnetic North Pole. The ship left Oslo, Norway, in June, 1903, and arrived in San Francisco in October, 1906. Until recently the small craft sat beached at the ocean end of Golden Gate Park. Today she is back in Norway at the National Maritime Museum.

Immediately outside the glass doors to the Grain Exchange (Chartered Bank of London) is a newsstand in a marble-lined corridor that connects this building with its independently owned neighbor. Walk through this passageway to the Art Deco lobby of 300 Montgomery.

Security Pacific Bank
• Basilica Interior
• 300 Montgomery Street
• George Kelham, 1918; The Capital Company, 1941

The internal passage from the Merchants Exchange leads to the Art Deco lobby of 300 Montgomery. The California Street end of the building with the banking hall was built in 1918 for the American National Bank. In 1941, when that bank was merged with the Bank of America, the Capital Company expanded the building to Pine Street, hence the Art Deco lobby at 300 Montgomery Street. Many important Financial District buildings interconnect like this. No signs tell of these hidden passageways; one learns about the shortcuts only by working downtown. Like the alleys that thread through the blocks, the "secret" interconnections of the Financial District channel the patterns of those who work here in a "private" circulation system that facilitates constant casual meetings between people just as pathways and quadrangles on a campus do. Inconspicuous and never elaborate, these private interconnections were prevalent in office blocks built between about 1890 and 1940. After that, prestige buildings made little effort to relate to one another either architecturally or in their patterns of circulation. Plazas and open spaces, many of which actually inhibit casual meetings, have superseded these simple and intimate internal "streets."

The Bank of America moved back to the heart of the Financial District in 1941 after twenty years at Number One Powell at Market, next to the Powell Street cable-car turntable and the Market Street streetcar lines. The building at 300 Montgomery is twelve stories high and was the first big structure built after the Depression.

The lobby leads to the back entrance of the impressive columned banking hall of the Security Pacific Bank, second in California and tenth in the nation. The hall is modeled after a Roman basilica. While we associate the word *basilica* with great churches, the first Christian basilicas were adaptations of Roman secular buildings. To the Romans a basilica was a large meeting hall used for law and public administration. The central space between the rows of columns is called a nave. The columns here have recently been given a *scagliola* finish, a form of imitation marble work. Such solemn bank interiors bring to mind the acid comment of San Franciscan Ambrose Bierce, author of *The Devil's Dictionary,* who claimed that Mammon was the god of the world's chief religion and that his holy city was New York!

11 Kohl Building
- 400 Montgomery
- Percy and Polk, 1901

The prime intersection of California and Montgomery has historically attracted important buildings. In 1901 Alvinza Hayward, an
associate of William Ralston's in the Bank of California, commissioned this elegant eleven-story, H-shaped, steel-frame block, clad in
gray-green Colusa sandstone. A persistent but unconfirmed Downtown legend has it that Mrs. Hayward's superstitious beliefs account
for the building's H-shape (only a U-shape is visible from Montgomery Street). The building was the latest word in design; its richly
modeled upper-story arcade is especially handsome. It was among
San Francisco's first "fireproof" buildings; it was so well built that not
only did it survive the earthquake but its upper stories escaped damage in the subsequent fire—the only Downtown block to partially
escape the flames. Willis Polk rebuilt it after the fire, preserving the
original design. The building is at the core of the Financial District
and central to the city's Edwardian architectural tradition.

12 Bank of America World Headquarters
- 555 California Street
- Wurster, Bernardi and Emmons; Skidmore, Owings and Merrill
- Pietro Belluschi; 1968
- Carnelian Room Bar, 52nd Fl., after 3, 433-7500

Cross Montgomery Street to the full block occupied by the Bank of
America complex, clad in reddish South Dakota carnelian granite.
Like a massive basalt outcropping or a great, dark tourmaline crystal,
the fifty-two-story, 779-foot-high, zigzag-faced tower dominates
the city's skyline the way the $80 billion bank dominates banking in
California. This composition of a tower, a low banking hall, and a
large plaza (with an auditorium underneath it) opened in 1968. It cost
over $120 million and reaches as high as San Francisco's downtown
zoning permits.

One of the constants in California towns is the inevitable central
location of the Bank of America. It is often the most substantial
structure in town and invariably faces the main street at the corner
of the principal intersecting streets. A rival bank, often a Wells Fargo
branch, is paired with it across the intersection. A flag usually flies
from the bank, punctuating the spot that is more the center of town
than the city hall, post office, church, or park. In the same way, the
monumental, opulent, exquisitely detailed Bank of America World
Headquarters stands at the intersection of California and Montgomery Streets.

The Bank of America is one of the most remarkable successes in
American banking history. It was founded as the Bank of Italy by

Amadeo Peter Giannini in 1904, with $285,000 in capital. The bank's first office was at 1 Montgomery Avenue, now Columbus Avenue, at the intersection of Washington Street, where this tour began. This put the bank between the Italian-American North Beach neighborhood to the north and the Financial District to the south. A.P.'s bank decided to serve "the little fellow" and built a financial giant whose multinational corporate headquarters is now not inaccurately described as a "world headquarters."

Giannini was born in San Jose, California, in 1870, the son of the Genoese-born owner of a small hotel. His father died when he was young and his mother then married Lorenzo Scatena, who moved the family to San Francisco and opened a wholesale produce business. Young A.P. was a genius with figures and had a way with customers. Lorenzo Scatena made his stepson a full partner at age nineteen. By 1904, at age thirty-four, A.P. founded his own bank with Antonio Chichizola, a wholesale grocer, as first president.

The Bank of Italy prospered with its philosophy of serving many small personal accounts through branch banks at the center of hundreds of California towns. In the nineteenth century, Italians were the single largest foreign-born immigrant group in California. They did not all cluster in the cities, but moved to colonize and farm the land. Italian-American farmers ("ranchers," in California parlance) were scattered across California. The Bank of Italy opened branches and courted them. Brochures and advertisements were printed in Chinese, Portuguese, and other languages. As California grew, so did the bank. By 1921 it had outstripped its Establishment rivals and become the largest bank in the West. The bank was a key instrument in developing California's municipalities, agriculture, stock-raising, dairying, and industry. It became first in statewide branch banking; in 1930 the Bank of Italy shed its immigrant beginnings and rechristened itself the Bank of America. When the Depression struck, the bank was seriously overcommitted in its loans to hard-hit farmers, and when President Roosevelt declared a "bank holiday" it seemed that "the little fellow's" bank might not reopen. Old-line San Francisco bankers were not upset at the prospect. But Roosevelt made it clear to the head of the Federal Reserve Bank in San Francisco that no bank in California would reopen unless "the little fellow's" bank opened too. This kind of logic was persuasive, and the bank reopened with all the rest.

The sudden economic boom of World War II, which turned California into the arsenal for the far-flung Pacific Theater, carried the bank to further advances. It continued its investments in California's phenomenally productive agribusiness, in wartime industry, and in municipal development. After the war, as California's suburbs boomed, so did the bank that expanded to serve them. Today the Bank of America is of national and international importance. It was, for example, instrumental in helping save New York City from bankruptcy, thus turning the tables on its "Eastern Money" rivals.

When the bank assembled the block at California and Montgomery, it was subdivided by two narrow alleys, Spring and Summer Streets. It was covered with low-rise, post-1906 brick buildings and 315 Montgomery, the large steel-frame office block on the northwest corner of Montgomery and Pine built in 1921 and designed by Kelham and Macdonald. The latter building was preserved and became the link between the low-rise banking hall and the tall tower. The east-west line of Summer Street is preserved in the space between the banking hall and 315 Montgomery. Spring Street was vacated for the plaza facing California Street in front of the tower. But the nineteenth-century pattern of subdividing blocks with secondary, principally pedestrian, streets was repeated in the underground concourse that cuts through from Pine to California parallel to Montgomery and provides direct access to the tower elevators without having to cross the plaza or enter the front lobby. These pedestrian circulation patterns carried through the massive development at the sidewalk level "root" the complex firmly into the historic patterns of Financial District public and private pedestrian circulation.

The tower contains both the head offices of the bank and plush rental office space occupied by lawyers, financial consultants, and the San Francisco offices of corporations and individual investors with regional and international interests. Some 7,500 people work in the complex. The garage underneath it has 420 spaces. The steel for the complex weighs 50 million pounds—enough for 12,500 pre-1970 automobiles. Thirty-two passenger elevators and two freight elevators serve the vertical transit needs of the tower and can zoom from the lobby to the top in thirty seconds.

The zigzag façade is curiously like the decorated zigzag Moderne poured-concrete abutments that anchor the suspension cables of the Golden Gate Bridge of 1937. The two-page spread in the Sunday supplement that announced the building paired a picture of the new tower with a collage of San Francisco Victorian bay windows and thus introduced even this radical departure in scale as nonetheless continuous with the city's architectural traditions. The sawtooth profile accommodates very large two-sided bay windows that may not seem especially impressive from outside but which reveal their true dimension and effect from within. The offices in the pointed bays enjoy superb views. From them the city, the bay, and the region lie spread out like an animated scale model. Since the building stands on the northern edge of the high-rise cluster, the view to the north of the Golden Gate and Mt. Tamalpais is unobstructed. Like Russian and Telegraph Hills and the ridge of Pacific Heights, the north (California Street) side of the tower enjoys one of the finest views to be had from the heart of any American metropolis.

The zigzag façade is regular along the sides but varied along the top, giving the tower an animated profile within a simple box shape.

This ornamental variation is subtle and understated. Perhaps this studied, underplayed quality (seen in the building's top and in the meticulous perfection of the detailing of the bronze handrails and other touches) speaks more to the heart of sophisticated Northern California design than any other feature. A more obvious reference to San Francisco tradition can be seen in the brilliantly lighted metal ceiling of the low-rise banking hall, a contemporary interpretation of the coffered ceilings of banking halls such as that in the old Bank of California. The mezzanine of the banking hall houses a dull but appropriate exhibit of office machines and an interesting photographic display that charts the history of the bank, and through it, the modern history of all California. Both the banking hall mezzanine and the steps of what was once Summer Street lead to A.P. Giannini Plaza, in front of the tower.

The plaza, like the sculptural tower for which it serves as a podium, is equally an expression of power and wealth. A quarter of this prime block of land in the heart of downtown is open space. A.P. Giannini Plaza measures 290 by 140 feet and is the epitome of the luxury of space in the most densely developed place in the state. The plaza was designed with a discipline and single-minded monumentality that is noteworthy if not particularly congenial to humans seeking sun, grass, or complexity. The tight wall of buildings across the street that defines the plaza seems human-scaled by comparison. A very large American and a California state flag (the bear flag adopted by Yankee insurgents under Mexican rule in 1846) are happy spots of color and movement in the severe plaza. They also exploit the wind currents that tall buildings generate along the ground.

The focal point of the plaza, and the chief ornament of the complex, is the polished black granite 13-by-30-foot sculpture by Masayuki Nagare. The tall, rectilinear, sharp-edged tower and Nagare's enormous polished pebble, both set uncompromisingly on a clean table of dull-finished carnelian granite, engage in a self-regarding conversation of sculptural forms. The pedestrian has entered a high-art landscape as serious in its design intent as a Japanese monastery's sand garden. While the sculpture and the tower seem so different, they are actually structurally identical. The tower is a steel frame, sheathed in 3.5-inch-thick slabs of mirror-polished granite from South Dakota. The seemingly monolithic sculpture is likewise an assemblage of polished black Swedish granite mounted on a steel frame. The stone blocks are of random sizes fitted together Inca-fashion. The official title of the piece is *Transcendence,* though San Franciscans have managed what seems a fitting irreverence by dubbing the black-rock piece "the banker's heart."

The most beautiful effect achieved by the prismlike tower occurs under certain light foggy atmospheres when the sun's rays strike the faceted surface at low angles. Then the building reflects the light in beams that seem to emanate from the building. It is an arresting and mysterious effect; the building becomes a softly gleaming crystal standing in a moving, diaphanous atmosphere.

13 The Russ Building
  - 235 Montgomery Street
  - First built-in garage, George Kelham, 1927

South along Montgomery and across Pine is the tan, terra-cotta-clad, Gothic-style Russ Building with its ever-alive, artistic elevator board in its lobby. The prosperity of the 1920s was expressed in the city's skyline by the erection of soaring skyscrapers, steel-frame, terra-cotta-clad buildings that met the sidewalk much like traditional office blocks but that rose much higher and were crowned with picturesque tops. The thirty-one-story Russ Building, the tallest building on the West Coast until 1964, opened in September, 1927, two years before the crash that halted large-scale construction for almost a generation. The Russ Building occupies the site of Christian Russ's 1847 residence and the later Russ House, a hotel popular with miners and merchants from the early 1860s. The $5.5 million skyscraper was financed in a novel way: shares were sold to the general public by a specially created corporation organized by two investment groups.

It was the marvel of its day, with 1,370 offices and every conceivable service. The building was designed as a self-contained miniature city for lawyers and businessmen, boasting a complete "shopping district," as it was called, for its tenants. The eleventh-floor corridor housed a barber shop, beauty salon, gym, buffet lunchroom, business-machine shop, drugstore, haberdashery, tailor, hotel-reservation offices, jewelry store, notary, optometrist, stationery store, valet service, women's clubroom, stenographer and translation service, and that latest in instruments for long-range business transactions, a room with the telephone directories of principal cities. On the twenty-fourth floor was a glass-shielded sun deck, a tiny park in the sky with benches and places for tenants to meet. It was also the first downtown building to accommodate the automobile; a 400-car garage was built underneath this Gothic exterior. The building is E-shaped with three wings to the west, permitting natural light and ventilation.

The Russ Building acted as a great magnet for financial-service establishments and anchored the Financial District to the Montgomery Street canyon. It epitomizes the vertical solution to downtown expansion.

Perhaps the most important aspect of the Russ Building is the straightforward, practical, and congenial way it meets the sidewalk. No blank wall or wind-swept "plaza" confronts the pedestrian. Instead, a two-story-high central Gothic entrance is flanked by two rows of small-scale, indented shop fronts tucked between the façade's vertical piers. This design allows the shop fronts to change without destroying the building's coherence. There is even a black-and-white, standardized See's candy shop tucked into the discreetly receptive front.

14 Mills Building and Tower
· 220 Montgomery Street and 220 Bush Street
· Early steel-frame, Chicago School, Burnham and Root, 1891
· First tower addition in San Francisco, Lewis Hobart, 1931

Darius Ogden Mills was one of the financial powers in the West and one of the key financiers of the great Comstock silver lode and the transcontinental railroad. Part of that wealth was invested in a large downtown office block, the Mills Building. The famous Chicago architectural firm of Burnham and Root designed the steel-framed, hollow-core block in 1891–92. They used a modified form of the Richardsonian Romanesque style with delicate exterior ornament. The most notable exterior feature is the great Romanesque arched entrance with its lively stonecarving. The base of the block has a white Inyo marble veneer. The upper stories are clad with buff brick and graceful terra-cotta ornamentation. It is a solid, four-square block giving the appearance of great strength enlivened by ornamentation, and is the only unaltered Chicago School–style building in San Francisco.

When it opened in 1891, it was a modern marvel. It boasted its own electric power plant in the basement, with Thomas Edison generators powered by steam. The engine exhaust was used to supply the building with steam heat. Excess electricity was used by shops on Kearny Street.

The structure was so well built that it rode out the earthquake of 1906 with no major damage. The building superintendent and his family felt the early morning shocks in their penthouse atop the building, but only some crockery was broken. The superintendent fired the boilers at the usual hour and started the elevators. The building remained open until two in the afternoon but finally had to be abandoned to the approaching fire. The general conflagration burned out the building's interior but left the shell unharmed.

Willis Polk was in charge of the restoration and carefully retained the original exterior design. He also designed two compatible additions on the Bush Street side in 1914 and 1918. In 1931, Lewis P. Hobart, another San Francisco architect, designed still another addition to the Mills Building, a twenty-two-story tower with an entrance at 220 Bush that complements the old block perfectly. The tower was built with $1.1 million paid to the Mills estate for the site of the San Francisco International Airport south of the city; the 50-foot-by-137.5-foot lot was bought from the Coit estate for $300,-000. The Mills Building reconstruction, additions, and Tower represent continuity and imagination in the sensitive retention of the city's architectural fabric—a sound idea that has been repeated by many local investors, including the Fairmont Hotel, the Pacific Gas and Electric Company, the Southern Pacific Railroad, the St. Francis Hotel, the Bank of California, and others.

The Mills Building has always housed lawyers, and recently insurance companies. The San Francisco Bar Association established club rooms on the top floor; the Downtown branch of the City Law Library is located in the building. Other distinguished tenants included the Paul Elder Bookshops (1898) and Podesta and Baldocchi, florists. It was also the original home of the Sierra Club. Today some 3,000 people work in the block and tower.

You have walked from north to south, following the course the downtown core has moved in a century and a half; it is only appropriate to continue from the ground to the sky. The best publicly accessible high-rise "observatory" in San Francisco is the Carnelian Room bar atop the Bank of America tower. There is an exhilarating view out over the Jackson Square Historic District, Chinatown, and North Beach to the great bay, the majestic Golden Gate, and Marin County. A regional view is an appropriate conclusion to this exploration of what men have built in San Francisco from the Gold Rush to the skyscraper.

Tour 3

Eastern Pacific Heights

Victorian and Edwardian Houses and Mansions

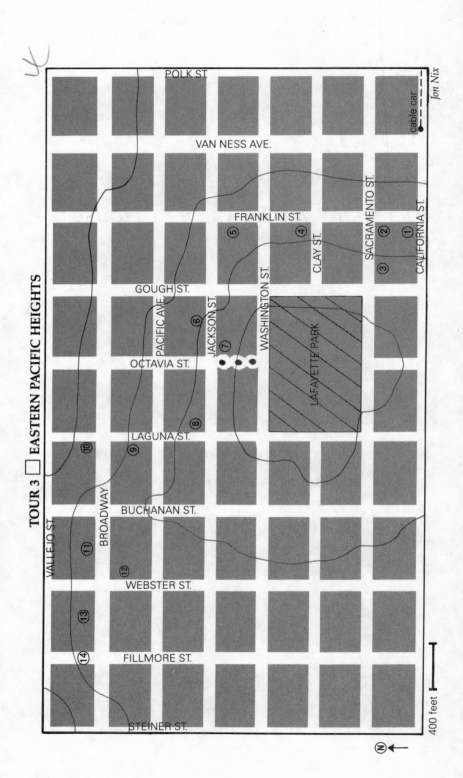

TOUR 3 □ EASTERN PACIFIC HEIGHTS

Jon Nix

POLK ST.

VAN NESS AVE.

FRANKLIN ST.

GOUGH ST.

PACIFIC AVE.

JACKSON ST.

WASHINGTON ST.

CLAY ST.

SACRAMENTO ST.

CALIFORNIA ST.

cable car

LAFAYETTE PARK

OCTAVIA ST.

LAGUNA ST.

BROADWAY

BUCHANAN ST.

VALLEJO ST.

WEBSTER ST.

FILLMORE ST.

STEINER ST.

400 feet

N

WHAT THIS WALK COVERS

This walk seeks out the surviving great Victorian and pre–World War I city mansions in this present-day apartment-house district. The walk charts the shift in taste from the Victorian (1860–1899) to the Edwardian (1900–1915) period along Pacific Heights, a spectacular ridge.

PRACTICALITIES

Best time for this walk: On Wednesday and Sunday afternoons, between 12:30 and 4:30, both the Haas-Lilienthal House (built 1886, donation $2, phone 441-3004) and the Whittier Mansion (built 1896, donation $1, phone 567-1848) are open with tours that allow a rare glimpse into two Victorian interiors. The only other Victorian house museum in San Francisco is the 1861 Octagon House at 2645 Gough Street, near Union, preserved by the Colonial Dames of America. It has a pleasant garden, but the first floor has been altered. Furnished with colonial antiques. (Open the first Sunday and the second and fourth Thursday of each month from 1:00 to 3:45 P.M., free, phone 885-9796.)

Parking: The perimeter of Lafayette Park is the most likely place to find a parking space. To return to the park by bus, see the instructions at the end of the walk.

Getting there by public transit: (1) Take the #45 Van Ness bus west on Sutter Street to Van Ness and California, alight and walk one block uphill to Franklin and California, the spot where the fire was stopped in 1906; or, (2) Take any cable car to Powell and California, transfer to the California Street cable car going west, and ride to the end of the line at California and Van Ness. Walk one block up California to Franklin, crossing Van Ness Avenue.

Cafés and restaurants: The #22 Fillmore trolley-bus goes downhill toward the bay to Union Street's many bars, restaurants, and shops. Downhill in the other direction, on Fillmore itself, are some small eateries, shops, etc. Or take the #55 Sacramento bus to Polk Street and its cafés, restaurants, and shops.

Returning: To return to Lafayette Park at the end of the walk, catch the #22 Fillmore trolley-bus at the southwest corner of Fillmore and Broadway. At Sacramento Street transfer to the #55 Sacramento Street bus going east (downtown). The #55 bus has three stops on the south side of Lafayette Park and continues to Nob Hill, Chinatown, and the Financial District.

The Haas-Lilienthal House, 2007 Franklin Street, built in 1886 in the Eastlake–Queen Anne style. Now the headquarters of the Foundation for San Francisco's Architectural Heritage and open to the public.

INTRODUCTION

Pacific Heights is an apt and beautiful name for San Francisco's choicest residential area, although the view is of San Francisco Bay, not the Pacific Ocean. It was part of the 500-block Western Addition to San Francisco, laid out in 1855 west of Larkin Street, north of Market, and east of Divisadero. Seven large squares were set aside for public parks. Pacific Heights covers 130 blocks from Van Ness Avenue on the east to Presidio Avenue on the west, and from California Street on the south to Union Street on the north. This east-west rectangle is now split in two at the line of the Fillmore Street trolley-bus. The eastern, or downtown, half is now an apartment-house district, but sequestered here and there are a few survivors from the first wave of development in the 1880s, some of the finest Victorian houses in San Francisco. Many of the largest are now nonprofit institutions and private schools.

West of Fillmore Street, all the way to the Presidio Army Reservation, is a later-built (1895–1925) neighborhood of single-family townhouses. These houses stand close together and form a protective ring around the many private gardens at the core of every block. At the western end of Broadway, high on a spectacular ridge up against the parklike Presidio and far from the city's hustle and bustle, is a string of great houses that fully deserve the description palatial.

Pacific Heights occupies the highest ground to the west and north of the downtown, a common location for luxury districts. The steep ridge along Broadway and the summit of Lafayette Park enjoy the best views, unsullied by industry. The great bay below collects the waters from the rivers that drain the Sierras and the enormous and abundant Central Valley of California. These waters, flowing west, have carved a channel, the Golden Gate, through the Coastal Range to the Pacific. To the north of the Gate is Mt. Tamalpais, often with its feet in the white fog, looking like a mountain in a Chinese scroll. With little industrial or automobile pollution upwind and steady westerly winds, Pacific Heights enjoys constant fresh air and sparklingly clear views. At night the lights on the opposite shores glitter like a long, low bank of embers.

Beyond the Golden Gate, where the waters of the land meet the waters of the sea, great banks of fog are generated, which flow through the Gate in the late afternoon. On a foggy night, when the trees are dripping wet, the glistening streets of Pacific Heights feel intimately connected with the sea. The foghorns in the Gate, each with a different voice, seem to answer each other's calls. They turn the neighborhood's stillness into passages of silence in an extended piece of music.

Pacific Heights' two principal parks are four-block-square Lafayette Park and Alta Plaza. (Four blocks is the minimum size necessary to create a spacious park within a gridiron street plan; the center of the park is a full block away from the city streets. Generous parks

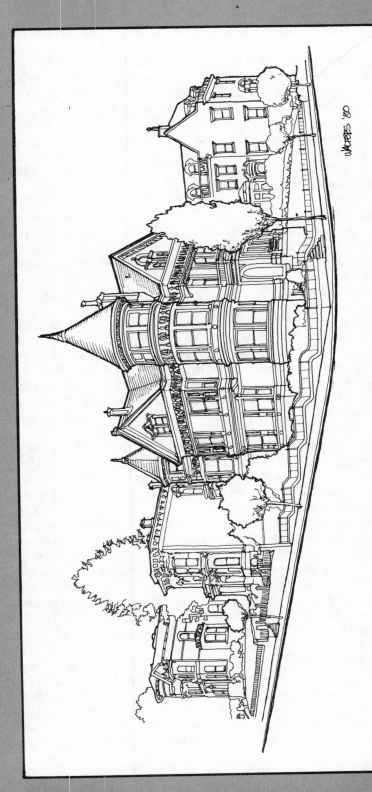

High Victorian mansion group on the northwest corner of California and Franklin Streets. Left to right: 1834 California, 1818 California, 1701 Franklin, and 1735 Franklin.

characterize the whole Western Addition and are the work of an anonymous surveyor who must have realized that the few, small parks in the old part of the city east of Larkin Street, laid out only eight years previously, were entirely inadequate. This was an important step in the creation of San Francisco's superb system of over 160 neighborhood parks and squares.) Lafayette Park is laid out as a romantic English landscape with large lawns falling away from a wooded peak—swept at night by the beacon of the Alcatraz lighthouse. It embraces 9.46 acres and was, like all of San Francisco, originally barren and windswept. Irrigation and forestation have changed the barrenness, but most of the trees in Lafayette Park lean eastward, away from the prevailing westerly winds.

The true San Franciscan will find a species of plant to grow absolutely anywhere. In the nineteenth century San Franciscans imported plants from all over the globe to cultivate in their artificially watered paradise. Desert plants like date palms, fan palms, yucca trees, New Zealand cabbage palms; many varieties of Australian eucalypti; Italian pines, Norfolk Island pines, trees from the Himalayas, cypress trees from the Monterey peninsula; mosses and ferns that flourish in dank places, plants that thrive in sand—all were lovingly cultivated. Today virtually every house, apartment, restaurant, and business-place is alive with plants. It borders on a collective mania. One nineteenth-century visitor remembered being astounded to find a small spring bouquet standing in a broken cup in a blacksmith's shop. Today San Francisco has a higher per-capita consumption of cut flowers than any other American city. The city's magnificent parks are but one manifestation of this horticultural passion.

In the 1840s and 1850s much of the land west of the present Downtown was occupied by squatters, some in the pay of real-estate speculators, who built fences and shacks and took over unprotected property. This led to a generation of lawsuits and counter-suits. Neither army land nor park land was sacred. One man, Samuel Holladay, even occupied the top of Lafayette Park. About 1867 he built a large white house there, Holladay's Heights, which became a mecca for literary society. Holladay built an astronomical observatory on the hill in 1879, the first in the West, and successfully held off the city for his lifetime. Not until 1936 did the city raze the house and reclaim the site. The trees Holladay planted around his house became the grove with a hollow center at the summit of the park. The St. Regis Apartments on the eastern edge of the park is the last evidence of these incursions into public reserves.

Van Ness Avenue, the eastern border of Pacific Heights, was named after Mayor James Van Ness, one of the men responsible for passing ordinances in the 1850s that clarified the confused land titles west of the city. The Van Ness ordinances reserved spaces for streets and schools and allowed those in possession of the land to clear their title to it. In essence this allowed squatters to take over most of the city's public Outside Lands. Today Van Ness Avenue is Highway 101, the principal highway through the city. It was not intended to be a major traffic artery, but rather a quiet and grand boulevard lined with mansions. In 1888, Hittell's guide to San Francisco noted, "On Van Ness Avenue, and the street lying to the west of it, the visitor may see a larger number of handsome wooden residences than he will find elsewhere within the same space in any city in the world." Churches and clubs also favored Van Ness. Most of the oldest Protestant congregations and the Roman Catholic cathedral relocated near Van Ness Avenue as the Downtown expanded.

In the era of privately owned streetcar lines, Pacific Heights' well-to-do residents enjoyed the best transit connections of any neighborhood in San Francisco, with the possible exception of Nob Hill. The lines on Pacific Avenue, Jackson, Washington, Sacramento, and California Streets meant that most residents had to walk only one block to catch a cable car. It was written in the 1880s that "the streetcars are so cheap, and run at intervals so brief, and are generally so clean and convenient, that relatively little use is made of cabs. On account of the hilly character of the site Hansom cabs cannot be used to advantage." Even wealthy families found it unnecessary to keep a horse and carriage. The cable-car crews often knew most of their passengers by name; operators would ring their bells when passing friends, pretty girls, and children. Public transit did not, however, disturb the tranquility of the area's two most prestigious streets, Van Ness Avenue and Broadway. The last cable-car line in Pacific Heights, the Washington-Jackson line, shut down on September 1, 1956. A band playing funeral dirges preceded the last car on its final journey. Today Pacific Heights is poorly served by noisy diesel buses that sometimes fail to make the steep grade on the approach from Nob Hill; but then many residents, certainly most in the western half of Pacific Heights, have automobiles. Today the relative lack of public transportation increases the isolation and social exclusivity of the neighborhood.

When the earthquake and fire struck in 1906, Van Ness Avenue, the widest street in the city (five feet wider than Market Street), was chosen as a fire break. Army Engineers dynamited some of the mansions on Van Ness to stop the fire from spreading westward. The Pacific Heights mansions that survived to the west were all slightly damaged. At the Rudolph Spreckels home at Gough (pronounced "Goff") and Pacific, one observer wrote,

> The lawn was riven from end to end in great gashes, the ornamental Italian rail leading to the imposing entrance was a battered heap and Rudolph Spreckels, his wife, his little son, his mother-in-law and sisters-in-law and maid servants had set up their household on the sidewalk, the women wrapped in rugs and coverlets and huddled in easy chairs hastily rolled out. They were having their morning tea on the sidewalk and the

silver service was spread on the stone coping. At house after house of the wealthy and fashionable this scene was repeated.

After the fire and earthquake Van Ness Avenue, the edge of the surviving residential area, became the temporary home for downtown stores in houses not destroyed by fire or dynamite. Surviving buildings on the west side were turned into shops with large plateglass-windowed additions built over front gardens. Temporary frame buildings were built along the east side. As one observer said,

> A glance up and down the Avenue . . . suggested the main street of a seaside resort rather than the principal retail street of a big city. Strangers familiar with Atlantic City promptly noted the fact that the modern buildings and the liberal display of bunting reminded one of the boardwalk of the New Jersey watering place. There was an air of unsubstantiality which made it easy for the visitor to accept the statement that like the prophet's gourd it had sprung up in a night.

Van Ness was permanently rebuilt only after the Downtown was reconstructed. Many of the large buildings that line the avenue today were built between 1910 and 1930. In the nineteenth century, the side streets between Van Ness and Polk Street had been the location of many livery stables. In the early twentieth century Van Ness became San Francisco's automobile row. The automobile was still a luxury then, and some of the showrooms are impressive architectural monuments to the prosperity of the Coolidge years—especially the former Packard showroom designed by Bernard Maybeck at Van Ness and O'Farrell.

Though Pacific Heights and its great houses escaped the flames in 1906, another force almost as irresistible swept away many of its gingerbread castles in the early twentieth century: rising real-estate values. The good name, good views, and good transit connections with downtown made this a prime area for luxury apartment houses. One by one the great Victorian houses were torn down. Many of those that survived became boarding houses. The luxury suburbs on the Peninsula south of the city started drawing the rich out of the city in the 1890s. Those who inherited big, old-fashioned houses in Pacific Heights usually had modern houses of their own and sold off the family mansion to liquidate the estate. They were bought by developers who constructed luxury apartment houses.

The apartment houses built in Pacific Heights between the wars were often of superior design. Most were elevator buildings between six and eight stories high. Although there was no height limit, economic forces and the technology of the day made this size building optimal. An architecturally coherent district developed. Big, white, reinforced-concrete apartment buildings, many with vertical bands of shallow bay windows, filled the ridge west of Van Ness. From across the bay the big white blocks blend with the white, cubist form of San Francisco. In the twenties and thirties apartment lobbies were things of splendor. Marble, custom metal-work, and polished brass continued to be used in the Art Deco of the thirties. After 1960, higher land costs, building costs, and calculations of the optimal investment increased the height of the typical apartment building to about twelve stories. Most lack bay windows, have vast expanses of glass, and sport open balconies (almost useless in this climate).

Today eastern Pacific Heights is no longer the exclusive preserve of the very rich. It has a varied population—mostly adult, quiet, and hard-working. Many of its apartments are home to single men and women who work in offices Downtown. A second distinctive ingredient in the population is widows who sold their suburban homes to live in more convenient city apartments and condominiums.

THE TOUR

1 California and Franklin Streets, northwest corner
· Victorian Mansions
· 1701 Franklin
· Queen Anne, W.H. Lillie, 1895

The large Queen Anne house at the northwest corner of California and Franklin was built for Edward Coleman. Coleman owned the Idaho Mine in Grass Valley, California, and made a fortune in gold mining and timber. The house he built on this prominent intersection displays the San Francisco Queen Anne style at its most assured. The house is distinguished by a round corner tower with curved glass windows. Notice the smooth curve where the tower meets the wall; this curve is echoed in the low retaining wall around the garden. There is a faceted tower to the rear, on the California Street side. The house is a suave exercise in geometric forms: by the late 1890s the best San Francisco architects had learned how to integrate a wide variety of geometric forms and still produce a harmonious whole. The interior is designed around a central hall with a staircase lighted by a large stained-glass window on the north side of the house. The original paint scheme was gray. The house saw a long period of decline when it was used as a card club and rooming house. It was restored in 1975 and converted to law offices. At that time a lively but tasteful modern paint scheme was applied, which emphasizes the white scratchwork that embellishes the house. Typical Queen Anne motifs—wreaths, garlands, and flaming torches—decorate the exterior. Most of this fancywork is cast plaster, not carved wood.

First Church of Christ, Scientist
· Franklin and California Streets, northeast corner
· Tuscan Revival, Edgar A. Matthews, 1911

The fire that followed the 1906 earthquake destroyed all the buildings from the Downtown to this corner. In 1911, Edgar A. Matthews designed a church for the site, which, like all Christian Scientist properties, is immaculately maintained. The church is in the Tuscan style. Its handsome square tower makes a nice pair with the round turret of 1701 Franklin Street. The church is clad with tapestry brick and beautifully colored terra-cotta ornament.

1818 California Street
· Italianate, 1876

Walk around the corner of the Coleman house to 1818 California Street. This house was built in 1876 by Louis Sloss as a wedding present for his daughter and her husband, Ernest Lilienthal. It is in the Italianate style, so called because its redwood ornament was loosely derived from Italian Mannerist designs. Louis Sloss dealt in mining stocks and also formed the Alaska Commercial Company, which secured an exclusive concession from the United States government to harvest sealskins on the Aleutian Islands. This concession became the foundation of a large fortune. While the east wall of the house shows handsome architectural elaboration, the west wall of the building is purely utilitarian, with windows poked in where needed and pipes and telephone wires visible. Exterior plumbing is a typical economy in San Francisco building and is possible because the temperature never drops below freezing. The house has been converted into two flats.

1834 California Street
· Italianate and Queen Anne, 1876 and 1895

This fascinating house combines the first and last of the three principal Victorian styles popular in San Francisco. The right-hand side was built in 1876 in the Italianate style, characterized by the slant-sided bay windows. The left side was added in 1895 and displays the rounded bay windows of the Queen Anne style. It is a unique architectural amalgam that neatly sums up the evolution of Victorian domestic styles between 1870 and 1890. The original house was built for Samuel Sussman, a pioneer San Francisco merchant, the "S" in S&W Fine Foods. In 1895 the house was bought by John C. Coleman, the brother of the man who built 1701 Franklin. Coleman had ten children and every reason to want a larger house.

John Coleman was active in the development and consolidation of public utilities. He had holdings in the Pacific Telephone and Telegraph Company, the Pacific Gas and Electric Company, and the North Pacific Coast Railroad. He was also a director of the California Street Cable Railroad, which passed by his front door—and which set up its temporary headquarters in his house immediately after the 1906 earthquake. Coleman died in 1919 at the age of 95. His daughter, Miss Persis Coleman, has preserved the house like a fly in amber. Its quiet gray color scheme, green shades, and white curtains have never changed. Various grayed tones were the original colors of nearly every San Francisco Victorian house. Poet George Sterling dubbed San Francisco "the cool, gray city of love" for both its pearly fogs and its gray houses.

This cluster is among the most important groups of high-Victorian houses remaining in San Francisco. It was unusual both then and now to find such large gardens surrounding San Francisco houses. The symmetrical tree between 1818 and 1834 California is a Norfolk pine.

2 Bransten House
· 1735 Franklin Street
· Georgian Revival, Herman Barth, 1904

Walk back to Franklin Street, turn left, and look at the red-brick-veneered, two-story, Georgian-style house at 1735 Franklin. The spacious lawn between the corner Coleman house and the Bransten house is a rare piece of open space in what has always been a densely built-up part of the city. This lawn, the corner house, and 1818 California owe their survival to the fact that the Bransten family purchased them in order to preserve the light and view of this red-brick house. Number 1735 Franklin has its entrance on the side, a common pattern in San Francisco. This freed the street façade for a large bay window. The Branstens were coffee wholesalers, and MJB coffee is still sold in San Francisco. Here and there in the old parts of town, the strange ads for MJB coffee with their enormous question mark and cryptic slogan "Why?" survive to puzzle passersby.

3 1900 Block of Sacramento Street, South Side
· Victorian row houses
· Italianate and Colonial Revival, 1870s to 1895

The row of five small Victorian houses at 1911, 1913, 1915, 1919, and 1921 Sacramento is one of the few surviving groups of standard Victorian row houses in this part of Pacific Heights. While grand houses were built on Van Ness Avenue, and elaborate houses on Franklin and Gough Streets, the side streets were once filled with more modest houses such as these. Houses like these, with their flat roofs, were built in the late 1860s or early 1870s and are typical variations on the Italianate style. Number 1911, with its graceful window moldings, exhibits a less frequently encountered kind of ornament. Although only one of these houses has a bay window on the façade, bay windows were widespread throughout the 1870s, 1880s, and 1890s.

Number 1919 Sacramento is a fine example of the Colonial Revival style. The Palladian window on the first floor, the circular window on the second floor, and the gable roof with dormers are all hallmarks of the style. This house was built in 1895. The delicate windows and the fine quality of the ornament are typical of the elegant decorative elements in late Queen Anne and Colonial Revival houses.

Victorian houses had to conform to two contradictory requirements: the need for extreme economy in land use (hence the tight row-house arrangement), and the desire for seeming opulence (thus the application of elaborate redwood ornament to the front of an essentially simple frame structure). San Francisco's Italianate row houses evolved to meet both these requirements. They provided so fine a solution to the housing needs of the rapidly expanding middle class—their principal buyers—and recognized economy and profitability for their builders that they still remain the most distinctive element in San Francisco's architectural mix.

Housebuilding in San Francisco was marked by the prevalence of the piecework system; parts of houses such as bays and ornaments were mass-produced in mills south of Market Street and then attached to a frame. These houses were not designed by architects but rather constructed by builders following standard plans. Since in this tightly packed city there was little room for gardens or the horizontal extension of buildings, a feeling of spaciousness was contrived by accentuating the verticality of the house. Tall, narrow windows and doors and high ceilings were universal—this last despite the obvious problem in heating. Flat roofs evolved during the nineteenth century as an economy measure in a city where the rains are rarely heavy. Richly molded cornices were devised to define the top of the house and to make a more impressive streetscape.

Return to busy Franklin Street and see 1901 Franklin at Clay.

4 The Golden Gate Church
· 1901 Franklin Street, at Clay
· Baroque Revival, 1900

This restrained, Baroque Revival house was built in 1900 for one of the Crockers. Though it appears to be stone, it is actually built of wood. Its simple landscaping is typical of nineteenth-century San Francisco taste. The gumdrop-shaped evergreens were characteristic of Northern California horticulture in the 1840s and after. The house was acquired by Rev. Florence S. Becker and is now a Spiritualist church.

5 Haas-Lilienthal House/San Francisco's Foundation for Architectural Heritage
· 2007 Franklin Street
· Eastlake–Queen Anne, Peter R. Schmidt, 1886
· Open Wednesday and Sunday, 12:30–4:30; $2; 441-3304

Walk down Franklin to the great, gray Haas-Lilienthal House at 2007 Franklin. This house was built in 1886 for William Haas, a Bavarian-born wholesale grocer. It cost $18,500 to build. A description of the house published one year after its construction noted that "an air of comfort and elegance pervades the house; convenience has been consulted; electricity flies at the command of the slightest touch." The Haas-Lilienthal House is a transitional building and is best described as an Eastlake house with a Queen Anne tower. Today the house is a rare survivor, but in the 1880s there were many such houses on Nob Hill and in Pacific Heights. A frontal view of the Franklin Street façade shows a bold and extremely complex forcing together of elements underneath the gable. This gable is repeated in three other gables on the garden side of the house. The gables make it appear that the house has a peaked roof, but in fact, the roof is flat. The Eastlakes of the late 1880s were undoubtedly the boldest architectural experiments San Francisco house building ever saw. Wild, mannered manipulations of cubes, cylinders, pyramids, cones, and exaggerated gables were improbably used in asymmetrical juxtapositions. Sleight of hand in the juggling of elements is the essence of these designs.

Photographs and drawings in the ballroom chart the history of the building and its neighborhood. Some changes have been made, such as early-twentieth-century revisions of the front main floor, the addition of a chimney and bathroom on the south wall, the addition of a sleeping porch in the back, and a new roof. In 1927 a wing was added, with a garage on the ground floor and bedrooms above, designed by noted San Francisco architect Gardner Dailey. The house has been kept as it evolved over time as one family's home and has not been "brought back" to the 1880s. The south side garden, originally a separate lot, was purchased in 1898 and gives the house more space than was usual for a San Francisco Victorian. The large tree is an English holly.

Today the Haas-Lilienthal House is a house museum; it also contains the offices of the Foundation for San Francisco's Architectural Heritage, a member-supported nonprofit organization dedicated to the preservation of buildings and places important to San Francisco's architectural and historic character. Organized in 1971, Heritage acts as an advocate for the preservation of significant buildings, provides technical and financial assistance, encourages city policies that recognize and protect architecturally and historically significant buildings and neighborhoods, and sponsors public education programs to fos-

ter a greater appreciation of San Francisco's architecture and the need
to conserve it.

6 Glenlee Terrace
- 1925–55 Jackson Street
- Mission Revival, Arthur J. Laib, 1913

Leave the Haas-Lilienthal House, turn left at Jackson Street, and see
the white stucco, Mission-style Glenlee Terrace at 1925–55 Jackson.
Between 1900 and 1930, when former single-family house sites were
being redeveloped into apartment houses, court-shaped buildings
such as this one were built on Russian Hill and Pacific Heights. On
flat or steep sites, there has never been a better configuration for a
San Francisco apartment building. In Shingle, Mission, Pueblo, and.
other styles they offer some of the most civilized high-density housing ever built in San Francisco. Like a cell within a larger cell of the
regular city block, each compound has its own definite identity.
There is a sense of place here, even if achieved with stucco over frame
and wire-lath. The palm trees were old Victorian favorites; here they
give the right exotic touch. Visible far overhead are the trees atop the
salmon-colored luxury apartment building at 2006 Washington
Street, another example of the San Franciscan's ability to grow a plant
absolutely anywhere.

Royal Swedish Consulate
- 1950–60 Jackson Street
- Georgian Revival, Walter Bliss, 1918

Across the street, at 1950 and 1960 Jackson, are the twin Georgian-
style orange brick-and-terra-cotta houses built by Swedish-born
Captain Matson's widow in 1918. Appropriately enough, they are
now the Royal Swedish Consulate. A lovely white marble statue can
be seen through the right-hand gate. The south-facing front garden
in the court formed by the two L-shaped houses almost always has
flowers in bloom.

From the intersection of Jackson and Octavia there is a fine view of
the bay and the cluster of simple clapboard, green-roofed buildings at
Fort Mason. This military reserve dates from the initial American
occupation of California in the 1840s and boasts handsome landscaping. Notice how the westerly winds have sculpted the fort's trees.

7 Spreckels Mansion
- 2080 Washington Street, at Octavia
- French Baroque, George Applegarth, 1913

Farther up Jackson, at Octavia, is a view of the back of the white Utah
limestone mansion built in 1913 for Adolph Bernard and Alma de

Bretteville Spreckels. Adolph Bernard Spreckels was one of the thirteen children of Claus Spreckels, the western sugar king. In the heyday of the giant trusts, Spreckels senior had divided the country with Havemeyer in New York; Spreckels's share was everything west of the Rockies. The Spreckelses held vast tracts of cane- and beet-producing lands in California and Hawaii including a 40,000-acre plantation in Hawaii. Adolph married French-born Alma de Bretteville in 1908; five years later the couple moved into their new French Baroque mansion on Washington Street. Seven or eight houses had previously occupied the large site, and Mrs. Spreckels insisted that they be saved and moved.

The Washington Street façade of the mansion has pairs of giant composite three-quarter columns with decorated lower shafts. Elaborate gardens were planned to cascade down this side of the property but were never planted. This block of Octavia was curved, landscaped, and paved with brick to discourage through traffic.

Architect George Applegarth had studied at the École des Beaux-Arts in Paris for six years. The same combination of patron and architect that built this mansion also endowed San Francisco with one of its finest Beaux-Arts buildings, the California Palace of the Legion of Honor in Lincoln Park, opened in 1924. The period French furniture on exhibit in that museum gives a good idea of how mansions such as this one were furnished.

Visible to the east of the Spreckels mansion is the salmon-colored tower of 2006 Washington. After the first World War the rich no longer built great mansions in the city; such development moved beyond the suburban fringe. In town, the wealthy preferred large apartments. Number 2006 Washington was built in 1925 during the first wave of luxury apartment-house construction. This splendid, discreetly decorated building was built with only one apartment per floor, each as large as a sizable house; it is one of the poshest such buildings in San Francisco. A beautiful garden faces the Spreckels mansion and a garage is unobtrusively tucked under the building. The salmon color has a warm glow at sunset.

Cross Octavia and continue west on Jackson; on the north side of Jackson is a varied array of eclectic styles popular from the 1920s to 1940s.

8 Whittier Mansion/California Historical Society
· 2090 Jackson Street
· Richardsonian Queen Anne, Edward R. Swain, 1896
· Open Wednesday, Saturday, and Sunday, 1–5; $1; 567-1848

This elaborate mansion faced in red Arizona sandstone was built in 1894–96 for widower William Franklin Whittier and designed by San Francisco architect Edward R. Swain (who also designed the McLaren Lodge in Golden Gate Park in 1896). Whittier came to California from Maine in 1854, was a member of the Committee of Vigilance in 1856, and eventually became a partner in the largest West Coast paint and white-lead company with profitable sidelines in imported glass, mirrors, oils, etc. The company eventually became W.P. Fuller and Co. Before the construction of the apartment houses around it, this house had a magnificent view of the north bay and the Golden Gate. The house cost some $150,000 to build.

Stone houses are unusual in San Francisco. The abundance of excellent timber in California and Oregon, the lack of good building stone, and the threat of earthquakes combined to make wood the favored building material on the West Coast. Between about 1895 and 1915, however, some wealthy San Franciscans built in brick and stone, probably as a way of distinguishing their houses from all the others. Pacific Heights is the principal part of San Francisco where such houses are found. The Whittier house is built of steel-reinforced brick walls with a sandstone facing. The house went through the earthquake of 1906 with virtually no damage. The weathering of the soft sandstone, however, has been severe. Surface coatings of preservatives have slightly changed the color of the exterior.

When the house was built it was described as "Renaissance in feeling." Today we would call it a Richardsonian Queen Anne house with Classical elements. The round corner towers are the most distinctively Queen Anne feature of the house. The rigid symmetry of the façade, the Classical portico, and the curious Ionic temple front that seems suspended on the façade's second-story center, however, show the influence of the more "correct" Neoclassical styles of the period 1895–1915. San Francisco's wildly picturesque, asymmetrical, somewhat naïve late-Victorian styles gradually gave way to more sober styles in the Edwardian period. The Whittier mansion is a transitional design halfway between the late-Victorian Queen Anne style and the "modern" Neoclassical styles of the turn of the century. The almost independent temple façade on the second story is an intimation of things to come; a decade later such academic design would no longer be mere detail in a larger design but would become the design itself.

Underneath these antique embellishments, however, is a thoroughly modern building. The Whittier house was built with a 5-foot-square Otis hydraulic elevator, a transformer to convert city streetcar power to house current, gas-and-electric fixtures, and electric auxiliary heaters. (Whittier was on the board of what eventually became the Pacific Gas and Electric Company.) The true glory of this house is its rich interior. An extraordinary array of fine woods was used to panel the interior: golden oak, Honduran mahogany, Guatemalan primavera, tamano, birch, cherry, bird's-eye maple, waxed redwood, and other fine woods. One of the most fascinating rooms in the house is the circular, Turkish-style smoking room in the northwest turret with its rich polychromed arched ceiling and built-in humidor.

After Whittier's death in 1917, his daughter used the house as her pied-à-terre in San Francisco during the winter social season. The house was later sold and eventually purchased by the German government for a consulate in 1941. This interlude proved to be very brief; two months later the United States declared war on Nazi Germany and the house was seized by the Alien Property Custodian. It was auctioned in 1950.

In 1956 the California Historical Society bought the mansion for its Northern California headquarters. The original furnishings had been dispersed by that time, and CHS furnished the house with interesting nineteenth-century furniture and an outstanding collection of California paintings, including superb examples of the work of William Keith, Thomas Hill, William Hahn, Edwin Deakin, Raymond Yelland, and Grace Hudson. Some are loans from the Louis Sloss, Jr., Collection. The sweeping landscapes of California's natural wonders and early towns preserve images of a fresh new world now so far away. The second floor is now a gallery that mounts interesting changing exhibitions.

Behind the Whittier mansion, on the southeast corner of Pacific and Laguna is Schubert Hall, formerly the John D. Spreckels house, at 2099 Pacific Avenue. It houses the Library of the California Historical Society, one of the foremost libraries devoted to California and Western history. It also houses the California Genealogical Society collections and the Kemble Collection.

Across from the CHS Library, on the northeast corner of Pacific and Laguna, are two six-story, white, bay-windowed, reinforced-concrete apartment buildings with fanciful ornamentation typical of the Spanish-intoxicated 1920s. In strong light these buildings dazzle the eye. From across the bay this kind of large structure fits in perfectly with the white, cubist profile of San Francisco. While gray was a favorite color for San Francisco's Victorians, in the early twentieth century white and Mediterranean pastels (light pink, mustard, "landlady's beige") became the fashion. Light colors make even the most dissimilar buildings blend. Such colors are especially felicitous under this city's peculiar light.

9 2535 Laguna Street
· Brown shingle house, Ernest A. Coxhead, c. 1904

The three-story (with garage), brown shingle house with green roof, metal chimney, and glossy black trim was designed by the inventive English-born San Francisco architect, Ernest A. Coxhead. It was one of four houses that Coxhead designed for Mrs. Florence Ward between 1898 and 1904. English vernacular buildings of the Medieval period fascinated certain Bay Area architects, and their clients, at the turn of the century. The entrance is deep in the middle of the side of the house, permitting the narrow street frontage to be used for bay windows. One effect of this floor plan is to make the house seem bigger once inside it; it is a long walk back to the front room. The building's Georgian-inspired ornament is spare but beautifully modeled. (Presidio Heights, especially the 3200 and 3300 blocks of Pacific, is the treasury of this style.)

Walk down Laguna. Fresh water was extremely scarce among the sand dunes of San Francisco. Laguna Street got its name from a fresh-water lagoon near the bay where laundries clustered in the mid-nineteenth century, when that area was far beyond the outskirts of town. Turn left on Broadway.

10 2000 Broadway
· Modern residential high-rise, Backen, Arrigoni and Ross, 1973

This twelve-story, gray concrete apartment building was designed in 1973. Definitive architectural categorizations usually take at least two generations to evolve; for want of a better name such present-day designs are usually labeled Concrete Brutalism. This massive, high-density building is arranged around a brick-paved court and epitomizes the agitated, cut-out rectangular forms favored by contemporary high-style designers and sometimes called the Third Bay Tradition. Like the Eastlakes of the late 1880s, this style exhibits a tense, arbitrary juxtaposition of varied geometric forms and window shapes. Eastern Pacific Heights has a wider variety of periods and styles of buildings than any other part of San Francisco; investors continue to build high-fashion buildings along this dramatic ridge. In the nineteenth century they built large mansions; today they build large condominiums.

11 Hamlin School/originally James Leary Flood Mansion
· 2120 Broadway
· Baroque Revival, 1901

The three-story Baroque Revival mansion with the Ionic portico and bronze fence at 2120 Broadway was built in 1901 by an unknown architect for James Leary Flood. (Flood *père*'s Connecticut brownstone mansion atop Nob Hill, built in 1886 by Augustus Laver, is now the Pacific Union Club. See Tour 5.) This house, though it looks like stone, is actually built of wood. Its severe formality is characteristic of the simple lines of the Baroque Revival styles that succeeded the agitated late Victorians. The interior is organized around a skylighted Great Hall, two stories high and paneled in oak and walnut. Other features include a Chinese Room finished with red lacquer and a bamboo ceiling, and a mosaic-tiled solarium that extends across the back of the house with a magnificent view of the Golden Gate.

In 1928 the house was bought by the Sarah Dix Hamlin School for Girls, which had been founded in 1863 as the Van Ness Seminary. When the house became a school, the third floor servants' quarters became rooms for boarders. In 1967 a modern concrete school building was constructed down the steep slope behind this building. The new building was designed by Wurster, Bernardi and Emmons and exhibits the unadorned purity of the early work of that famous San Francisco firm. In 1970 a third building was built between the other two; its roof is used for a playground and enjoys a sweeping view of the bay. The two stone lions that flank the mansion are affectionately known as Leo and Leona. Detour left up Webster Street.

2 Bourn Mansion
· 2550 Webster Street
· Georgian Revival, Willis Polk, 1896

This imposing dark-clinker-brick Georgian townhouse was built for William Bourn in 1896. Bourn was head of the Spring Valley Water Company (now the San Francisco Water Department), the Pacific Gas and Electric Company, and the Empire (gold) Mining Company. He was a prime mover in the financing of the great Panama-Pacific International Exposition of 1915. Bourn also commissioned Polk to design his country seat in San Mateo, Filoli (a name derived from the contraction of Bourn's motto: "Fight, Love, Live"), an estate larger than Monaco situated on the watershed of the Spring Valley Water Company. Filoli, with some of the finest gardens in the country, is now a property of the National Trust for Historic Preservation.

Bourn needed a city house where he could receive callers; this house was designed for this purpose. Beyond the massive front door are two waiting rooms, one for ladies in the French style to the right, and one for gentlemen in dark colors to the left. A hallway on the first floor leads to an impressive staircase and the *piano nobile* above. A butler would lead callers up this grand staircase to a beautifully decorated waiting room embellished with Bruce Porter murals of peacocks. Beyond a handsome wood archway was Bourn's princely reception room, with an enormous fireplace at one end and Bourn's gigantic desk and a bay window with a view of the Golden Gate at the other. This impressive room, which extends the width of the house, is expressed on the exterior by the large central window over the front door. This overscaled window is characteristic of the curious predilection of turn-of-the-century Bay Area architects to explode the scale of one piece of exterior ornament. Undoubtedly, those who called on Mr. Bourn were suitably impressed, if not actually oppressed, by the forceful design of this townhouse. In keeping with the purpose of the building as a place to receive callers, the reception areas are grand beyond imagining, while the bedrooms on the third floor are tiny and unimpressive. William Bourn died in 1936, one of the last of the West's legendary empire builders.

13 Convent of the Sacred Heart School/originally James Leary Flood Mansion
· 2222 Broadway
· Renaissance Palazzo, Bliss and Faville, 1912

Return to Broadway and see 2222 Broadway, now the Convent of the Sacred Heart (girls') School but originally the second palatial home of James Leary Flood, the son of the Nevada silver king. This superb steel-frame mansion, clad in Tennessee marble, was designed in the style of a Renaissance palazzo and is among the finest houses ever built in San Francisco. The design is quiet and elegant; the materials, workmanship, and detailing exhibit a standard of opulence and perfection no longer possible in modern building. Each block of stone in the façade was carefully matched with the grain of its neighbor. The carving around the door is delicate and subtle. The front door's metal grille looks like black lace when illuminated from behind at night. Walk around the right-hand side of the building to the court on the east side. The extraordinary bay window with its double row of small arches had stained-glass windows inserted into it when that part of the mansion was converted into a chapel. Exotic tree ferns grace the courtyard.

Two red-brick neighbors flank the mansion and make its Tennessee marble façade even more resplendent by contrast. The house on the right is now the Convent of the Sacred Heart and is connected to the school by a bridge. The house to the left was built about 1905 for Andrew Hammond, a lumber and railroad magnate. In 1956 it became the Stuart Hall School for Boys.

14 Panorama of Bay and Golden Gate
· Broadway and Fillmore

(View of) Palace of Fine Arts
· Beaux-Arts, Bernard Maybeck, 1915

From Broadway and Fillmore there is a spectacular view of the north bay, the Golden Gate, and the Marin headlands. This area was known as Harbor View in the nineteenth century. The white, low-rise Marina district along the bay shore was originally a tidal marsh filled in for the mammoth Panama-Pacific International Exposition held in 1915. The dome of Bernard Maybeck's Palace of Fine Arts is the last survivor from this great fair that celebrated the opening of the Panama Canal and the reconstruction of San Francisco. The present structure is a reinforced-concrete replacement of the original "temporary" building. The romantic imagery of the Palace was inspired by Bocklin's painting, "The Isle of the Dead." The reconstruction of the Palace demonstrates the power of one well-loved architectural fantasy to outlive the materials it was originally built of.

Looking up Broadway presents an almost equally fascinating view of western Pacific Heights. This favored valley was built up in the late 1890s and early 1900s. Here and there are a few houses built in the 1940s by famous San Francisco architects on the grounds of demolished mansions. From this spot there is a rare view of the interior of one block on the opposite slope. The heart of every block is filled with trees and lush gardens. The streets are also lined with trees that are pruned every year so that they do not block the light or views. Every house here is different and all are architect-designed, not builders' row houses. Western Pacific Heights extends from here to the Presidio and is among the choicest residential areas in the country.

To return to Lafayette Park or the Downtown, see page 130.

Tour 4

Mission Dolores and the Mission District

The Heart of San Francisco

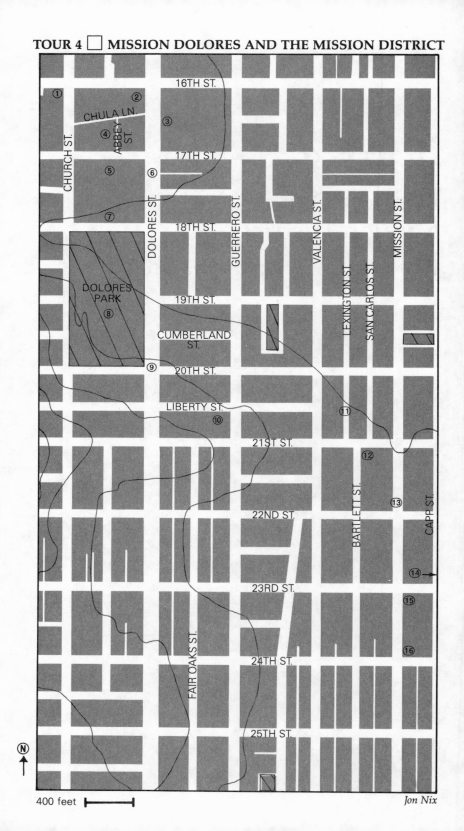

400 feet

Jon Nix

1 Everett Junior High School
2 Mission Dolores
3 Notre Dame School
4 Chula Lane and Abbey Street
5 3639–41 Seventeenth Street
6 Dolores Street
7 Mission High School
8 Dolores Park
9 Dolores Street, Cumberland to Liberty
10 100 Block of Liberty Street
11 Lexington Street Row
12 Bartlett and Twenty-first Streets
13 Mission Street
14 Capp Street
15 Bank of America Mural
16 BART Subway Station

WHAT THIS WALK COVERS

This walk passes through the sunniest and most historic valley in San Francisco, from Padre Junípero Serra's Mission Church of San Francisco de Asis of 1791, the oldest building in San Francisco, to Dolores Park and Liberty Street's Victorians, and then to Mission Street and the Latino Inner Mission and the modern BART station at Twenty-fourth Street. Give yourself a half-day for this walk; it is a bit longer than the others, but rewarding.

PRACTICALITIES

Best time for this walk: Ten o'clock Sunday morning is the best time by far. Families are on their way to church and the neighborhood is relaxed and happy. Mission Dolores is open daily, 10:00 A.M. to 4:00 P.M.

Getting there by public transit: From downtown Market Street take the J, K, L, or M streetcar and alight at Sixteenth and Church. *Return:* The walk ends at the BART station at Twenty-fourth and Mission.

Cafés and restaurants: The blocks near Twenty-fourth and Mission have many different Latin-American restaurants. La Rondalla (Mexican) at Twentieth and Valencia is good. And the Roosevelt Tamale Parlor at 2817 Twenty-fourth Street is also worth mentioning—for its name as well as its food.

Gallery: A focal point of the contemporary Mission's Latino culture is La Galeria de la Raza at 2851 Twenty-fourth Street, phone 826-8009 for exhibits and hours.

Returning: The walk ends at the Twenty-fourth Street BART station, where you can take a train to Downtown.

INTRODUCTION

The history of the succession of peoples in the Mission district is in microcosm the history of the city and, to a degree, that of the entire state of California. After the Mexican era, Yankee squatters simply occupied plots in the valley in the 1840s and 1850s. Next came a substantial wave of German-speaking and Scandinavian immigrants in the 1860s. They were followed by the Irish and then the Italians, especially after 1906 when the South of Market and North Beach districts burned. The Irish flavor in the Mission was especially strong during the first half of this century. The "Mish" developed its own accent, said to be like that of Brooklyn. Since 1960 there has been a great influx of Latino families into the Mission. The Mission has been a revolving door into American society.

The Mission is famous in a foggy city for its welcome sunshine. Sheltered from the cold west wind and fog by Twin Peaks, and facing

Mission Dolores, built of adobe in 1791 and designed by Father Francisco Palou. To the right is the Churrigueresque Revival basilica, built in 1913. To the left is the walled cemetery, the oldest burial ground in San Francisco.

east and south, this valley was chosen by Franciscan missionaries as the most benign spot near the strategic Presidio on the Golden Gate.

The Mission period of California history is almost impossible to uncover, buried as it is under a strangely, for America, pious romanticism. The coming of the gray-clothed Franciscan friars was not as one thinks St. Francis would have had it. The Spanish and Mexican soldiers and priests who penetrated California, and the Yankees who followed them quickly and massively, were not the salvation but rather the utter obliteration of the native peoples. It was, as anthropologists would call it, "a fatal impact." Murder, barbarity, terror, and absolute cultural contempt were effectively accompanied by smallpox and other "new" diseases that wiped away the entire race in a couple of generations. The Christians' God of Love was accompanied by extinction.

The tribe that the Franciscans gathered at Mission Dolores were known as the Ramaytush, one of the Costanoans, or coast people, who populated the area from the Golden Gate to Monterey Bay. The area was originally an intricate patchwork of differing language groups and most early explorers were struck by the tremendous variation of languages and tribes in the Bay Area. The Mission at San Francisco embraced eighteen tribes in 1816. Before the coming of the Europeans, the Costanoans enjoyed a relatively simple material culture, living on shellfish, especially mussels, and acorns. The gentle climate and abundance of acorns permitted a culture almost free of Adam's curse.

These seasonally nomadic native tribes were forced by the Spanish soldiers to leave their favorite sunny places around the bay and cluster in a European-shaped village around the Mission church. Here the native peoples saddened, sickened, and died. A visitor, Louis Choris, observed in 1816, "After several months spent in the mission, they usually grow fretful and thin, and they constantly gaze with sadness at the mountains which they can see in the distance." Births never equaled, or even came close to, the number of deaths. Another visitor noted that "San Francisco contains about a thousand Indians. The number of deaths in the last year exceeded 300. . . ." By 1850, a United States Indian Agent found but one survivor, Pedro Alcantara, who said, "I am all that is left of my people—I am alone."

Yet images of peace and beauty cling to the popular conception of mission and rancho days. It was not the first wave of Yankee settlers who started the cult glorifying Early California. That began in popular literature in the 1890s and became immensely popular as a visual idiom, Mission architecture, in the prosperous 1920s. In the early twentieth century the missions were restored—a mild word; in many cases they were totally reconstructed. The early colonial days provided a unifying architectural image of white stucco walls and red tile roofs as California boomed.

Somewhere tomorrow morning, a California architect will sit

down and design an almost-always-pleasing Mission-style structure, be it house or bank, crematorium, school, club, or utility substation. With frame and stucco, or steel and concrete, he will recreate the effect of thick adobe walls. Flat roofs will have tacked-on fringes of red clay tiles to look like pitched roofs, even if the structure is only one story high but larger than four football fields. The Mission style, California's own Colonial Revival, has been the favorite style, judged simply by the number of attempts at it. Fortunately, mediocre Mission is always better than mediocre anything else. And, when the Mission or Mediterranean style is good in California, as it often is, it can be very good indeed.

The Mission district is not the place to see Mission-style domestic architecture; most of the neighborhood was built in the Victorian and Edwardian eras. (See the streets around the Sunset Reservoir, and the adjoining Parkside district built in the 1920s, for the endless invention in stucco and red roof tiles that can all be put under the umbrella of California Mission architecture.) But during the heyday of the Mission style in the 1920s many of the schools, churches, and institutional buildings in the populous and politically powerful Mission were rebuilt in variants of the Mission style. It was a golden age for school-building, and this walk picks out two of the best examples. Even the tree-planting in the Mission has become increasingly Mediterranean. About 1920, Dolores Street was handsomely planted with palms, and in the 1970s palm trees were planted (along with some of the worst modern street furniture) on the commercial artery of Mission Street itself.

THE TOUR

1 Everett Junior High School
· Sixteenth and Church Streets
· Byzanto-Mission, John Reid, Jr., 1925

Roman Catholic Archdiocese
· 1955

On the southwest corner of Sixteenth and Church Streets is the massive, red-tile-roofed Everett Junior High School built in 1925 and designed in the Byzanto-Mission style. It is a handsome, solid, and very California school building. Its polychrome tiled vestibule and front entrance on Church Street are not visible from here. Schools and churches dot the Mission; the Mission has always been a family neighborhood with many children.

Facing Everett Junior High School, at 441–45 Church Street, is a bland white-stucco four-story office building, the almost-anonymous headquarters of the Roman Catholic Archdiocese of San Francisco, built in 1955 on part of the site of Mission Dolores's long-gone adobe compound. Though San Francisco has always had a large Catholic population and many churches, the Catholic Church has historically had a low profile here. A pastoral rather than a political tradition has been characteristic of the archbishops of San Francisco. This modest headquarters is, therefore, exactly appropriate.

2 Mission Dolores
· Sixteenth and Dolores Streets
· Adobe with Baroque façade, Padre Francisco Palou, 1791
· Restoration, Willis Polk, 1918

Mission Dolores Basilica
· Churrigueresque Revival, 1913

Walk a block east along Sixteenth Street to the red-tile-covered dome of Mission Dolores Basilica, facing palm-lined Dolores Street. (The title "basilica" is an honor conferred by the pope. Pius XII conferred this dignity in 1952, and a pontifical red and gold umbrella and coat of arms flank the altar.) The 1913 basilica is not really worth entering, but is worth looking at from the outside and comparing with its venerable neighbor to the south, Mission Dolores—officially the Mission San Francisco de Asis—built in 1791. Here is a great example of what happens when historical styles are "revived." The modern church is far grander than anything Spanish or Mexican California actually built; it echoes not the simple missions but the luxuriantly rhetorical styles of Baroque Mexico's wealthiest cities, which in turn echoed the designs of Mexican architect Churriguera. The strong contrast between the plain walls and the complex (if indifferent) ornament around the windows and doors of the basilica works well under San Francisco's bright skies. This church replaces a red brick Gothic-style structure that fell in 1906.

The first mission church, probably only a brush shelter, was about five blocks to the east, at the edge of an intermittent swamp called Laguna de los Dolores, the Lagoon of Sorrows, named after the Virgin of Sorrows because Spanish explorers discovered it on her feastday. But the ground there was too soft, and sometime between 1776 and 1782 the mission was moved back to this spot. The cornerstone of the present Baroque mission was laid in 1782 and it was completed and dedicated in 1791. Father Francisco Palou designed the church. He is buried near the south wall in the adjoining cemetery. The 114-by-22-foot structure exhibits the use of an imported building technique, adobe, a beautiful but extremely fragile material; adobe buildings naturally wash away. This building has been stuccoed with a hard shell of cement plaster to preserve it.

Designs from Costanoan baskets were used for the painted ornamentation on the ceiling. It is one of the most beautiful ceilings in the city. It looks different when seen straight up than at an angle; then the chevron patterns turn into another design. When the eye travels down to the far end of the tunnellike church, it meets the altar, a piece of Baroque Spain, strained through northern Mexico. The door of the tabernacle came from Manila, another part of the Spanish empire, the greatest of the day. The background (reredos) to the altar came from Mexico, brought by land rather than sea, on the backs of mules. It has been repainted many times but not changed.

The church is still used as the baptistry for the parish, and there is a Victorian marble font. Above it is a lunette made in the 1930s, representing the baptism of an Indian child by a Franciscan priest. The altar rail and the hand-wrought ironwork around the baptistry are probably original, perhaps from the 1820s.

This structure enjoyed a sophisticated restoration in 1918. Willis Polk did not approach this building with a heavy hand. His idea was to try to bring it back and to make concessions only where necessary and in such a way that one's attention is not drawn to them.

Leave the church through the door to the right of the altar. Outside is a contemporary Mission-style veranda with an interesting series of pictures of what the Mission used to look like. In the small museum at the end of the veranda is a glass window in the left-hand wall that allows a glimpse of the adobe construction beneath the modern cement stucco. A series of photographs shows the semi-ruined California mission chain at the turn of the century. In the center case are the original chalices and monstrances of the Franciscan mission. Mounted high on the wall is a model of how the struts and the ridge-joints of the rafters were originally bound with thongs of rawhide. Behind the museum is a well-designed paved courtyard installed in 1978 with a gate to the mission cemetery.

The romantic, vine-entangled cemetery on the sunny south side of the mission is punctuated by yew trees, flame-shaped and dark-green, ancient symbols of everlasting life. More than 5,000 of the Costanoans were buried here. After 1857, when the mission church was returned to the Church and the parish was a heavily Irish one, this became the cemetery for the pioneers. Cemeteries fix people in one spot and permanently enshrine mankind's social arrangements. Here the high-rise marble obelisks of the rich face the street, while humbler tombs, the vast majority unmarked, are in the back of the plot. Burial next to the wall of the church was reserved for priests and governors. Father Francisco Palou, the designer of the mission, and Captain Louis Antonio Arguello, the first Mexican governor of Alta California, are buried here. Some of the oldest cast iron in San Francisco ornaments a few of the tombs. It is the same kind of New York and Philadelphia ironwork that was exported to New Orleans. The most interesting monument in the cemetery is in the far corner toward the front—a large brown sandstone Victorian extravaganza decorated with firemen's helmets and upside-down torches. Here lies James "Yankee' Sullivan, an early pugilist, who, it was said, hanged himself while awaiting trial by the Vigilance Committee of 1856. Nearby is an atavistic rock Grotto of Lourdes built in 1920. Plants and vines have overgrown the once-bleak cemetery and make it a place to linger and search the tombstones. Roses flourish here in the peace and sun. The dazzling white wall of the mission is often the foil to the clinging bougainvillaea, which bursts in magenta sprays.

Leave the cemetery and return to Dolores Street.

3 Notre Dame School (Ursuline Convent)
· 347 Dolores Street
· Mansarded Period Revival, c. 1907

At Number 347 Dolores Street, across from the mission, is the Notre Dame School. In its style, it is a building of the 1850s or 1860s, although it was built after the earthquake and fire of 1906. The fire that began downtown consumed everything from the bay to here; it destroyed half of the Mission district, as far south as Twentieth Street, but stopped across the street from historic Mission Dolores, at the wall and iron grill in front of the school. The ironwork survives from the prefire school building. Notre Dame is an Ursuline convent and school, and is reminiscent of New Orleans architecture in its flavor and form.

4 Chula Lane and Abbey Street
· Backstreet and Victorian cottages

Walk past the shrine to the Virgin Mary in the mission cemetery wall, turn right, and walk up Chula Lane to Abbey Street, a quiet cul-de-sac of modest nineteenth-century houses on narrow, crooked streets. Children play in the streets here and cars slow down to a crawl. The Mission district is not just its busy north-south main streets; to its residents the Mission is a honeycomb of out-of-the-way backstreets. Farther up Chula Lane the houses are set at a saw-tooth angle to the sidewalk. The lots reflect the unsystematic sub-divisions inside the regular gridiron extended into the Mission Addition in the 1850s.

Walk up Abbey Street. The richly ornamented tower in the distance caps Mission High School. Number 37 Abbey Street is a simple one-story flat-front Italianate. Facing it, at Numbers 40–42, is a plain three-story frame building of a type known locally as Romeo flats, because of the balcony at the second floor for the open stairway. Continue to Seventeenth Street.

5 3639–41 Seventeenth Street
· Italianate, 1874

Numbers 3639–41 Seventeenth Street is a bay-windowed Italianate house built in 1874 with a small front garden complete with ferns, fuchsia, and jade plants. The side wall is also visible from the sidewalk.
Walk east on Seventeenth back to Dolores.

6 Dolores Street
· John McLaren, c. 1920

Turn right at Dolores Street, one of San Francisco's few tree-lined streets. The handsome date palms were planted by John McLaren in the early twentieth century. In the 1920s, palm trees swept over California along with Mission architecture as the state reinvented its heritage and built buildings and landscapes far grander than anything actually resembling desertlike early California. The Dolores Street palms make elegant a street solidly lined with apartment houses, flats, and churches. Walk south (downhill). In the median is a cast-iron replica of a mission bell on a pole that looks like a shepherd's crook. It marks *El Camino Real,* the Royal Road—just a trail, really, that passed up the California coast and linked the twenty-one missions together. The road was marked by the California Women's Club in the early days of motor touring in the 1920s. Each marker originally had a legend giving the number of miles to the next mission. Souvenir hunters have long since stolen most of them.

Dolores Street is lined with bay-windowed, three-story frame apartments and flats, mostly built between 1910 and 1920, in the area burned in 1906. It is a very agreeable street to walk along: all the buildings are similar but each has its unique ornamental treatment, so the street has both unity and variety. It also preserves the old Victorian house lot sizes, which give the blocks a human scale of 25-foot building fronts. There are no vast, bleak walls, rather an intricate pattern of doors and staircases. Most buildings have parking on the ground level and small, unobjectionable garage doors. (Despite its famous anticar philosophy, San Francisco has done more to accommodate the automobile under its housing than any other American city.) The coherent, unbroken, bay-window-studded blockfronts of the early twentieth century *are* the Mission district. The heights of the buildings relate to the width of the streets and allow light to reach all the rooms. The centers of the blocks are open and let light into the back rooms. The Mission still has buildings painted the light, traditional whites, beige, gray, and pale green colors that were universal in San Francisco in the early twentieth century. Now, as buildings are bought and spruced up, they are often painted strong colors such as forest green, blue, and brown. But the strong sunlight and fogs of San Francisco eventually turn the deepest colors into chalky, pale pastels.

7 Mission High School
· Eighteenth and Dolores Streets
· Mission, John Reid, Jr., 1926

This large, red-tile-roofed high school with its lofty tower shows the influence of Bertram Goodhue's fair buildings in Balboa Park, San Diego, built in 1915. Large blank walls and rich, concentrated ornament at the entrance and tower make a stark, effective contrast. Here is the white-walled, arcaded, red-tile-roofed heritage of the early California missions adapted for a modern concrete structure—the imagery of adobe and stone in reinforced concrete and factory-cast terra-cotta. The school was completely reconstructed, and its ornament more securely fastened, in 1978 as part of the reinforcement of all the public schools in California.

8 Dolores Park
· Jewish cemeteries, 1861; city park, 1905

Mission High faces two-block Dolores Park, the largest park in the Mission. These two blocks were originally purchased in 1861 for two Jewish cemeteries by Temples Emanu-El and Sherith Israel. This spot was chosen because it was on the edge of the city and because it rises gently up the slope of Dolores Heights. From the far corner (Twentieth and Church, at the southwest) of the spacious open rectangle, there is a sweeping panorama over the Downtown to the northeast and the bay beyond. Cemeteries occupied much of the high ground west of the city in the nineteenth century. They and some fenced-in amusement grounds/beer gardens were the best landscaped parts of the early city.

The city closed almost all the cemeteries around the turn of the century. In 1905 the park was simply but agreeably laid out as a large lawn with clusters of palms in the corners and an axial path along the line of Nineteenth Street. Unfortunately an ugly little park building mars the very center of the park. Also, unfortunately, more of a blight than an ornament in the green park, a massive concrete monument with a replica of the Mexican "liberty bell" was installed at Dolores and Nineteenth in 1962. The bell itself might have been attractive in the park, but the completely unnecessary concrete "plaza" is of stunning ugliness and provides just one more piece of concrete where there could be grass. The principal function of this Maginot Line-like emplacement is to provide a target against which to throw beer bottles.

Up the slope, on the western side of the middle of the park is a bronze statue of Fr. Miguel Hidalgo y Castilla, Mexico's George

Washington. Hidalgo is holding one hand to his heart, looks south toward Mexico, and gestures with his other hand toward the Mission district itself. The statue is not only unattractive, it is inaccurate as well. Unlike every other California *barrio,* the Mission is not a predominantly Mexican-American district. The Mission's Latino population comes from Central America, the Caribbean, and northern South America as much as from Mexico. The restaurants along Mission Street are Nicaraguan, Salvadoran, Venezuelan, and Costa Rican as well as Mexican. The movement of many Irish families from the Inner to the Outer Mission (south of Army Street), and later to the semidetached suburbs of Daly City and Pacifica, was accompanied by the immigration of Latino families looking for large, inexpensive flats. In 1950 only 11 percent of the Mission's population was Latino; by 1970 almost half the Mission's 50,000 people were Latino. About 30 percent of the population is under eighteen years of age.

Dolores Heights, with its agreeable mixture of small houses and rich vegetation, rises to the southwest (see Tour 10).

9 Dolores Street, Cumberland to Liberty

Walk up Dolores Street to Cumberland Street (opposite the south part of the park), an attractive and typical street of flats and apartments. On the corner is the competent Period Revival Second Church of Christ, Scientist, designed by William H. Crim, Jr., in 1915, which makes an interesting contrast with its red-brick Gothic neighbor, Ascension Lutheran Church, built in the style popular with traditionalist congregations.

Continue up Dolores to Liberty Street. From this crest there is a sweeping view north down palm-lined Dolores to the fortresslike, streamlined United States Mint designed by Los Angeles architect Gilbert Stanley Underwood and built atop Blue Mountain in 1937. That very 1930s stripped classical structure made the old Mint at Fifth and Mission obsolete.

10 100 Block of Liberty Street
· Victorian Cluster, flat-fronted Italianate to Queen Anne,
  1870s–1890s

Turn left at Liberty Street and see Number 159, the large Italiante house atop the high retaining wall. It was built by Judge Daniel Murphy in 1878, during the brief period when it was thought that the Mission "warm belt" might develop as San Francisco's luxury suburban district. Commodious houses with flower-filled gardens were built by prominent San Franciscans here and there. But the conquering of the hills by the cable car in the 1870s turned the tide of fashion north, not south, and Pacific Heights with its marine views became the poshest residential district. The Murphy house is among the largest surviving in the Mission and is noted for the visit to it made in 1896 by Susan B. Anthony, an early leader of the woman-suffrage movement. The house was built on high ground to give it a view of the then distant city. It has since been subdivided into several units.

The row of houses downhill from Number 159 displays several styles once popular in San Francisco. The house immediately to the east (downhill) was probably built about 1917 on what had been the side yard of Number 159. It is in an aggressive Craftsman style and is like the housing that was built during the first World War period on the East Bay hills and in some hilly western districts of the city.

Next down the hill is a good example of the Queen Anne style of the 1890s, with scratchwork plaster ornamentation and a round corner tower. Next are three Stick-style houses of the 1880s. Last in the row, Number 109, is a flat-fronted Italiante of 1870 with elegant window moldings.

The fancier houses on this block were built on the south side so as to look out over the city. More modest houses were built on the north (viewless) side of Liberty Street. At the turn of the century, denser apartment houses were built on the main streets in the Mission. They define the side streets and enclose them, creating a room-like effect within each side street, such as here.

Number 110 Liberty, a late Queen Anne–Tudoresque house, a very pleasant house with a gable roof, dates from the 1890s.

From the corner of Liberty and Guerrero one can see 827 Guerrero, a late 1880s Queen Anne house with a Moorish arch and as many architectural embellishments as its architect could conceive of. Notice the rich texture of the walls; virtually every surface (and originally the roof as well) was treated as an opportunity for pattern and ornamentation. The house has its original iron fence.

Across Guerrero on Liberty, in the center of the block, is a row of three Italiante buildings with slant-sided bay windows. They vary in density from what was once a single-family house to a six-unit building. Their similar architectural style helps unify buildings of greatly varying density. All the buildings on Liberty Street are worth close examination; it is one of the architecturally richest streets in the Mission.

11 Lexington Street Row
· Italianate, 1876

At Valencia Street turn left, walk up to Twentieth Street, the edge of the fire in 1906, cross Valencia, go east a few yards on Twentieth, and turn right into Lexington Street. At Valencia Street the district changes from what was originally professional and middle-class housing on the high ground to working-class housing on the flat land. The contrast between palm- and residence-lined Dolores Street and stark Valencia is dramatic. Valencia could hardly be bleaker; its embellishment consists of a row of utilitarian street lights.

But the small-scale side streets in the Mission, blessedly free of through traffic, harbor architecturally coherent and socially diverse residential enclaves. Side streets such as Lexington Street, which is only three and a half blocks long, have a strong sense of visual definition. The closed-in vistas at the ends of the street define a cell within a neighborhood. In a city of endlessly continuous streets, such defined pockets are welcome. This is one of the accidental graces of the speculator-subdivided Mission.

Lexington Street was built up with two-story Italianate working-class housing in 1876–77. Most were originally two-family houses with one floor per family. It was noted by visitors to late-nineteenth-century San Francisco that the "mechanic class" (skilled workmen) could afford their own houses in San Francisco.

At Lexington and Twenty-first Street look back up Lexington. Note how the turn-of-the-century apartment houses on the main streets, with their larger bulk, extend farther than the small row houses and thus frame the end of the street like bookends. It is an accidental but welcome pattern.

12 Bartlett and Twenty-first Streets
· Victorian houses

Turn left (east) on Twenty-first; in a few yards Bartlett Street intersects from the south. On the southeast corner is a trio of old Victorian houses. The one on the corner, 3243–45 Twenty-first Street, has settled unevenly into the soft ground. It was built after 1880 and has remarkable Eastlake turned-wood ornaments.

The vast parking lot across the street robs the whole area of its form. The Mission was built with the streetcar system, not the automobile, in mind. The present-day need to accommodate the car has destroyed housing and the area's visual coherence as well.

13 Mission Street
· Commercial artery

Continue left along Twenty-first Street to Mission Street. Turn right on Mission, walk down one block of Mission to Twenty-second Street.

Mission Street follows the oldest path of travel from San Francisco south. This valley and the path through it were San Francisco's only land connection with the rest of California till the late 1930s, when the two great bridges were built. A plank road here built in the 1850s was soon followed by San Francisco's first railway in 1857. In the early 1860s horse-drawn cars began operation between the Downtown and the Mission. Because of its relatively sunny climate and accessibility, the Mission was developed with race tracks and beer gardens, such as Woodward's Gardens near Mission and Thirteenth Street.

By the 1870s and 1880s this early exurbia was well served by streetcar lines, and rows of Victorian houses rapidly filled up the valley. By 1870 there were 23,000 Mission residents; by 1900 there were 36,000. Mission Street, with its frequent streetcars, became the main thoroughfare for the district. By 1900, Mission Street was a continuous strip of shops. There was little need for Mission residents ever to go to Market Street downtown; Mission Street provided nearly every possible service. The street was probably at its peak during the 1930s. The enormous movie marquees that still punctuate the street were added in that period. The street retains the scale and intricacy of use established by the streetcar between 1880 and 1930 but has lost its larger department and furniture stores.

Today Mission Street, and its one-block extensions along the east-west side streets, is still lively if not immaculate. There are virtually no empty shops. The older buildings with their generally lower rents make ideal locations for small businesses without much capital to start. The ethnic succession in the Mission has been mirrored in its shops. Today's Latino population is evidenced in the many small restaurants and grocery stores. The area near Twenty-fourth Street and Mission has a marked Latin-American flavor.

14 Capp Street, between Twenty-second and Twenty-third Streets
· Stick-Eastlake row houses, T.J. Welch, 1889–94

Walk down Twenty-second Street one short block to Capp Street and turn right. From the corner of Twenty-second and Capp is a capsule view of the new and old in the Mission. The enormous 1960s high-rise (ironically enough the "Bay View" Savings Building) epitomizes the danger of overdevelopment. It is the only building of its size in the entire valley and breaks the horizontality of the entire Mission district. Its south side is an ugly uninterrupted concrete wall capped by a too-large electric sign. Behind the massive, out-of-scale tower, eating its way into the once coherent side streets, is a very large parking lot—landscaped, it's true, but nonetheless a parking lot. Finally, most objectionable because of the mixture of fear and arrogance that it embodies, is the riot-proof ground floor. These are the gilded fortresses of the present. Notice the open and pleasing shop fronts across Twenty-second Street. They have no need of barricades to protect them from their neighborhood.

Facing the Bay View parking lot is the finest surviving uninterrupted row of Stick-Eastlake row houses in San Francisco. All were built between 1889 and 1894 by Australian-born architect T.J. Welch for developer Baroness Mary E. von Schroeder. Most of them have miraculously survived with very little alteration. The "flash glass," for example, the small colored squares surrounding the main window pane, survives on many of them. Traditional pale colors also survive here. So too does the original treelessness of Victorian San Francisco; note the total lack of greenery. It was only in the twentieth century that (annually pruned) street trees were planted to soften the harshness of the city's streets. The row is very beautiful, its mass-produced woodwork fanciful.

Walk down Capp Street past this rare row, turn around, and look north. Beyond the lacy row of Victorians rises the wooden spire of Gothic-style St. Mark's Lutheran Church, built as late as 1901. This beautiful, if no longer properly maintained, church is typical of American church architecture in the nineteenth century. The spire is a delightful piece of work. The church was built for a German-speaking congregation that has since dwindled and is a reminder of the German and Scandinavian residents of the Mission before 1900.

At the other end of Capp Street, at Twenty-third Street, is the Mission United Presbyterian Church, built in 1891. This congregation is also not what it once was, and this fine old wooden church is sadly in need of repairs. It is an excellent example of the Romanesque style so popular for city churches in America during the 1890s and was designed by Percy and Hamilton.

Capp Street epitomizes the basic pattern of the Mission: behind the commercial streetcar corridor along Mission Street are dense rows of wooden houses, here and there punctuated by large wooden churches.

To the east, on filled-in Mission Bay, was San Francisco's—and California's—first large industrial district. Many of the Mission's earliest residents worked in those early factories. Most walked to work. Today the James Lick Freeway is the approximate dividing line between the residential Mission and the industrial bayshore. To the present day, many of San Francisco's unions have their meeting halls in the Mission.

15 Bank of America Mural
· Mission Street at Twenty-third
· Chuy Campesano, Luis Cortazar, Michael Rios

Turn right and walk up Twenty-third Street to Mission. The Bank of America branch here has a superb mural over the banking counter depicting the present-day Latino population of the Mission. It is an exhortation to work, struggle, and study. Chuy Campesano, Luis Cortazar, and Michael Rios painted the roughly 10-by-100-foot mural on panels a few blocks away. A well-hidden and impolitic seven-headed cobra of the SLA was discreetly painted out before its unveiling. It is in the tradition of the Mexican muralists: a people-crowded story in strong colors and bold forms.

16 Bart Subway Station
· Mission and Twenty-fourth Streets
· Hertzka and Knowles, 1973

Exterior Mural
· Michael Rios, T. Machado, R. Montez, 1975

Round the corner to the left and continue down Mission Street to the corner of Twenty-fourth Street. Here is one of two BART stations in the Mission. The interior of the station is more attractive than its exterior; the barrel-vaulted underground station was opened in 1973 and is attractively tiled in colors reminiscent of the painted ceiling of old Mission Dolores. More interesting than the station (and the ugly modern street furniture that was installed when BART went in) is the mural painted on the west wall of a building on the northeast corner of the intersection. This large work was painted by M. Rios, T. Machado, and R. Montez in 1975. The construction of a futuristic transit link between the Downtown and the Mission was perceived as a threat to the lively low-rent district. The artists depicted the sleek silver BART train resting on the backs of the people.

Tour 5

Nob Hill

The Imprint of the Railroad and Silver Barons

TOUR 5 ☐ NOB HILL

The Picture Map Company

1 Pine Street Wall
2 Joice Street
3 California and Powell Streets
4 Mark Hopkins Hotel
5 Pacific-Union Club
6 Fairmont Hotel
7 Brocklebank Apartments
8 Huntington Park
9 Taylor Street to Pleasant Street
10 The Clay-Jones
11 Chambord Apartments
12 Grace Cathedral

WHAT THIS WALK COVERS

There are two Nob Hills, the summit and the slopes. Those with strong legs and good lungs should explore the slopes and hidden side streets (Numbers 1, 2, 3, 9, and 10). Others may wish to walk only the level blocks at the summit where the Flood Mansion, the Stanford Court, Mark Hopkins, Fairmont, Huntington Hotels, and Grace (Episcopal) Cathedral cluster.

PRACTICALITIES

Best time for this walk: This tour can be done morning, afternoon, or night. On a clear night the view from the summit or from the Top of the Mark (Mark Hopkins Hotel) is extraordinary. Grace Cathedral often has organ concerts on Sunday afternoons (phone 776-6611). Or walk this tour and then take the cable car to Polk Street for an inexpensive lunch or dinner and watch the sidewalk scene.

Parking: There are two parking garages on the top of Nob Hill, one on California Street between Mason and Taylor, and another under the Masonic Auditorium on California and Taylor. A less expensive city garage is located under St. Mary's Square on California between Kearny and Grant; take the cable car up the California Street hill.

Getting there by public transit: The California Street Cable Rail Road serves Nob Hill. It runs from the Hyatt-Regency Hotel on The Embarcadero, through the Financial District, and over Nob Hill to Polk Street and Van Ness Avenue.

Cafés and Restaurants: The great hotels boast expensive restaurants. Cocktails at the Top of the Mark are a local tradition. The Vienna Coffee House in the Mark Hopkins serves excellent breakfasts and pastries. Mama's on Nob Hill at California and Jones is moderate and tasty. Le Club in the Clay-Jones at 1250 Jones is very expensive and most agreeable. The Big Four Restaurant and Bar in the Huntington Hotel is a virtual museum of memorabilia of the railroad barons. Fournou's Ovens in the Stanford Court Hotel and the Nob Hill Restaurant in the Mark Hopkins are posh and excellent. Polk Street, at the western foot of the hill, has many good, moderate-priced restaurants, and one lunchtime jewel: Swan's Oyster Depot, serving the best cold seafood in San Francisco and a tradition since 1907. The Palms Bar and Café, also on Polk, is the best place to watch the passing parade. Victor's Pizzeria at 1411 Polk serves some of the best pizzas in the city.

INTRODUCTION

How did Nob Hill get its famous name? For an answer, we have our choice between etymology, myth, and geography. The etymolog-

View from Huntington Park atop Nob Hill of the 1100 Block of Sacramento Street with residential high-rises and a French-style town house, remodeled in 1968.

ical explanation, and the most ingenious, is that the name is a contraction of *nabob*, a British slang word for the rich that in turn comes from the Hindu *nawwab*, meaning viceregent or governor. Londoners used the word to describe the ostentatious ex-colonists who came back to the English metropolis with riches gained in India. The home-grown, mythological explanation sometimes heard is that Nob is a contraction of the loathsome word "snob." Most unlikely. The geographical, and most probable, explanation is that Nob is a contraction of the plain English word "knob" meaning an isolated rounded hill or mountain. Before the 1870s, Nob Hill was simply called the California Street Hill after the main thoroughfare that climbs its precipitous flank from the Financial District to the east. It was the railroad barons—the Big Four—and the Nevada silver kings whose elaborate mansions made this steep, sandy hill the epicenter of wealth in nineteenth-century California and who gave the hill its indelible cachet, which has survived earthquake, fire, and even the income tax.

Nob Hill (elevation 338 feet) was not the first roost for San Francisco's millionaires. That distinction belongs to Rincon Hill, a much smaller mound south of Market Street now absorbed under the approach ramp of the Bay Bridge. There the wealthy built Greek Revival and Gothic houses surrounded by ample gardens in the 1850s. But as the port expanded, and after a deep cut was made through the hill in 1869 to allow Second Street traffic easy passage at grade, Rincon Hill lost its bucolic remoteness and was swallowed up in the industrial district south of Market.

Money began its northwestward migration: first to Nob Hill, then Russian Hill, then later to the ridge of Pacific and Presidio Heights. One observer credited the shift of fashion to the advent of the cable car and to a "growing appreciation of marine scenery." San Francisco began to conform to what is a highly regular pattern: the clustering of luxury residential districts to the north and/or west of the city core, and the development of industry, commerce, and working-class housing to the south and east.

Crocker, Huntington, Hopkins, and Governor Stanford, the Big Four of the Central Pacific (transcontinental) Railroad, only followed, if on a gargantuan full-block scale, the tastes of the earlier rich. In the late 1850s, William Walton, a wealthy merchant, built a grand house at Taylor and Washington Streets on what we now call Nob Hill. It was subsequently purchased by Maurice Doré, a wealthy banker with an appropriate name. Other social leaders followed. William T. Coleman built a white Roman villa set in a walled garden, and Senator George Hearst, father of the publishing magnate, built a Spanish palace of white stucco. Modest frame houses also peppered the hill before the millionaires assembled their half- or full-block parcels in the 1870s.

Robert Louis Stevenson described the summit of Nob Hill in 1882:

The great net of straight thoroughfares lying at right angles, east and west and north and south, over the shoulders of Nob Hill, the Hill of palaces, must certainly be counted the best part of San Francisco. It is there that the millionaires are gathered together vying with each other in display. From thence, looking down over the business wards of the city, we can descry a building with a little belfry, and that is the Stock Exchange, the heart of San Francisco: a great pump we might call it, continually pumping up the savings of the lower quarters to the pockets of the millionaires upon the Hill.

The Junior League's architectural survey commented, "The Nob Hill householders of the 1880s and 1890s were not the sole proprietors of the state of California—but they may well have represented the majority interest."

Though this walk centers on the posh crest of the hill, there is more to Nob Hill than its famous hotels. There are really two Nob Hills, the small area at the summit, and the much more extensive and usually overlooked slopes. The earthquake and fire of 1906 wiped away all but two buildings on the hill, the brownstone Flood mansion and the steel-frame Fairmont Hotel. Today the summit is crowned with tall steel-frame and reinforced-concrete hotels and luxurious condominiums mostly built in the booming 1920s and 1960s. The slopes, on the other hand, are blanketed with an even-scaled development of three- and four-story frame apartments and flats built between 1906 and about 1915. These postfire, bay-windowed buildings house a representative cross-section of San Franciscans of moderate, even modest, means. The great majority of the apartment buildings on the north and west slopes of the hill are now owned by Chinese-Americans who began moving west out of Chinatown in the 1960s. Recently reduced maximum height limits will help conserve this area. The famous hill is today a lively, varied, and very San Franciscan neighborhood accommodating many races, classes, and cultures.

THE TOUR
The determined walker should begin this tour at the northwest corner of Powell and Pine Streets. The cable cars from Union Square stop at this intersection.

1 The Pine Street Wall
· Corner of Powell and Pine Streets
· Engineers of the Central Pacific Railroad, mid-1870s

The massive granite retaining wall surrounding the block on which the houses of Stanford and Hopkins stood was designed by engineers from the transcontinental railroad and built with blocks of Sierra granite. The wall is said to have cost as much as the houses that once surmounted it. One last relic of the ornamental iron cresting of the

Hopkins mansion survives atop a chimney on the Pine Street wall. This wall, the foundations of the United States Mint at Fifth and Mission Streets, and Fort Point on the Golden Gate are the premier examples of the mason's art in San Francisco.

The high wall and cut-down street are reminders that nearly every inch of San Francisco was either graded or filled at very heavy expense. Building plots and roadways were hacked out of the hills as the gridiron pattern was imposed on the undulating topography. Fitzhugh Ludlow wrote in the 1860s, "The candid visitor must regret that the grading of San Francisco seems to have been done by a Giant armed with a fish-slice and a coal-scoop under the influence of Delirium Tremens." It was drastic, but the means were more prosaic. Irishmen with picks and shovels, aided by steam-driven shovels nicknamed "steam paddies," did most of the work.

2 Joice Street

Walk downhill on Pine Street half a block and turn left. The relentless grid was often subdivided by alleys and short service streets within the uniform blocks. Joice Street is one of these, once the service alley behind two rows of Victorian houses. Such welcome variations in an otherwise repetitive plan are found throughout San Francisco and invariably harbor secluded enclaves. Joice Street is half stairway and half roadway. This pocket of three- and four-story flats and apartments has the quiet intimacy and unexpectedness that make for memorable residential pockets. Here ordinary architecture of only a generation ago creates an extraordinary cell sheltered within the modern city.

Continue up the stairs to the crest of Joice Street. The three towers of the Hyatt Hotel, Timothy Pfleuger's 450 Sutter Street, and the Union Square Holiday Inn rise to the south. To the north are the twin spires of Saints Peter and Paul Church in North Beach. The simple wood-sheathed three-story twelve-unit apartment house with parking on the ground level at 50 Joice Street was singled out in 1949 by the San Francisco Museum of Modern Art as an important architectural work. It was designed by John G. Kelley and exhibits the reticence, refinement, and simplicity of what is now called the Second Bay Region tradition (from 1930 to the late 1940s). Continue to California Street, turn left, and walk up the hill to the small maroon-and-gold wooden signal tower at the intersection.

3 California and Powell Streets
· Cable-Car Signal Tower

This signal tower watches the blind spot where San Francisco's two surviving cable-car lines intersect. The California Street cable, as the older line, lies over the Powell Street cable. Powell Street cable cars coming up from Union Square must drop their cable to cross the intersection. Because visibility coming up Powell and California Streets is so poor, a watchman is needed to control the cable-car signals mounted on the tower.

From California and Powell look down California Street to see the red-brick bulk of the Southern Pacific Company's headquarters at the foot of California and Market Streets. It was money from this dominant real estate and transportation company that made Nob Hill famous. Today this corporate giant, once known in California as "The Railroad," has fixed assets of some $4 billion, holds 3.8 million acres of western lands (some of these holdings date back to the Congressional land grants of a century ago), and still carries a majority of the freight business in the West. Chartered in 1862, the corporation is also involved in trucking, real estate, pipelines, title insurance, and most recently, transcontinental microwave communications. Early directors of the railroad, Leland Stanford in particular, formed the California Street cable-car line in 1874 and began the prestigious redevelopment of Nob Hill.

The University Club
· 800 Powell Street
· Brick palazzo, Bliss and Faville, 1912

Across the street, on the northeast corner of California and Powell, a spot usually crowded with visitors waiting for the cable car to Fisherman's Wharf, were Leland Stanford's opulent stables. The site is now occupied by the University Club, a men's club designed in the style of a Florentine Renaissance city palace. This was the style adopted by most of the men's clubs in San Francisco after 1906. Women's clubs preferred Georgian models. There is a good view of the 1886 square-rigger, the *Balclutha*, from this intersection. See Tour 12.

The Stanford Court Hotel
· 905 California Street
· Creighton Withers, 1911; Curtis and Davis, 1972

In 1874 Leland Stanford, one of the Big Four of the transcontinental railroad, formed the California Street Cable Rail Road and secured a city franchise in 1876. The line made a direct link between Kearny Street at the edge of the Downtown, the crest of Nob Hill, and Fillmore Street in the residential Western Addition. During the heyday of privately owned transit, the California Street Cable Rail Road was a blue-chip investment. The same year that Stanford secured the franchise, he began the construction of a large Italianate-style frame house at California and Powell Streets behind the massive granite retaining wall that now surrounds the Stanford Court Hotel.

Stanford, a lawyer born in Troy, New York, took to his railroad riches with enthusiasm. His horse-breeding ranch, now the campus of Stanford University, consisted of 9,000 choice Peninsula acres south of San Francisco. His vineyard was the largest in California. His Italianate city mansion, designed by S.C. Bugbee, was notable for the mechanical conveniences it boasted. Stanford had a passion for inventions. Typically, he had the interior of his house and stable thoroughly photographed by the famous photographer Eadweard Muybridge.

In that house Leland Stanford, Jr., began a boy's hoard of rare and wondrous things: interesting stones, miniature steam engines, crystals, a boy's magpie collection of wonderful curiosities. The Stanfords doted on their only child. He was privately tutored and extensively traveled. Then, at sixteen, he died in Florence while on a European tour with his parents, perhaps from an overdose of culture. When Leland Junior died his parents decided to endow a university in his memory. Today, in a room at the University Museum at Leland Stanford Junior University south of San Francisco, one can see some of the things that a young boy collected in his parents' Nob Hill mansion. That childlike curiosity, that most marvelous of capacities, should be the genesis of a world-renowned seat of learning seems happy indeed.

When Governor Stanford died in 1893, he donated his house to the people of San Francisco with the proviso that it never be demolished. His widow, the redoubtable Jane Stanford, converted the deed to the then-floundering Stanford University. The fire of 1906 failed to defer to Stanford's wish and the house disappeared in the flames. In 1911 the Stanford Court was built on the site—a luxury apartment house designed by Creighton Withers in the Parisian manner with a large open court. Its reserved, classically detailed yellow-ocher bulk exudes a feeling of stability. It became a favorite last home for frail but wealthy San Franciscans who left their large homes to retire in the heart of the city. In 1972, Curtis and Davis remodeled the luxury apartment building with its shallow bays into a 400-room luxury hotel with two phones and two TVs per suite. The idea was a good one and money was spent freely on the $17 million conversion, with fine green marble floors in one café, for example. But it is regrettable that the lobby has only an ordinary ceiling height; great public rooms need to be two stories high. (Compare the lobby of the Stanford Court with that of the Fairmont or St. Francis.) The roof over the courtyard, despite the stained-glass dome over the fountain, spoils the effect of the principal feature of the building, its great court. How appropriate a glass roof would have been here!

4 The Mark Hopkins Hotel
· 999 California Street (at Mason Street)
·Weeks and Day, 1925

Leave the Stanford Court and walk up California to the small, brick-paved plaza in front of the Mark Hopkins Hotel at Mason Street. This was the site of the house of Mark Hopkins, another of the Big Four of the Central Pacific (later Southern Pacific) Railroad. The Stick-style Hopkins house was by far the most elaborate pile of carved-and-sawn redwood California ever saw. It was a monument not to the personal style of Mark Hopkins but to that of his wife. Riches hardly changed Hopkins's personal needs at all. He was, for example, a vegetarian and liked to cultivate his own garden. He had been happy living in a simple frame house. In fact, Hopkins did not enjoy the mansion on California Street for very long. He died in a company car at an obscure railroad siding in Arizona in 1878, shortly after having moved to the top of Nob Hill. Mary Hopkins, on the other hand, had a passion for possessions. She eventually accumulated houses in New York City, two in Massachusetts, one on Block Island, and the architectural mirage on Nob Hill.

Her second husband, Edward T. Searles, a decorator who first met Mrs. Hopkins when he asked to see the plush interior of the legend-ary pile, donated the house to the San Francisco Art Association (now the Art Institute) in 1893. It perished in the fire of 1906. The art school built a temporary wooden building before selling the valuable site and moving to Russian Hill in the 1920s.

In 1925 Weeks and Day designed the Mark Hopkins Hotel, a twenty-story steel-frame building notable for the assured way it defines the southeast corner of the top of the hill. Its plaza makes a welcoming gesture to arriving guests. The tall central tower and its two wings are clad in buff brick and accented with 1920s Gothic Revival terra-cotta ornament. In 1936, Timothy Pfleuger designed the rooftop cocktail lounge, the world-famous Top of the Mark (since remodeled). Big bands used to broadcast from "the Mark." Today a radio station has its studios behind the hotel. The large spotlighted American flag flying proudly from its pinnacle ripples and snaps on windy nights.

831, 837, 843, and 849 Mason Street
· Townhouses, Willis Polk, 1917

From the plaza look across the street at 831, 837, 843, and 849 Mason Street. The elegant detailing of these four identical townhouses is typical of Polk's sure touch. (Polk was not responsible for the "im-provement" of Number 849.) The blockfront of which the Polk townhouses are a part is compact, articulated, and distinctly San Franciscan.

Across the southwest corner of Pine and Mason Streets is 903 Pine Street, a four-story frame apartment house typical of building on the slopes after the fire of 1906. Its height, its bay windows, its pleasing stock architectural ornament, and its scale and urbanity are characteristic of the south, west, and north slopes of Nob Hill. Increasingly, however, Pine Street is being invaded by buildings of a totally different scale and orientation: tall, visually impoverished concrete highrises. Grosvenor House, across the intersection from the postfire apartments at 899 Pine, epitomizes the bleak type.

1001 California Street
· Morsehead Apartments, Houghton Sawyer, 1915

Cross the street from the Mark Hopkins plaza to 1001 California Street, the Morsehead Apartments. This ritzy French Baroque–style apartment house is one of the handsomest on the hill. The lobby is ornamented with statuary and mosaic work. It has housed such notable families as the Hearsts. A discreet discotheque is tucked into its corner.

Next door is one of the most frequently noticed buildings on Nob Hill, 1021 California Street, once described as standing "like a quiet, well-dressed child among grownups." New Yorker George Schasty designed this three-story townhouse (with five stories to the rear) in 1911 for Herbert Law, a patent-medicine millionaire who eventually owned the Fairmont Hotel across the street. The enclosed Standard Oil Garage next door was designed in 1956 by Anshen and Allen.

5 Pacific-Union Club/originally The Flood Mansion
· 1000 California Street
· Italianate, Augustus Laver, 1886; Willis Polk, 1912; George Kelham, 1934

In 1885 James Flood commissioned Augustus Laver to design a palatial $1.5 million house built of Connecticut brownstone. Flood, one of the Comstock (Nevada) silver kings, had visited New York City and been impressed by the vogue for brownstones there. The Flood Mansion was one of the most resented buildings in nineteenth-century San Francisco. Its dark color and the use of a "foreign" building material offended architectural and public opinion alike. It was said that Flood employed one man full-time simply to polish his $30,000 brass fence. Fanciful serpents' heads and other designs are worked into its gates. The gates flanking the main stairs to the house are particularly intricate and imposing. The fence, like money, is undoubtedly better with the patina of age.

This was the only Nob Hill mansion not built of wood and was the only one to survive the fire of 1906. Its burned-out shell was reconstructed in 1912 with additions designed by Willis Polk. The building became the bastion of the Pacific-Union Club, San Francisco's most prestigious and exclusive men's club (locally referred to as the PU).

The remodeled building is better proportioned than the original. The addition of the wings and the partial suppression of the tower make the building look more comfortable on its site. The perception of the building's scale has also changed now that the mansion is surrounded by far larger buildings. Notice where Polk inserted third-story windows when he changed the building from two to three stories to accommodate more bedrooms. The lighter-colored balustrade at the top of the building is painted sheet metal, not brownstone. Polk's hand in the redesign is subtly evident in the bronze handrails flanking the front steps. The supports for the side handrails are beautifully proportioned miniature Doric columns cast in bronze. This is typical of Polk's love of classical forms, his playful sense of scale, and his use of historical allusions in unexpected places. He also created outstanding club rooms inside as fine as any on the East Coast, and a Minoan-columned plunge in the basement with an electrically illuminated stained-glass ceiling that ranks among the most astounding, and inaccessible, rooms in San Francisco. The landscaping around the mansion is restrained and conservatively elegant. The red border begonias dotted around the lawn complement the chocolate-colored stonework perfectly.

6 The Fairmont Hotel
• 950 Mason Street
• Reid Brothers, 1906; Mario Gaidano (tower), 1962

Cross Mason Street and approach the Fairmont Hotel. This grand hotel occupies the block assembled by James G. "Bonanza Jim" Fair, another of the Comstock silver kings. His marriage broke up after he assembled the block but before he got to build his house. His daughter, Tessie Fair Oelrichs, decided to build the grandest hotel in San Francisco on the commanding site. It was ready to open when the earthquake and fire struck in 1906. The shell of the building survived though the fire consumed all of the brand-new building's contents. The hotel was reconstructed and opened one year to the day after the disaster of 1906.

For many years the Fairmont Hotel dominated the skyline of San Francisco. Passengers on approaching ferry boats saw the great hotel looming white and luminous over the hilly city. The Fairmont is faced with matte white terra-cotta; its cornice is as delicate as a fluted piecrust. The upper-right-hand southwest corner of the cornice recently fell off and was expediently replaced (alas!) with flat stucco.

Enter the hotel through the main entrance. The lobby is one of the great public spaces in San Francisco. Walking across the vast patterned carpet with its swirling leaves makes one a bit giddy. Walk straight through the lobby, past a staircase, all the way to the Venetian Room (one of the great showcases of American song), and turn left. Go down the corridor and turn right. Around the corner is an enormous and beguiling rendering by the Reid Brothers of the hotel with its original gardens, which stepped down the downtown side of the hill. Also note the extensive collection of photographs of the earthquake and fire of 1906 to the left. Continue down the hall to the elevator. A tower designed by Mario Gaidano was added to the hotel in 1962. Its exterior elevator offers one of the unique experiences in San Francisco. Take the agreeably slow glass-walled elevator to the Crown Room. As it ascends, the Financial District high-rises seem to grow up out of the ground. The effect is extraordinary and the panorama is breathtaking. Chinatown is at one's feet, the Financial District straight ahead, North Beach to the left, and the Navy Yard to the far right. Come back out through the lobby to Mason Street.

Walk north (toward the bay) and cross Sacramento Street.

7 The Brocklebank Apartments
· 1000 Mason Street
· Weeks and Day, 1926

The Brocklebank, at 1000 Mason Street, is an elegant ten-story apartment building with surprisingly small windows. Its brick-paved court, like that of the Mark Hopkins by the same architects, defines a corner of the hill's summit, in this case the northeast.

The Brocklebank was the pride and joy of Mrs. M.V.B. MacAdam, an extraordinary woman who decided, as she wrote in her sad memoir, to build an apartment house "which would be a credit to San Francisco and to myself." She oversaw every step of its design and construction. The architects must have had great patience. She climbed to the roof of the Fairmont across the street to make sure that the color of the roof tiles was just right. She even designed the uniforms of the multitudinous staff.

During the boom of the late 1920s she sank her entire fortune into this project. When the budget seemed insufficient to furnish the 277 rooms, she sold off an apartment house on Sutter Street and forty-six sand lots on the beach to assure that the appointments were as good as the building. Most unhappily, her $1 million dollar loan was foreclosed during the depths of the Depression. Even the furnishings in her own apartment were threatened. As she wrote years after the catastrophe, "Added tears are futile: so, with outward calm I passed through the door which closed upon my little world wherein I had lived in supposed security." But the monument to her care is still proudly there, just the way she wanted it.

From the intersection of Sacramento and Mason Streets there is a sweeping view. Down the slope to the north is the red-brick cable-car barn at Mason and Washington Streets, where the great flywheels drive the steel cables. In the distance is Russian Hill, with its peculiar mixture of large high-rises, smaller-scale apartment buildings, and brown shingle houses. The small, dark, shingled building with the white windows visible at the very top of Russian Hill was architect Willis Polk's own house. The Baroque church in the valley is Nuestra Señora de Guadelupe; it marks the original location of San Francisco's post-Gold Rush Latin town.

The Park Lane
· 1100 Sacramento Street
· Apartment building, Edward E. Young, 1924

The Park Lane Apartments on the northwest corner of Sacramento and Mason, 1100 Sacramento, reflects the opulent twenties.

Up Sacramento is the empty lot once occupied by the Sproul mansion (pronounced Sprool) on Sproul Lane.

The Nob Hill
· 1170 Sacramento Street
· High-rise residential building

Across Sproul Lane is the Nob Hill, one of the most luxurious new high-rise apartment buildings on Nob Hill. A driveway circles through the ground level of the building. Along its west side is a sliver of a garden.

1172 Sacramento Street
· Townhouse, built c. 1908; remodeled by Ted Moulton, 1968

This bijou townhouse is one of the most-loved confections on Nob Hill. It is in the spirit of the lost Hopkins Mansion, although on a miniature scale. Notice the fancy cast-iron grillwork over the plate-glass windows and its handsome second floor. From across the street the illusionist effect of the converging lines on the mansard roof and the fanciful iron cresting at the top of the building are most effective.

Both the townhouse and the Nob Hill high-rise were commissioned by Edward T. Haas in the 1960s. The townhouse is actually an extensively reworked postfire two-family flat built about 1908. It was remodeled by Ted Moulton, who even used mahogany for part of the façade. He transformed a typical postfire building with two bay windows into a 1960s version of an eighteenth-century French townhouse.

8 Huntington Park
· Donated 1915

Cross Sacramento Street and enter Huntington Park with its sand-boxes and its beautiful bronze-and-marble replica of the Tartarughe (Tortoise) Fountain in Rome's Piazza Mattei. The original fountain was commissioned by Pope Alexander VII and sculpted by the Florentine Taddeo di Leonardo Landini in 1581. San Francisco's copy lacks the bronze tortoises along the rim of the basin that give the fountain its name. The four graceful bronze youths are among the city's most delightful ornaments.

Huntington Park was the site of the mansion built for David Colton in 1872 for $75,000. One source noted that "the design, or picture, of the original was brought from Europe by ex-U.S. Senator Milton S. Latham, in 1868." The architect is unknown. It was unique among the millionaires' palaces in that it was the only one that showed any architectural restraint.

Colton was the chief lawyer for the railroad and was derisively known as the One-Half of the Big Four and One-Half. At his death his widow was sued by the Big Four, who claimed that Colton had embezzled railroad funds. During the trial, Mrs. Colton produced a series of six hundred letters written to Colton by Huntington that described how the railroad had bought politicians in Washington and Sacramento. It was one of the most sensational trials of its day, revealing the seamy underside of the great fortunes that made Nob Hill famous. A bitter but victorious Mrs. Colton sold the house in the 1880s and left San Francisco.

Strangely enough, Collis P. Huntington, another of the Big Four, bought the property in 1892 for $250,000. The house survived until 1906 and was the scene of a famous burglary in which a good deal of silverware was spirited away. In 1915 Huntington's widow donated the land to the city for a park. One story has it that Mrs. Huntington originally wanted only children with governesses to use the park!

Today, Huntington Park is one of the finest parks in San Francisco, with its view of the Cathedral House and Cathedral towers to the west, the brownstone Flood Mansion to the east, and elegant hotel and apartment buildings all around. It is a sunny, urbane park. Its statuary includes the central fountain and a charming, small bronze sculpture, "Dancing Sprites." One very Nob Hill touch is the pillared and red-tile-roofed public toilet, which looks like a small temple.

The Huntington Hotel
· 1075 California Street
· Weeks and Day, 1924

Across California Street facing the park is the unostentatious brick-

faced Huntington Hotel. It is perhaps the finest hotel in a city noted
for its hotels. The hotel's green-liveried doorman's shrill, hollow
whistle calling for taxis is a familiar sound on the hill.

Masonic Memorial Auditorium
· 1111 California Street
· Albert E. Roller, 1958

Also visible from Huntington Park is the slick, white-marble-clad
California Masonic Memorial Temple. The stripped classical portico
shelters two strange objects, tall pillars capped by globes. The long
tradition of Masons' and Odd Fellows' buildings in the center of
California towns here culminates in a well-located, functional, but
sterile building. This was once the site of the A.N. Towne residence,
a Colonial Revival brick-and-frame house built in 1891 and destroyed by the fire in 1906. Its marble portal survived and was moved
to Lloyd Lake in Golden Gate Park. It is known as "The Portals of
the Past" and is one of San Francisco's two memorials to the 1906
earthquake. (The other is the depressing mural in the Rincon Annex
post office.)

9 Taylor Street to Pleasant Street
· Post-1906 flats and apartments

Leave Huntington Park. Note the low, granite retaining wall around
the park which survives from the Colton house. Walk north and cross
Sacramento Street to see 1110 Taylor Street. This one-story frame
building with its classical pediment is thought to have been the home
of Flood's coachman, though how it survived the fire is a mystery.
   Nearby is 1138–40 Taylor Street, a three-story flat. This elegant
and congenial small building shows how fine the buildings that were
built after the fire of 1906 could be. It has a garage and entryway on
the street level, a beautiful window at the middle of the second floor,
a large bay window on the third floor, and a windscreen along the
top sheltering a roof deck. The entire 1100 block of Taylor Street is
intact and boasts an outstanding group of three- and four-story
postfire apartments and flats.
   Walk to the intersection of Clay and Taylor Streets. This was the
terminus of the world's first cable railroad, the Clay Street Cable
Railroad promoted by Andrew Hallidie. Look down Clay Street to
the soaring, 853-foot-high Transamerica Pyramid. Look up Taylor
Street to Russian Hill. Note the coherent cityscape of the postfire
apartments and flats that blanket the slopes. At this intersection there
is a small commercial cluster with a corner grocery store, a barber-
shop-hairdresser, a café, and other neighborhood conveniences.
   Cross the street and see 1153–57 Taylor Street, a three-story frame
flat with corner bay windows typical of turn-of-the-century San

Francisco. From here to Van Ness Avenue this building type predominates.

Walk under the trees and look at 1133–43 Taylor Street. This four-story, gray shingled flat is an excellent example of early-twentieth-century San Francisco building. It was built in 1908 for artist Emil Pissis and designed by Bakewell and Brown, the architects of City Hall. It has careful, restrained ornament and an interesting elevation on Pleasant Street. It has been lovingly maintained and enhanced.

Turn the corner and walk up Pleasant Street. This aptly named street is a delightful example of San Francisco's quiet byways. Continue up Pleasant, turn right at Jones Street and walk to the intersection of Clay and Jones.

10 The Clay-Jones
- 1250 Jones Street
- Art Deco, Albert H. Larsen, 1929

The slender, Deco-styled shaft of the Clay-Jones, with its radio tower (which now serves taxis and other two-way radios), has been a Nob Hill landmark since 1929. The Clay-Jones was one of the earliest residential high-rises in San Francisco and is still one of the best, despite some later alterations to its top. It was converted into condominiums in 1973.

Up and down Jones Street are the bulkier high-rises that have succeeded the slim towers of the thirties. The massive buildings of the 1950s and 1960s are far less appealing, both from the street and from a distance, than the light, slender towers of just a generation ago. The smaller windows of the older buildings conserve energy, while allowing stunning views, and their relatively larger, light-colored wall areas reflect more daylight and harmonize with the cityscape when seen from afar. These blocks have seen intensive development since the 1960s.

Turn around, walk south on Jones Street to the corner of Jones and Sacramento.

11 The Chambord Apartments
- 1298 Sacramento Street
- Beaux-Arts, James F. Dunn, 1921

The Beaux-Arts apartment building on the northeast corner of Sacramento and Jones is an architectural curiosity of the first rank in San Francisco. It is a building so different, and so intriguing to the public, that it has earned constant misattribution. This unique design of billowing poured concrete has attracted to itself the legend that this is a building by the Barcelona architect Antonio Gaudí. It is not. It was designed by South of Market–born San Francisco architect James

F. Dunn in 1921 for James Witt Dougherty, son of a wealthy rancher.

The billowing balconies and bay windows of the animated exterior reflect the building's unique floor plan. As originally designed, each apartment had a perfectly oval living room fifteen feet by twenty feet. The ends and sides of these oval rooms stacked in the southwest and southeast corners of the building protrude from the wall plane and form the shallow bay windows. The balconies were originally highly ornamented with rich Beaux-Arts decoration. These embellishments were stripped away to make the building conform to modern seismic requirements. The top floor was built as a penthouse with an open court facing the cathedral across the street. In 1926 patent-medicine tycoon Herbert E. Law bought the Chambord, altered the fifth floor, and added a sixth-floor penthouse of no particular distinction. The present owners intend to gut the building and attach it to a soaring, slim condominium tower behind it on Jones Street. The Chambord is a city landmark, but San Francisco's landmark ordinance protects only exteriors, not interiors.

The Cathedral School for Boys
· 1275 Sacramento Street
· Rockrise and Watson, 1965

The Cathedral School for Boys, at 1275 Sacramento, southeast corner of Jones, uses its roof for exercise areas and almost vanishes into its sharply sloping corner site. The handling of the reinforced concrete is ingratiating rather than brutal. It is a human-scaled and friendly building—a most conducive place for education. The blue-blazered students spill onto the #55 Sacramento bus in the afternoons on their way west to Pacific Heights and home, their red-and-gold-striped school ties askew in their mannerly rambunctiousness.

1200 Block of Sacramento, north side
· Post-1906 flats and apartments

Walk down the 1200 block of Sacramento, between Jones and Taylor, a handsome row of small-scale apartment houses that includes two other Beaux-Arts or French-style buildings. Enter the cathedral grounds by walking up the staircase behind the Diocesan offices at 1055 Taylor Street near the corner of Sacramento.

Grace Cathedral Block

The block bounded by California, Sacramento, Jones, and Taylor was assembled, or almost assembled, by Charles Crocker, another of the Big Four. Only one parcel eluded him, a lot with a small frame house owned by Nicholas Yung that stood where the rear carriage gate that now leads to the cathedral's parking lot is. Yung kept raising his price, and Crocker became infuriated. In revenge, Crocker built a forty-foot-high spite fence around three sides of Yung's lot, depriving him of sunlight. Neither man would give in. It took the death of both before Crocker's heirs were able to buy the last lot on the block. The spite fence became a notorious attraction. In 1877 Dennis Kearny's Workingman's Party staged a boisterous demonstration on the top of Nob Hill against the rich and the Chinese brought into California to work on the railroad. The spite fence was the rallying point for the angry mob.

Crocker commissioned Raun and Taylor, San Francisco architects, to design him a grand house on the California Street side of his block. The result was a vast Second Empire–style wedding cake. Later a second house was built on the California and Jones corner for Crocker's son. Both houses burned in 1906; all that remains of them today is the granite and basalt wall on Sacramento and Taylor Streets, built with stone from the railroad's quarries at Rocklin and Cordelia, California. After the fire, which also destroyed old Grace Church, the Crocker family donated the block to the Episcopal Diocese of California.

12 Grace Cathedral
 • Lewis Hobart, 1911; completed 1964

Grace Cathedral, consecrated in 1964, combines the memory of Gothic forms with San Francisco's earthquake-conscious building code. The result is a monolithic, steel-frame, concrete Gothic cathedral, twentieth-century building methods recreating the shapes achieved by medieval stonemasons piling stone upon stone minus the flying buttresses. "To those who admire reinforced concrete Gothic cathedrals," says *Here Today*, "this massive church, for which George Bodley drew the plans and which Lewis Hobart executed, may be considered the finest example of that style in the west." Hobart's chief inspiration was Notre Dame in Paris.

If the structure of the building is not medieval, its curiously embedded context is. The Cathedral House (built in 1911 for the Church Divinity School of the Pacific and designed by Austin Whittlesey) and its companion Diocesan House on Taylor Street wall in the front of the cathedral. Medieval cathedrals were often embedded in a thick crowd of buildings before nineteenth-century improvers provided them with front yard plazas. The block on which Grace stands has a pleasing randomness and intimacy created by the huddling of the Cathedral House and its companion in front of the Cathedral.

The small plaza between the buildings with its three olive trees and the tiny strip of garden leading to the parking lot are pleasing, human spaces. Near the steps is the Washington elm, a small tree propagated from the famous elm tree that grew on the Cambridge, Massachusetts, commons and under which George Washington ac-

cepted command of the American troops. The Cathedral steps, with
their treasure at the top—a cast of Lorenzo Ghiberti's "Doors of
Paradise" at the Baptistry in Florence—face the sheltered and sunny
space. When people mill about after the service, the hospitableness
of the accidental plaza becomes apparent.

A sad sign of a general decline in civility was the necessary re-
moval of the small white frame Wayside Chapel that used to nestle
so securely under the shadow of the Cathedral on its California Street
side. This meditation chapel had to be removed because of vandal-
ism. It and the Cathedral used to present an engaging dialogue between simplicity and grandeur.

If reinforced-concrete Gothic cathedrals are not one's particular
favorites, the treasures inside the Cathedral are indisputable joys.
They include a fourteenth-century Catalonian crucifix, a fifteenth-
century Flemish altarpiece in the Chapel of Grace, a fine Renaissance
terra-cotta bas-relief of the Madonna and Child by Mino di Gio-
vanni, a contemporary woodcarving of Hosea by California sculptor
David Lemon, and, ranged along a wall in the north ambulatory, a
collection of medieval Bible pages showing the history of the repro-
duction of the sacred scripture in script and type.

The sonorous Aeolian-Skinner organ with 100 ranks and 7,000
pipes, the 44-bell English carillon, and Grace Cathedral's fine musical
program make the whole building a vast musical instrument. Here
flourishes a proud and ancient patronage, an official Cathedral organ-
ist. To experience the very best Nob Hill can offer, time your walk
to conclude with a concert in this house of worship and harmony.
Organ recitals are often held on Sundays at 5:00 P.M. The carillon is
played on Wednesdays and Sundays at 3:00 and 5:00 P.M.

No doubt the most appreciated treasure of the Cathedral is the
great rose window, made in 1970 in Chartres by Gabriel Loire. It is
illuminated from inside at night and its colors burn bright and beautiful to inspire the passerby. Its wheel of light makes visible through
color St. Francis of Assisi's "Hymn to the Sun."

Tour 6

Chinatown

A City Within the City

The Picture Map Company

1 Chinatown Gate
2 400 Block of Grant Avenue
3 St. Mary's Square
4 Old St. Mary's Cathedral
5 Commercial Street
6 Portsmouth Square
7 Soo Yuen Benevolent Association
8 Temple of Tien Hon
9 Kong Chow Benevolent Association and Temple
10 Spofford Alley and Old Chinatown Lane
11 Old Chinese Telephone Exchange
12 Chinese Historical Society of America Museum

WHAT THIS WALK COVERS:

This walk explores both the main streets and the alleyways of Chinatown, a post-1906 red-brick district of extraordinary density and activity that preserves the scale of Civil War San Francisco beneath its exotic signs and façades. Grant Avenue, Portsmouth Square (San Francisco's original Plaza), Waverly Place and the Tien Hon Temple, and the Chinese Historical Society Museum are the highlights of this tour.

PRACTICALITIES

Best time for this walk: Chinatown is alive almost around the clock and can be savored day or night. Check temple and museum hours (Nos. 8 and 12). Sunday afternoon, when Chinese-Americans flock to Chinatown from all over the Bay Area, is the liveliest time. Chinese New Year, usually in early February, is the district's chief holiday time when the dancing lion and his loud drummers come to accept an offering from each shop.

Parking: Public transit is the best way to get to Chinatown, since parking is impossible. The public garages under Portsmouth Square and St. Mary's Square are convenient but often full.

Cafés and Restaurants: Chinatown has more restaurants than any other part of San Francisco, but only a few stand out. Among the best are Sun Hung Heung (744 Washington), Cantonese, and Yenching (939 Kearny), Szechuan cuisine. The best *dim sum* (steamed pastry) lunch is at the Hong Kong Tea House, 835 Pacific. Two other excellent Chinese restaurants are located outside Chinatown—the Szechwan (2209 Polk) and the Hunan (924 Sansome). The Yet Wah at 1801 Clement in the Richmond district is also good.

INTRODUCTION

Chinatown can be described as a city within a city. It has been, and is, an extraordinarily conservative city. It is clustered around San Francisco's original Mexican plaza (Portsmouth Square) and along its first street (Grant Avenue), which became a Chinese quarter after the Gold Rush of the 1850s. Within a dozen years San Francisco's business center moved a few blocks east and then south, on bayfill, to where the Financial District is today. Old San Francisco (Yerba Buena) became Chinatown.

Because it was such a poor, if lively, area the buildings in Chinatown were subdivided and added onto but not drastically changed. When the district burned down completely in 1906 it was almost immediately rebuilt (most of it with salvaged bricks) to be much like the downtown Civil War city. Chinatown was rebuilt in an Edward-

The Ying On Labor and Merchant Benevolent Association at
745 Grant Avenue, a typical post-1906 brick associational building
with shops, residences, and a meeting room with a loggia on the
top floor, whose façade was remodeled in 1920.

WILLIAM
WALTERS

ian style like all the rest of San Francisco. It was made "Chinese" during the tourist boom of the 1920s, when Chinese cornices, loggias, and portals were added to otherwise ordinary buildings.

In this small district, nestled at the base of the modern high-rises, is a pocket of city buildings of an extraordinary density and variety of uses. Chinatown's population density per acre is second only to Manhattan's; since the 1950s its population has grown from about 30,000 to some 75,000. About 10 percent of San Francisco's population is of Chinese ancestry.

Chinatown is ever at work. Some small factories, restaurants, and shops are busy even late at night. As one observer wrote in 1888, "In the Chinese workshops there is no cessation of toil. In the multitude of their shops and cellars they make cigars, or boots and shoes, or bend over sewing-machines, with backs that never tire. The cobbler is at work, seated on his box on the sidewalk, while a customer waits nearby. . . ."

There are two Chinatowns. One consists of the uninterrupted string of shops and restaurants along Grant Avenue, and the other, the real Chinatown, exists above and behind this particular industry.

According to all objective measurements Chinatown is a slum, yet it is nonetheless a vital—and literally attractive—part of San Francisco. People from all over the world come to see this place; they come to see an Asian city within a Western one.

For oceans do not only separate, they unite; their currents link opposite shores in webs of trade and migration. San Francisco was born as a seaport, and what was most important was the sea, not the port. The Japanese Current links Canton and the region at the mouth of the Pearl River, Kwangtung Province in southern China, with San Francisco, the principal nineteenth-century port on this side of the ocean. Emperor Ch'ien Lung's edict of 1757 made Canton, a port not too far from Hong Kong, China's only window to the West. The dialect, cuisine, and customs of San Francisco's Chinatown are all from Kwangtung province.

The Chinese who came to California (which was romantically called "Mountain of Gold" in Chinese) must be seen as one chapter in the extraordinary phenomenon of the *huagiao*, the "Overseas Chinese." All around the Pacific basin there are Chinese colonies. San Francisco's Chinatown is only the oldest and largest on this side of the ocean.

Before their exclusion, the Chinese came to California to seek gold, to work on the construction of the railroad and later on the reclamation of land, or to engage in trade. Chinese settled in small clusters in nearly all Gold Rush California towns. But a wave of anti-Chinese feeling during the depressed 1870s drove nearly all of California's Chinese into San Francisco, the port that first received them and their eventual refuge. Anti-Chinese agitation inside San Francisco never dislodged this tiny city within a city. Appropriately enough under the shoulder of Nob Hill, Chinatown survived as California's only significant Chinese community. Exclusion in 1882 by the federal government prevented the growth of the Chinese population in California.

The Chinese who came to America organized themselves in three different kinds of organizations: family clans, regional groups, and "tongs," or trades. A tight and intricate organizational framework helped secure a place within America for the Chinese sojourners. Most of these family and regional associations bought real estate from the French, Italians, and Germans and established meeting places on the top floors of mixed commercial-residential buildings. They are the fabric of Chinatown, and account for its old-fashioned configuration.

The intense conservatism in real estate in Chinatown has deep roots. It is generally an older, more conservative generation that heads family and local associations, and their values are preserved in Chinatown. They own 20 percent of Chinatown today.

The Chinese-Americans in Chinatown, so distant from China and isolated by a political separation only beginning to be bridged, exhibit all the conservatism of a colonial offshoot in clinging to the ancient customs inherited at the time of settlement. San Francisco's Chinatown is much like Quebec Province in Canada—customs and attitudes survive there longer than in France herself.

Nineteenth-century American customs that have disappeared everywhere else also survive in Chinatown. This includes everything from the scale of the streets, to inscribing the date of the construction of a building at the top of its façade, to funeral marches with brass bands that mark the passing of local worthies.

Important funerals are usually scheduled for midday on Sunday, when the full procession passes down narrow Grant Avenue on its way out of Chinatown. A full brass band (mostly Italian-American musicians) playing slow dirges precedes such ceremonious exits. An open car with a large photograph of the deceased propped up in the back seat always heads these ceremonious departures. The mourners display little outward emotion as the cortege threads its way down Grant Avenue toward the freeway ramp and the road to the Chinese cemeteries south of the city with their vaults and courtyards.

There are no supermarkets or large department stores in Chinatown. Shopping, especially food shopping, is still as it was since time immemorial, a daily ritual of going from shop to shop for different items. Shoppers exchange greetings as they trudge from the live poultry vendor to the fish dealer, to the butcher, to the greengrocer. And perhaps, this day, there is a stop at some beat-up station wagon parked along the curb whose entrepreneurial owner has imported cages full of squirming live green frogs for sale at bargain prices.

Most of the greengrocers have open shopfronts with crates brimming with Chinese vegetables fresh from California's valleys. The abundance of produce available demonstrates that California's valleys are a Garden of Eden. Early in the morning the smart shopper and the alert visitor are on Grant (near Pacific) or Stockton Street with the eager housewives sifting through every crate for that one imperceptibly larger or fresher bunch of greens. Among the first things the Chinese pioneers did in California was to establish small gardens for specialty produce, many where Union Street is now.

Sprinkled among the food shops and curio stores are herb shops, some new, some old, with row upon row of small unlabeled drawers lining their walls. Customers enter with an herb doctor's prescription and an individual concoction is blended. The appropriate elixir is drunk as a tea.

At 947 Grant, near Jackson, is the Tin Bow Tong herb shop, a spot well worth a detour and a peek in the window. Behind its old plate glass is a room unchanged in seventy years. Rows of small wooden drawers line the wall behind the counter. Square, old-fashioned Chinese stools and chairs line the other wall. An old brass scale resting on the countertop is identical to the instruments that weighed out the gold dust of the Gold Rush of 1849. A Victorian clock, undoubtedly saved from the fire, ticks away on the far wall. Within this bare room is contained the slow rhythm of San Francisco's Chinatown.

San Francisco's Chinatown today is much like New York's Lower East Side at the turn of the century. The density is similar and so is the hunger and respect for two things: learning and money. The great achievement of Chinese-American culture is not visible in Chinatown but in the universities of the state of California. At Berkeley, for example, when the undergraduate library is closed at night, 70 percent of the students still studying are Asian-Americans. The head of the school system in San Francisco has said, not entirely in jest, that if the merit high school selected its students only by the criteria of academic merit, the school would soon have only Asian-American females.

THE TOUR

1 Chinatown Gate
· Grant Avenue at Bush Street
· Clayton Lee, 1970

At Bush and Grant is the ornamental entrance to Chinatown, appropriately embraced by two hamburger stands. Here the width of the street changes. The Chinatown side of Grant is narrow and preserves the early, narrow width of San Francisco's streets. The Downtown part of Grant was widened in the 1860s and became a fashionable shopping street for San Francisco.

On the northeast corner of Bush and Grant, to the right of the entry gate, is a circa-1910 postfire French Baroque building with

1920s Chinoiserie additions along the top. Chinatown is an occidental city in oriental dress.

2 400 Block of Grant Avenue
· Post-1906 shops with residences above

Walk up Grant to Pine Street. This block, the only pronouncedly uphill block on Grant Avenue, harbors several of Chinatown's more expensive furniture and jewelry stores and is close to fashionable Union Square. Farther on, the goods become less pretentious. The City of Hankow Tassel Company (a flavorful name if there ever was one!) is on this block.

On the northwest corner of Grant and Pine are two typical postfire buildings that were never made to look particularly Chinese. They are Neoclassical.

The Grant Avenue Hotel, on the southwest corner of Grant and Pine, like so many Chinatown buildings, has a meeting room at its top. That room has stained-glass windows with, among other designs, a picture of the Portals of the Past in Golden Gate Park.

3 St. Mary's Square
· Donated, 1912; underground garage, John Jay Gould, 1955; landscaping, Eckbo, Royston and Williams; statue of Sun Yat-sen Beniamino Bufano, 1937

Cross Pine Street, turn right, cross Quincy Street (really an alley), and enter St. Mary's Square, in part a donation of the Catholic archbishop in 1912. Note the view of old St. Mary's down Quincy Street, now pleasantly bordered on one side by poplar trees. The motto on the church tower reads, "Son, observe the time and fly from evil"—an admonition particularly appropriate in San Francisco.

Today St. Mary's Square is the landscaped roof of a parking garage. From this platform there is a spectacular view of the Financial District high-rises. The statue is of Dr. Sun Yat-sen, the first president of the Chinese Republic. Sun Yat-sen was a political exile and revolutionary fund-raiser in San Francisco's Chinatown in the early twentieth century. This stainless-steel and pink-granite statue was sculpted by Beniamino Bufano in 1937 under the Works Progress Administration and is typical of Bufano's streamlined work. The statue looks east toward the encroaching Financial District. Immediately to the east is the dark, imposing Bank of America world headquarters. This is the edge of Chinatown, a very sharp city edge with a most extraordinary perspective on the high-rises of the present.

Chinatown has surrendered part of its eastern edge at Kearny and Pine to the expanding Financial District but retained its old core (Sacramento and Grant). But it has expanded to the north into the alleys of North Beach, up Pacific Avenue through the pass between

Russian and Nob Hills, and skipped out with the bus lines to the western Richmond district (Clement Street). Chinatown is the only original ethnic enclave in San Francisco to have expanded since World War II.

4 Old St. Mary's Cathedral
• Crane and England, 1853; rebuilt, 1906

St. Mary's Rectory
• 660 California Street
• Skidmore, Owings and Merrill, 1964

Pass through St. Mary's Square to California Street. Across the street is the red brick tower of St. Mary's Roman Catholic Church, a famous San Francisco landmark. Though it burned in 1906, it was reconstructed to look much as it did in the early 1850s. It is the Catholic church closest to downtown and was the first Catholic cathedral in the city. The beautifully harmonious red-brick rectory to its right was designed by Skidmore, Owings and Merrill in 1964 and harbors a small courtyard to its rear. SOM also designed the thirty-three-story white high-rise, the Hartford Building, at the same time.

Sing Fat Building/Sing Chong Building
• Southwest corner/Northwest corner, California and Grant Streets
• T. Patterson Ross and A.W. Burgren, 1908

Across Grant from St. Mary's are two paired corner buildings with pagoda ornaments, which create an architectural conversation between east and west with the gothic church tower. The building to the left (the southwest corner) is the Sing Fat Building, built in 1908 and designed by the Scottish-born San Francisco architect T. Patterson Ross. The yellow-brick building on the right (the northwest corner) is the Sing Chong Building, also built in 1908 and also designed by Ross and A.W. Burgren. This prominent pair, standing half way up the California Street hill between the Financial District and Nob Hill, serves as another visual gate for Chinatown.

There were no Chinese-American architects in the post-1906 era. Ross and Burgren secured several important commissions from Chinese associations and were credited with introducing the "pagoda style" on a few key sites in the rebuilt district. The principal architectural journal in the city noted that "Where previously the rigid lines of cheap occidental building construction had provided perpendicular walls, now the fantasy of the Far East has been borrowed and in the Chinatown of today the pagoda style quite generally predominates." But this was true only on a few key corners; most of Chinatown's new buildings were actually plain.

When the Sing Chong Building opened it housed a Chinese emporium. Its tower was studded with electric lights. It was described as "a startling but pleasing combination of flamboyant, Far Eastern gaudiness of color and clear-cut Yankee enterprise and up-to-dateness." It was stuffed with bronzes, porcelains, ivory, ebony, furniture, jewelry, screens, silk embroideries, kimonos, cloisonnés, satsumas, handkerchiefs, shawls, gowns, beads, bedspreads, and silken underwear. Today a wax museum occupies the ground-floor corner.

The view north down Grant Avenue from California Street presents the vision of a fragment of an Asian city embedded in an American one. Chinese-style cornices, "pagodas," streetlights, phone booths, signs, and banners create a picturesque jumble of exotic shapes and colors. In slightly foggy weather, when the old neon signs are blurred, it is a magical view.

Walk along Grant and cross Sacramento Street. This block of Sacramento between Grant and Kearny was the location of the first Chinese stores in the 1850s. Among the older Chinese-Americans, Sacramento Street is still called Tong Yan Gai or "Chinese Street." Notice that the street signs here are in both English and Chinese.

5 Commercial Street
· Post-commercial brick buildings with a nineteenth-century scale

Continue along Grant to narrow Commercial Street and turn right. Along this brick-paved street is preserved the scale of mid-nineteenth-century San Francisco. The street originally led to a wharf. Today the Ferry Building tower terminates the view. There are even two-story buildings here, though we are only two blocks from the fifty-two-story Bank of America. This street was rebuilt after 1906 to look much like what it had in the late 1850s. The architecture is simple; since this is not a tourist street, the buildings were never made to look exotic. Behind these anonymous façades with their fabric-screened windows is the real Chinatown, a place of poverty and hard work, and not necessarily romantic.

Walk down Commercial Street to Kearny. The view back up Commercial, with Chinatown in the foreground and Nob Hill's high-rises beyond, shows how Chinatown nestles at the base of the hill. On the southwest corner of Commercial and Kearny is a heavily ornamented postfire building with a French or Art Nouveau flavor. It was once a luxury shop but now houses the information agency of the People's Republic of China and has been painted yellow and black.

6 Portsmouth Square
· Plaza of Yerba Buena, 1837; underground garage and park, Royston, Hanamoto, and Mayes, 1960

Turn left on Kearny, cross Clay Street and enter Portsmouth Square (now the roof of another parking garage, built in 1960). This was San

Francisco's original plaza, laid out in 1837 under Mexican rule, and was the heart of the boom town of the 1840s. The plaza was named for the U.S. warship *Portsmouth*, which brought Captain Montgomery to California in 1846. The original shoreline was only a block east.

The Mexican Custom House once stood in the plaza. Later Portsmouth Square attracted a swarm of gambling halls during the Gold Rush and eventually was the site of the town's first schoolhouse. City Hall was across Kearny Street. But the Downtown quickly shifted to the filled land of the cove to the east, and the old part of the town became the Chinese quarter.

The only major interruption of the square's scale is the Holiday Inn designed by Clement Chen and John Carl Warnecke and Associates, and built in 1971 on the site of the old Hall of Justice. This exaggerated structure looks like an air-conditioning vent, and its utterly superfluous pedestrian bridge (the bridge over the river Kearny) casts a dark shadow over the children's sandbox in the northeast corner of the square. This project was part of the "urban renewal" of San Francisco.

Portsmouth Square was scooped out and an underground parking garage inserted in 1960, with the park, Chinatown's principal open space, atop it. The benches in the park were painted red, a traditional good-luck color, and scaled to the height of the users. Though the square seems unattractively cluttered, it does work as a lively social space, especially for the older Chinese-American men who gather here daily to enjoy the sun and play checkers. Very early in the morning the square is sprinkled with devotees of *Tai Chi Chuan,* slow-motion gymnastics of extraordinary grace.

The modern Zen Buddhist temple on Washington Street on the north side of the square follows, behind its contemporary façade, the pattern of the older buildings in Chinatown. The top floor houses a meeting room with a loggia and a view.

The signs and dates set in at the tops of many of the buildings surrounding the park proclaim the ownership of these structures by family associations. Number 747 Clay Street, on the south side of the square, has a gold-and-black sign that tells the street that this is the Jin Family Association's building. There is commerce on the ground floor, no doubt residence above, and a meeting hall on the top. The Wo Hop building at 759 has an eagle atop it, a standard piece of turn-of-the-century ornament.

The signs and calligraphy in Chinatown are always fascinating. There is a complete spectrum of signs: ink on paper scrolls, carved and gilded wood panels, inscribed marble, a lot of old neon, and modern plastic too. Chinatown is a visual salad of graphics. Many of the doorways in Chinatown are flanked by twin orange paper banners with black ink calligraphic inscriptions. They are purchased in February during the New Year celebrations and are taped to the doorposts. They proclaim good wishes. A sample pair of inscriptions might read, "The country will be strong and the people will be happy," on one side and on the other, "In the wintertime all the people come together and sing."

7 Soo Yuen Benevolent Association
· Northwest Corner, Grant and Clay Streets
· c. 1910; remodeled, Albert Schroepfer and Edward G. Bolles, 1922

Leave the square via Clay Street to see the highly decorated building on the northwest corner of Grant and Clay. This building is owned by Soo Yuen Benevolent Association and was a plain building when built after the fire. But in 1922 it was given its Chinese dress by two San Francisco architects, Albert Schroepfer and Edward G. Bolles. It has a meeting hall on top, residences below, and shops along Grant Avenue. Typical of the use of every scrap of space in Chinatown is the newsstand and sundries shop along the Clay Street wall of the building. This sidewalk shop is closed over at night with boards but during the day keeps this busy corner very lively.

Dick-Young Apartments
· 823 Grant Avenue

At 823 Grant, on the west side between Clay and Washington, is the Dick-Young Apartments. A small bronze plaque to the right of the doorway reads, "The Birthplace of a Great City. Here, June 25, 1835, William A. Richardson, Founder of Yerba Buena (later San Francisco), erected its first habitation, a tent dwelling, replacing it, in October, 1835, by the first wooden house, and on this ground, in 1836, he erected the large adobe building, known as 'Casa Grande.' "

8 Tien Hon Temple
· 125 Waverly Place
· O'Brien Brothers, 1910

Continue up Clay to Waverly Place. The view north up Waverly pierces the real heart of Chinatown. This remarkable street shows just how Chinese Chinatown got to look, especially after the 1920s. Nearly all these buildings are owned by family associations that proudly embellished their headquarters with loggias, Chinese cornices, etc. All are capped by meeting halls and white flagpoles. For years the only flag flown in Chinatown—other than the American— was the Nationalist flag with its large white sun. In the last few years the flag of the People's Republic has appeared at rallies and in wall posters. But it is still the Nationalist flag that flies from Chinatown's innumerable association flagpoles on festive days.

Walk halfway down the block on the left-hand side to 117–19

Waverly, the Yee Fung Toy Building. This was once the offices of the *Chinese Times,* where the day's newspaper was posted in the window for all to peruse. This yellow-brick building was designed by Hamilton Murdock. When it was built in 1908, its top-floor meeting room was noted for its solid-walnut doors, iron thresholds, oak floors, and decorative skylight. It was "resplendent with imported carvings, screens, hangings, draperies, altar stand, furniture, [and] vases."

At 125 Waverly is the Shew Hing District Association Temple. This is one of the only temples in Chinatown easily accessible to visitors (open 10:00 A.M. to 5:00 P.M. and 7:00 P.M. to 9:00 P.M.). Climb the stairs to the top floor. This temple was founded in 1852 and dedicated to Tien Hon, revered as the Queen of Heaven. Sailors, travelers, fishermen, wandering minstrels, actors, and fallen women look to her for protection. She is the protectress of the sojourner and is an appropriate presence in this immigrants' colony. Pious families provide the tins of vegetable oil used to keep the temple lamps burning. Oranges are favored offerings because they are a pun on the Chinese word for wealth. Tien Hon is also called Tou Mu. Her tantric form is the Goddess of Light holding the sun and the moon. To the Chinese this street has always been called Tien Hon Miao or Street of the Tien Hon Temple. The temple houses antique fragments from other Chinese temples, or joss houses (so called because of the sticks of incense continually alight), dismantled when the Chinese were driven out of remote towns in Northern California in the 1880s.

Leave the temple and head back to Clay Street. At 109 Waverly is the beautiful red-and-white signboard of the Buddhist Association of America and the Chinese Library of America. Waverly Place is an important street for Chinese-Americans, especially the older generation. The Masons and American Legion also have meeting rooms on the street.

From Waverly and Clay, looking south down Waverly to Sacramento, on the left-hand side, the 1907 clinker-brick-faced First Chinese Baptist Church is visible. Protestant missionaries were very active in late-nineteenth-century Chinatown, and many Chinese-Americans today are Christian.

9 Kong Chow Benevolent Association and Temple
· 855 Stockton Street
· Ed Sue, 1977

Continue up Clay past Spofford Alley to Stockton. Grant Avenue is the visitor's Chinatown; Stockton Street is the residents' shopping street. Open-fronted vegetable, fish, poultry, and meat stores line the street to the north. Chinese-American housewives crowd the sidewalks, all laden with full shopping bags.

Across Stockton Street on the southwest corner is the new Kong

Chow Temple Building. On the ground floor is the Chinatown branch post office, and the top floor is a new home for Chinatown's oldest temple.

Chinese Six Companies Headquarters
• 843 Stockton Street

Next door to it is the elaborate polychromed and ornamented headquarters of what was traditionally the most important institution in Chinatown, and among all the Chinese in America—the famous Chinese Six Companies, whose formal name is the Chinese Consolidated Benevolent Association. Actually, there are seven district associations, representing seven areas of old China. They are the Kong Chow, Ning Yung, Sam Yup, Sue Hing, Yan Wo, Yeung Wo, and Hop Wo associations. The Six Companies once acted as labor contractors and brought Chinese laborers to California. They helped build California with their *ku li,* which translates as "bitter toil" and gave us our word *coolie.* Later the institution, always controlled by the merchant class, evolved into the highest board of arbitration among the Chinese in America. Conflicts between businessmen or groups from different districts would be resolved by the Six Companies. The Six Companies also functioned as the official representative of the Chinese in America. Today it is a nonprofit community organization with less power but considerable prestige. There is a freestanding gate over the entrance with yellow, green, and gilded tiles. Dragons, fish, birds, flowers, and guardian dogs embellish the façade. The building serves a host of community activities.

Kuomintang Headquarters
• 844 Stockton Street
• post-1906

Facing the Six Companies, at 844 Stockton, in an anonymous stucco-fronted building, is the headquarters of the Kuomintang, the Chinese Nationalist Party founded by Dr. Sun Yat-sen. This is another important conservative force in Chinatown whose influence over the younger generation is now waning. The glassed-in notice boards on the front of the Kuomintang headquarters record in photos and Chinese captions the daily life of Chinatown: school bands, awards from the Chinese Chamber of Commerce, testimonial banquets, etc. It is a window into the Chinatown community.

Return to Clay Street. On the northeast corner, at 902 Stockton, is St. Mary's [Chinese-American] School, built in 1911. Its windows are always alive with seasonal classroom art projects and are always a delight; pumpkins, turkeys, candles, snowflakes, hearts, rabbits, Easter eggs, and other art works—all the same but each one different

—chart the passing seasons of the year. Today Chinatown has more young children than ever before, and long strings of hand-holding schoolchildren led by their teachers are a lively sight. Across Stockton at 925 is the Neoclassical home of the Presbyterian Church in Chinatown, a typical 1907 postfire building never ornamented with Chinoiserie.

Farther up Stockton, on the northwest corner of Washington is the "pagoda"-and-cross-capped Methodist Board of Home Missions building, designed by Henry H. Meyers and built in 1911. Chinatown's most important political and religious institutions cluster along this part of Stockton Street.

10 Spofford Alley and Old Chinatown Lane
· Chinatown alleys and jewelry district

Walk back down Clay a few steps and turn left into Spofford Alley. Chinatown preserves a network of such nineteenth-century alleys; this one has a slight dogleg. Here is a classic piece of old Chinatown, a quarter rebuilt in 1906 but somehow preserving a much older atmosphere. Walk along Spofford; the doorways seem more ancient than they are. Small fortune-cookie factories, garment shops, social clubs, and other typical uses fill the street levels. Apartments and furnished rooms huddle above.

From the corner of Spofford and Washington, looking west up the hill, you see the pagoda-capped Methodist Church once more and, two buildings up, the ocher Commodore Stockton School Annex. It is a delightful building with attractive Chinese wooden loggias and ornaments, which happily were reinforced rather than stripped away when the school was reconstructed in 1976 to meet contemporary earthquake codes.

On Washington Street, Chinese jewelry stores are tucked into narrow shops. Their windows display rich yellow gold jewelry (Chinese-Americans prefer a heavier, yellower, less alloyed gold) and lustrous, delicately colored jade. Prized spinach-green jade adorns many of the women of Chinatown.

Cross Washington Street and enter the narrow alley of Old Chinatown Lane. This was once known as the Street of Gamblers; these side streets once teemed with brothels and gambling dens. The early immigration of Chinese to America consisted nearly exclusively of able-bodied laborers; only the merchant class could bring wives with them. Thus prostitution was an important element in Chinatown's early life. It is virtually invisible today. Gambling is another question; the Chinese have always loved to gamble. Travel agencies in Chinatown do a brisk business chartering buses to Nevada. And the rapid click, click, click of the Mah-Jongg tiles can be heard from behind many closed doors. Since the Gold Rush there's always been gambling near Portsmouth Square.

Chingwah Lee Art Studio
· 9 Old Chinatown Lane

Today Old Chinatown Lane is a dreary-looking concrete alley, but one with a hidden treasure at its end. This is the Chingwah Lee Art Studio at Number 9, open the first Saturday of each month between 2:30 and 5:00 P.M., a famous treasury of antique Chinese art. In the 1930s it was described as "a rare collection of porcelain, bronzes, ancient snuff bottles, paintings, ancient weapons of warfare, and a large collection of Chinese gods (many from temples formerly situated in towns and camps throughout California, which eventually will be housed in a new temple)." A peek through the window is a peek into ancient China. A beautiful wooden figure of Kuan Yin, the Goddess of Mercy, presides in serenity against the back wall.

1 Old Chinese Telephone Exchange
· 743 Washington Street
· Built 1909

Walk back to Washington and downhill to Grant Avenue, cross Grant, and see the small pagoda-shaped building, now a branch of the Bank of Canton, at 743 Washington. It was built in 1909 to house the Chinese Telephone Exchange, which functioned as a separate Chinese-language telephone system from 1894 until 1949. In the old days the manual operators each knew all 2,477 subscribers. Every operator was fluent in English and all of Chinatown's dialects. Today the modern telephone booths along Grant Avenue are disguised to look like pagodas.

Fidelity Savings
· 845 Grant Avenue
· Ed Sue, 1971

The most extravagant modern Chinese-style building in Chinatown is the Fidelity Savings building at 845 Grant. It has a massive gold-tile-roofed gate for its façade and two ferocious guardian dogs behind its iron fence.

Continue down Grant. Note the Sun Sing Theater at 1021. Chinese opera is no longer performed, but Chinatown has several Chinese-language movie houses. They often broadcast the sound track of the film to the sidewalk. Plaintive melodramas and loud Kung Fu productions are the favorites.

Ping Yuen Housing Project
· Pacific Avenue
· John Bolles, 1950; 1961

Cross Pacific Avenue, the easiest grade to the west and the old path of travel out to the Presidio. On both sides of Pacific are the balconied buildings of pale green concrete, the Ping Yuen (Tranquil Gardens) housing project, built between 1950 and 1961 by the city. These apartments are some of the best housing in Chinatown and have very low crime and turnover rates.

12 Chinese Historical Society of America Museum
· 17 Adler Place
· Remodeled, 1966
· Open Wednesday, Friday, and Saturday, 1–5; 391-1188

Continue up Grant and turn right into Adler Place a few steps short of Broadway. At Number 17 is the museum of the Chinese Historical Society of America. It is a postfire red-brick building appropriately remodeled in 1966 with a rich tile design and an elegant gilded sign.

Inside are the mementos, treasures, and work tools of the Chinese-American pioneers who helped build California. Notice the wheelbarrow made from small pieces of wood and wire. On the walls are some old scrolls, the treasured possessions of Chinese pioneers in California.

Tour 7
Russian Hill
An Essay in Regional Taste

TOUR 7 ☐ RUSSIAN HILL

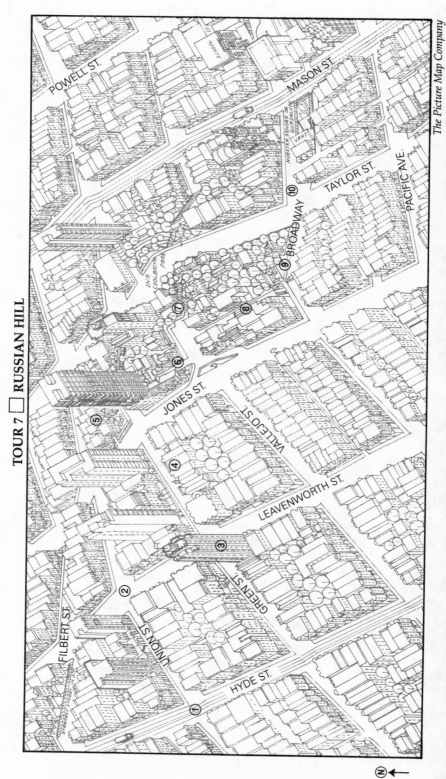

The Picture Map Company

WHAT THIS WALK COVERS

This walk explores the southern, or highest, peak of Russian Hill and includes two enclaves of vintage houses that escaped the fire in 1906. The heavily landscaped brown shingle cluster by some of the Bay Area's best-known early-twentieth-century architects at Vallejo Street is the highlight of this walk.

PRACTICALITIES

Best time for this walk: Almost any time is good.

Getting there by public transit: From Union Square or the Hyde-Beach turntable near Ghirardelli Square take the #60 Powell-Hyde (not the #59 Powell-Mason) cable car to Union and Leavenworth. Or take the #30 Stockton from Sutter and Stockton to Washington Square, transfer to the #41 Union trolley-bus west to Union and Leavenworth.

Parking: If driving, park near Broadway and Taylor, walk up the Broadway steps, turn right (north) at Jones Street, walk two blocks, turn left on Green and walk up one block to Green and Leavenworth. This puts you one block from Union and Leavenworth and the start of this walk. The route of the walk will bring you back to your car.

Cafés and Restaurants: At the end of the walk, Chinatown with its many restaurants is only a few blocks downhill.

INTRODUCTION

How Russian Hill got its name is shrouded in obscurity. The Russian empire reached only as far south on the California coast as Fort Ross, sixty miles north, and never penetrated San Francisco Bay. Still, the most popular undocumented legend is that some Russian sailors were buried somewhere on the high hill. If so, the reason is simple to understand; this 312-foot-high hill is one of the three hills that hemmed in Yerba Buena Cove, and it enjoys a sweeping view of the bay and the Golden Gate. Explorers and colonists were often buried within view of the sea that had brought them from afar. But the hill has always had what Californians call an Anglo population. (Russians did come to San Francisco, in four waves: in 1905–06, in 1918 after the revolution, in the 1930s via China when Japan occupied China, and after World War II when Russians from Eastern Europe settled in the Richmond District in the western part of the city.)

If the hill's name is not easily accounted for, its eventual identity is. In the nineteenth century Russian Hill was just far enough away from Downtown to attract a colony of writers and artists. Many of San Francisco's late-nineteenth-century artistic luminaries lived on

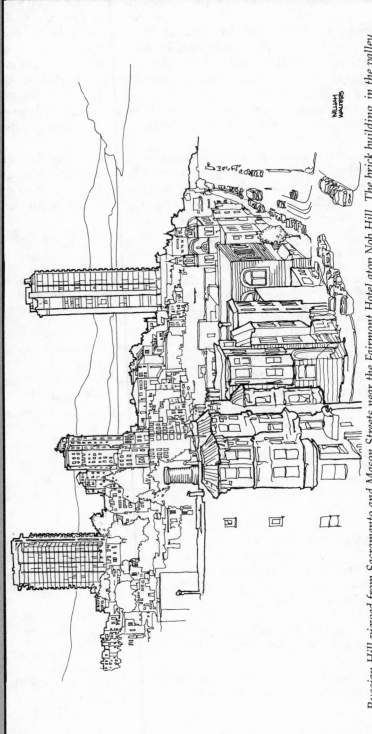

WILLIAM WALTERS

Russian Hill viewed from Sacramento and Mason Streets near the Fairmont Hotel atop Nob Hill. The brick building in the valley with the arched windows is the Cable Car Powerhouse and Museum at Washington and Mason Streets, built in 1887 and rebuilt in 1907.

this then relatively secluded, wild-mustard-covered hilltop. Among them were Frank Norris, George Sterling, Ambrose Bierce, Joaquin Miller, Ina Coolbrith, Will Irwin, Gelett Burgess, and John Dewey, all writers; William Keith, the best-known landscape painter of the period; and sculptors such as Douglas Tilden and Haig Patigan. The early residents of Russian Hill were described as "people of moderate means but superior tastes." Today Russian Hill is one of the poshest enclaves in San Francisco, with chic apartment houses and condominiums within walking distance of the Financial District.

The artistic spirit and consummate style traditional on Russian Hill are best expressed by a vignette from 1906. James Hopper, a San Francisco writer, wandered across the city during the three days of the uncontrollable fire. At the top of the Jones Street hill on Russian Hill he thought he heard the sounds of music.

> It was no hallucination. Upon the top of the Jones Street hill, in the middle of the street, the only thing standing in that direction for miles was a piano. A man was playing upon it. I could see his hands rising and falling, his body swaying. In the wind his long, black hair and loosened tie streamed. The wind bore the sounds away from me, but in a lull I finally heard the music. It was Saint-Saëns' *Danse Macabre,* "The Death Dance." His hands beat up and down, his body swayed, his hair streamed, and from the crest down over the devastated city [his music] poured, like a cascade. . . .

In 1919, Edward A. Morphy commented that Russian Hill "also harbors that perhaps not wholly unconscious pride of superiority to its environment which is the privilege of every place that becomes the abode of the intellectuals."

THE TOUR

1 Edwardian Commercial Crossroads
· Hyde and Union Streets
· Cable-car stop

Here two transit lines (cable and electric trolley-bus) cross and a small, pleasant neighborhood shopping area developed. It is a classic bit of Edwardian San Francisco, an intersection defined by bay windows at all four corners. Walk up Union on the right-hand sidewalk toward Leavenworth.

1145 Union (19–21 Sharp Street)
· International style townhouse, c. 1960

At 1145 Union, at the southwest corner of Sharp Street, is a two-story duplex in the local version of the International style but with a square glass bay window overhanging the sidewalk. Reticent almost to the point of anonymity, the house is very "city-wise."

2 Union and Leavenworth Streets
· Bay-windowed, Edwardian flats and apartments

Russian Hill has two summits; the intersection of Union and Leavenworth Streets is located in the saddle between them. This tour explores the southern, or higher, peak and includes several enclaves on the eastern side of the hill facing the Downtown. It is the extraordinary cluster of prefire survivors on the hill, and the basic fabric of the reconstruction-era flats, that give Russian Hill its sense of architectural identity. Though it is a residential district extremely close to downtown, Russian Hill has always stressed its remoteness and cultivated a rural image. The neighborhood and its residents have perpetuated a certain attitude or style, with an emphasis on expensive simplicity that is evident in Russian Hill's architecture, gardens, and the clothing and jewelry of its women.

Today Russian Hill exhibits an extreme, jarring contrast between its horizontal three-story postfire buildings and the gargantuan reinforced-concrete post-1930 high-rises that sprout abruptly from the top of the hill on a line along Green Street from Hyde to Mason. No more will be built: in 1974 a forty-foot height limit was put on the hill to prevent hypercongestion of the neighborhood. The high-rises are here for the same reason that the shingled shacks were built here in the 1880s and 1890s: for the exhilarating view. Russian Hill commands one of the most extraordinary panoramas of any American city. It looks south to the dense downtown high-rises and north to the spacious bay, the Golden Gate, and the hills beyond.

From the southwest corner of the intersection of Union and Leavenworth, there is an excellent view of Coit Tower and the top of Telegraph Hill at eye level to the east. The tower, the bronze statue of Christopher Columbus to its left, and Joseph Esherick's buff-colored Garfield grammar school at the head of Filbert Street are all clearly silhouetted in this hilltop-to-hilltop view. To the north down Leavenworth is Alcatraz, with wooded, pyramid-shaped Angel Island behind it.

While one key block at the top of Russian Hill escaped the fire in 1906, the rest of the hill burned. Most of the buildings at this intersection date from the reconstruction period, 1906 to about 1925. The row of three-story, bay-windowed flats marching up from the southeast corner of Union and Leavenworth shows typical postfire construction. Flats and apartment houses sprang up in place of destroyed Victorian houses. The even rhythm of their bays accounts for much of the area's character. Looming over the three-story flats is a tall concrete high-rise, typical of building on the hill from 1930 to 1974.

3 1101 Green Street
· Skyscraper with Spanish ornament, H.C. Baumann, 1930

Walk up Leavenworth to the corner of Green. Straight ahead, to the
south down Leavenworth Street, is an excellent view of the tight,
ordered cluster of high-rises at the top of Nob Hill. The street in the
bottom of the trough between the two hills is Pacific Avenue, the
natural pass from the harbor to the Presidio and a busy road in the
nineteenth century, especially for walkers. The Edwardian apartment
houses clinging to the slopes present a happy collage of light colors,
almost like paint chips in a rack. To the west, down Green Street, is
a view of the high-rises of Pacific Heights and the green, man-
planted forests of the Presidio. To the east, down Green Street, is an
extraordinary juxtaposition of low and high buildings. Along this
short, three-block long spine is a mix of soaring, futuristic high-rises
and a pocket of nineteenth-century two- and three-story frame
buildings. From this intersection, contemporary and turn-of-the-
century San Francisco collide.

The twenty-story white Spanish-Deco skyscraper at 1101 Green
Street was built in 1930. It is the earliest, and probably still the
handsomest, residential high-rise in San Francisco. Its slender white
tower, rich movie-palace-Spanish ornamentation, and many bay
windows rise with mannered elegance from the lofty corner. The
building is exuberantly ornamented at the top and ground levels. The
corner entry is emphatic and dignified and relates well with the
walker's sidewalk. The building's slim shape, white color, and sensi-
bly sized windows mean that the structure reflects a great deal of
light and stands gracefully on the city skyline.

Next door, downhill, is 1111–33 Green Street, a complex of gable-
roofed, Tudor-style apartments perched high atop a retaining wall.
A steep flight of steps leads to a courtyard at the side of the building.
Beyond it, also perched high atop a cement retaining wall, is a brown-
shingled, Tudor-style building typical of Russian Hill's search for the
country cottage despite the need for the radical surgery of the precipitous site and the unromantic apartment-house density.

On the northwest corner of the intersection, at 1907 Leavenworth,
is a three-story shingled apartment house with green trim that combines both the brown-shingle imagery of the Russian Hill of the
1890s with the denser, citified apartment houses of the 1906–25
reconstruction period.

4 1000 Block of Green Street
· Cluster of historic houses, Octagon to Pueblo Revival, 1857–1920s

Cross Leavenworth Street toward the pocket of old houses and see
1088 Green Street, originally a firehouse built in 1907 to house Engine

Company Number 31. It was sold in 1957 and preserved by the new owner as a pied-à-terre and an example of turn-of-the-century firehouse architecture in San Francisco. It contains a small residence above and a large party room on the ground floor. A peek into the front doorway reveals the relocated pole once used by firemen to slide down from the second floor.

Across the street is a varied collection of houses from the late nineteenth and early twentieth centuries. The oldest building is the Fusier octagon house built in 1857, with a mansard roof and cupola added in the late 1880s. The fad for these houses was sparked by Orson Fowler's *A Home for All*, which advocated octagonal houses as a more healthful design for living. (Only one other octagonal house survives in San Francisco, at Gough and Union Streets, maintained by the Colonial Dames of America. Admission by donation on the first Sunday of the month and the second and fourth Thursdays, 1:00 to 4:00 P.M.)

Next door is 1055 Green Street, an Italianate house built in 1886 and thoroughly modernized by Julia Morgan in 1916. Its symmetrical façade is delightful and elegant. The entrance is tucked in at the ground level. Discreetly emphasized living-room windows on the second floor look out over the street. Julia Morgan's designs were always noted for their livability and domesticity. Classical and Renaissance designs and ornamentation were revived in San Francisco in the first decades of the twentieth century; the symmetry and repose of this stucco-fronted house are characteristic of the best of that period. The garage visible down the driveway echoes the façade of the house.

The small shingled and turreted building to the east, 1045 Green Street, looks as if it, too, should have been a firehouse but has probably always been a single-family residence. It appears to have been built in the 1880s and imaginatively improved over time.

Number 1039–43 Green Street, next door, is a typical Italianate building of the 1880s, which was moved to the top of the hill after the fire of 1906. An extraordinary curved stairway and vintage iron fence distinguish this building.

Across the street, behind a red-brick wall and green hedge, is 1030 Green Street, an interesting stucco Pueblo Revival house from about 1918.

Number 1011 Green Street is almost impossible to see, tucked as it is behind and atop its ivy-covered garage. An interesting brown-shingled house with dark black sash and trim, designed by Ernest Coxhead about 1905, it is a brilliant piece of San Francisco design. Its radically cut-out shape can be best appreciated from across the street. A curious iron bracket braces the brick chimney. The reticence, almost invisibility, of the building is typical of the low-key style of Russian Hill.

Summit Apartments
· 999 Green Street
· Streamlined, Claude Oakland and Associates, 1965

From the intersection of Green and Jones Streets, you can see down the hill to Fisherman's Wharf, Alcatraz, Angel Island, and the north bay. To the south appears the startling contrast between the futuristic Summit Apartments at 999 Green Street and its Mediterranean neighbors, the backs of a group of townhouses on Russian Hill Place designed by Willis Polk. The massive, streamlined concrete base of the Summit Apartments ignores the traditional scale and texture of the hill but, of course, the tower enjoys panoramic views. The Summit was built by Joseph Eichler, a builder who developed vast parts of the west of San Francisco in the 1940s with affordable middle-class stucco row houses. Now that there is a forty-foot height limit on the hill, this giant can be regarded as an architectural dinosaur, the last of its kind. Mr. Eichler reserved the two-story penthouse at its top for himself. There is an inaccessible and little-used park between the residential tower and its parking-garage base.

5 Macondray Lane
· Pedestrian lane with embowered cottages

Walk north down Jones Street, halfway down the block to Macondray Lane. From this corner is a good view of the Mediterranean-style tower of the Art Institute four blocks to the north, designed in 1926 by Bakewell and Brown. It was built in the form of an ancient monastery though constructed of reinforced concrete. Its red-tile roof, greenery, and tower stand as a monument to the influence of northern Italian and Mediterranean design in early-twentieth-century California. The Art Institute houses an art school, a curious Diego Rivera mural, and changing galleries of contemporary art.

Turn right into Macondray Lane. Notice the typical postfire apartment house to the right; its shingled exterior harks back to the earliest houses on the hill. Macondray Lane harbors an extraordinary variety of small houses and apartments, all happily unified by the tunnel of greenery that embowers them. While the architecture is mostly conventional, the overall effect is extraordinary. At 19–21 Macondray Lane is an interesting contemporary apartment house with balconies and a spiral staircase. The windows of the building were slanted to take advantage of its spectacular view. The building next door, at 15–17, has plaster ornamentation over its simple windows.

The Belgian block paving here is treacherous but picturesque. Walk as far as the top of the wooden stairs at the end of the lane. From here there is a sweeping vista of the bay, North Beach, and Coit Tower atop Telegraph Hill, and a close-up view of San Francisco's characteristic roofscape. Here is the essence of postfire San Francisco's agreeable urban fabric. These simple clapboard buildings with their flat roofs and sheet-metal chimneys create a pattern and a beauty distinctive to San Francisco. The bay-windowed apartment houses climb the hill like steps. Each occupies a twenty-five-foot-wide lot, lots originally subdivided for single-family houses but rebuilt to a higher density and accidentally uniform height after 1906. Before leaving this spot, note the ancient fig trees sheltered against the slope, most probably planted by an Italian family.

6 Russian Hill Place
· Townhouse row
· Mediterranean, Willis Polk, 1915

Turn around and retrace your steps up Macondray Lane; walk up Jones past the Summit and follow the ramp straight ahead, turn left onto Vallejo (pronounced "va-LAY-ho") and walk up the staircase toward the sign RUSSIAN HILL. This is one of Russian Hill's two summits and is 312 feet high. When the classically detailed concrete retaining wall was built, several skeletons were found, leading some to say it was the old Russian sailors' burial ground.

Russian Hill Place is a pleasant, brick-paved cul-de-sac. The four attached townhouses on the west side, like the Art Institute which we saw from a distance, bring Mediterranean or Italian architectural imagery to this Mediterranean climate. The townhouses seem inspired by North Italian hill towns. Note the bronze plaque on Number 7, which reads, AVEC SOUCI.

7 1000 Block of Vallejo
· 1013–19 Vallejo
· Brown-shingle cluster, Willis Polk, 1893

Return to Vallejo Street. The two brown-shingled, gable-roofed houses at 1034 and 1036, built in 1884, are known as the Marshall houses. They escaped the fire in 1906. A third building to the east, at the edge of the cliff, was torn down for a high-rise that was never built. The site will probably be occupied by a three- or four-story condominium.

Walk to the balustrade at the crest of the hill. Like visual bookends symbolizing the history of San Francisco, the sailing ship *Balclutha* is visible to the north, and the contemporary high-rises dominate the view to the south. The curious brown-shingled, gable-roofed, white-windowed building at 1013–19 Vallejo Street was built in 1893 as two houses: one for architect Willis Polk and his family and one for his patron, Mrs. Virgil Williams. The shingle house seems small from this side, though the tiny scale of the white-framed windows makes it look larger than it is. Set on a steep slope, the other side of the building steps seven levels down the hill. (We shall see that side later from Taylor and Jackson Streets.)

To the right of this house, hidden in the trees, is another shingled building that dates from the Civil War period but was later remodeled by Polk: 1045 Vallejo Street, the Horatio P. Livermore home. This cluster of buildings on the southeast corner of the hill escaped the flames in 1906 and is among California's most important architectural ensembles. Most of the property was owned at one time by the Livermore family, who hired creative architects to design their houses. All the buildings are on generous lots with extensive landscaping; all use brown shingles and simple construction to achieve a rural effect within the city. (The other place in the Bay Area where such houses survive is Northside Berkeley, where professors built Craftsman houses at the turn of the century that are now overgrown with vines and trees.)

This group of buildings epitomizes the search for the rustic and the seemingly simple in California house design from the 1890s to the 1920s. Simple vernacular forms, brown-shingle exteriors, and unfinished redwood interiors—all set among vines and trees—create a romantic, woodsy architectural style much loved in Northern California. The roots of the "organic" architectural styles of the 1960s in this region can be discovered in these buildings. Explore a bit of the staircase that cascades down the hill in front of Polk's house, but return to the top of the hill and walk back down Vallejo, and to Florence Street.

8 Florence Street
• Pueblo Revival Group, Charles J. Whittlesey, others; c. 1920

Florence Street is a surprisingly coherent enclave of the Pueblo Revival architecture popular in the 1920s. A view of Grace Cathedral terminates the one-block-long street's vista. Number 1071 Vallejo, on the southwest corner of Florence and Vallejo, is a particularly striking design with windows sunk deep into its walls and a heavily emphasized cubistic shape designed about 1918 and built for H.P. Livermore.

Farther down the street are Numbers 35, 37, and 39 Florence Street, apparently all built at one time. All have rough stucco exteriors, deep-sunk windows, and projecting second levels. They are an interesting amalgam of Pueblo and Mission styles. Note their meticulously pruned shrubs.

Facing them at Number 30 is a contemporary interpretation of the same Pueblo effect. It is a simple stucco cube of surprising elegance.

Walk to the staircase at the end of Florence Street; visible to the south are the hotels and high-rises of Nob Hill. Walk down the staircase.

9 1000 Block of Broadway
· Brown-shingle cluster

Walk along the retaining wall that interrupts Broadway to the other side of the street. There is a bench built into the wall at the head of the stairs where you can sit and admire the old house across the street. The rambling stucco house built around an old tree is 1032 Broadway. The core of the house was built in the early 1850s. It has narrow, round-headed Italianate-style windows that could date from Civil War–period remodelings. In 1900, Willis Polk substantially expanded the building. There is a pleasing, random quality to the design of the house, rooted in the way in which it grew over time and the way it respects the tree around which it was built. The gardens that surround the house are abundant and picturesque. It was undoubtedly the great abrupt retaining wall that prevented the flames from destroying these buildings in 1906. The grading of the street here resulted in privacy and protection. The wooden balustrade that caps the wall was most likely designed by Polk. When Polk remodeled 1032 Broadway, he had an inscription placed over the front door that reads, "Except the Lord build the house, they labor in vain that build it. Except the Lord keep the city, the watchman waketh in vain" —an appropriate admonition for a house that looks down on the very heart of the city.

1020 Broadway
· Craftsman, Julia Morgan, 1917

Walk halfway down the steps on the right side and see 1020 Broadway across the street. This fine Northern California shingled house was built in 1917 and altered in 1927 and 1930. It epitomizes the rustic, Craftsman aesthetic popular in Northside Berkeley and Marin and to some degree in Presidio Heights. Its simple materials are used here with exact appropriateness. The massive shingled chimney shape is a motif now used by many contemporary designers. The simple green tarpaper roof is particularly pleasant. A wisteria vine climbs the eaves and links the house to its garden. Houses like this remind us of the observations that Charles Keeler made in 1902:

. . . here and there through city and town, homes have been reared in the . . . simple fashion—plain, straightforward, genuine homes, covered with unpainted shingles, or built of rough brick, with much natural redwood inside, in broad unvarnished panels. The same reserve which has characterized the building of these homes has likewise been exercised in their furnishing. A few antique rugs, a few good pictures or photographs of the masters, and many good books, with plain tables and chairs, constitute the furniture. To find this spirit, which would have been a delight to William Morris, so strongly rooted as to assume almost the aspect of a cult, is, I take it, one of the most remarkable features of a civilization so new as that of modern San Francisco.

10 Broadway and Taylor Streets
· View of Nuestra Señora de Guadalupe
· Shea and Lofquist, 1907

From this intersection at the base of the stairs, the twin white Baroque spires of Nuestra Señora de Guadalupe church of 1907 can be seen silhouetted against Telegraph Hill and the bay. It stands as the only reminder that this slope was San Francisco's Latin district in the 1850s, with many Peruvians and Chileans living here. As late as 1940, it was the only Catholic church with Spanish-speaking priests in the city. It is reputed to be the first church in the United States built of reinforced concrete. Below the street here is the Broadway Tunnel, bored in 1952, which passes under Russian Hill and relieves the neighborhood of through traffic. Broadway and Taylor is also the western edge of Chinatown, which has expanded up the low pass of Pacific Avenue to embrace the slopes of both Nob and Russian Hills.

There is a Chinese-style prefabricated-metal gas station on the southwest corner of Pacific and Taylor, the next intersection—a remarkable piece of contemporary San Franciscana.

11 View from Taylor and Jackson Streets
· South side of brown-shingle cluster

Because of the high slope on which the brown-shingle cluster between Vallejo and Broadway stands, the best view of it is from the northeast corner of Taylor and Jackson Streets. The jumble of shingled shapes cascading down the hill, partially hidden behind dense greenery, is a unique island in the very heart of the city. The cluster has a medieval look to it and has grown increasingly complex over time. (Note how the balconies of the Summit have accumulated small plants.)

12 Taylor Street Apartment Houses
· Bay-windowed, postfire apartment buildings
· Falk and Knoll, 1913

Walk up Taylor to 1360–70, Hillgate Manor apartments. This stucco, court apartment house built in the 1920s has a startling view of the Transamerica Pyramid through its gate.

On the southwest corner of Taylor and Washington, at Number 1255–57, is La Granja Apartments, with highly exaggerated brackets supporting pillared balconies on the third and fourth floors.

From here the walker has two choices, either to continue up level Taylor Street to Nob Hill and Grace Cathedral and the California Street cable line, or turn down Washington one block to the cable-car powerhouse and museum.

13 The Washington and Mason Cable Car Powerhouse and Museum

The Washington and Mason Cable Car Powerhouse and Museum is open daily from 9:00 A.M. to 6:00 P.M. and is well worth visiting. Inside, the satisfying roar of the engines and the giant red and yellow wheels that drive the cables fill the cavernous room. Here is a rarity indeed, a functioning piece of industrial antiquity, the last cable car powerhouse in the world.

The cable car was an attempt to bring the power of the stationary steam engine out onto the road for passenger transport. The cable railroad was invented by a San Francisco wire-rope manufacturer, Andrew Hallidie, who built the world's first cable railroad on Clay Street from Kearny to Jones in 1873. Hallidie formed a trust that successfully patented the new technology and forced other lines to pay a royalty for its use. Twenty-eight other American cities once had cable lines before the introduction of the far more efficient electric streetcar in Richmond, Virginia, in 1888. After that superior system was perfected, cable lines survived only where extremely precipitous grades precluded electric streetcars.

Cable-car lines are very expensive to construct; with their brick-vaulted underground conduits for the cables, they are mechanically complex and difficult to operate, cannot make up lost time on schedules, and, most important, are relatively energy-inefficient. Between 60 and 80 percent of the energy generated by the system is used just to propel the cable; only about 4 percent is used to move the cars and their passengers. The heyday of the cable cars was between 1881 and 1888, the same years that Victorian San Francisco boomed.

San Francisco's cable cars were originally powered by steam but were converted to electric motors in 1911. The cables travel at an average speed of 9.55 miles per hour, or 840 feet per minute. Each cable is 1.25 inches in diameter and is composed of six strands of sixteen wires each, surrounding a manila hemp core. The breaking point of the cable is 155,000 pounds, twice the pull exerted by all the cable cars at any one time. The average life of a cable is from 45 to 120 days.

Each cable car acts independently. A "grip" on the cable car, which Hallidie patented, operated by the gripman, reaches through the slot between the tracks like a pair of pliers and clutches or releases the steadily moving underground cable. The cable pulls the cars along the street and up the hill; it also holds the cars back on the downgrade. To stop the car, the gripman drops the cable and applies the wheel or track brakes. The conductor in the rear of the car sometimes helps with braking on the steepest grades of the Hyde Street lines.

There are two surviving types of cable cars. The California Street line uses double-ended cars with an enclosed center cab. Their livery is maroon, cream, and tan. The California Street Cable Rail Road was the top of the line in its day, and its sumptuous standards were adopted by other transit lines across the country, who called their larger cars "California type."

The Powell and Mason and the Powell and Hyde lines use smaller, single-end cars, half open and half closed. They sport a green, cream, and tan livery. San Francisco's Municipal Railway must rebuild each car itself as they wear out. By now, every car has been rebuilt at least once.

In the museum is the very first cable car built in 1873 for Hallidie's Clay Street Cable Rail Road. This small experimental car owes its survival to the fact that it was sent to Baltimore for an exhibition in 1905 and so escaped the earthquake and fire in San Francisco the following year. When Baltimore experienced a great fire in 1907, it was thought that the relic was lost. But in 1939 the car was discovered in a junkyard in Baltimore and returned to its native city. In the back of the museum is a complete collection of models of all the various cable cars and streetcars once used in San Francisco.

The introduction of the cable car radically changed residential patterns in San Francisco. Previous to its introduction in the 1870s, level streets close to downtown, such as Sutter Street, were favored by the wealthy. The sandy, inaccessible hilltops were sprinkled with ordinary houses. The cable car inverted this pattern; the wealthy bought hill property to enjoy "marine views," and the level lower streets increasingly attracted commerce and less costly housing. Today the surviving cable-car lines all operate in areas burned in 1906 and rebuilt in the Edwardian period. Three- and four-story, bay-windowed flats and apartments march up and down the hills where the cable cars run producing an even, repetitive rhythm of bays, doorways, and cornices. Surprisingly few of these congenial city buildings have been demolished or unrecognizably altered. The result is one of the most extraordinary urban experiences in the nation, an historical urban whole of vintage public transit traveling at an agreeable 9.55 miles per hour through an intact and unique turn-of-the-century architectural zone.

The cable cars were saved from cost-cutting extinction by Mrs. Hans Klussman's Citizens' Committee to Save the Cable Cars in 1947. In 1964 the entire system was placed on the National Register of Historic Places, making the wooden cars the only moving national landmarks.

Tour 8
The Haight-Ashbury
Old Shell, New Snail

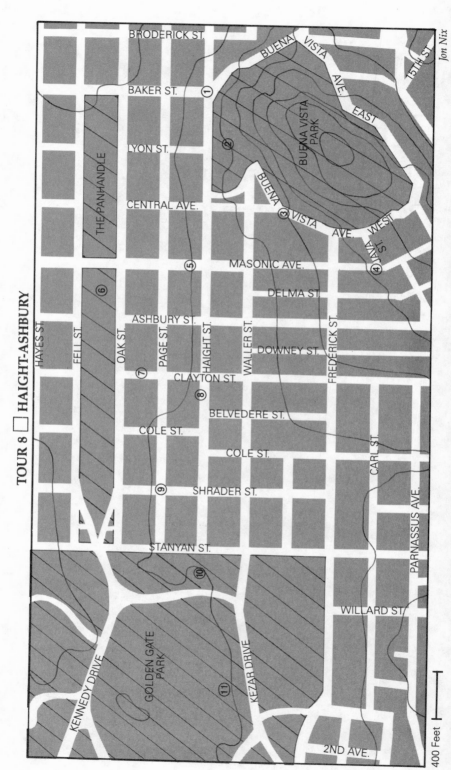

TOUR 8 ☐ HAIGHT-ASHBURY

Jon Nix

BRODERICK ST.

BUENA VISTA AVE. EAST

15TH ST.

BAKER ST. ①

②

BUENA VISTA PARK

LYON ST.

THE PANHANDLE

CENTRAL AVE.

BUENA ③ VISTA AVE.

JAVA ST. ④

BUENA VISTA AVE. WEST

MASONIC AVE. ⑤

⑥

DELMA ST.

ASHBURY ST.

FREDERICK ST.

HAYES ST.

FELL ST.

OAK ST.

PAGE ST.

HAIGHT ST.

WALLER ST.

DOWNEY ST.

⑦

CLAYTON ST.

⑧

BELVEDERE ST.

COLE ST.

COLE ST.

CARL ST.

⑨ SHRADER ST.

STANYAN ST.

PARNASSUS AVE.

⑩

WILLARD ST.

KENNEDY DRIVE

GOLDEN GATE PARK

⑪

KEZAR DRIVE

2ND AVE.

N ←

400 Feet

1 1100 Block of Haight Street
2 Buena Vista Park
3 Buena Vista Avenue West
4 Java Street to Masonic Avenue
5 Haight Street to the Panhandle
6 Golden Gate Park Panhandle
7 400 Clayton
8 1600–14 Haight
9 510–12 Shrader Street
10 Golden Gate Park and Alvord Lake
11 Children's Playground

WHAT THIS WALK COVERS

This walk threads its way through a late-Victorian neighborhood famous for its recent alternative subculture. Also included are Buena Vista Park as well as the Panhandle and southeast corner of Golden Gate Park.

PRACTICALITIES

Best time for this walk: The Haight can be foggy in the morning and chilly in the afternoon. The best time is between ten and three. You may wish to see the neighborhood first and then stroll down Haight Street itself to see its shops and sample its restaurants. There is a Haight Street fair in the summer. It is not necessary to dress up to visit the Haight.

Getting there by public transit: From downtown Market Street take the #7 Haight trolley-bus or the #71 Haight-Noriega or #72 Haight-Sunset bus and alight at Haight and Baker Streets.

Cafés and Restaurants: Haight Street has many varied small restaurants and increasingly interesting shops selling fine crafts and near-antiques.

INTRODUCTION

The Haight-Ashbury, as its compound name implies, embraces two distinct areas. The Haight, once known as Pope Valley, lies in the flatlands along the Golden Gate Park Panhandle. Ashbury Heights, always a richer area, rises to the south, up the slopes of Mt. Sutro, crowned by the Empire-waisted television tower. Haight Street serves as the dividing line between the two.

Most of the building in the Haight-Ashbury took place between 1885 and about 1910. The flat areas built up first; development only gradually crept up the slope of Ashbury Heights. The Haight-Ashbury fuses an ideal density of city housing (dictated by the economics of late-nineteenth-century land subdivision and public transit networks), and a deliberate effort by the nature-conscious Victorians to create a better urban residential environment, one surrounded by an ample cushion of parks.

The first house in what became the Haight-Ashbury was built in 1870 by F.W.M. Lange, a German immigrant. It stood on a nine-acre dairy farm near Cole and Grattan Streets. Small ranches with a few cows or vegetable patches dotted the valley by the late 1870s.

The area went from ranches to city blocks when public transit reached out west toward Golden Gate Park. Fortunes were quickly made as the land changed hands—and use. The Haight Street cable-car line that ran from Market Street to Stanyan was owned by "The

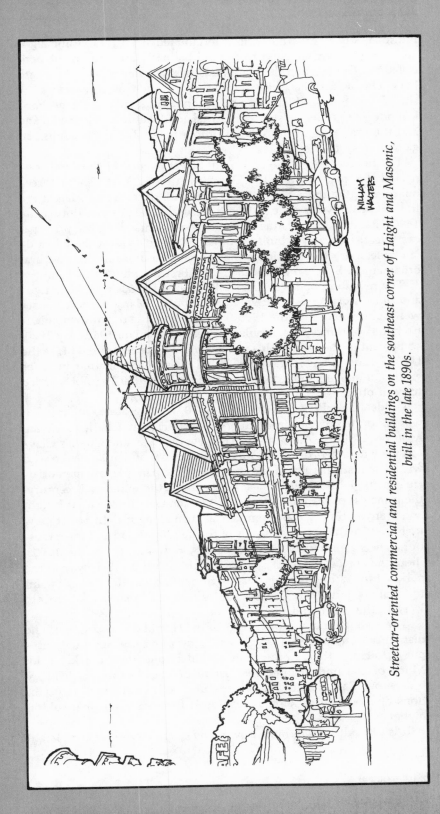

Streetcar-oriented commercial and residential buildings on the southeast corner of Haight and Masonic, built in the late 1890s.

Railroad," the Southern Pacific. It terminated at a turntable at Haight and Stanyan Streets, close to the old ballpark, an amusement park called the Chutes, and the main pedestrian entrance to Golden Gate Park. The block of Haight between Clayton and Cole Streets was the site of the Chutes, which had a menagerie, vaudeville, and a mechanical ride like a roller coaster that carried gondolas up an inclined plane and then released them to splash into a pond. Ten cents admission gained entry to the Chutes.

The first cable-car line up Haight Street opened in 1883 and connected this plateau with the Downtown to the east. About three-quarters of the more than 1,000 Victorian houses in the Haight are in the Queen Anne style, the architectural style popular during the 1890s. Most of the existing flats and apartments along the principal east-west streets were built between 1900 and 1915 in the Edwardian style, a dry Neoclassicism that provided a unifying architectural ornament in San Francisco during the first decade of this century.

The neighborhood was first built up in the 1880s with large two- and three-story, one- and two-family houses. Many of these houses were subdivided after the 1906 fire destroyed the downtown neighborhoods or during the population peak of the late 1940s. By 1970, 48 percent of the households in the Haight were composed of, as the U.S. Census put it, "unrelated individuals"—a term that includes groups of single people and couples living together but not married to each other.

Golden Gate Park was begun in 1870, when a State Commission was appointed by Governor Henry Huntly Haight. Charles Stanyan, Monroe Ashbury, A.I. Schrader, R. Beverly Cole, and Charles Clayton were members of the Board of Supervisors of San Francisco who were also instrumental in the creation of the park. All are memorialized in the local street names. Throughout the nineteenth century, the principal pedestrian entrance to Golden Gate Park was at Haight and Stanyan Streets. The commercial strip along Haight Street grew up to service the everyday needs of the neighborhood and the recreational needs of visitors to the park. On weekends in the 1890s, thousands of people passed down Haight Street on their way to the park. At the terminus of the Haight Street line was the transfer point for the Park and Ocean Railroad, a steam railroad that ran out Lincoln Way to the ocean and the Cliff House.

The eastern, or downtown, edge of the Haight developed first. The district built up in a spotty way with clumps of, say, six row houses put up at one time by carpenter-builders and then quickly sold. Much of the undeveloped real estate in the Haight was held by prosperous San Franciscans for speculative investment. Large sections of blocks were kept undeveloped for years and then sold at higher prices later.

It is difficult to determine how many of the houses in the Haight were originally owned by single family owner-occupiers, and for how long. Evidence indicates that much of the area was always held by absentee landlords. This was a pattern rooted in the original patterns of land ownership, subdivision, and relatively large-scale development. Many of the original buildings were two-family houses; thus at least half of the population were renters from the start. We know that by 1939, about two generations after the start of development, only 10 percent of the houses in the entire Haight were still single-family dwellings. As the city and region grew, the Haight changed from an upper-middle-class suburban fringe in the 1880s to a working-class inner-city district by 1930.

The high point of the streetcar system in this part of the city was reached in 1912 when the Haight Street line increased its scheduling from thirty cars per hour—one every two minutes—to forty-one cars per hour. The early streetcars were as colorful as they were convenient; the Haight Street line was painted a vivid red, the Oak Street line was green, and the Ellis Street cars were deep blue.

By 1924 the Haight was a faded but comfortable neighborhood. One resident wrote that "There is a comfortable maturity about the compact little city that San Francisco knows as Haight-Ashbury. Not the maturity that is suspicious of down-at-the-heel old age, but a nice upholstered, fuchsia garden sort of grown-up-ness, just weathered enough to be nice, and new enough to be looking ahead to the future instead of sighing futilely over the past."

Lowell High School, the finest one in the city, was nearby at Masonic and Hayes. In 1928, when the Sunset Tunnel opened (the tunnel runs under Buena Vista Park), development in San Francisco spread west of Twin Peaks. The Haight-Ashbury, which had been a fashionable neighborhood up until that point, began to lose its appeal.

In the 1930s, during the Depression, maintenance levels in the Haight fell drastically. Many fine houses were converted into rooming houses owned by landlords who had moved to the western fringes of the city or to the suburbs. The resident population, never particularly stable, began to change. As is typical of development in the Bay Area, it was the flatlands (along the park Panhandle) that decayed most rapidly. The slopes held their own longer (and later recovered faster in the 1970s). The Works Progress Administration made a real-property survey in 1939 and found that between Waller and Oak Streets 15 percent of the buildings were substandard.

San Francisco saw its maximum population in the late 1940s. Streetcar usage also reached its peak during those years, but without adequate maintenance and continued investment the overburdened system quickly deteriorated. The number of buildings in the Haight remained stable but the number of living units increased dramatically. In 1919, there were 4,715 living units in the Haight. By 1940 there were 8,040. By 1950 there were 8,770: an overall increase of 85 percent.

Cities are like pools of water; a stone thrown in one spot causes changes to ripple out to other areas. In the 1960s, when the city Redevelopment Agency began the wholesale demolition of the adjoining Western Addition, the Haight began to change dramatically. An indication of the changes is the percentage of the black population between Oak and Waller and Stanyan and Baker. In 1950 it was 3 percent; in 1960, 17 percent; and in 1970, 50 percent. The existing population, not itself in any way necessarily long rooted in the district, began to drift away. Rents in the Haight did not go up as much as in the rest of the city and the Haight became a relatively cheap place to live.

When rents in North Beach began to rise due to the booming tourist trade, the low rents prevailing in the Haight began to attract San Francisco's bohemians, then known as beats, to the Haight-Ashbury. Students from San Francisco State University also settled in. It was to prove the beginning of accelerated change in the Haight-Ashbury and eventual world fame for the "fuchsia garden comfort" of the Haight.

From 1967 to 1969 these few blocks became the mecca for the hippie movement. During the "summer of love" in 1967 some 200,-000 young people flooded this foggy, park-encircled neighborhood temporarily abandoned by the middle class. This sudden high was immediately followed by a sudden crash. By 1970 the area was nicknamed "the Hate" or the "Haight-Ashcan." But the downturn was very brief. The social, racial, and cultural heterogeneity of the area became an irresistible magnet for an educated, energetic, determinedly nonconformist population. Now the Haight is less flamboyant, much more private, but still an unquenchably utopian village lodged within the larger city. About half the residents are married and about half unmarried. Professionals account for about one-quarter of the population, half are classed as skilled, and another quarter are unskilled laborers. According to the 1970 census (which especially here is not to be taken at face value), 45 percent of the adult working force earned $4,000 to $10,000, 21 percent earned $10,000 to $15,000, and 21 percent earned less than $4,000. Running against these modest incomes are the increasingly high prices currently being paid for both commercial and residential real estate in the area. Rents are rising faster than incomes, and the result is a constant turnover in the population, with the richer steadily replacing the poor.

But even those with higher incomes move here because they value the cultural uniqueness of the Haight. The upper-middle-class and professional people buying houses and renovating in the Haight can be just as hip as the hippies. One sure measure of the recent changes in the Haight is its taverns. By 1979 gay bars outnumbered straight ones, five to three. The value of real estate has soared, and, most important, owner-occupancy has increased from 14 percent to 54 percent between 1970 and 1977. This is the single most important long-term change in the history of the neighborhood since its development.

THE TOUR

1 **1100 Block of Haight Street**

• 1080 Haight Street
• Queen Anne, Fred P. Rabin, 1896

• 1081 Haight/1–3 Buena Vista East
• Flatiron Queen Anne, John J. Clark, 1894

• 1128 Haight Street
• Queen Anne, 1891

• 1132–36 Haight Street
• Flats, c. 1915

Begin at the intersection of Haight and Baker Streets. On the northeast corner is 1080 Haight Street, a large three-story Queen Anne house built in 1896 and designed by Fred P. Rabin, a German-born architect. The original owner was Dr. John C. Spencer, a local philanthropist. The dining room had an aquarium built into the wall. The spacious attic was used by the Spencer children as a tennis court. The front porch is distinguished by Richardsonian Romanesque arches.

The flatiron building with the corner tower to the south is another Queen Anne, 1081 Haight/1–3 Buena Vista East.

This intersection, with its four turrets to the east, epitomizes the Queen Anne style as it evolved in the Haight. The corner towers are especially effective at the top of a hill, as here; this crest defines the eastern edge of the Haight, and the cluster of towers serves as a gateway to the neighborhood. The service station's open corner epitomizes the invasion of this streetcar environment by the automobile.

The 1100 block of Haight Street, facing the park, was a very desirable block when it was first developed. About half the original houses remain, some grievously altered and others more or less intact. Two Queen Anne houses remain to the west of the service station. Number 1128 Haight, with a corner turret and intricate shingle work between the first and second floors, is typical of the first wave of housebuilding in the area and was built in 1891 for George Pringle. Between the two Queen Annes is 1132–36 Haight, a three-story Edwardian apartment house with semicircular bay windows built early in this century.

2 Buena Vista Park
• Reserved, 1868; landscaped by John McLaren, c. 1910

Cross Haight Street and approach the stairs to Buena Vista Park. From here, look up Buena Vista East, an irregular street once known as Hill Park Drive, which produced strange-shaped lots that attracted interestingly sited houses. Climb the stairs and take the branch to the right.

From the top of the stairs you can look to the northeast out over the western districts of San Francisco. In the distance to the left is Alta Plaza, a large, terraced park, and beyond it is the summit of Angel Island. To the right of Angel Island and Alta Plaza are the green plumes of Lafayette Park's eucalyptus trees rising above the white apartment buildings of eastern Pacific Heights. Farther to the right are the downtown high-rises and beyond them the Contra Costa hills across the bay.

View of St. Ignatius Church
• Renaissance Revival, Charles J.I. Devlin, 1929

Continue up the path to the right. Halfway up is a spectacular view to the northwest. The large church to the left is St. Ignatius, a Renaissance Revival Jesuit church built in 1929 on the campus of the University of San Francisco.

View of Lone Mountain College
• Collegiate Gothic, H.A. Minton, 1932

To the right of the church is the square tower of Lone Mountain College, designed by H.A. Minton in 1932. On the far horizon is Mt. Tamalpais. Between the mountain and ourselves rise the twin red piers of the Golden Gate Bridge. From here can be seen the close weaving of green parks and dense white housing so characteristic of San Francisco's cityscape.

At the intersection, take the high path to the right. Note the low stone walls that border the path and the marble-paved gutter between the path and the wall. The marble was salvaged from the ruined front steps of the old city, and a few headstones, after the earthquake of 1906.

Continue to the children's playground. Here there are places to sit and look out over the neighborhood. This complex, beautifully fitting playground was a gift of the Land and Water Conservation Fund in 1975. From here there is a good view of the Golden Gate Park Panhandle, the strip of great eucalyptus trees to the north, and Marin and Mt. Tamalpais in the distance.

View of Third Church of Christ, Scientist
· Tuscan Revival, Edgar A. Matthews, 1918

Below, on Haight Street, is the Third Church of Christ, Scientist, a fine Tuscan Revival building with warm colored brickwork on its exterior and Romanesque terra-cotta ornamentation.

The valley below, once known as Pope Valley, was part of a land grant given to José de Jesús Noe in 1845. Noe was the *alcalde,* or mayor, of the village of Yerba Buena and took his pay in land rather than money. His was one of the earliest Mexican land grants on the San Francisco peninsula.

Buena Vista Park, thirty-six forested acres with a peak 569 feet above sea level, is one of the oldest parks in San Francisco, dating as a public reserve from 1868. It was originally known as Hill Park and is now wooded with pine, acacia, cypress, and live oak. Although there were some groves of native oaks in spots, extensive tree planting by John McLaren in the early twentieth century accounts for most of the park's dense, seemingly primeval greenery.

In the 1890s, when the summit of the park was still unforested, Buena Vista Park did, indeed, have a good view. De Witt's guide of 1888 noted, "A grand view of the entire city, from the Cliff House round the City front [the Embarcadero] to Hunter's Point, can be had. The Farallones and Point Reyes can also be discerned as can Mt. Tamalpais and Mt. Diablo."

The park was partially forested by schoolchildren on Arbor Day, a holiday actively observed on this originally treeless peninsula. The seedlings were provided by Adolph Sutro, an engineer who made his fortune by designing the water-drainage system for the Nevada silver mines. He invested most of his money in San Francisco real estate and was avidly interested in forestation. He sentimentally called his trees the children of his old age. Other examples of Sutro's forestation are Yerba Buena Island (now bisected by the Bay Bridge tunnel), and Mt. Parnassus, now known as Mt. Sutro. It is almost impossible to visualize just how bleak the city was before such extensive forestation and landscaping. Buena Vista Park was made, as the city parks commissioners described it in 1917, a "deep tangled wildwood."

Early San Francisco, the area to the east of Van Ness Avenue, was laid out in the 1840s, to maximize "useful"—that is, buildable—land. Very few parks were provided in the old part of the city. Only later did people begin to realize that an adequate city plan demanded more than just the maximum number of building plots. Provision had to be made to preserve, or rather enhance, pockets of nature in the man-made environment.

When the western fringe of the city was laid out in the 1850s, provisions were made for well-placed parks to relieve the oppression of an uninterruptedly built-up city. The area west of Van Ness and east of Divisadero eventually acquired many spacious hilltop parks.

On the far western edge of San Francisco the finest of all the parks was created in the 1870s, Golden Gate Park, which reaches from the old city to the Pacific. The Haight-Ashbury is fortunate to be virtually surrounded by fine late-nineteenth-century parks, parks that only now, after a century of continuous care, are at their peak.

3 Buena Vista Avenue West

Leave the park and walk to Buena Vista Avenue West. In the middle distance is Kezar Stadium, built in 1925 on the edge of Golden Gate Park on the site of the park's original nursery. To the right is a three-story shingled building reminiscent of the kind of housing built in Presidio Heights in the early twentieth century and rare in this part of the city.

Walk up the sidewalk to the left alongside the park. Across the street at 815 Buena Vista Avenue West is the St. Francis Residence, an ordinary but appropriately scaled and sited building with plantings typical of San Francisco. Number 767 Buena Vista Avenue West is a hideous four-story apartment building representative of modern blight.

Floyd Spreckels Mansion
· 737 Buena Vista Avenue West
· Queen Anne–Colonial Revival, Edward J. Vogel, 1898

Number 737 Buena Vista Avenue West, a large Queen Anne with Colonial Revival details, is one of the grandest houses on Ashbury Heights; it was built in 1898 for Floyd Spreckels. The central pediment is original; the two dormer windows are later additions. The house sports delicately scaled Queen Anne details—garlands, swags, and ribbons below the cornice, fanlights over the windows, and a semicircular porch framed by classical columns. Small cherub heads emerge from the capitals of the columns. The large pair of gates to the right came from the Hills brothers' estate. The exotic spiky plants in the yard are typical of late-nineteenth-century landscaping. The top floor was, at various times, the studio of Jack London and of Ambrose Bierce.

Descend the staircase and walk to the intersection of Buena Vista Avenue West and Frederick Street. The corner house (639 Buena Vista West), a simple two-story classic stucco building with an elegant entrance, exhibits the refinement of Baroque Revival architecture in San Francisco between 1915 and the late 1920s. It is a competent Renaissance-inspired design.

Continue up Buena Vista Avenue West. The next house, Number 635, is also classically simple and elegant. Number 615 is a large two-story house with a Tudor-style central gable and a shingled exterior. Note the generous windows facing the park.

601 Buena Vista Avenue West
• Queen Anne, William Armitage, 1895

Number 601 is a good example of the Queen Anne style in an upper-middle-class house. The band of ornament above the second floor is scratchwork, a kind of plaster-and-burlap composition that replaced carved wood in the 1890s.

Cross Java Street. Look down its one-block length to the view of the eucalyptus forests blanketing Mt. Sutro in the distance. An observer of the late 1890s wrote, "No tree but the eucalyptus seems to thrive in this climate, as the soil is of a sandy nature and entirely unfit, and the strong winds from the ocean make it almost impossible to raise anything else." Java Street is typical of the *ad hoc* street pattern in the hillier central section of San Francisco.

Number 595–97 Buena Vista Avenue West, on the southeast corner of Java, is a modern building on a corner site typical of contemporary Bay Area construction and design. It uses simple forms and large windows that take advantage of the view of the park across the street.

555 Buena Vista Avenue West
• Concrete apartment house, "Spanish" style, c. 1930

Number 555 Buena Vista Avenue West, a 1930s building with an emphatic neo-Churrigueresque entrance, is typical of the large apartment houses built in San Francisco in those years. It is a reinforced-concrete structure with industrial sash windows. The entryway and the fire escape that rises above it give the building a dramatic presence. The original lobby is intact and mildly reminiscent of the movie-palace architecture of the period.

4 Java Street to Masonic Avenue

Return to Java Street, walk through to Masonic, and turn right. The house on the corner, 1482 Masonic, a large shingled house, has a third floor that projects beyond the floors below in medieval style. Notice its welcoming entryway. The house has hints of Mission Revival forms incorporated into it and has been extended on the Java Street side. This was, and remains, one of the wealthiest parts of the Haight-Ashbury; income and topography drop from here.

1450 Masonic Avenue
• Eastlake–Queen Anne, A. J. Barnett, 1891

Walk down Masonic Avenue. Notice the prevalence of early-twentieth-century Tudor Revival buildings along this stretch. Number 1450 Masonic is a large Eastlake–Queen Anne with a curious turret.

It has modern stained-glass windows inserted at the second floor. Strange copperwork has replaced the plaster scratchwork at the cornice level, below the turret, and on the front porch.

Number 1421 Masonic across the street has a boxy three-story stucco front. But behind this early-twentieth-century addition is an 1890s shingled Queen Anne house with a bell-shaped turret.

Casa Madrona Apartments
• Frederick Street
• Mission, 1920s

Walk downhill to the corner of Frederick and Masonic. To the left, in the middle of the block, are two large apartment houses. The white stucco building with the red-tile roof is the Casa Madrona, a Mission-style apartment complex built around a central court in the 1920s. California in the twenties! The courtyard shelters a large clump of banana trees. The entrances to the right and left of the court present silhouette copies of Mission campaniles complete with fake mission bells. The "bells" mask lights.

130 Frederick Street
• Apartments, "Spanish" style, 1930s

The large terra-cotta-colored three-story cement and stucco apartment building at 130 Frederick Street is notable for its industrial sash windows and its pasted-on neo-Churrigueresque ornamentation. This was a combination particularly popular for public schools in the 1930s.

Notice the progression of architectural styles as you walk down Masonic Avenue. At the corner of Masonic and Java, we saw several Tudor-style and shingled buildings of the early twentieth century. In the 1300 block we see a good row of Stick-style buildings. Farther down the block are several Queen Anne houses from the early 1880s.

Number 1349 Masonic is the Villa Satori. This two-story Queen Anne, with its multicolor paint scheme and magical Indian designs, is the home of one of the oldest communes in the Haight.

1322–42 Masonic Avenue
• Row of six Stick-Eastlakes, c. 1885

Across the street are six Stick-Eastlake row houses, all identical in form but each painted in an expressive, if eccentric, color scheme. Stick-style buildings are characterized by wooden ornaments, "sticks," which rise from the ground level straight to the cornice. They were built about 1885.

Today's responses to these houses are as warm as one imagines those of the original occupants were. But in the 1920s, when they were in their middle age, they seemed dowdy and sad. They had neither the freshness of youth nor the mellowness of age. One writer who lived in Ashbury Heights described her block in the 1920s: "[The houses] sit there with their poker faces like close-mouthed Yankees refusing to divulge any secrets." The intersection of Waller and Masonic has good examples of Queen Anne row houses.

1214–56 Masonic Avenue
· Row of eight Queen Anne tower houses, Cranston and Keenan
· 1897

On the east side of the 1200 block is a fine cluster of eight Queen Anne houses with gables and towers. Most are intact, but some have lost their ornament.

The west side of the 1200 block of Masonic, facing the Queen Anne row, has an uninterrupted row of Edwardian flats and apartments built in the early 1900s. Notice that the street widens at this intersection as it meshes with the older grid of the flatlands.

1200 Masonic Avenue (corner of Haight)
· Shops and apartments, Martens and Coffey, 1896

Continue down Masonic Avenue to the corner of Haight. On the southeast corner, 1200 Masonic, is a Queen Anne commercial and residential building built for a Mrs. Bogart, a cashier at the *San Francisco Examiner.* A dentist occupied the second-story corner bay. On the northeast corner is another Edwardian apartment and commercial building, originally a corner drugstore, which during the hippie era was the Drogstore, a café and hangout later called Magnolia Thunderpussy's. It was one of the last survivors from "flower power" days. It is part of an uninterrupted row of three-story Edwardian apartment buildings with shops on the street level. They are part of a continuous ribbon of such buildings that sprang up along the east-to-west streetcar lines.

5 Haight Street to the Panhandle

The history of this row of restaurants, shops, and bars has had three phases. In the late nineteenth century and early twentieth, when the strip served as the gateway to Golden Gate Park, an amusement park, the ball grounds, and the transfer point to the Ocean Railway, the strip served both local residents and those who came from all over the city for recreation.

With the ascendancy of the automobile, areas far beyond the city limits developed as the city dwellers' playgrounds. The car also broke the monopoly of the Haight and Stanyan entrance to the park and made all the peripheral entrances equally accessible. The Haight

Street strip became a neighborhood shopping area exclusively.

Today, Haight Street has increasingly become a street with city-wide appeal. Shops that have opened since 1975 have often aimed at citywide, but not yet regional, clienteles. Neighborhood services such as barber shops, launderettes, and small grocery stores are being replaced with shops selling expensive, hand-made furniture, art, or gourmet foods. Opponents of the trend call it the "Union Streetization" of the Haight. Handbills, political grafitti, and wall posters seem to be the local cottage industry. Any boarded-up shopfront or construction boarding instantly accumulates a tattered collage of layers of posters and messages. Visitors are advised not to stand too long at street corners lest they be mistaken for a lamppost and have a poster attached to them.

Haight-Ashbury Children's Center
• 1101 Masonic Avenue
• Neoclassical, 1906

Cross Haight Street and continue down Masonic. Number 1101 Masonic is the Haight-Ashbury's Children's Center. This wooden, Neoclassical building was constructed in 1906 as a single-family house. It is now a nursery school for children from low-income families. About half of the schoolchildren in the Haight have only one parent at home.

1482–84 Page Street
• Queen Anne, Newsom and Meyer, 1899

Number 1482–84 Page Street, at the northeast corner of Page and Masonic, is a large two-family Queen Anne–style house. Before the earthquake it was rented to Isaac Magnin, the owner of a small dry-goods business downtown, the seed of today's famous clothing store.

To the right are two buildings by the same architects, 1480 and 1478 Page Street, mirror images of each other. They were built in 1899 for Mrs. L. Gassner. Her husband owned a plumbing and gasfitting business. They mix elegant Georgian ornament with shingle exteriors. Other than the insertion of a garage under 1480, the differences between these two buildings are quite subtle. Compare their windows, dormers, front doors, and ornamentation and discover the many differences between these deceptive "twins."

St. Agnes Rectory/originally St. Agnes Church
• 1025 Masonic Avenue
• Welch and Carey, 1907

Number 1025 Masonic, an elegant wooden box with a façade modeled after a Greek temple, was originally St. Agnes Church. It was converted into the church rectory when the larger church was built next door. Four wooden pilasters rise from the first to second story; a triangular pediment capping the composition betrays its conception as a temple. Notice the prevalence of Neoclassical ornamentation in this vicinity.

6 Golden Gate Park Panhandle
· Landscaped in 1870s by William Hammond Hall

Continue down the hill and enter the Panhandle. Oak Street, now a one-way street, was originally the route of another streetcar line. The Panhandle is a good place to rest and reflect on the recent history of the Haight. This strip—one block by eight, a total of 23.4 acres—adjoins the main part of Golden Gate Park and was the first part to be improved. It was originally enclosed by a fence that was locked at 9:00 P.M. It shelters the park's oldest trees and was laid out with a curving carriage drive that became the most fashionable gathering place for San Francisco's high society. On Sundays in the 1870s, glistening, lacquered carriages and high-spirited teams thronged the Panhandle.

Though the Panhandle itself received much attention, the streets around it did not. In 1888 the Panhandle Improvement Club, later the Panhandle and Ashbury Heights Improvement Club, was formed. Its president, Dr. C.C. Salfield, had a gift for attracting attention to his neighborhood's needs. To get the city to provide streetlights, he invited all the supervisors to an elaborate dinner, "setting forth the very best in food and moisture." He instructed the hackmen who transported his guests to hit every chuckhole and rut on the way. Within a few weeks forty streetlights were placed in the neighborhood. To call attention to the poorly paved streets, which got such heavy traffic going to the park, Dr. Salfield took advantage of a flooded sewer, which he helped along with a board or two, to launch a rowboat on Oak Street. He had himself photographed rowing across Oak Street. The streets were improved.

After the earthquake in 1906, the Panhandle became the neighborhood refuge. Eleven babies were born here that first night! Eventually the park housed thirty thousand refugees, first in tents and later in wood cottages. A post office was opened in the park when it became an instant city.

In 1951 the Department of Highways of the State of California planned to use the Panhandle as the convenient site for part of a freeway. This outrageous plan sparked the famous "Freeway Revolt" in San Francisco, the first time any American city stopped the completion of a freeway network through its mature districts. When the Trafficways plan was announced in 1951, a botanical survey was made of the Panhandle. Over three hundred different kinds of plants were found to grow here.

McKinley Monument
· Robert Ingersoll Aitkin, 1904

At the head of the Panhandle, on Baker Street between Oak and Fell Streets, is a monument to the assassinated William McKinley, the twenty-fifth president of the United States. The monument, consists of a beautiful fifteen-foot-high bronze female figure, emblematic of the Republic, extending, as is her way, a palm leaf in one hand and a sword in the other. She stands atop a ten-foot high granite base with a bas-relief of McKinley. The monument was built in 1904 with money raised by popular subscription. It and the Victory monument in Union Square are the prime examples of Beaux-Arts commemorative art in San Francisco. It stares in disbelief at the offices of the Department of Motor Vehicles across Baker Street.

By the early 1960s, the Haight had faded. The white middle class was moving away or aging. Blacks were moving in from the Western Addition as redevelopment demolished whole blocks. Students at San Francisco State also discovered the area. Rents were low; $175 a month would rent the two bottom floors of a Victorian townhouse with elaborate mantels and fireplaces and painted-over plaster ornamentation.

A decor of sensual indulgence blossomed. Patterned Indian cotton bedspreads hung from high Victorian ceilings turned what had been the formal parlors of the respectable bourgeoisie into instant, exotic pleasure palaces. Joss sticks perfumed the air and masked the heady fragrance of another kind of smoke. Eclectic junk-shop kitsch, Victorian clutter revisited, became the local style. Lithographs of Hindu icons—dancing elephants with many heads—served as signs of some half-perceived confusion.

Outside were the mature parks. As one resident who arrived in the mid-1960s remembered it: "The proximity of nature in Golden Gate Park added a magical, almost cosmic quality to life in the neighborhood." Memories of those far-off early days were recently published in San Francisco:

> The actual composition of the Haight was diverse. Among the things that brought people were traditional bohemian impulses of artistic self-assertion and the romantic search for mystery and authentic experience; the search for nonviolent social forms; curiosity about the meaning of psychedelics; the lure of the drug marketplace, for both customer and dealer; rejection

of a comfortable social upbringing; loneliness and rejection in other communities; uncertainty about goals; desire to evangelize, organize or bust the people already in the Haight; and the sheer momentum of the phenomenon.

Lives became theatrical quick-changes. Costumes of old lace, velvet, sewn denim, jewelry, and body painting created a tribal garb; hippie beads became a social badge. The cold cement sidewalks and cool green parks became outdoor stages for the enactment of fantasies both private and collective. Beautiful girls with long flowing hair danced down Haight Street like ethereal Isadora Duncans. People passed out flowers on the streetcars. A permanent state of carnival seemed to have arrived. Everyone who saw it preserves at least one extraordinary image from those halcyon days.

Ken Kesey staged a Trips Festival at Longshoreman's Hall. Thousands came. The word "hippie" emerged. A Human Be-In, peaceful and massive, happened in January, 1967, in Golden Gate Park.

In 1967 *Time* magazine announced that the Haight had become "the vibrant epicenter of America's hippie movement." Publicity turned the attention of America's internal exiles to this beautiful Victorian neighborhood with the foggy weather. Change accelerated. The Haight was on its way to being burnt out by klieg lights, journalism, and heroin.

In the spring of 1967, the Gray Line began taking tourists in sealed coaches on what was advertised as the "Hippie Hop: the only foreign tour within the continental limits of the United States." Hippies trotted alongside the buses—which were crawling their way through the traffic jam—holding mirrors up to the bus windows. Others dropped by, including British historian Arnold Toynbee and Beatle George Harrison.

By 1967 the scene had already spread out. Individuals and groups moved on to rural communes, spaced suburbs, in Northern California. The Haight attracted to itself all the alienated. Toward the end of the hippie era, Haight Street degenerated and became Skid Row. Derelicts both young and old preyed on one another. About two-thirds of the merchants on Haight, old and hip, closed up by 1971. The streets turned cold and vicious. What began with grass, joss sticks, acid, costumes, and flutes culminated in knifings, speed, smack, and plywood nailed over shopfronts. Multiple drug abusers and ambulatory schizophrenics once abounded; few are to be seen today. A suspicious flood of cheap heroin wiped out the Haight in 1970–71.

After the deluge, all was quiet. Allen Ginsberg, Timothy Leary, and Ken Kesey stayed away. A curious cultural efflorescence began in the beat-up neighborhood. Out of the ashes, phoenixlike as befits this city, the Haight has reemerged as a vital neighborhood in the 1970s. Today the Haight is alive with all kinds of shops and spaces.

The old Victorian houses are being given fresh coats of bright (often very bright) paint. A new wave of prosperity has swept the Haight.

A recent comment on the Haight noted, "What's missing, of course, is the mystique of the 'Hashbury,' the sense that the neighborhood is surfing the crest of some historical wave. But the Haight has a new mystique . . . that it's gone through hell and pulled itself out. A chastened mystique, but still, like the old one, one of hope."

Walk two blocks west of Masonic, down the center of the Panhandle, to Clayton Street. Number 1539 Oak Street is a Neoclassically ornamented stucco-fronted former firehouse. It once housed those bizarre rubber-tired converted cable cars that delight conventioneers and disconcert San Franciscans.

7 400 Clayton Street
· Ernest Coxhead, 1895

Leave the Panhandle, cross Oak Street and go up Clayton Street. On the left is 400 Clayton Street, the only Ernest Coxhead–designed house in this part of San Francisco. It was built in 1895 for $7,261. Coxhead often used Classical elements in a strange way. The parts are always correct but their scale or placement is often exaggerated or unexpected. In this house, a highly regular composition, the entrance is not in the center where one might expect it, but off to the side. And over the door is a triangular pediment and a garlanded oval window, but notice how illogically the window breaks into the pediment.

409–11 Clayton Street
· Row of six Queen Anne houses, Soule and Hoadley, 1893

Across the street is a row of six Queen Anne buildings constructed in 1893 as two-family houses. It is one of the best intact rows in this part of the Haight. Notice the slot between 407 and 405. This was devised as a way to get light and air into the middle of the buildings. Number 409 is particularly well-preserved, with all its scratchwork intact. This is 409 House, part of the Haight-Ashbury Free Clinic, which attempts to cope with the health needs of the area. It was set up with reading and meditation rooms on the first floor, a psychiatric facility on the second floor, and the publication office of *The Journal of Psychedelic Drugs* in the attic.

414 Clayton Street
· Eastlake cottage, 1880s

Number 414 is an early one-story Eastlake building. Almost all of the houses built here were of two or three stories; by 1885 the land was too costly for anything else. A few of the earliest houses, however, were one-story cottages. Number 414's neighbor to the left was probably identical before its "improvement."

Farther up the block, on the northwest corner of Page and Clayton Streets, is a particularly offensive thirteen-unit apartment house with open garages on the ground floor. This one building destroys the continuity of the entire block. It is a good example of the banality of much contemporary building and the comparative richness of nineteenth-century architecture.

At Haight Street the predominant building type changes from houses to apartment buildings with shops on the ground floor. At the intersection of Clayton and Haight Streets, parks and open spaces are visible in all four directions. Parks terminate the vistas down nearly every street in the Haight.

8 1600–14 Haight Street
· Commercial-residential buildings, Peterson James Company, 1911

The large three-story corner building at 1600–14 Haight may have originally been a hotel. Shops fill the Haight Street frontage. The apartments are entered from Clayton Street.

Old Superba Theater
· 1660 Haight Street
· Beaux-Arts, 1910

Turn right on Haight Street. Number 1660 Haight Street was originally the Superba Theater, built in 1910. Its richly molded Beaux-Arts façade is a welcome ornament to the street.

Continue west on Haight Street. Across Belvedere Street, on the southwest corner, is the United California Bank, a handsome, one-story Neoclassical structure. Up Belvedere is an uninterrupted row of Edwardian apartment houses.

Number 1677–81 Haight Street is a three-story building with shops on the ground floor and flats above, designed by James F. Dunn and built in 1904. Its bow front, French windows, and Baroque decoration strive to recall Parisian buildings. There are only a handful of such "Modern French" buildings in San Francisco.

Continue up Haight Street. At the corner of Haight and Cole Streets was the old Haight Theater, a focal point for much of the artistic ferment in the Haight during the hippie era. At that time it was used for a multiplicity of events, and laconically renamed the Straight Theater.

Old Masonic Lodge
· 1748 Haight Street
· c. 1914

At 1748 Haight is a large three-story frame commercial building with shops on the ground floor and a large meeting hall upstairs, which housed the Park (Masonic) Lodge No. 449, organized in 1914. At the turn of the century this block was the site of the Chutes amusement park. The city's neighborhood Masonic lodges had their greatest membership right before the crash in 1929. A second peak in membership was achieved in the World War II era, but in the 1950s an irreversible decline set in and the Masons' Park Lodge gave up its hall. Today the cavernous space has been reborn as a gay disco, thus neatly framing the neighborhood's social history.

The view south from Haight Street, up Cole Street toward Mt. Sutro, shows Edwardian apartment houses close to Haight Street, Queen Anne houses two blocks up, and, in the distance, modern box-shaped buildings scattered across the heights.

9 510–12 Shrader Street
· Eastlake cottage, 1891

Continue up Haight Street to Shrader Street and turn right. Here the neighborhood begins to disintegrate; parking lots and brutalized houses scar this part of the Haight. Tucked between two larger buildings is 510–512 Shrader Street, a beautiful 1891 Eastlake cottage on a raised basement.

1901 Page Street
· Colonial Revival, Edward J. Vogel, 1896

Directly across the street is the side wall of 1901 Page Street. This is a mixed Queen Anne and Colonial Revival house. Notice the curious placement of the porthole-shaped windows; while nearly every aspect of the building is rigidly symmetrical, there are only three of these windows where one might expect four. The upper right-hand window frame has a strange little rectangular window stuck right up through it. Though the design of the wall is formal and rigidly calculated, expediency intruded in typical San Francisco fashion. This house was once the home of author Kathleen Thompson Norris. Later a workshop was set up here to embroider church vestments and altar cloths. Unlike most of the houses in the Haight-Ashbury, it is set off by front and side yards and still boasts its original iron fence.

1890 Page Street
· Queen Anne, Samuel Newsom, 1889

On the northeast corner of Page and Shrader is 1890 Page Street, a three-story Queen Anne with extensive and intricate shingle work and swallow's-nest stucco work, designed by Samuel Newsom (an important early California architect), and constructed by an Irish-born master carpenter, L.C. Sweeny, in 1889. Notice the beautiful ornamentation between the second and third stories.

1900–02 Page Street
· Eastlake–Queen Anne, 1890s

On the northwest corner is 1900–02 Page Street, a very large, three-story Eastlake–Queen Anne building with a great variety of window shapes.

1922 and 1928 Page Street
· Queen Anne, W. H. Lillie, 1892

Turn left on Page Street and walk west toward Golden Gate Park. At 1922 and 1928 Page Street are two small Queen Anne cottages on raised basements.

10 Golden Gate Park

As Golden Gate Park flowered, the commercial properties across the street increased dramatically in value. In the 1880s property along the park on Stanyan Street was selling for from $25 to $50 a front foot. Eleven years later, in 1891, the same property was selling for $125 to $250 a front foot. Across from the park on Stanyan were roadhouses, restaurants, coffeehouses and the ominously named Terminal Hotel. The supermarket and fast food franchise at the corner of Haight and Stanyan are near the former sites of the Haight Street Cable Car barns and the terminus of the Park and Ocean Railroad.

Alvord Lake
· 1894

In the small depression straight ahead is Alvord Lake, donated by park commissioner William Alvord in 1894. This small, cement-bottomed pond is sheltered from the winds by tall cypresses and clumps of coast live oak. In the 1890s the pond was described as "surrounded by artistically arrayed rocks, ferns, and pampas grass, which present a very romantic appearance. A fountain plays from its center, and under its sprays gambol rare specimens of swans."

Alvord Lake Bridge
• Reinforced concrete underpass, Ernest Ransome, 1889

Beyond the lake is Alvord Lake Bridge, a pedestrian underpass. This was the first reinforced-concrete bridge in the United States. Its revolutionary building material was disguised to look like stone; new building materials were often made to look like traditional ones in the nineteenth century. Underneath the bridge are fake stalactites to heighten its romantic effect. A plaque affixed to the "keystone" reads: "National Historic Civil Engineering Landmark: Alvord Lake Bridge." (While well-intentioned, the plaque defaces the bridge.) Golden Gate Park also once boasted an early metal pedestrian suspension bridge by John A. Roebling, the engineer of the Brooklyn Bridge.

11 Children's Playground
• 1886; redesigned, 1978, Michael Painter and Associates

Pass through the tunnel to the other side and walk to the Children's Playground, designed by William Hammond Hall and landscaped by John McLaren. The unenforced signs here read: "This area is a children's playground. Adults are not allowed unless accompanied by children." Pass through the playground to the festive carousel, alive with children and old-time waltz music. De Witt's guide in 1897 said, "A cup of tea and a light lunch can be had here. On the grounds are countless swings, and springboards, and a fine, old merry-go-round, with its ever-romping horses and chariots—of never-ceasing delight to the children. In addition, there are real little donkeys, upon which the children can ride, and little carts drawn by goats." The tired donkeys and goats are gone.

Sharon Children's House
• Richardsonian Romanesque, Percy and Hamilton, 1886

North of the carousel is the Sharon Children's House built with a $50,000 bequest left by William Sharon. It is a handsome two-story sandstone building in the Richardsonian Romanesque style, one of the only buildings of its type in San Francisco. Sharon was quite a ladies' man, and one newspaper wondered if the city could afford a house for all of Sharon's children. Walk around the building to its front. Though designed by Percy and Hamilton, a San Francisco firm, the building is a faithful echo of the fine public libraries that Henry Hobson Richardson scattered across New England in the 1880s. The semicircular Romanesque arches have an emphatic rhythm. The date, 1887, is carved into the pediment. The building is alive with fine stonecarving; there are even heads emerging from the capitals of the columns. The building suffered heavy damage in 1906 but was rebuilt within the year. In front of the Sharon Children's House is a spacious meadow and a low rise beyond. This rise was Hippie Hill, now just a pleasant grassy slope, but once the heart of the "Hashbury" that is no more. One can walk from here to McLaren Lodge to explore Golden Gate Park, or return to Haight Street and its restaurants. All the transit lines that run east (downtown) on Haight Street go to Market Street.

Tour 9

Golden Gate Park

A Man-made Eden

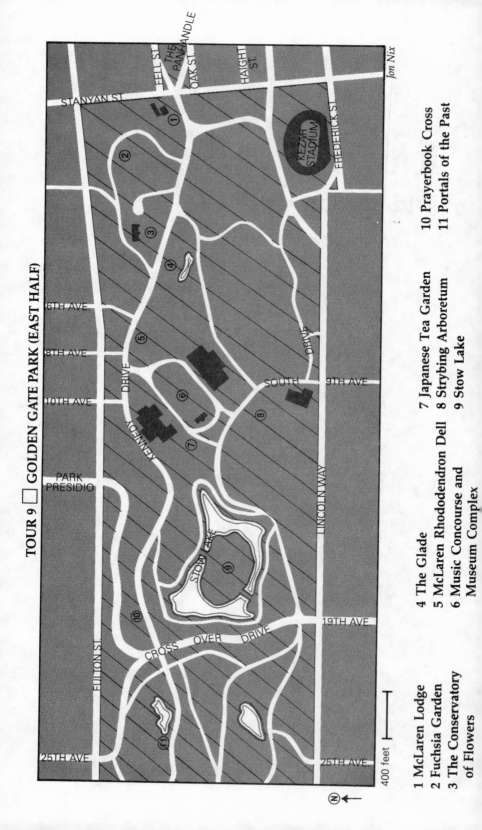

TOUR 9 ☐ GOLDEN GATE PARK (EAST HALF)

Jon Nix

1 McLaren Lodge
2 Fuchsia Garden
3 The Conservatory of Flowers
4 The Glade
5 McLaren Rhododendron Dell
6 Music Concourse and Museum Complex
7 Japanese Tea Garden
8 Strybing Arboretum
9 Stow Lake
10 Prayerbook Cross
11 Portals of the Past

400 feet

Ⓝ ←

STANYAN ST
FELL ST
THE PANHANDLE
OAK ST
HAIGHT ST
FREDERICK ST
KEZAR STADIUM
16TH AVE.
8TH AVE.
10TH AVE
KENNEDY DRIVE
PARK PRESIDIO
SOUTH DRIVE
9TH AVE.
LINCOLN WAY
STOW LAKE
CROSS OVER DRIVE
19TH AVE.
FULTON ST
25TH AVE.
25TH AVE.

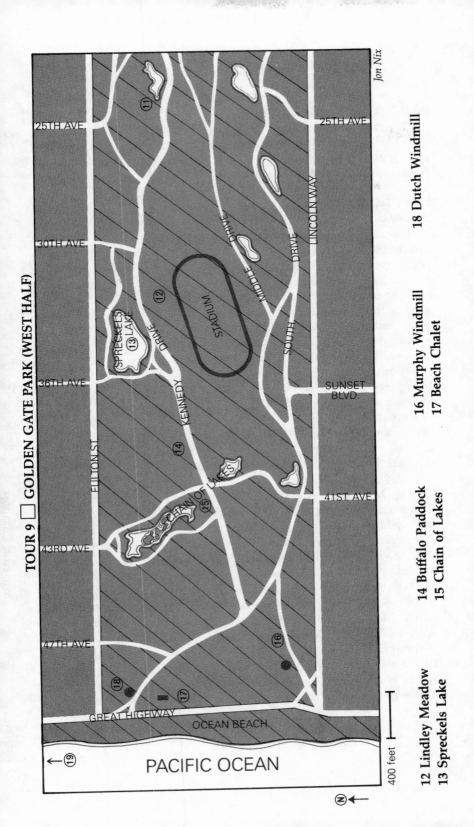

TOUR 9 ☐ GOLDEN GATE PARK (WEST HALF)

Jon Nix

12 Lindley Meadow
13 Spreckels Lake

14 Buffalo Paddock
15 Chain of Lakes

16 Murphy Windmill
17 Beach Chalet

18 Dutch Windmill

WHAT THIS WALK COVERS

This walk explores both the natural wonders and cultural landmarks of Golden Gate Park, beginning with McLaren Lodge and ending at the Ocean Beach or, if you choose the alternate route discussed at the end of the chapter, the Cliff House.

PRACTICALITIES

The best ways to see Golden Gate Park are: (1) on foot, walking slowly, (2) by bicycle, especially on Sundays when some roads are closed to automobiles, or (3) by car on a rainy day, when the park becomes your vast, private garden.

Best time for the walk: Early in the morning and from 10:00 A.M. to 3:00 P.M. The park chills rapidly when the afternoon fog rolls in. But rain and fog transform the park into a Corot landscape of smokelike trees and meadows peopled with only occasional figures. The soothing, romantic quality of this late-nineteenth-century work of landscape art awaits the explorer unconventional enough to savor the park when others don't.

Getting there by public transit: Many routes are possible. The quickest is to take a #71 Haight-Noriega or #72 Haight-Sunset bus from downtown Market Street and alight at Stanyan Street at the edge of the park and near the bicycle rentals on that street. (You will have to bring your own lock and chain for the bike if you wish to go inside the park's museums.) Please respect others in the park and stay on the bike paths.

Walkers: Most walkers will find the park too long to walk end to end (three miles). In that case, walk the first half of this tour and cut off at Lloyd Lake to Fulton Street and Twenty-fifth Avenue. There take a #5 Fulton going west to the ocean (or east back downtown). If you wish to go to the Cliff House and Seal Rocks, take the #5 Fulton to the end of the line and transfer to a northbound #18 Sloat to the crest of the Great Highway and the Cliff House (refreshments). From there the fastest return to the downtown is via the #2 Clement bus, which has its terminus at Point Lobos Avenue and Forty-eighth Avenue. The #2 Clement passes a long string of restaurants in the Richmond district.

Cafés and restaurants: There are several places mentioned in the tour where it is possible to eat and drink.

Returning: Alternate routes are given at the end of the tour.

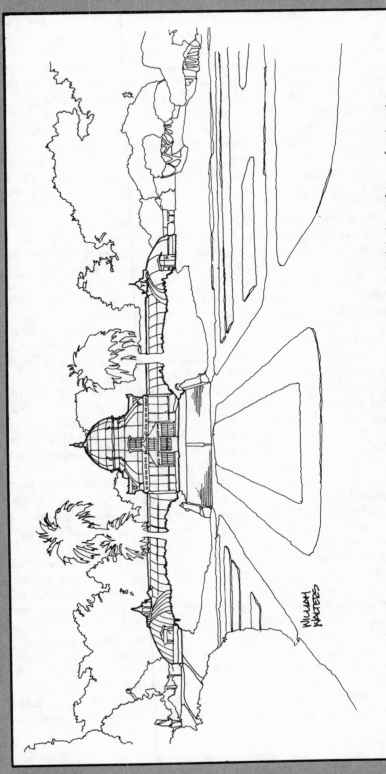

The 1875 Victorian Conservatory of Flowers on Kennedy Drive in Golden Gate Park in its parkscape of mature trees.

INTRODUCTION

In the Bible, when the prophets wished to devise a symbol for mankind in a perfect state, they wrote of the Garden of Eden. In San Francisco, Golden Gate Park is that 1,017.4-acre Eden. (New York's Central Park, by comparison, is 840 acres.) It is one of the most dramatic demonstrations of the wonders of irrigation in California. And it is one of the premier works of Victorian landscape design in North America.

In the 1860s this three-mile-long, half-mile-wide parcel stretching from the edge of the city to the Pacific was described as "A mass of white, trackless, moving sands, without vegetation, and not pleasing to any of the senses." What very few trees there were were described as "stunted growths, seemingly ashamed to claim membership in the tree family."

The land that was transformed into this evergreen park was originally one-sixth of the public Outside Lands west of the city. As in most of post–Gold Rush California, squatters illegally built shacks and fences here and claimed ownership of the city fringes by right of possession. In 1864 Supreme Court Justice Stephen Field upheld the city's claim to the Outside Lands west of Twin Peaks, but well-connected squatters and land speculators refused to vacate. A politically acceptable compromise was struck; in return for giving title to the occupiers to five-sixths of the lands, one-sixth was surrendered to the city. Of course the sixth given over to the public was the part with the most sand and the least water.

The Outside Lands Commission began planning for the park. The early prognosis was not encouraging. The press attacked the idea. When Frederick Law Olmsted, America's foremost landscape architect and the designer of Central Park in New York, was shown the site he declared it impossible to create a park here and suggested that the city look for a more auspicious place.

Nonetheless, Mayor Frank McCoppin and Governor Haight persisted, and on April 4, 1870, the legislature passed "An Act to Provide for the Improvement of Public Parks in the City of San Francisco." The governor appointed a Park Commission and the "impossible" project was begun.

(The State of California has always been an avid and dedicated gardener. From Golden Gate Park, to today's freeways, to the flowerbed-bordered parking lots around nearly every state building, a passion for horticulture marks every state project, no matter how ordinary the architecture or utilitarian the facility. The city of San Francisco did not assume responsibility for its great park till 1900.)

The Park Commission put the topographical survey and park plan out to public bid and awarded it to a twenty-four-year-old surveyor and engineer who came in with the lowest price, $4,860. William Hammond Hall produced a detailed topographic survey and preliminary park plan in only six months. The commissioners were so pleased that they appointed him the first superintendent of the park in 1871.

In five short, frustrating years Hall created the basic plan for the park, its principal roads, and plans for its forests, meadows, hills, and valleys. Landscaping began in the Panhandle and the eastern end of the park. In 1873 he completed the Main Drive to the beach. But Hall's experience in the Army Corps of Engineers and the federal Coast Survey had not prepared him for the complications of politics, and a State Assembly committee accused him of waste and extravagance. The legislature cut his $30,000-a-year park budget and Hall resigned. (He later became California's first State Engineer and made a handsome return on land he bought in Cherry Valley, which he foresaw would be needed for San Francisco's Hetch-Hetchy water system. He was roasted in the press for this. He died in 1924.)

Between 1876 and 1886 the park had three superintendents and no clear direction. In 1886 the governor fired all the park commissioners and called Hall back as consulting engineer. Hall agreed to return, but only for one year, and only in order to handpick his successor.

Hall chose a Scottish-born gardener, John McLaren, who had experience working on the large estates of the wealthy south of the city. He chose well. McLaren dedicated his life to filling out the park plan, planting trees, fighting meddlesome politicians (and statues of politicians), and in so doing earned the undying affection of San Franciscans.

In 1917, when "Uncle John" reached the city's mandatory retirement age of seventy, a special ordinance was passed exempting the Superintendent of Parks from this rule. His pension was canceled and his salary doubled. McLaren continued as chief of all the city's parks for twenty-six more cycles of the seasons. He died in 1943 at the age of ninety-six, still at the head of the parks, after fifty-six years of nurturing Golden Gate Park. Stories and legends about the indomitable, plant-loving old man in the tweed suit flourish and continue to grow like the countless trees he planted. Of him it can truly be said, "If you seek his monument, look around you."

The Park's Basic Design

Hall's design for a "natural" park involved massive grading of virtually the entire site. He turned the shifting sands into a complex honeycomb of valleys and low hills to create meadows walled in by wind-breaking stands of trees. Each meadow acquired a different designated use, from baseball to polo. Like a grand hotel with many different rooms, Golden Gate Park accommodates many, many different activities. But since each use is screened by bands of trees, a visually restful landscape is the result.

The shifting sands at the ocean end of the tract were subdued with dune-reclamation techniques adopted from the Gulf of Gascony in France. Imported sand grass, *Ammophilia arenaria,* held down the moving sand and permitted the systematic landscaping of the bleak wasteland.

Once the land was graded and planted with grass, trees were set out. Some one hundred species of conifers were planted, ranging from the hardy Monterey pine and cypress to Torrey pines and pines from New Zealand. Evergreen conifers were selected because they absorb the moisture in the foggy winds. Thus Hall and McLaren actually redesigned, or at least tempered, the park's climate!

Many varieties of Australian eucalypti were also planted. Flowering and deciduous trees (those that drop their leaves) were only infrequently used. McLaren carried on a worldwide correspondence with scientists and botanical gardens. There was a steady exchange of information, seeds, cuttings, and plants. Specimens came from the Mediterranean, South Africa, China, Japan, and especially Australia and New Zealand.

The trees McLaren planted were generously provided for. Tree holes six feet square and six feet deep were filled with straw, manure (McLaren secured a monopoly on the sweepings from the city streets), and loam. He was a perfectionist and personally selected the location of many trees. If the result did not please his fastidious eye, the tree would be dug up and moved or turned just a bit till it looked right.

Once inside the park the attentive eye begins to see an infinity of shades of green. The silhouettes and individual textures of the trees become important. The jagged shapes of the Monterey cypress, the random profiles of the old pines, and the soft, globular clouds of the tall eucalyptus trees are played off one against the other. Of special importance in Golden Gate Park are the bush or shrublike pittosporums from New Zealand, which serve as low, continuous sheltering bands or "walls" enclosing the foreground of most of the meadows. Their fine leaves and dense branching patterns make them ideal "background" planting. McLaren limited color to flowerbeds placed at strategic spots where their sudden appearance would be heightened by the unbroken green backdrop.

The park can be divided into two parts, with Stow Lake and Strawberry Hill at the center. The eastern end of the park houses cultural activities and the more exotic plants. The western end of the park has more open space, a more relaxed landscape, and physical activities that need space, such as horseback riding, archery, and polo. The land slopes gently from east to west.

The best way to see the park is to follow Main Drive, now John F. Kennedy Drive. As you travel along the drive you enjoy the romantic theater of nineteenth-century landscaping. The sequence of views is as thought-out as a movie or an extended piece of music; each passage has its moods: from the exotic to the "natural," from the complex to the simple, from the cultural to the recreational, from the dense to the spacious, from the city to the sea.

The sequence of the park is, first the Panhandle and its carriage drive (see the Haight-Ashbury walk); then McLaren Lodge, the park headquarters; then the Fuchsia Garden, harboring San Francisco's most extraordinary flowering plant; next the glass Conservatory with its tropical plants and seasonal displays; a primeval glen of fern trees; next the museum complex, which houses music, art, and sciences (the scientific displays embrace the land, the seas, and the heavens); next the Japanese Tea Garden, another piece of exotica; and then Stow Lake. Strawberry Hill rises almost in the dead center of the park and is the highest point in the park. From its peak there is a dramatic panoramic view. Next is Rainbow Falls, which recreates a stream in the Sierras. Then a string of gentle meadows and lakes unfolds. One alley of geometrically placed trees serves as the only reminder that all of this is man-made. At the western end of the park the landscape becomes simple, with low shrubs and bushes. Two windmills serve as reminders of the importance of irrigation to the park. Between the two windmills is the Beach Chalet, with its superb 1937 fresco cycle recapitulating the history of recreation in San Francisco. Lastly, appearing almost as a surprise, is the aptly named Pacific Ocean.

THE TOUR

1 McLaren Lodge
· Edward R. Swain, 1896

The most appropriate place to begin this tour is McLaren Lodge, north of John F. Kennedy Drive, at the head of the Panhandle. This handsome sandstone and tile-roofed building was occupied jointly by the Park Commission and John McLaren. The building is noteworthy for its restful horizontal lines, porch, and loggia. Its stonework is quite fine. The hard sandstone was quarried in San Francisco at Twenty-sixth and Douglas. Its red-tile roof gives a hint of the Mission Revival that was to come. The park's first nursery once occupied the site. Today this building and its unobtrusive annex are the headquarters of San Francisco's Recreation and Parks Department. From here San Francisco's superb system of over 160 parks is administered.

Some five thousand species and varieties of plants grow in the verdant park. McLaren Lodge itself is agreeably overgrown with vines. This seems appropriate; McLaren was continually struggling to hide the park's "embellishments" with plants. In front of the lodge is a large Monterey cypress affectionately known as Uncle John McLaren's Christmas Tree.

Visible to the south is the giant orange-and-white-striped tripod of the Sutro television tower completed in 1973. At 980 feet, it is the tallest structure in San Francisco. Called a candelabra configuration, the $12 million steel structure was designed by Albert C. Martin and

Associates in Los Angeles and fabricated in Columbia, South Caro-lina. On a clear day, the tower can be seen for fifty miles. It was built by a consortium of television stations and also serves FM radio sta-tions and some other uses. While a generally unloved structure, its Empire-waisted design is a handsome piece of utilitarian engineering more pleasing than the pseudo-Seattle space needle that the City Planning Commission actually approved. At night the tower's wink-ing red beacons look like an enormous light sculpture. It generally improved television reception in this hilly city.

2 Fuchsia Garden

Follow the signs to the Fuchsia Garden. Here, under tall trees, is an incredible assortment of fuchsia plants of every imaginable color and size. The fuchsia is a plant particularly well adapted to San Fran-cisco's cool climate. Thick, indestructible old fuchsia bushes can be found in the backyards of all the Victorian districts in San Francisco. Some fuchsia are nearly always in bloom, although the peak season for this garden is July and August.

3 The Conservatory of Flowers
· Erected by Lord and Burnham, 1878

Continue to the Conservatory. This enormous white Victorian green-house is one of the half-dozen most important treasures in San Fran-cisco and is the oldest building in the park. It is an architectural, horticultural, and social landmark.

The Conservatory was ordered in 1875 by James Lick, a San Fran-cisco real-estate millionaire, from the Hammersmith works in Dub-lin. Lick intended to erect it at his estate in San Jose but died before his new toy could be uncrated. Leland Stanford and others purchased the disassembled structure for $2,600 and donated it to the park with the stipulation that it be assembled within eighteen months. The firm of Lord and Burnham from Irvington-on-Hudson, New York, was engaged to erect the Conservatory. F.A. Lord himself came west to supervise its erection in 1878.

In 1883 fire destroyed the central dome and all its exotic plants. Charles Crocker donated $10,000 for its restoration. The wood-frame structure was unharmed in the 1906 earthquake. Today the Conserv-atory remains much as it was in the nineteenth century but in fragile condition. This delightful Victorian bauble serves as San Franciscans' Temple to Flora and is among the most loved places in the city. The building is distinguished by an octagonal dome and two low, spread-ing wings with pavilions at each end.

Enter the building and examine both it and its contents. Slowly. There is no need to rush. The large carved jardiniere in the vestibule came from the Italian cloister of the Panama-Pacific International

Exposition of 1915. Canaries once sang in the vestibule's cupola. The central dome houses enormous palm trees and other tropical plants. A band of brilliantly colored glass serves to brighten the interior of the dome. Walk through to the right. This east wing houses truly fantastic greenery; the pavilion at its far end contains the water-lily pond. In the pond are enormous Japanese carp that sparkle in the filtered half-light.

Walk back to the other, or west, wing, passing by the orchid case on the right-hand wall with its rich array of orchids of every size and color. Continue to the west pavilion. Here seasonal flowers are displayed at the peak of their bloom. The cycle includes cyclamen, cinerarias, Easter lilies, calceolaria, schizanthus, tuberous begonias, chrysanthemums, and poinsettias. It is remarkable that there are no guards at the Conservatory. People respect the plants, and there is blessedly little damage to the building or its fragile inhabitants.

This is a good place to reflect on San Franciscans' love of plants. The harshness of this sandy site and the relative lack of native vegetation led the Victorians to import plants from all over the world. Ferns, palms, eucalypti, fuchsia, orchids, and every other imaginable plant were brought to San Francisco and lovingly cultivated. Today it is nearly impossible to enter a house or apartment, and even many business places in San Francisco, without seeing flourishing plants.

On the slope immediately in front of the Conservatory is San Francisco's floral welcome mat: a large plot covered with small colored plants arranged as pictures with changing themes throughout the year.

The grounds in front of the Conservatory are laid out as a formal flower garden always ablaze with color. It looks like an enormous oriental carpet—which is appropriate, since the finest carpets were inspired by Islamic gardens. The trees around the Conservatory are perhaps the best composition in the park. Turn around slowly to savor this work of consummate environmental art.

4 The Glade

Directly across the drive from the Conservatory is a small, seemingly primeval glade of prehistoric-looking fern trees, acanthus, and banana trees. One almost expects to see dinosaurs foraging here.

5 John McLaren Memorial Rhododendron Dell

Down the drive to the left is the four-acre John McLaren Memorial Rhododendron Dell. The rhododendrons here are at their peak in May. McLaren spent most of his life fighting the introduction of statuary (which he called "stookies") into Golden Gate Park. And so, with fitting irony, he is commemorated by—a statue! Unlike some of the statuary in Golden Gate Park, it is a very fine piece of work.

McLaren stands with his bow tie, his goatee, and his vested suit, contemplating a pinecone in his left hand. Behind him is the stump of a tree fern that touches the back of the figure so that the statue merges with the vegetable kingdom. As a minor concession to McLaren's hatred of statuary, the green bronze statue is placed directly on the ground and not on a stone pedestal. The thing that "Uncle John" would have liked best about the statue is that it almost disappears against its backdrop of greenery. And overhead is a tree dropping cones of the type McLaren holds in his hand. The statue is by M. Earl Cummings and was the gift of A.B. Spreckels in 1944.

Up the drive, nearly hidden in its McLaren-inspired setting, is a statue of the Scottish poet, Robert Burns. Another well-hidden statue, at the corner where one turns left for the Music Concourse, is the large bronze statue of Thomas Starr King on a pink granite base. King, an ecumenically minded Unitarian minister who died in 1864, was one of the men chiefly responsible for keeping California in the Union during the Civil War. He was a noted orator and was the first San Francisco clergyman to open his pulpit to all faiths. This statue was modeled by the famed American sculptor Daniel Chester French in 1892.

6 Music Concourse and Museum Complex

The most prominent statue as one enters the Music Concourse is that of Padre Junípero Serra, the founder of the California missions. He is shown striding forward, his cloak in agitation, with both hands raised, one holding up a cross. This statue was dedicated in 1907 and is the work of Douglas Tilden.

Pass the bust of U.S. Grant and see the bronze statue of the Cider Press. This bronze shows a nude male operating a press and a child kneeling at his feet. It was given to the park by the Executive Committee of the California Midwinter Fair of 1894. During that exposition a sixty-acre fairground was constructed in and around the low depression that now shelters the Music Concourse. It was California's first great fair and it is fitting that it should be commemorated by a statue that reminds us of the state's agricultural abundance. The fair was held in midwinter to advertise California's benign climate and to distract the populace from the 1893 depression, when eighteen banks failed in San Francisco. Several large, eclectic pavilions were built, mostly in the Moorish or Mission styles, some to house exhibits from the great Columbian Exposition in Chicago. The fair generated its own electricity, which was used to illuminate a huge steel tower in the center of the Concourse.

Directly across from the cider-press monument is a grove of old palm trees and two curious sphinxes by young Arthur Putnam. They date from 1903 and once stood guard before an Egyptian-style museum saved from the fair. It was the first public art museum in San

Francisco, one of those curious late-nineteenth-century museums stuffed with an astounding variety of not always accurately attributed curios.

That Egyptian building was replaced by a modern art museum, the De Young Museum, to the left, completed in 1921. The De Young is now, thank God, a plain building, but when originally built it was covered with terra-cotta ornamentation in flamboyant Spanish Renaissance style. All the ornament was stripped from the building because it was an earthquake hazard. Of outstanding interest is the superb Avery Brundage collection of Asian art in the west wing and El Greco's gray-and-green mystic vision of St. Francis in ecstasy. The De Young is open seven days a week, 10:00 A.M. to 5:00 P.M.

At the eastern end of the Music Concourse is a memorial to Francis Scott Key, the lyricist (if that's the word) of our national anthem. It was recently reerected after a long period in storage. The monument was originally erected in 1887 as a bequest of James Lick and seems to be inspired by the Albert Memorial in London.

Descend into the Music Concourse. The building to the south is the California Academy of Sciences, which contains a natural-history museum, a planetarium, and an aquarium housed in a building that was begun in 1917 by Lewis P. Hobart and has expanded somewhat frighteningly since then.

At the western end of the concourse is the classically styled Music Pavilion, a gift of Claus Spreckels, designed by the Reid Brothers and constructed in 1899 of Colusa sandstone. This grand structure replaces a simpler wooden bandshell erected during the Midwinter Fair of 1894. The present bandshell is typical of the kind of architecture San Franciscans used for large office buildings and public institutions at the turn of the century. Its cornices and ornamentation are enjoyed by humans and pigeons alike. The concourse, with its carefully pollarded English plane trees and gravel floor, is a congenial place for Sunday-afternoon band concerts. Its place in the park is that of contrast. It contains the only noticed deciduous trees in the evergreen park. Its formal French axial design is completely different in spirit from the (equally man-made) "natural" English landscape park in which the Music Concourse is embedded.

7 Japanese Tea Garden
· George Turner Marsh, 1894

To the right of the bandshell and immediately west of the De Young Museum is the Japanese Tea Garden. The garden was built for the 1894 fair by George Turner Marsh, an Australian-born dealer in oriental art who opened America's first oriental art store in the arcade of the old Palace Hotel. (The firm still exists at 522 Sutter Street.) Marsh laid out the garden, and even imported seventy-five rickshaws to cart around visitors to the fair. But Japanese-Americans protested that in America there were horses to perform such labor and boycotted the picturesque conveyances. Marsh then hired Germans in costumes.

When the fair closed, the popular tea garden remained. From 1907 to 1942 the Hagiwara family ran the tea garden as a concession. In 1909 the world's first fortune cookies were introduced in the teahouse. They made such a hit that restaurants in Chinatown adopted them and they became known as Chinese fortune cookies. In 1942 the Hagiwaras were sent to detention camps in Utah and the city changed the garden's name to the Oriental Tea Garden. The original name was restored in 1952.

Appropriately enough in polyglot San Francisco, even the Japanese Tea Garden has its foreign element. When the 1915 exposition closed, a Siamese pagoda was moved to the garden. The sculptural treasure in the garden is the great one-and-a-half-ton, ten-foot-eight-inch bronze Buddha cast in Tajima, Japan, in 1790. It is the Amazarashi-no-hotoke Buddha, "the Buddha who sits through sunny and rainy weather without shelter." It is one of the largest bronzes to leave Asia.

The glory of the garden, of course, is the plants. Many are very old bonsai. Though the garden is only five acres, the artistic placement of the plants makes it seem much larger. From March to May the azaleas are in bloom. The best time to see the garden is in the fog or rain. It is open from 8:00 A.M. to 7:00 P.M.

Near the intersection outside the tea garden is the stone Japanese Lantern of Peace dedicated to the pioneers from Japan who came to California starting in 1869.

8 Strybing Arboretum
· Robert Tetlow, 1937

Across the road is the Strybing Arboretum, a gift of Mrs. Helen Strybing. It is a sixty-acre garden-within-a-garden alive with over three thousand species of plants. Ducks, swans, and even peacocks wander at will throughout the arboretum. The Strybings were not people in the public eye but they were friends of John McLaren's. All the plants here are labeled; it is a zoo of plants. Among its embellishments are a simple fountain with a large jet of water, an 1847 Mexican bell installed in 1967, and, most happily, a statue of St. Francis erected in 1967.

At the edge of the arboretum is the Hall of Flowers where San Francisco's annual county fair—a flower show!—is held. (San Francisco is both a city and a county, and the state provides each county with funds for a county fair.) The Hall of Flowers has an active program for garden clubs and all those who love flowers. The arboretum is open from 8:00 A.M. to 4:30 P.M. on weekdays and from 10:00 A.M. to 5:00 P.M. on Saturdays, Sundays, and holidays. There is an excellent map available at the entrance kiosk. Free guided tours every Tuesday through Saturday at 1:30 start in front of the Hall of Flowers.

9 Stow Lake

From the arboretum continue to Stow Lake. Rowboats, pedal boats, and electric motorboats may be rented by the hour at the boathouse on the north side of the man-made lake. The boathouse is a delightful island of quiet in the city, and refreshments of a carbonated sort can be secured here.

In the middle of Stow Lake is Strawberry Hill, a man-made hill with an altitude of 428 feet. Two bridges—one garnished with giant, cyclopean boulders—connect the shore of the lake with the hill. A gentle dirt roadway corkscrews to the top of Strawberry Hill, where wild strawberries once grew.

Climb to the top of the hill. The empty rusticated rock reservoir at the top of the hill was the starting point for Huntington Falls, an artificial waterfall that cascaded from here to Stow Lake, the largest reservoir in Golden Gate Park (which requires over 4 million gallons of water every day). The lake is named after the park commissioner who persuaded Collis P. Huntington to donate the money for it. In the nineteenth century this was one of the busiest spots in the park. The hill was capped by a large, two-story coliseum-shaped observation tower run by a politician named Sweeney. McLaren considered it a monstrosity. It was destroyed by the earthquake of 1906 and never rebuilt. Pieces of pink-colored foundation work are still visible buried in the sand at the top of the hill.

Today the summit of Strawberry Hill is thickly wooded with cypress, eucalyptus, and long-leafed acacia and offers tantalizing partial views of the city. No single clear perspective is possible from here but, more importantly, San Francisco can be seen as a mosaic of neighborhoods of dense white housing and large green parks. To the east are the tops of the Financial District high-rises; to the south is the slope of Twin Peaks with its dense eucalyptus forest; farther around to the right is the low slope of the Sunset district with its even rhythm of pastel cubes marching as far as the sea; to the west, obscured by trees, lies the Pacific Ocean. To the north and west is the most splendid view of all, the Golden Gate Bridge with the open Marin County hills beyond. Mt. Tamalpais and the twin red spires of the bridge punctuate the vista. From this small man-made hill at the center of the park one sees and feels what is essential about San Francisco: First, the sand underfoot, shifting dune sand sculpted and held down by man. Next, the dense man-planted greenery that flourishes, when irrigated, on these foggy slopes. And beyond lies the third part of the triad: the dense, white city spilling across the valleys and reaching from the bay to the sea. From this vantage point it is possible to believe that not all of man's approaches to the earth need be brutal.

Leave the summit of Strawberry Hill and slowly descend the spiral road. A quarter of a turn down the road is a glimpse of the golden onion dome of the Russian Greek Orthodox Cathedral of the Holy Virgin on Geary Street in the Richmond district silhouetted against the Golden Gate. The Richmond district is home to many Russian-Americans.

10 Prayerbook Cross
· Ernest Coxhead, 1894

Farther west along Kennedy Drive, atop a rare natural bluff, is Prayerbook Cross, inspired by an ancient Celtic cross on the Scottish island of Iona. From the top of the bluff on which the cross stands cascades Rainbow Falls, a tribute to the powers of pumping and irrigation. This bluff is a perfect example of set-piece nineteenth-century landscape design. Its obvious inspiration was a mountain stream in the High Sierras. McLaren once noted that he often went on walks in the countryside and, when he found a striking effect in nature such as a "bonnie brook," he would come back and attempt to duplicate it in the park.

11 The Portals of the Past
· Ionic portico

Continue to Lloyd Lake. Along the way is the elevated roadway of Cross Over Drive. Reflected on Lloyd Lake's still surface are the six Ionic columns of the Portals of the Past. They once framed the entrance of the A.N. Towne residence atop Nob Hill, designed by Willis Polk in the late 1890s. The house was destroyed by the fire of 1906. An inspired photographer took a picture of the city's ruins through its still-standing columns and entitled it *The Portals of the Past.* In 1909 the portico was reerected here. The white portico reflected in the tranquil lake (really another reservoir) creates a dreamy and romantic view. There is a sense of melancholy here appropriate to San Francisco's only architectural monument to the earthquake and fire of 1906.

12 View of Lindley Meadow

Leave Lloyd Lake and continue west along Kennedy Drive. Beyond the next rise there is a glimpse of Lindley Meadow, a large, grassy lawn surrounded by high banks and dense foliage. The curving, flowing drives and the relaxed, informal placement of the eucalyptus and cypress trees knit these spaces together in a harmonious and unobtrusive way. A casual traveler through the park would think it nothing but trees and greenery, so well-hidden are its many recreational uses.

Farther up the drive, on the left-hand side across a grassy meadow, rises a totemic sculpture entitled *The Goddess of the Forest*. It was carved in 1939 by Dudley C. Carter for the Treasure Island fair. The goddess is represented as a crouching nude female figure carved out of an enormous redwood tree trunk. She supports a bear (California's emblem) in her lap and holds an owl in her hands; an eagle protects the back of her head. The unvarnished redwood sculpture has achieved the soft, grayish-green patina characteristic of the way wood weathers in Northern California's climate. Like some enormous fetish, the goddess is accumulating the paired initials of lovers all around her base. She seems contented with the view.

▌3 Spreckels Lake

Still farther along the drive, to the right, is Spreckels Lake, the model-yacht pond, held up like a shimmering, reflecting platter at the northern edge of the park. The light, stuccoed Richmond district is visible through a screen of cypress trees. The surface of the pond is usually flecked with seagulls and ducks. There is a water fountain here.

The next area along the drive, skillfully hidden in the landscape, is the Golden Gate Park Stadium, originally the Polo Field.

▌4 The Buffalo Paddock

Continue along Kennedy Drive and pass the Buffalo Paddock on the right-hand side. This low meadow houses a herd of buffalo, an institution in the park since 1892. The buffalo are large, shaggy, unwieldy-looking creatures that stand motionless for hours. Their sudden apparition, especially if you come across them in the fog, is altogether surreal. They are a curious reminder that San Francisco is part of the Far West.

At different times, before the opening of Fleischhacker Zoo in the 1930s, Golden Gate Park housed an aviary, goats, moose, elk, deer, kangaroos, bears, seals, and elephants. Now only the buffalo and the peacocks and ducks in the Arboretum remain in the park. However, as the park's forests mature, especially in the western section of the park, raccoons and other small mammals have moved in and flourish in this "natural wilderness."

▌5 Chain of Lakes

The Chain of Lakes, really a string of three artistically landscaped reservoirs, helps supply the park with its daily 4 million gallons of water. Willows once flourished here when all around was sand. The eleven islands in the lakes are the only parts of the park not accessible to the visitor. Each island was originally landscaped differently. The edges of the lakes are scalloped and irregular. The tiny islands are disposed randomly, but with all the art of a few rocks in a Japanese sand garden. The illusion of natural lakes is perfect.

About one-third of the park's water comes from processed sewage, another third comes from the city water system (ultimately from the High Sierras), and only a third is pumped from the park's own wells. An underground river runs under the Arboretum and the western end of the park. McLaren tapped this convenient source when the water company was privately owned. Municipalization of the water system in the 1930s lowered the cost of water to the park and led to the atrophy of the park's own water sources. The windmills at the ocean end of the park were part of McLaren's desire to decentralize water sources. The park's water system also irrigates Lincoln Park, which *is* on the Golden Gate, an umbilical link between the park and the gate.

Farther up the drive is the turnoff for horse rentals. The park is threaded with bridle paths. This small stretch of the drive is one of the only places where the trees are planted in rigid lines, forming an alley of obviously man-planted trees.

At the intersection turn left. A short way down the hill and on the right is an almost invisible road that leads to the Richmond-Sunset sewage-treatment and water-pumping system. It lies hidden at the westernmost edge of the park. There are visiting hours on Thursdays from 9:00 A.M. to 4:00 P.M. It is not a lovely structure. A large perpetual torch burns off the poisonous gases released from the treatment of the sewage.

16 The Murphy Windmill and Keeper's House
· 1905

Outside the sewage-treatment plant is the restored Murphy Windmill, built in 1905, and its small red-brick Colonial-style Keeper's House. Parts of the giant wooden vanes of the windmill lie rotting on the ground. It was once one of the largest sail windmills in the world, 114 feet across, and it pumped 40,000 gallons of water per hour from an underground river. Leave the Murphy Windmill and bicycle or walk north along the edge of the Great Highway.

17 Beach Chalet
· Willis Polk, 1921

Continue to the two-story, white-pillared Beach Chalet on the park side of the highway. This is a convenient place to secure refreshments.

This building contains one of the very finest pieces of public art in San Francisco. Here, between 1936 and 1937, under the auspices of the WPA, Lucien Labaudt executed a series of frescoes. Immediately inside the front door is a large, rectangular barroom with frescoes covering all the wall surfaces (1,500 square feet). Over the inside of the front door is a phrase from a poem by Bret Harte: "Serene, indifferent of fate thou sittest at the Golden Gate."

The theme of the murals in Coit Tower is the working life of California. The theme of these murals is play and recreation. The two cycles complement each other. This cycle makes a complete tour of the city.

The scene surrounding the front door shows a man feeding pigeons and a woman knitting a sweater in Union Square, a place of rest in the very center of the city.

Continue left. The next figure, an architect standing between the two windows, represents Arthur Brown, Jr. He holds the plans for Coit Tower, another public embellishment of the 1930s. Behind him rises the Beaux-Arts Civic Center and the splendid City Hall. A Corinthian capital is at his feet and steelwork behind. Here is perfectly summarized the final phase of the Beaux-Arts movement in San Francisco architecture, which stretched from the 1890s to the 1930s.

Next, in the southwest corner, are boaters at the St. Francis Yacht Harbor; the bay has been a continual source of recreation for San Franciscans. The quotation over the center of this wall, "Sails are furled from furthest corners of the world," is a phrase from Joaquin Miller.

To the left are sightseers at Land's End looking out over the Golden Gate. A ship lies wrecked on the rocks below. On the headlands rises the Moderne, vaguely Mayan, Veterans' Hospital built in 1933. Also visible is a view of Baker Beach at the Presidio.

Next, on the wall over the right-hand side of the bar, is a large fresco representing recreation in Golden Gate Park. From left to right in the background are visible the Portals of the Past, the Conservatory, the de Young Museum, and the Japanese Tea Garden. In the foreground, among all the users of the park, is a man in a green plaid suit who seems to be blessing and accepting a new seedling. It is "Uncle John" McLaren.

In the center of this wall, over the bar, is a quotation from Ina Coolbrith: "Fair city of my love and my desire." At bar level is a small painted-in plaque that reads, "Federal Art Project, 1936–1937, Lucien Labaudt."

The left-hand side of the bar represents picnickers at Land's End with the Marin hills in the distance and a single tower of the unfinished Golden Gate Bridge (completed in 1937).

In the corner of the north wall is a scene representing the catching and selling of crabs at Fisherman's Wharf. The quotation in the center of this wall reads, "At the end of our streets, the stars," from a poem by George Sterling.

Beyond that, in the corner at the left, is a scene on the waterfront at Pier 26 with docks, sailors, and fishermen. The man pushing the cart was the then-controversial head of the Longshoremen's Union, leftist Australian-born Harry Bridges.

Finally, completing the cycle, between the two windows, is a scene with Chinatown in the background and a policeman and a florist in the foreground. It is a curious pairing, representing perhaps the opposite ends of the spectrum of life in a big city.

The murals have hardly faded at all; here, awaiting discovery, is an artistic treasure unaccountably neglected.

18 The Dutch Windmill

Leave the chalet. Visible to the north is the bladeless Dutch Windmill, built in 1903. A small tulip garden nestles at its base. Cross the Great Highway to the beach. The concrete wall was designed by city engineer Michael O'Shaughnessy and reaches down twelve feet below low tide. Beyond is the vast Pacific Ocean.

Returning: There are three ways of returning to the eastern end of the park. The first is to retrace one's path along John F. Kennedy Drive. The second is to return along the South Drive through the park. The third and perhaps the most interesting way to return, and the most direct but most hazardous, is to bicycle down Lincoln Way. This is the busy street that serves as the park's southern border.

Lincoln Way

Lincoln Way presents a sharp edge between park space and built space. To the right is the edge of the Sunset district, built in the 1920s and 1930s and, like the park itself, replacing an endless stretch of shifting sand dunes. The ride back along Lincoln Way is very slightly uphill as far as Thirty-fourth Avenue; after that it is a gentle descent all the way to Stanyan Street.

The architectural styles along Lincoln Way are remarkably eclectic and exhibit the full range of the stylistic possibilities of frame and stucco construction. Many of the houses are surrounded by characteristic San Francisco residential landscaping: closely trimmed, geometrically shaped bushes and shrubs, and a surprising array of imported plants.

If you have more time, rather than going to Lincoln Way, you can go on to the Cliff House.

The Cliff House and Seal Rocks

The rugged headland at the western tip of Point Lobos, north of the Ocean Beach, is the site of the famous Cliff House. The #18 Sloat bus at the corner of the Great Highway and Fulton Street goes up the hill to the Cliff House, where refreshments can be secured. The first building on this dramatic site was built in 1858. The present bland building is the fifth to be built here; it opened in 1909 and was modernized in 1950. It is, alas, nothing like the bold French chateau-style Cliff House that Adolph Sutro built here in 1896 and that burned in 1907. That particular building, now long lost, is the one architectural work that lives on in the city's memory and in countless postcards and drawings. A seven-story gingerbread pile perched so improbably on its high rock, it seemed to sum up the daring act of building on this barren, isolated peninsula and was, in its way, a symbol of the flamboyant Victorian era. It was replaced by a modern concrete building sober to the point of boredom.

The magnificent site, however, is as dramatic as ever. The surf boils among the rocks below; some four hundred feet offshore are the Seal Rocks, a favorite spot for Steller sea lions. The lusty barking of the gregarious, polygamous seals is a happy sound. The Seal Rocks were deeded by Congress to the city in 1887, and the sea lions have been under the protection of the Recreation and Park Commission ever since. Visible on the horizon on clear days are the Farallon Islands, a cluster of rocky islands thirty-two miles west of Point Lobos. They too shelter sea lions and have been a protected bird sanctuary since 1909. The name is a Spanish nautical term for a small, pointed island. A lighthouse has warned mariners away from these rocks since 1855. North of the Cliff House are the ruins of the concrete tanks of the Sutro Baths, a favorite resort of San Franciscans that closed in 1952 and burned in 1966. Built by Adolph Sutro and opened in 1896, the baths covered three acres and boasted the world's largest indoor pools of both fresh and salt water. In 1977, the National Park Service purchased the Sutro Baths site and the Cliff House for $3.9 million and incorporated them into the Golden Gate National Recreation Area.

Returning: To return to Union Square, take the #18 Sloat bus back down the hill toward Golden Gate Park, alight at Cabrillo and La Playa, and transfer to the #38 Geary or the #38 Geary Express bus.

Tour 10

The Castro and Noe Valley

San Francisco Now

MARKET ST.

17TH ST.

POND ST.

PROSPER ST.

①

FORD ST.

DORLAND ST.

②

18TH ST.

CASTRO ST.

EUREKA PLAYGROUND

HANCOCK ST.

COLLINGWOOD ST.

19TH ST.

HARTFORD ST.

CUMBERLAND S

20TH ST.

③

NOE ST.

RAYBURN ST.

LIBERTY ST. ④

⑤

⑥

21ST ST.

HILL ST. ⑦

SANCHEZ ST.

22ND ST.

ALVARADO ST.

23RD ST.

VICKSBURG ST.

⑧

ELIZABETH ST.

⑨

24TH ST.

DIAMOND ST.

Ⓝ

400 Feet

⑩

Jon Nix

WHAT THIS WALK COVERS

This walk-and-bus-hop begins at the head of Market Street in Eureka Valley, goes up to the crest of aptly named Hill Street with its sweeping panorama of Victorian residential districts, then goes down the other side of the hill to Noe Valley. On one side of the hill, in the Castro, is one of the most dynamic gay male neighborhoods in the world. On the other side, in Noe Valley, is a well-educated, heterogeneous, politically and culturally liberal population with its own street scene.

PRACTICALITIES

Note: This walk includes some steep sidewalks and a half-block of stairs.

Best time for this walk: Daytime from about 11:00 to 2:00 is good. Sundays are best; the most people are out then.

Getting there by public transit: From downtown Market Street take the #8 Market/Castro trackless trolley-bus, which runs from the Ferry Building to Castro Street. Many other Market Street lines stop at Castro, but the #8 seems preferred by the locals.

Cafés and restaurants: Twenty-fourth Street in Noe Valley has many good small eateries and bars. The Noe Valley Bar and Grill at 3945 Twenty-fourth Street with its redwood interior is perhaps the best.

INTRODUCTION

In 1887 the Castro Street Cable Line opened, connecting the head of Market Street with Twenty-sixth Street. The ivory cars spurred the development of Eureka and Noe Valleys at the base of Twin Peaks. It was a quiet, leisurely line that served two shopping streets; three cars were all it needed. Even though the parent Market Street Railway switched from cable cars to electric streetcars, the steep 17 percent grade of the Castro Street hill preserved cable cars on this line until April 6, 1941. On that day the last Castro Cable Car made its eight-mile-an-hour trip over the hill.

With the convenient streetcars came dense development where dairy cattle once grazed over open hills. Speculators bought the Mexican ranches, leased them to dairies, and waited for the city to grow in their direction. With the streetcars, developers laid out grids of streets and sold off blocks and lots to builders and homestead associations. Contractor-builders, often following stock plans, then built the Victorian houses and cottages that still mantle the hill and its two valleys to the north and south.

Strings of row houses sprang up here and there, which were sold

Row of Queen Anne-style cottages on the south side of the 500 Block of Liberty Street between Castro and Noe Streets, built in the late 1890s.

to working- and lower-middle-class families. German, Scandinavian, and later more and more Irish-American families populated the western fringe of the city at the base of Twin Peaks. There were many homeowners, but many renters as well. The area has never suffered neglect, and, with every year, the gardens behind the houses and the twentieth-century pruned street trees soften more of the harshness of these precipitous streets. Because of San Francisco's justifiably famous marine views, the "inland" cityscapes are frequently overlooked. In this part of the city, where the Victorian residential districts lie draped over the furrowed slopes of Twin Peaks, remarkable views of nothing but nineteenth-century houses with twentieth-century gardens are memorable to those who look for them.

With the prosperity that came after World War II, many families, or their children, bought houses in new suburbs such as Daly City and Pacifica. Since about 1970 two new waves of migration have reinvigorated the two valleys. Eureka Valley, close to Market Street, has become world famous overnight as a significant focal point for young gay men from all over the United States. The sexually unorthodox have always sought out cities, specifically certain cities, and more specifically certain sections of certain cities. There has gathered there what some call a ghetto and others a community. This process is at its most intense in Eureka Valley's Castro district. Energetic and restoration-minded, the new residents of the Castro have repaired and refurbished dowdy old houses and made them resplendent.

Up the Castro Street hill on the summit, and in Noe Valley on the other side, a second, quieter, but equally significant immigration has brought new vigor to an old part of town. Many professional families with young children live here; a discernably committed-to-the-city population, including many artists, makes this one of San Francisco's most agreeable neighborhoods. The side streets on the southern slope of the hill are quiet, serene, and well worth random exploration.

THE TOUR

1 Market and Castro Streets
· Transit node and commercial crossroads

At Castro Street, Market Street is deflected from its straight course by the base of the hills at the center of the city that includes Twin Peaks. Visible at the foot of Market is the tower of the 1896 Ferry Building, framed by the huge downtown high-rises. In the other direction, to the west up the hill, is the Sutro television tower, built in 1973.

This is now a busy intersection of public transit, automobiles, and pedestrians, but at the end of the nineteenth century, this area was the westernmost edge of the city. Before the opening of the Twin

Peaks trolley tunnel in 1917, San Francisco's built area stretched from here to the Ferry Building on the bay. The fire unleashed by the earthquake in 1906 did not reach the western half of the city, and almost all the buildings here except those on the corners (two gas stations, a bank and a contemporary credit union) are Victorian.

The Castro is sometimes now referred to as Castro Village, no doubt after Greenwich Village in New York. In its urban form (if not in its population!) it is a microcosm of the typical nineteenth-century California town. Like them it consists of a gridiron of residential streets, with one, Castro Street, as a commercial strip of continuous shops with banks on the corners and a 1922 movie-palace marquee. The commercial strip of Castro is only two blocks long and ends abruptly where the steep slope begins. One block behind this 100 percent commercial street are the local church and public grammar school with its ballfield. All else is housing. Most housing (houses, flats, and apartments) are two or three stories high. Almost all of it is frame construction. Though not readily visible from the public sidewalk and street, most blocks here have green centers of individually fenced-in backyards.

The Twin Peaks Bar on the southeast corner of Castro and Seventeenth Street is a sociological if not an architectural monument. It was the first gay bar with floor-to-ceiling plate-glass windows looking out on the world. The bars along Castro draw locals and people from all over the world. The valley bounded by Market and Church Streets to the north and east, and Twenty-first and Eureka Streets to the south and west, is the most visibly gay neighborhood in the city.

Some of the most interesting galleries and shops in the Castro are not on Castro but on the south side of Market Street on the 2300 block between Sixteenth and Seventeenth Streets. Here the latest fashions and the latest revivals are showcased in old shopfronts.

The Castro Theater was built in 1922 and designed by Timothy Pfleuger, one of the best movie-palace designers of the splashy 1920s. It was recently made a city landmark and survives as one of the best intact movie palaces in San Francisco. The resplendent reinforced-concrete façade is in Spanish Renaissance style. Over the neon-trimmed marquee is a great central window flanked by elaborate ornament and surmounted by an empty niche. It fulfills that place in the cityscape traditionally occupied by churches. These elaborate and dim houses of celluloid fantasy were central to all California settlements in the 1920s and 1930s. The interior of the Castro Theater is —and this is very rare—original.

The other important institution and building on this block is the round-cornered Bank of America, originally Bank of Italy, at 400 Castro Street. This Beaux-Arts branch bank was built in 1921 and designed by Edward T. Foulkes. It was originally covered with terra-cotta imitation stonework and had an elaborate cornice and frieze.

Like many San Francisco buildings, it was stripped and modernized with stucco.

2 Castro and Eighteenth Streets: "Castro Village"
· Victorian and turn-of-the-century commercial strip

Walk down the west side of the lively 400 block of Castro to the corner of Eighteenth Street. Once there was a rose garden here; now it is the "Times Square" of the present-day Castro. Visible ahead is a picturesque city silhouette of peak-roofed cottages blanketing the slope. The valleys built up first in San Francisco, but by the 1890s artisans' cottages were climbing the hills in this area. Each of these originally low-cost two-story houses has its own backyard and enjoys sweeping views of the city. The two- and three-story, bay-windowed apartments and flats that line Castro Street wall in blocks of delightful small hill cottages behind. We will see these cottages from their street sides atop the hill.

On the southeast corner is a branch of the Hibernia Bank that can stand as a symbol of what is happening in California design today. When the 1929 bank had to be expanded to serve the hard-working and affluent local population, the corner Beaux-Arts building was retained and a contemporary glass-and-concrete addition was built in 1979. The architect for the new section was Robert Sarnoff. He introduced a small "plaza" area in front of the new bank, which, unlike almost all such "public spaces," works well. Sunny and sheltered, the spot has become a hangout on the street, nicknamed "Hibernia Beach." The building is cut back at a 45-degree angle, the signature of late 1970s design.

At 527–33 Castro are the semicircular bay windows of the three-story turn-of-the-century Komsthoeft Building, with shops on the first floor and two stories of flats above. At 531 is a mini-complex of boutiques and a restaurant with an outdoor eating area in the backyard. This backyard garden lets the visitor see the back of this typical building and the characteristically Northern California way in which it has been transformed with wooden decks and lavish planting, especially of constantly blooming fuchsia.

3 700 Block of Castro Street, above Twentieth Street
· Stick-Eastlake row, 1880s

On Castro, across from the new Hibernia Bank, catch the #24 Divisadero bus up the Castro Street hill. How much more fun the cable cars must have been! Above Twentieth Street, on the east side of the street in the 700 block of Castro, is a striking row of Victorian flats. On the southeast corner, at 701, is a whimsical one-story house with a round turret built in 1897 by the prolific housebuilder Fernando Nelson for himself. It was originally in the back of its lot and had a stable underneath it for Nelson's retired firehorse Bill, who hauled lumber to construction sites. A later owner moved the house to the corner and built the brick garages underneath. Many San Francisco houses have had similarly peripatetic histories.

Immediately up the hill is a row of five houses, one Queen Anne and four Stick-style, all built by Fernando Nelson in 1897. The curiously shaped porch columns with their odd donut capitals were among Nelson's favorite signature details. The same man built seven more modest cottages on Liberty Street up the hill.

4 Liberty Street and Steps
· 500 block of Liberty Street
· Queen Anne cottages, 1890s; Art Deco flats, 1940s

Those who can navigate steep hills should alight at Liberty Street and see the peak-roofed row of cottages on the 500 block. Here is a prime example of a street of Victorian cottages built by a developer for speculative sale to prosperous "mechanics." They epitomize the first wave of tract-house building in California. The row of five houses at 563–77 Liberty Street were built in 1897 by John Anderson, contractor. Another row of five peak-roofed houses at 541–59 Liberty Street was built by Carlson and Anderson. The seven cottages with the gingerbread drips and donut capitals were built by Fernando Nelson. With their steep wooden stairs, fancy gingerbread trim, and flower-filled gardens they preserve the look of old San Francisco. Here even a repetitive house design is enlivened by the stepping-up-the-hill effect of this rugged terrain.

Walk up Liberty Street to Noe Street. The white Art Deco complex at the Liberty Street steps was built in the 1940s and is one of San Francisco's most ambitious Deco developments in any neighborhood. Climb the steps. Partway up, turn back to enjoy one of the most attractive views of this attractive city. White houses and dark green trees cover the steep amphitheater of hills. The red rock mass of Corona Heights to the north and the grassy slopes of Twin Peaks due west frame the horizon. Houses of every style, color, and shape merge into the distinctive San Francisco cityscape. All over these neighborhoods the stucco and asbestos-shingle "improvements" of a generation ago are being pried off, and Victorian and period houses are being restored to their original visual richness. Often the afternoon fog stands over Twin Peaks, keeping Eureka and Noe Valleys sunny and bright. From the top of the steps, San Francisco Bay and the Contra Costa hills appear to the east.

5 Rayburn Street to Twenty-first to Sanchez Street

Walk down Rayburn Street to Twenty-first Street. The top of the hill was sprinkled with modest, one-story cottages. Rayburn Street is lined with wooden garages and simple cottages. Walk up the slight incline of Twenty-first Street to Sanchez Street.

6 Twenty-first Street and Sanchez Street
· Panorama of downtown high-rises

At the corner of Twenty-first and Sanchez there is a sudden and spectacular view of the downtown high-rises with the dark Bank of America and white Transamerica Pyramid seen as a pair from this angle. To the left are the slender residential high-rises of the Pacific Heights ridge and the north bay beyond. The white peaked-hat-shaped structure in the distance is St. Mary's Roman Catholic Cathedral built in 1971. The red-tile-roofed church with the dome and towers rises in the valley next to a long, low, rectangular structure with a tile roof. That is the 1791 Mission Dolores (see Tour 4). The great green dome in the middle distance, modeled on that of St. Peter's in Rome, caps Bakewell and Brown's City Hall of 1915 in the Beaux-Arts Civic Center.

Rolph House
· 3690 Twenty-first Street
· Tudor Revival, c. 1913

The houses here are modest even if the view is extraordinary. Only 3690 Twenty-first Street, on the northeast corner of Sanchez, stands out. It is a tree-embowered Stockbroker Tudor house with a fine garden built about 1913 by San Francisco's beloved "Sunny Jim" Rolph, who served as mayor from 1911 to 1930 and then as governor of California. The large bronze fountain of Leda and the Swan is said to be from Florence. The stuccoed, slate-roofed house enjoys a good view of Rolph's City Hall below.

From the fire-alarm box on the southeast corner of the intersection is a view of Mission Valley below, Potrero Hill with its peaked-roofed cottages, the blue bay, Oakland, the Contra Costa ridge, and pyramidal Mt. Diablo, the highest peak in the region.

7 Hill and Sanchez Streets
· Panorama of Victorian district

Walk the one block at the crest of the hill to Hill Street. At 849 Sanchez, on the northeast corner, is a typical two-story streamlined stucco house of 1938 with porthole windows. Abstract modern stained-glass inserts show that even houses of this recent vintage have become prized possessions. Catercorner from this house, on the southwest corner, is a fine view to the south of the densely built Mission district. Two tall steeples punctuate the valley. The needle-like steeple in the distance belongs to St. Paul's Catholic Church, built in 1911. Its bells peal out over the quiet valley regularly. The wind and occasional distant trucks and diesel buses are the only other sounds heard atop this quiet hill set in the very center of the city. Hilltop parks—some forested, some open hills—frame the horizon. The forested peak in the center is St. Mary's Park Playground. The scattered trees and meadows beyond are part of enormous McLaren Park, the second-largest city park but little used. The largest mass of trees to the right (southwest) stand on the ridge this side of Glen Canyon Park.

8 Noe Valley Church
· 1021 Sanchez Street
· Stick-style, Charles Geddes, 1888

Walk down the hill toward the near steeple. On the southeast corner of Sanchez and Twenty-second Street is a typical two-story 1880s corner grocery building with a recessed corner entrance and a square-sided bay window placed at a 45-degree angle to the intersection.

At 1021 Sanchez is the Noe Valley church, a Stick-style church with a Gothic-style porch designed by Charles Geddes and recently restored. This part of the city and the Mission district have the oldest Victorian frame churches in San Francisco, since the fire of 1906 destroyed all the older churches downtown. This church is a handsome example. Though the woodwork seems rich to us, it is actually a plain building for its period, 1888. The detailing on the steeple is pleasant, as are the various kinds of fancy shinglework in the gable. This church was known as "Lebanon Presbyterian" because its steeple was said to be constructed of Lebanon cedar—if true, an extraordinary thing.

The wide streets and sidewalks and small houses along this part of Sanchez Street, plus the light colors and general stillness, lend this side of the hill a strangely pleasing bleakness—almost a serenity—that is the "feel" of San Francisco's myriad of clean, tucked-away neighborhoods. Behind these rows of buildings are small, green gardens, even more peaceful and remote from the hustle and bustle of the city all around.

9 Twenty-fourth Street Commercial Strip
· Victorian and turn-of-the-century commercial buildings

Twenty-fourth Street is the shopping strip for Noe Valley and includes a small supermarket, service shops, bookstores, galleries, restaurants, and cafés. It is a post-hippie, post-Vietnam, post-sexual-revolution zone with organic food, charts of the heavens and spiritual books, and imported gourmet foods. Young families and small children enliven the street. Browsing in these stores, scanning the flyers attached to walls and street poles, picking up the free neighborhood newspaper, and just watching and listening to the people here is a good way to see the new generation of San Franciscans (usually from somewhere else) who have committed themselves to living in the city. This is an urban migration as important, in a reverse way, as the shift of the poor into the central city after World War II.

Such has been the economic boom along Twenty-fourth Street that the City Planning Commission has had to prevent shops and offices from seeping up to the second and third floors of shops and apartment buildings along the street. This has prevented over-development and congestion along the street and also preserved socially valuable rental housing in the city. Virtually no one is building moderately priced rental housing in the city. This, plus the enormous profits from conversion of existing rental units to condominiums, has made rental housing an endangered species in San Francisco.

10 Noe Valley Branch Library
· 451 Jersey Street near Twenty-fourth and Castro
· Renaissance Revival, John Reid, Jr., 1916

One place to see this revitalizing migration by those who can choose where they live is the branch Public Library at 451 Jersey Street, one block south of Twenty-fourth and Castro Streets. This terra-cotta-clad Renaissance Revival jewel was paid for with part of the $750,000 given to the city for this purpose by steel magnate Andrew Carnegie. This fine public facility is only one of twenty-seven intimately scaled public branch libraries scattered throughout the city. Books, lectures, and films make it truly the "peoples' university." The work of some of the many, many neighborhood artists, painters, potters, photographers, etc., are exhibited here. At night, lectures and films attract the working people in the valley and make the library a vibrant community center. The recently assembled Noe Valley Community Archives are housed here. Twenty-fourth Street has several pleasant restaurants. To return to Downtown, take the #11 Hoffman bus east on Twenty-fourth Street to Mission Street and alight. Here you have your choice between BART, the modern subway, or several slow surface lines that run on Mission Street to Downtown and the Ferry Building. Twenty-fourth Street east of Mission Street has the city's widest selection of Latin-American restaurants.

Tour 11
Great San Francisco Interiors
Eight Architectural Gems

TOUR 11 ☐ GREAT SAN FRANCISCO INTERIORS

SAN FRANCISCO BAY

FERRY BUILDING

BAY BRIDGE

freeway

MARKET ST.

MISSION ST.

MONTGOMERY ST.

FINANCIAL DISTRICT

POWELL ST.

COLUMBUS AVE

THE EMBARCADERO

FISHERMAN'S WHARF

FORT MASON GGNRA

MARINA BLVD.

LOMBARD ST.

VAN NESS AVE.

GOUGH ST.

SACRAMENTO

CALIFORNIA ST.

GEARY BLVD.

FULTON

YON ST.

ARGUELLO BLVD.

PRESIDIO

TO GOLDEN GATE BRIDGE

UNION SQUARE

#47

#38

#5

#2

#69

#4

#7

#1

#3

#6

#8

#5

San Francisco Department of City Planning

MAJOR STREETS AND AREA NAMES   TRANSIT LINES AND UNION SQUARE

1 Hibernia Bank
2 Church of the New Jerusalem
3 Palace Hotel
4 City Hall
5 Temple Emanu-El
6 V.C. Morris Store
7 St. Mary's Cathedral
8 Hyatt-Regency Hotel

WHAT THIS WALK COVERS

The eight architectural gems presented here are scattered throughout the city and can't be visited in a single walking tour. Perhaps the best thing to do is to select the periods that most interest you and visit the interiors that exemplify them. Directions are given for reaching each site by public transit.

INTRODUCTION

Buildings are like shoes. The way the inside wears turns out to be more important than the way the outside looks. These publicly accessible San Francisco interiors present a chronological selection of the best of each surviving period of San Francisco building. Most are great in size; all are great in idea, intention, design, and effect. Each of these interiors speaks for a locally important era of design.

THE TOUR

1 The Hibernia Bank
- 1 Jones Street, at McAllister Street off Market Street (near Civic Center)
- Beaux-Arts, Albert Pissis, 1892, 1907
- Open Monday to Friday, 10–3, banking days

Getting there by public transit: Take any line on Market Street and alight at Jones Street.

Completed in 1892 on a prominent corner site just off Market Street, this steel-frame, granite-clad architectural gem was designed by Albert Pissis, the leading Beaux-Arts-trained San Francisco architect of his day, and was widely considered to be among the most beautiful buildings in San Francisco. The Hibernia Bank is one of the oldest financial institutions in the city and was founded in 1859 by John Sullivan and incorporated in 1864. The Irish Catholic Tobin family has historically had a strong interest in the Hibernia Bank.

This elegant Corinthian-columned bank utilizes its corner site dramatically, with a colonnade and dome sheltering the bronze doors of the corner entrance. It is a free-standing building; the granite façades on all four sides were originally white but have now weathered to gray. The well-built structure withstood the earthquake but was gutted by the fire in 1906. It was then carefully reconstructed and added onto (including the second, oval skylight inside) and has been perfectly maintained and preserved ever since. Walking into the high-ceilinged, opulently detailed banking hall with its extravagant plasterwork (the best in San Francisco), and beautiful stained-glass

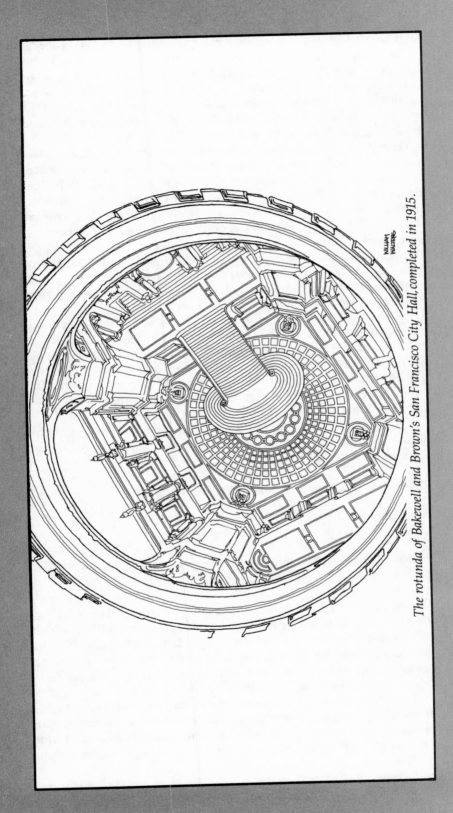

WILLIAM
WALTERS

The rotunda of Bakewell and Brown's San Francisco City Hall, completed in 1915.

skylights is like walking into San Francisco's fabled past. Few spaces in the entire city are as handsome, or as historically evocative, as this one. It is one of San Francisco's hidden treasures, waiting to be discovered in one of the city's least explored areas. The Hibernia Bank epitomizes the pride of the San Francisco-based banks and the truly extraordinary care with which fine old buildings are maintained to serve generations of history-minded San Franciscans.

The great banking hall has been painted a pleasing tan, gold, and pale mauve, which delicately accentuates the richly molded plaster-work. A frieze of shields and torches encircles the hall. The twin steel doors to the vaults on the north wall are framed in red and green marble. Above them, in the frieze, is a splendid clock with a sunburst design. The two skylights, one round and the other oval, glow with soft, pearly colors.

When everything burned down around this sturdy bank, the two gore lots flanking the bank were rebuilt with two sympathetic build-ings, the Shaw Hotel and 1072–80 McAllister, which frame the view of the bank from Market Street. This cluster of three buildings shows why San Francisco was fortunate to have the fire and rebuilding when she did; this kind of sympathetic, compatible building design is what was best about Edwardian city-building. Number 1072–80 McAllister, on the northeast corner of Jones, has strikingly propor-tioned, tripartite, Chicago windows on its two upper floors. The Shaw Hotel's green copper cornice echoes the Hibernia Bank's richly detailed dome.

On the northeast corner of McAllister and Jones is San Francisco's most delightful sidewalk flower stand, shaped like a miniature Mar-ket Street trolley-bus.

2 Church of the New Jerusalem (Swedenborgian)
· 2107 Lyon Street, at Washington Street (Presidio Heights)
· Tuscan Revival façade, A. Page Brown, 1895
· Open most afternoons, closed during weddings

Getting there by public transit: From Downtown, take the #55 Sac-ramento bus and alight at Lyon Street. Walk three blocks uphill to the church.

The simple brick exterior of this small neighborhood church gives no hint of the delights within. The arched façade is modeled on that of a village church near Verona, Italy. Half the lot consists of a pleasant garden with an olive tree, a cedar of Lebanon, and a redwood *(Sequoia sempervirens).* In one corner is an old Franciscan cross from Mission San Miguel in the Salinas Valley.

Enter the church through its modest portal. The interior, and what it says, is the work of Reverend Joseph Worcester, a Swedenborgian minister from Massachusetts with a love for California nature. Inside the church there is the sense of the forest. Madrone-trunk roofbeams from Santa Cruz brace the ceiling. Large oil paintings of California forests by William Keith line one wall. The scent of the wood burnt in the fireplace lightly perfumes the air. There are a few green plants, and, over the altar, a bristlecone pine from the Sierras, earth's longest-lived tree. The two softly glowing stained-glass windows by Bruce Porter depict water. The round window in the gable shows a dove perched on a fountain. The blurry, beautifully colored mystical window on the side wall shows St. Christopher carrying a glowing child across a blue river.

The fine chairs, designed by young Bernard Maybeck, son of a woodcarver, combine the sense of solidity desired in the 1890s with the Arts and Crafts aesthetic. Made of hard, satin-finished maple, and tule rushes from the Sacramento Valley, these chairs are both comfortable (always important in a chair!) and beautiful. Sturdy, and with low backs, the chairs seem almost a lesson in the enduring religious virtues. And, like a religious congregation, they are more as a group than they are as individuals. The chairs are designed to fit together in compact rows, pewlike. When gently pushed together they "click" like billiard balls.

This church, with its warm, intimate, lodgelike feeling, is San Francisco's favorite wedding chapel. Nature—the seacoast, forests, mountains, and deserts—is where most Californians worship. Joseph Worcester brought the power and beauty of the forest into this modest but artistic city church, using the best talents of turn-of-the-century San Francisco.

3 Palace Hotel
· Market Street at New Montgomery Street (downtown)
· Beaux-Arts, Trowbridge and Livingston, 1909
· Open always

Getting there by public transit: Any Market Street line will take you to the Palace.

The old Palace Hotel that stood on this site from 1873 to the fire of 1906 was *the* hotel in San Francisco and the West. It claimed to be the biggest in the world when it opened with 755 rooms (in a city of 250,000 people). The building was a seven-story hollow brick rectangle with a glass-roofed Grand Court. The Crystal Roof Garden, just beneath the glass skylight, was alive with flowers and permitted a view down into the court where carriages entered to deposit guests.

William Ralston, the head of the Bank of California, was the splashy investor behind this grand hotel. He had his chief architect, John P. Gaynor, travel to see other great hotels before designing the bay-windowed extravaganza that became the biggest building in San Francisco. Unhappily, Ralston drowned five weeks before the Palace opened in 1875. William Sharon took over the hotel.

The great hotel was part of a larger real-estate scheme of this enterprising buccaneer banker. Ralston watched the Financial District shift south down Montgomery Street to Market and formed a syndicate that secretly purchased lots south of Market, across from the foot of Montgomery. They cut their own street, New Montgomery Street, from Market to Mission and put the front door of the Palace Hotel not on Market Street but on their own New Montgomery Street. The plan did not work out, however. The big hotel blocked the movement of prestige uses down New Montgomery and became the edge of the downtown district, not the generator of an expansion of the core across the Market Street line.

It was written in 1878 that "If you wish to hide from an enemy who dwells at the Palace, the safest thing to do is to board there yourself. There is slight chance of your ever meeting him. . . . It is annexing a state to get a bedroom." California's and the West's magnates all gravitated to the Palace, especially during the winter social season. From May to September, San Francisco high society moved *en bloc* to the great resort hotels, particularly the now-lost Del Monte Hotel built by the Southern Pacific Railroad on the Monterey peninsula, and vacationing Easterners filled the Palace. (Today the Del Coronado Hotel of 1886 in Coronado, near San Diego, is the last great Victorian seaside resort hotel in California.)

In the 1890s the two top floors of the Palace housed millionaire regular residents. Dinners at the Palace were lavish and endless, featuring Pacific oysters, salmon, bass, shrimp, mountain quail, duck, venison, even grizzly-bear steaks. State banquets were served on the renowned Palace gold service. The Palace Grill was one of the city's most famous institutions. As one newspaper noted, "Here hobnob the European nobleman or celebrated scientist, the great stars of the stage and the world of music." Enrico Caruso, for example, was a guest at the Palace the morning of the earthquake of 1906. The panic-stricken Caruso ran out of the hotel in a towel, carrying an autographed picture of President Theodore Roosevelt and vowing never to return.

The fire gutted the grand hotel, though its steel-reinforced brick walls survived. The old walls were razed and a new structure was built atop the old brick water reservoir under the basement. A new $10 million grand hotel with a stunning, glass-roofed interior court and a sober, light Milwaukee brick exterior was designed by Trowbridge and Livingston of New York City. Young George Kelham, an architect who was to leave his signature in San Francisco with landmarks such as the Russ Building on Montgomery Street, was sent out west to supervise the construction.

At 1:00 P.M. Thursday, December 17, 1909, the doors of the new Palace were unlocked for the first time; the key was attached to four balloons, which carried it away. It was a declaration that the doors to the great hostelry would "remain open for all time." Every corridor was converted into a dining room to accommodate the 1,469 diners on opening night; the hotel's loyal clientele filled it to overflowing. Once the new Palace was open, there was an agreed-upon feeling that the city was back from the ashes. (The Fairmont had reopened on April 19, 1907, and the St. Francis Hotel on Union Square reopened that November.)

The new hotel replaced the traditional Grand Court with the glass-roofed Garden Court (originally the Palm Court), sometimes called the most elegant room in San Francisco. The room is 120 feet long, 85 feet wide, and 45 feet high. The pillars are covered with scagliola, plaster painted in imitation of marble, and the ceiling is hung with crystal chandeliers. The best way to experience this great room is to attend its lavish Sunday buffet brunch served from 10:30 A.M. to 2:30 P.M. While the cuisine is not what it was in the Edwardian age (Green Goddess dressing was invented here), the setting is still the same.

The most historic event in the Garden Court was Woodrow Wilson's famous, if ill-fated, League of Nations speech. And, on August 2, 1923, President Warren G. Harding died at the Palace while still in office. The last king of Hawaii also died at the Palace.

The other famous room in the Palace is the Pied Piper Room, with its large Maxfield Parrish mural of the Pied Piper of Hamelin and his sprightly entourage. (Parrish had previously painted the famous mural of Old King Cole in New York's Knickerbocker Hotel, now in the St. Regis.) The bar was an ice-cream parlor during Prohibition.

The third room of the Palace of architectural interest is the richly wood-paneled Happy Valley Bar, a fine masculine Edwardian interior, dim and inviting. Its name commemorates the small valley in the sand dunes on this spot, where pioneers built small frame cottages in the 1850s.

In 1937 there was a famous eighty-seven-day strike at all of San Francisco's best hotels in an attempt to unionize this important San Francisco industry. The strike failed, but during World War II the Palace, Fairmont, Mark Hopkins, and St. Francis Hotels were declared essential war industries, and unionization and the five-day workweek were introduced.

In 1973 the Palace was purchased by Kokusai Kogyo of Japan, and it is now managed by Sheraton Hotels. Historical collections, including old photos, and part of the famous solid-gold service, are displayed in cases along the hotel's principal corridor, which parallels New Montgomery Street.

4 City Hall
· Polk Street between McAllister and Grove Streets (Civic Center)
· Beaux-Arts–Renaissance, Bakewell and Brown, 1915
· Open business hours

Getting there by public transit: The #5 McAllister on Market Street passes City Hall. Alight at Polk Street.

The great domed City Hall, completed in 1915, is the centerpiece of San Francisco's Beaux-Arts Civic Center of municipal, state, and federal office buildings. The 1906 earthquake reduced the old City Hall (which stood where the Main Library is today) to picturesque ruins. At the same time, a strong wave of civic reform ousted the corrupt, boss-ridden municipal government, and the city began with a clean slate.

Great plans were made for a monumental municipal complex, and in January, 1912, an $8.8 million bond issue was approved by the voters at the urging of the new reform mayor, James Rolph, Jr., known to everyone as "Sunny Jim." Rolph was to continue as mayor from 1911 to 1930 when he was elected governor of California. Under his long administration a vast number of public buildings were built: schools, hospitals, libraries, fire and police stations, and many other civic facilities. All were characterized by excellent design and honest construction. The City Hall, the most important symbol of the new city, was the finest of all. In 1916 *The Architect,* a journal published in San Francisco, called it "the greatest architectural triumph of the greatest building period San Francisco has ever seen, a period not merely of rebuilding but of better building." When Rolph died in 1934, he lay in state under the dome he built.

A competition with a $25,000 first prize was announced limited to San Francisco architects. Bakewell and Brown's design was chosen over seventy-two other entries. Arthur Brown, Jr., had trained at the École des Beaux-Arts in Paris; his design is usually described as French Renaissance in style, but it could just as well be called American Renaissance. It was the highlight of the City Beautiful Movement in San Francisco. Christopher H. Snyder was the engineer, and John Galen Howard, Frederick H. Meyer, and John Reid, Jr., were the consulting architects. Jean Louis Bourgeois designed most of the interiors, and the sculptures in the pediments were carved by Henri Crenier, both also trained at the École des Beaux-Arts.

The City Hall is a rectangle 400 feet long and 300 feet wide, consisting of two office wings with central light courts joined by a 301-foot-5½-inch-high lead-clad copper dome capping a 186-foot-6-inch-high ceremonial rotunda within. There are actually three domes—the exterior one, the coffered one with the central "eye" seen from inside the rotunda, and an inner dome between these two with the cartouche depicting a ship visible through the "eye." The building has a steel frame under its exterior of gray granite from Raymond, California. The lofty dome, which rises higher than that of the national capitol, rests on four 50-ton and four 20-ton girders. The dome proper begins 191 feet above ground level, and its diameter at that point is 86 feet. A ring of free-standing Doric columns surmounted by tall urns surrounds the drum of the dome on the exterior. A slender steeple crowned with a torch caps the dome. When the city council is in night session, the light in the lantern is lit.

The École des Beaux-Arts, while often thought of as merely training its students in correct Classical- or Renaissance-inspired ornament, actually provided an education in spatial planning as much as in symbols. Brown arranged the building's functions with a deliberate purpose. Once inside the building the citizen is flanked by his responsibilities: to the south is the Tax Collector, and to the north is the Registrar of Voters. Above this ground-floor material and political base are the three branches of the municipal government: Straight ahead, up the grand staircase that rises from the center of the rotunda, is the chamber of the Board of Supervisors, the eleven-member city council. The windows of the supervisors' chamber face the neighborhoods to the west. Paired with this great room is the mayor's office on the east, or downtown, side of the building's second floor. Above the "political" branches, on the third floor, are the municipal courts and the law library. Brown's arrangement gives pride of place to the legislative branch but also clearly expresses the role of the executive and judicial branches. This is not just architecture; it is a civics lesson. Surrounding the organs of government is the city bureaucracy. At the center of everything is the great public rotunda. The first landing of the grand staircase serves as the city's municipal stage for inaugurations, ceremonial occasions, and, on election night, as the place where vote tallies are officially announced.

In contrast to the sober Doric columns of the exterior, the rotunda is ornamented with elaborate Corinthian capitals with their leafy exuberance. The interior of the rotunda is faced with light-colored Indiana sandstone and is paved with light-pink Tennessee marble. The splendid branched electric torchères and florid railings were executed in iron and bronze by Leo J. Myberg and are perhaps the finest metalwork in the city. Over the sunburst clock on the east wall is a figure of Father Time facing a torch-bearing youth and the inscription, "San Francisco, O Glorious City of our Hearts that hast been tried and not found wanting, Go thou with like spirit to make the future thine."

The ceremonial entrance to City Hall is on the Polk Street, or downtown, side. The mayor's office opens onto a second-floor balcony overlooking the two-block-square Civic Center Plaza. The pediment on this side is ornamented with an allegorical group carved by Henri Crenier showing San Francisco flanked by the riches and resources of California to one side and Commerce and Navigation on the other. The pediment on the Van Ness Avenue side, which faces the setting sun, depicts Wisdom flanked by Arts, Learning, and Truth on one side and Industry and Labor on the other. At the building's dedication one speaker urged the municipal government "to try to rise to its surroundings," a lofty ideal indeed. Perhaps more than any other building, City Hall embodies the pride of San Francisco.

5 Temple Emanu-El

· Lake Street and Arguello Boulevard (Presidio Heights)
· Byzantine Revival, Schnaittacher and Bakewell and Brown, 1926
· Open Monday to Friday, 9–5

Getting there by public transit: From Downtown take the #55 Sacramento bus and alight at Arguello Boulevard.

The history of the Jews in San Francisco is an important and happy one. They came to San Francisco with the first steamers of the Gold Rush era and have flourished with the city's growth, which they in no small measure stimulated. Migrants came from the Eastern seaboard and the interior and from Bavaria, France, Alsace, Poland, England, and Russia. They came to a growing city which, while by no means free from prejudice, was relatively open. Here various congregations were organized, as with Roman Catholic parishes, often along ethnic lines. The first synagogue, Temple Emanu-El ("God is with us"), was formed in 1850 by Bavarian-born German-speaking Jewish merchants. These men were sons of the liberal tradition of progressive nineteenth-century German Judaism, and Temple Emanu-El pursued the reform of Jewish ritual and the harmonizing of traditional Jewish values with secular American culture. With prosperity came a strong and continuing tradition of philanthropy, first to specifically Jewish institutions (burial society, orphanage, schools, hospitals, etc.), and then, by the second generation, to the city as a whole, as important supporters of civic causes and patrons of cultural institutions. The history of the Jew in San Francisco is one of responsibility and generosity toward the city.

The stately temple with the great red-tile-covered dome at Lake and Arguello Streets was built in 1926 to replace the onion-domed synagogue at 450 Sutter Street downtown that burned in 1906. (Miller and Pfleuger's Mayan-Deco, bay-windowed Medical-Dental skyscraper of 1929 now occupies that site.) The congregation moved from the downtown Union Square area to Presidio Heights, near Pacific Heights and not too far from Seacliff, the city's wealthiest neighborhoods.

With a lot, defined needs (for classrooms, offices, rabbi's study, auditorium, etc.), and a desire for a sumptuous building, the trustees of the congregation turned to Sylvain Schnaittacher and Bakewell and Brown, associated architects; the hand of Arthur Brown, Jr., was the important one; he designed the City Hall, Opera House, Coit Tower, and many of San Francisco's other important buildings between 1915 and the 1930s.

Brown's inspiration was the dome and sublime massing of Justinian's Hagia Sophia in Constantinople. The Arguello Boulevard elevation best conveys this historic recall. Another important influence in the design of the temple was the memory of the courtyards and cloisters that linked together the massive buildings of the Panama-Pacific International Exhibition of 1915. Temple Emanu-El is like one single "cell" (cloister and great domed building) from that world's-fair megastructure. (Of the Panama Pacific International Exposition, the only remnant is a concrete replica of Bernard Maybeck's Palace of Fine Arts [see Tour 3], with its massive free-standing colonnade and rotunda.)

The desire for a grand building within a $1.2 million budget ruled out granite or marble, which were preferred, and mandated the use of steel frame and reinforced concrete with cement stucco—the best building material for large structures in earthquake country. The terra-cotta-tile roof harmonizes well with this material. To Brown, the dome surpassed all other architectural forms in impressive nobility and beauty. "It is," he wrote, "most appropriately used when men wish to give material form to their most exalted sentiments." Once the dome was decided on, the cloistered court followed, since it gave Brown the opportunity for a powerful contrast and play of masses. The dome was imposing; the temple has a volume larger than the Paris Opera and seats more than 1,700 people.

The cloistered court and its fountain set the House of God apart from the outside world, and yet link it to it. In the courtyard is a mosaic Star of David with symbols of the twelve tribes of Israel, and olive, fig, date, and cypress trees. From the court the front of the temple with its nichelike portal rises majestically to make a truly powerful architectural effect. A huge bronze lamp hangs in the niche above the doors. It is the *Ner Tamid* and burns continually as a symbol of God's eternal presence in the midst of His people. The play of light and shade across this entrance was eagerly studied by Brown.

Passing through the great portal, one enters the low, vaulted vestibule painted like a starry sky. This transitional social space links and separates the sky-covered court outside from the soaring dome within.

Entering the sanctuary, the worshipper has his attention immediately focused on the gilt-bronze and cloisonné enamel Ark, which contains the scrolls of the Torah, the first five books of the Bible. A soaring canopy with green marble columns shelters and frames the Ark. As Brown expressed it, "The austerity of the surrounding walls and vaults, depending on their form and proportion alone to give them beauty, serves as a contrasting foil to the splendors of the Ark itself." Flanking the Ark are two seven-branch candelabra, the menorahs, symbolizing the six days of creation and the Sabbath. There are two pulpits, the lower one for preaching and the higher one for reading from the Torah. Behind the pulpits are a Skinner organ and a choir loft which accommodates up to fifty singers.

The balanced motifs of the circle in the square, of the dome, and of the apse, govern the design and create exaltation, unity, harmony, and rhythm; a work of a distinctly religious character. To the south is the great portal with its lamp, to the north is the Ark with its holy book, and to the east and west are two contemporary stained-glass windows by California artist Mark Adams. To the east, where the bay is, is "Water"; to the west, where the sun sets, is "Fire."

6 Former V.C. Morris Store
· 140 Maiden Lane (off Union Square)
· Frank Lloyd Wright, 1949
· Open shop hours

Getting there: It's a half block east of Union Square.

Tucked into this narrow alley lined with small luxury shops is Frank Lloyd Wright's only work in San Francisco, the complete transformation of a 1911 structure. Seen from the narrow side street of Maiden Lane (once an infamous nest of brothels), the 46-foot-wide, 32-foot-high façade of tawny Roman brick invites the passerby to enter its one emphatic, semicircular-arched entrance. A short glass-walled tunnel lets one look inside even when the shop is closed.

The brickwork of the arch is set in concentric bands that make the entrance seem like an aura (the same effect achieved by Gothic cathedral portals). But the beautifully detailed façade is modern in spirit and method. Wright incorporated electric lights in the façade in a row of square white plastic-covered lights along the bottom with a Greek key design, in hidden lights behind the latticelike brickwork along the edge of the façade, and in a (now cemented over) three-quarter circle of lights set under glass in the sidewalk at the entrance. This careful use of light makes the façade attractive at night to strollers. Wright's signature appears in a square red tile set in the lower left-hand corner of the façade.

This façade, even if it stood all alone, would rank among the most important architectural designs in this architecturally creative nation. Its broad unadorned expanse, so artistically treated at entrance and edges, is one of Wright's most direct references to the great Louis Sullivan, Wright's teacher, whom he always referred to as *"lieber meister."* The façade recalls the fine handful of small-town banks that Sullivan designed in the last years of his tragic career. The use of simple planes and controlled ornament also testifies to the important influence of the Viennese Secession. The semicircular arched entry with its impost return is also a recall of the strong-looking designs of Henry Hobson Richardson, Sullivan's teacher. Here is a façade rich with references to American architectural history, but at the same time wholly new.

But the real surprise waits inside. Within this small, roughly cubic shop Wright's genius created unexpected grandeur—a true jewel of American architecture, and one of the best works from the often-uninspired late 1940s. Inside the two-story-high space Wright set a gently curving ramp that seems to rise weightlessly toward the translucent white ceiling of its own accord. The motif of the circle anticipated by the entrance is repeated everywhere, in round portholes, semicircular tables and low round benches, in the circular designs in the ceiling, and in a large round suspended planter. The V.C. Morris Store was designed to showcase china and crystal, round and globular shapes, many translucent. When filled with what it was so ingeniously designed to display, it seemed a room full of bubbles, light, and sparkle. The customer was smoothly led past all the stock in the store, and, from the top of the ramp, could look down on table settings to get an overall impression. Today it displays women's clothing, and sympathetic semicircular metal dress racks have been installed. The walnut furniture is Wright's.

The V.C. Morris Store has often been cited as a precursor of Wright's Guggenheim Museum in New York City completed in 1959. But the museum plans were published in 1946, before the construction of this shop. Wright also designed a house for Mr. Morris that was never built. In 1949, Wright unveiled a grand design for a concrete "butterfly" bay bridge at the San Francisco Museum of Modern Art. Wright's other completed works in the Bay Area include a hexagonal-modular house near Stanford University built in 1937, and his last major work, the futuristic Marin County Civic Center, constructed in San Rafael in stages beginning in 1962, after the architect's death.

7 St. Mary's Cathedral

· Geary and Gough Streets (Cathedral Heights)
· McSweeney, Ryan and Lee; Pietro Belluschi; and Pier Luigi Nervi
· 1971
· Open every day

Getting there by public transit: From Union Square take the #38 Geary bus and alight at Gough Street.

St. Mary's Cathedral's interior is no doubt the most important contemporary great space in San Francisco. Built in 1971, the prestressed-concrete hyperbolic parabolioid arches of its great 190-foot-high, Greek-cross-shaped cupola are a steel-and-concrete masterpiece.

The previous St. Mary's, built on Van Ness Avenue in 1887–91, burned down during the heyday of massive "urban renewal"—the complete demolition of old districts and changes in their use. Geary Street, which had always had the main streetcar line from the downtown straight west, was widened and made into a major automobile artery. On the southwest corner of Geary and Gough, the crest of the hill, the Redevelopment Agency built a new supermarket. Archbishop McGucken knew he wanted the new cathedral on a hilltop, so the new market was relocated to Eddy and Laguna Streets and the commanding site was sold to the church. The city also permitted a block of O'Farrell Street to be vacated to make the cathedral even more visible from downtown.

The huge two-block parcel is cleverly designed. Most people think only the cathedral occupies the site, but in reality a large courtyarded high school, a rectory, and a convent, along with a large auditorium beneath the cathedral, are tucked underneath and behind this $12 million complex. Its construction took five years.

The cathedral is credited to a local firm, McSweeney, Ryan, and Lee, but two other designers were really responsible for this fine design. Pietro Belluschi of Boston, Italian by birth and engineer by training, formed the concept of a Greek cross within a square that later became the design for the new cathedral. Belluschi's bold design called for an engineer of genius, and Pier Luigi Nervi of Rome, one of the master designers of the twentieth century, was called in as a consultant and visited the site twice. Nervi, also by training an engineer, fused the mathematical and the aesthetic in reinforced-concrete structures he called "stone in motion." The lightness and grace with which this cupola leaps from its four 15-by-24-foot sculptured piers proclaims Nervi's genius. A mathematical model made possible a computer analysis of the whole structure. Looking up into this flowing, cross-shaped vault persuades the viewer of the elegant logic of its construction. It is a consummate expression of the modern age and of the beauty of its technological prowess. Asked at the cathedral's unveiling what Michelangelo would have thought of this building, Nervi answered, "He could not have thought of it. This design comes from geometric theories not then proven."

The interior arrangement of the cathedral was also new. The Second Vatican Council in 1962, as part of its sweeping liturgical reforms, turned the altar around and made the priest face the congregation. This new cathedral expresses those reforms. The austerely simple stone altar is raised up on a platform and is surrounded by pews on three sides. Except for a cross and a baldacchino of hanging aluminum rods, there is no decoration in the sanctuary. Richard Lippold's baldacchino is like a rain of light falling on the altar. The stained-glass windows are by Hungarian-born Gyorgy Kepes and were made in Philadelphia. The four narrow windows in the cupola represent fire (west), sky (north), water (east), and earth (south).

But certainly, after the baldacchino, the most splendid sculpture in the clean, modern interior is the glorious organ on its freestanding, sculpted pedestal. Even when silent this instrument is a visual song. Ruffati Fratelli, an old family firm in Padua, Italy, built the instrument. Mr. Ruffati and his three sons came here to install it.

The Second Vatican Council also encouraged an outward-looking attitude; in the design of the cathedral this is expressed by the large clear glass windows in the building's four corners. They give views of the city, and make the city part of the cathedral. The view toward the slope of Twin Peaks to the southwest is particularly picturesque.

Tucked into the south end of the site is a high school with three courtyards. Underneath the cathedral itself are a large auditorium and many meeting rooms. A square marble-paved corridor links together the ground-floor meeting rooms. The corridor itself is beautifully handled; the high quality of the building is evidenced in places such as these.

Leave the cathedral through the western door behind the great organ. From the terrace on the west is a fine view of the city to the southwest. The old skyline of small, pale-colored cubes stepping up the many hills survives here.

From the terrace on the east (downtown) side of the cathedral plaza, there is an interesting view of towers all around. The red-brick church was built in 1880 for St. Mark's Lutheran congregation and is a typical example of the use of Romanesque forms for American city churches in the late nineteenth century. Also visible is the green copper dome of the City Hall, the finest ornament on San Francisco's skyline. Farther to the right are the Gothic spires of St. Paul's Lutheran Church, designed by A.J. Craft and built in 1894. Its lacy spires are among the most beautiful in the city.

A few summary observations on the cathedral can be made: Its plan, structure, and technology are better than its ornamentation. The interior is better than the exterior—and it looked even better before the installation of the first of the side altars in the handsome skylighted bays embarrassingly revealed the mediocrity—and worse —of this kind of contemporary "religious" art. Only Lippold's baldacchino saves the situation.

It is very much a building of its day—not only in its design, but in the fact that the sunken parking lot is far superior to the "plaza" and terrace (which should be open all the way around the cathedral). This is, in fact, probably the best parking lot in San Francisco. The plain, square, coffers of the poured-concrete roofs over part of the parking area directly and elegantly display the character of *the* contemporary building material. When free of automobiles these are handsome, abstract spaces, a purely Cartesian world of well-proportioned grids.

8 Hyatt-Regency Hotel
· Foot of Market Street at the Embarcadero (Embarcadero Center)
· John Portman & Associates, 1973
· Open always

Getting there by public transit: From Union Square take any cable car going north on Powell Street to Powell and California. Transfer to an eastbound (downtown) #61 California Street cable car. Ride to the eastern terminus of the #61 California Street cable line.

The twenty-story Hyatt-Regency Hotel, with its seventeen-story-high great interior space, opened in 1973. It is one of five buildings in Embarcadero Center, part of the Golden Gateway Redevelopment Project. The chief developers were David Rockefeller and Associates and the Prudential Insurance Company; and the chief designers were Atlanta-based John Portman and Associates. The hotel occupies a prime site where Market and California Streets meet the Embarcadero. The terminus of the California Street cable line is on one side of the hotel and the historic Ferry Building with its ferries to Marin (Sausalito and Larkspur) is across the Embarcadero. The site alone cost the developers $11.5 million in 1966. The hotel cost some $50 million.

The hotel is roughly triangular in shape. The Market and Drumm Street façades rise conventionally from the street. The north side, however, slopes back at a 45-degree angle, giving the rooms on that side small balconies with views of the bay.

Enter the hotel at the California and Drumm Street corner and take the escalator up two levels to the spectacular lobby. This vast modern space is 300 feet long, 170 feet wide, and 170 feet high. Restaurants, shops, cafés, bars, sunken conversation areas, and contemporary art animate the skylit space. The focal point for the great space is Charles Perry's four-story-high hollow sphere of golden anodyzed-aluminum tubes floating in a reflecting pool. Perry was trained as an architect but works as a sculptor in Rome. There is also a running "brook" and a row of full-size *Ficus* trees in the space. The lobby should be explored and looked at from various angles.

The space is almost always alive with people and is continually animated by the five glass-cylinder elevator cabs gliding up and down the southwest corner of the space. Each bronze-tinted glass cab is decorated with 400 tiny lights. The view of the lobby from the moving elevators is spectacular. One elevator leads to a revolving restaurant perched atop the hotel.

The south wall of the great space is festooned with ivy that cascades from some seventeen stories of planters along the open balcony-corridors that serve the 840 rooms upstairs. Trees, shrubs, and flowers are all around. (Unfortunately, the narrow skylight does not admit enough light for the trees, and artificial-sunlight lamps have had to be hung over them. Even then there is not enough light, and the trees must be periodically rotated with boxed trees kept outdoors.)

The huge lobby dictated that the structure consist of a series of modified A-frames. And, since this site was originally part of Yerba Buena Cove, the structure rests on a thick concrete mat atop prestressed concrete piles.

The Hyatt-Regency Hotel is in the southeast corner of the Embarcadero Center built between 1970 and 1980. The four office towers that comprise the rest of the multiblock development are all linked together by landscaped podiums connected by pedestrian bridges. Shops and restaurants fill the sidewalk and mezzanine level. The upper levels of the podiums are bright and sunny and worth exploring. The contemporary art in the Embarcadero Center is of the highest quality and includes some of the best public art in San Francisco.

Tour 12

Fisherman's Wharf: Ghirardelli Square to Pier 39

The City Meets the Bay

TOUR 12 □ FISHERMAN'S WHARF

Jon Nix

MUNICIPAL PIER

FORT MASON

AQUATIC PARK

HYDE ST. PIER

PIER 43

THE EMBARCADERO

VAN NESS AVE.

BAY ST.

POLK ST.

BEACH ST.

NORTH POINT ST.

LARKIN ST.

HYDE ST.

JEFFERSON ST.

LEAVENWORTH ST.

COLUMBUS AVE.

JONES ST.

TAYLOR ST.

MASON ST.

POWELL ST.

STOCKTON ST.

KEARNY ST.

cable car

cable line

#60 POWELL & HYDE LINE

cable line

#59 POWELL & MASON LINE

400 feet

N

WHAT THIS WALK COVERS

Fisherman's Wharf is one of most visitors' first destinations in San Francisco. The former military, manufacturing, and fishing activities of this nineteenth-century waterfront area have been replaced with recreation and tourism, important industries in San Francisco. Imaginative conversions of red-brick factories, historic ships, and some interesting modern designs are the highlights of this walk.

PRACTICALITIES

Best time for this walk: Day and evening are lively here, about 10:00 A.M. to 10:00 P.M. Weekends are often crowded.

Parking: Parking here is exceedingly difficult. Best to take public transit. From Sutter and Stockton Streets take the #30 Stockton going north. Alight at Columbus and Bay to get to Fisherman's Wharf; continue five blocks more, to Bay and Van Ness, to start this walk. The #59 Powell and Mason and #60 Powell and Hyde cable-car lines also connect Union Square with Fisherman's Wharf.

Cafés and Restaurants: Culinary San Francisco is substantial sourdough bread, fine Napa Valley wine, and, from the second Tuesday in November to late May or June, succulent Dungeness crab. The clean, cold North Pacific waters from Moro Bay to Eureka yield an abundance of these tasty crustacea. From the Costanoan tribes who lived on bay shellfish and river salmon, to the Chinese shrimpers of the 1850s, to the Greek, Genoese, Neapolitan, Calabrian, and Sicilian fishermen who succeeded them, seafood has been the local gustatory treat. But, though every first-time visitor to San Francisco heads immediately to Fisherman's Wharf to savor its seafood, most of the city's best seafood houses are not on "the Wharf." The best seafood houses in San Francisco are:

—Swan's Oyster Depot (cold seafood and the best clam chowder, lunch only), 1517 Polk near California, also the best retail fish market and the sweetest crab.

—Tadich's Grill (130 years old and a San Francisco favorite), 240 California in the Financial District, worth the wait in line.

—Scott's Seafood Grill (new but excellent), 2400 Lombard at Scott Street in "motel row."

—Scoma's on Pier 47, foot of Jones Street at Jefferson, on Fisherman's Wharf.

—Sam's Grill (plain, but an institution since 1867), 374 Bush near Kearny in the Financial District.

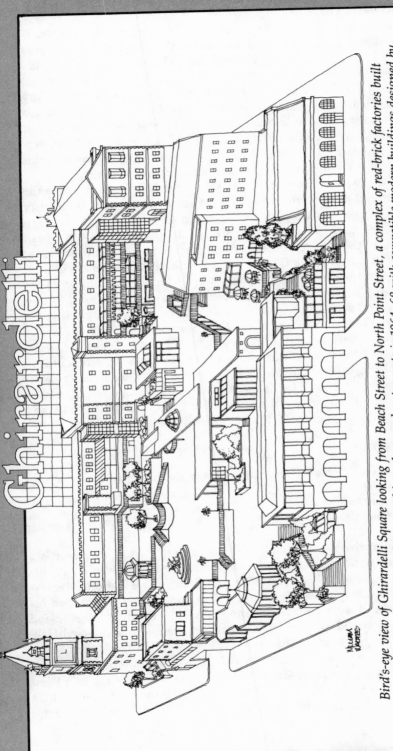

Ghirardelli

Bird's-eye view of Ghirardelli Square looking from Beach Street to North Point Street, a complex of red-brick factories built between 1864 and the 1920s and converted into shops and restaurants in 1964–68 with compatible modern buildings designed by Wurster, Bernardi and Emmons.

INTRODUCTION

Fisherman's Wharf was a colorful destination for nineteenth-century visitors to San Francisco. In those days a large fishing fleet was a significant part of the city's economy. The small wharf was surrounded by an early industrial zone of red-brick factories, metal sheds, and railroad yards. As these facilities were superseded by modern one-story plants beyond the city limits, these antiquated warehouses and factories were attractively converted into shops and restaurants to serve the growing number of visitors to San Francisco. Today the last bit of the real wharf is embedded like a fossil in this booming present-day hotel, restaurant, and retail district.

To the west of Fisherman's Wharf proper is Fort Mason, now the anchor and headquarters of the most important twentieth-century addition to the city's parks, the Golden Gate National Recreation Area. This park reaches around the Golden Gate, down the Ocean Beach, all the way to Fort Funston in the extreme southwest corner of the city. Across the Golden Gate, the GGNRA extends to Olema, more than twenty miles to the northwest. Much of this land was kept open as military reservations for the defense of the harbor. Military technology made such installations obsolete, so the army has given over vast tracts to the National Park Service starting in 1972. The GGNRA offers an extraordinary array of recreational activities. Phone 556-0560 for general information. There is an excellent free map of the GGNRA available at the Fort Mason headquarters with information about all the features of the park. The piers on the west side of Fort Mason are the scene of many fascinating events and organizations; phone 441-5705 for a daily recorded message.

THE TOUR

1 Fort Mason (Golden Gate National Recreation Area, Headquarters)
· Van Ness Avenue and Bay Street gate
· Victorian military housing and battery site

At the northwest corner of Van Ness Avenue and Bay Street is a small gate and the pedestrian entrance to the Fort Mason U.S. Military Reserve, now headquarters of the Golden Gate National Recreation Area. The massive gate to the fort and the red-tile-capped retaining wall were a project of the WPA in 1939. Enter the gate and walk up the sidewalk along MacArthur Avenue to McDowell Hall. It was the residence of the commanding general of the United States Army in the West from 1865 to 1943. It was the headquarters of the U.S. Army in the West during the subjugation of the American West from the 1860s to the 1880s. This frame building was begun in 1854 and has been frequently expanded. Its Stick-style appearance dates from the 1880s and is a rare survivor from its period. Today the building houses an Officers' Club, and a large, one-story addition has been built on the other side with dining rooms overlooking Aquatic Park and the bay.

Notice the beautiful palm and eucalyptus trees along the carriage drive in front of McDowell Hall. This is, perhaps, the oldest landscaping in San Francisco.

In the grassy circle in front of McDowell Hall is a granite block with a bronze plaque commemorating Colonel Richard Barnes Mason, after whom the post is named. Mason was the man who expelled the squatters from the reservation in the 1850s. Among those squatters was John C. Frémont, a one-time U.S. Army captain and leader of the Bear Flag revolt. Frémont had built a house on what was then Black Point with a commanding view of the bay. Colonel Mason expelled Frémont and pulled down the house.

California was a military conquest, and the first American government in the state was military. General Kearny, the first military governor, encouraged the occupation of the land by American squatters and settlers. With the exception of military reservations at strategic points, almost no land was put aside for public purposes. Within what eventually became San Francisco three large tracts were set aside for the military: Fort Montgomery downtown near the docks (eventually sold off), the Presidio on the Golden Gate, and what became Fort Mason on Black Point. As the reach of modern weaponry expanded, these in-town military reserves became strategically unimportant and eventually too expensive to keep. In San Francisco the military reservations have evolved into an informal extension of the city's park system. Along with their landscaping contemporary, Golden Gate Park, they shelter San Francisco's finest mature trees.

From the carriage drive in front of McDowell Hall is a view of the post's taut and economical frame structures. Visible to the west, with the forest of the Presidio as a backdrop, is a typical green-roofed, white-walled frame structure. Each army post in California developed a characteristic color scheme; Fort Mason's was white and green.

Walk up the sidewalk and driveway toward the cluster of small houses on Pope Street. (Along the way there is an excellent view of the apartment houses on Pacific Heights and the trees atop Lafayette Park.) This row of unpretentious frame houses constitutes an outdoor museum of California architecture since the earliest period of Yankee building in the 1850s. Number 231 Pope Street with the shingled skirt between its first and second floors is a simple Stick building. Number 232 is a much simpler and earlier Greek Revival house with considerable shed extensions flanking it. Here is the way California's frame vernacular architecture grows over time. Notice the interesting north wall of Number 231, with a large window in the stairwell. The giant eucalyptus tree in front of Number 232 is especially splendid, with an extraordinary girth. Number 235—the long, low building with the open porches—is a rare survivor, probably from the Civil War period. It is of a type usually found in the hot interior valleys of the state and was rare in the city where space has always been at a premium.

Across the street from these simpler houses are more pretentious ones built for the officers, which enjoy views of the bay. Brooks House Number 2, as the plaque in front of it says, was part of a larger structure built in the 1850s that was divided in 1864 and moved to this site for officers' quarters. In the nineteenth century, frame buildings were expanded and reworked, or moved—rarely demolished. Peek beyond the green hedge to see the house. It is a classic American frame building of great simplicity and beauty. It has been added onto over time, but always harmoniously. The simple color scheme—white with dark brown sash and green roofing—preserves the paint schemes of the nineteenth century. The house has Greek Revival or Carpenter Classic detailing. There is a superb view of Aquatic Park, the park's harbor with its small sailboats, and the great white ferryboat *Eureka* moored at the Hyde Street pier.

Turn back toward Number 235, turn right, and walk along the right-hand sidewalk under the trees. Walk to the wooden plaque that marks the spot of the Frémont home. Beyond the embankment to the left was the site of Batería San José, a fortification built in 1797 that boasted six small brass cannons. It was long gone by the Gold Rush period.

In 1863 this commanding bluff was terraced by U.S. Army Engineers for gun emplacements. These batteries were soon obsolete and were eventually landscaped as part of the post's grounds. Hardy cypress trees were planted on the embankments between the gun terraces to produce an intricate sequence of small pocket parks.

Continue straight ahead and descend the cement stairs. Walk toward the view of the Golden Gate Bridge to the left. From the bluff beyond the picnic area is a spectacular view of the Golden Gate and the bridge. Below are the red-roofed piers of Fort Mason's transport docks. A tunnel beneath the bluff connected these piers with the Belt Line Railroad and San Francisco's waterfront. As America penetrated the Far East, Fort Mason became the army's chief supply port for Alaska, the Panama Canal Zone, Hawaii, the Philippines, and East Asia. Officers and men embarked from here as the United States became a Pacific power. During World War II this was an important port for the Pacific theater: 1,644,243 soldiers and 23,589,000 ship tons of cargo poured through these piers during the war with Japan. Today the piers house a wide variety of community recreational and cultural activities and organizations.

2 Golden Gate Promenade
· View of bay, Golden Gate, and Aquatic Park

Today Fort Mason is the headquarters of the Golden Gate National Recreational Area, created in 1972 and administered by the United States Department of the Interior. This beautiful and vast new park system includes former military reservations, state and county park lands, and private land. The GGNRA includes all the waterfront from Fort Mason to the Presidio, and from the Presidio to the southwest corner of the city including Fort Funston. The Golden Gate Promenade is a 3.5-mile-long scenic trail along the bay shore that extends from Fort Mason to Fort Point under the Golden Gate Bridge. The promenade allows a spectacular view of the bay.

The Aquatic Park area, with its small attractive sandy beach, is a public improvement of the 1930s. In the late nineteenth century this was one of San Francisco's industrial districts and the waterfront was scarred with railways and debris. Starting in 1929 this scallop-shaped harbor was redeveloped and sand was trucked in for the beach. Fisherman's Wharf, which now lands more tourists than fish, lies to the east.

Across the harbor is the Hyde Street pier with its historic ships. In the far distance, beyond the piers and Fisherman's Wharf, rise the three masts of the sailing ship *Balclutha,* built in 1886 and open to the public.

Go to the pipe-railed walkway, walk down one flight of stairs, and follow the rail to the steep stairway at its end. From the head of the stairway, beyond the fence, is a fine view of the mid-nineteenth century officers' houses that stand on the tree-covered bluff.

Walk down the staircase to the street. Immediately to the left is the auxiliary pumping station, built in what can be called the Industrial Mission style, that is on constant standby to pump seawater into San Francisco's auxiliary high-pressure system of fire hydrants, built after the catastrophic fire of 1906. The building has four generous arches, a copper-and-red-tile cornice, and wrought-iron corbels as its principal ornaments.

Cross the street and look over the low stone wall. After the fire in 1906, much of the debris was dumped in this spot and is visible at low tide. The low wooden structure built out over the water is the home of the Sea Scouts.

Walk along the promenade toward the white streamlined building. Visible across the street is the entrance to the Belt Line Railroad tunnel under Fort Mason.

Visible over the grassy bank are the plastic-roofed bocce-ball courts, the favorite gathering places of old Italian-American men.

3 National Maritime Museum/Aquatic Park Casino
· Foot of Polk Street
· Streamline Moderne, William Mooser, Jr., 1939
· Open daily, 10–5, free, 556-8177

Despite industrial and railroad pollution, this area has attracted rowing, swimming, sailing, and fishing since the nineteenth century. Many of San Francisco's oldest swimming and rowing clubs are located in the line of gray and shingled buildings across the beach at the foot of Jefferson Street. They were fanciful late-nineteenth-century buildings with balconies and turrets; all have since been substantially extended and remodeled into simple boxlike shapes—the ultimate California architectural form. Only the roofs of the old buildings hint at what they once were.

In 1917 a group of San Franciscans organized to pressure the city into rehabilitating this part of the waterfront. In 1923 the state of California deeded the underwater lots beneath Aquatic Park harbor to the city. During the Depression of the 1930s the Works Progress Administration selected Aquatic Park as a public-works improvement. William Mooser, Jr., the branch manager for the WPA in San Francisco, designed the $1.8 million casino in 1939 and laid out the grounds in the Streamline Moderne style. The landscaping and architecture were integrated. The great, white casino stands like a ship moored on the land: it even has wind scoops on the roof. It is flanked by two large bleachers. Beyond the bleachers are two tall streamlined loudspeaker holders whose tops are shaped like the ends of the building. Beyond them, at the farthest points of the design and separated by the beach, are round combination rest rooms and observation decks—the men's room is far to the east and the women's room all the way on the other side. To create this attractive beach, a railroad whose trestle ran across the cove was moved to the broad esplanade. The bleachers were constructed so that spectators could watch swimming meets and sunbathe, but the waters of Northern California are far too cold for most people to swim in. The 5,000 planned-for swimmers never came. Only a few hardy souls, members of the local swimming clubs, actually swim here.

The ultramodern facilities of the Aquatic Park casino were described in the WPA Guidebook: "Each person returning from the water passes through a photo-electrically operated chlorinated shower and foot bath on his way to the dressing rooms and fresh water showers. He dries himself in currents of warm air and retrieves his street clothes from metal containers that will be sterilized with live steam before they are re-issued."

While the casino was never a success, the beach is. Children and dogs and strollers frequent the beach at all hours of the day. It is one of the most beautiful places easily accessible to the city dweller. The views of Marin county across the bay are extraordinary. It is a place for strollers, lovers, and all who wish to escape from the pressure of the city and experience the calm of the great bay.

The casino, without swimmers, needed a new function. It was eventually used for a senior citizens' center and, after 1950, for the Maritime Museum.

The National Maritime Museum is open every day of the week from 10 A.M. to 5 P.M. It is worth visiting both for its collection and for the casino itself. Walk around to the front of the building. (A ship's stern has been placed over the front door as the sign for the museum.) Every opportunity for architectural embellishment with nautical motifs was exploited. Even the terrazzo sidewalk in front of the museum has a wavelike design. The grayish, greenish slate which surrounds the front door was incised with shallow relief carvings by Sargent Johnson. Inside the buildings all of the walls of the principal space were covered with vividly colored undersea murals by Hilaire Hiler. The exhibits inside recount the long history of San Francisco's association with the sea. Ship models, maps, paintings, and photographs record the maritime life of the bay from the sleek clipper ships of the 1850s built for the New York–to–San Francisco run to the powerful steamships built to cross the Pacific. Only after World War II did San Francisco's port begin to decline. Today the major port on the bay is Oakland, where there is space for containerized cargo.

4 Ghirardelli Square
· Woolen Mill, 1864
· Model chocolate factory, William Mooser, Sr., 1893–1916
· Modern buildings and adaptive reuse, Wurster, Bernardi and
    Emmons, 1964–68

Across Beach Street is red-brick Ghirardelli Square. Rapallo-born Domingo Ghirardelli came to San Francisco via Peru in the 1850s and began a chocolate business downtown on Jackson Street. In 1893 his sons bought this block, which contained an old red-brick woolen mill built in 1864, one of the earliest factories in the West. Around this structure (placed at an eccentric angle because it was oriented to the original shoreline, not the street grid) the Ghirardellis began the development of a large chocolate factory. Architect William Mooser, Sr., the father of the man who designed the Aquatic Park casino, designed the new buildings here between 1893 and 1916. It was a model factory and exemplifies the personal pride associated with the best early-twentieth-century industrial design. The sturdy utilitarian buildings were constructed of brick and timber and trimmed with white cast stone. Eventually the complex ringed the entire block, with some lawn and trees in the center. One of the last buildings constructed was the powerhouse, now the Ghirardelli Cinema, on the northwest corner of the block. It is a simple but elegant brick structure with a row of eight generous arches marching across its Beach Street façade.

Cross the street, turn left, walk to the powerhouse, and walk up the red-brick staircase to Rose Court.

When the chocolate plant became obsolete in the early 1960s, it was threatened with demolition and probable replacement with high-rise buildings (such as the view-blocking Fontana Towers of 1962 to the west). William M. Roth, a civic-minded San Franciscan, bought the old jumble of buildings and decided to turn it into a complex of quality shops and restaurants. An underground parking garage was tucked below the site and a modern structure, the Wurster Building, was built on the Beach Street side. The arches of the Beach Street arcade under the Wurster Building repeat those of the old powerhouse. The architects for this ingenious conversion were Wurster, Bernardi and Emmons, and John Matthias. The landscape architects were Lawrence Halprin and Associates.

Ghirardelli Square exploited both accident and design to create a complex and delightful shopping space. From Rose Court, you see the north side of the 1864 Woolen Mill, where the Mandarin Restaurant is now. There is also an interesting concrete wall fountain in the court by Lawrence Halprin. Walk up the stairs to the left to the lower plaza. From the terrace you can see the happy blending of the old buildings to the right and the modern buildings to the left. Continue up the stairs alongside the Woolen Mill. Inside the Woolen Mill the old brick-and-timber interiors were retained; wooden columns support the floors above.

Continue up the stairs to the west plaza. The square is divided into two sections, a west and east plaza, with an information booth in a modern pavilion in the center. At the information booth, obtain a detailed map of the square, helpful in your explorations of this fascinating complex of specialty shops.

Walk through the east plaza to the delightful bronze fountain sculpture of the two nursing mermaids, by Ruth Asawa. This fountain, named "Andrea," was installed in 1968. The two mermaids are surrounded by tortoises, lily pads, and dancing frogs.

The square is the perfect blending of old and new; the old buildings were restored and adapted and the new buildings, while uncompromisingly modern, respect the color, appearance, scale, and texture of the old. The landscaping is informal and includes large terra-cotta pots of flowers and mature olive trees. Both the space and the landscaping have an intricacy and visual interest that turn everyone into an explorer. Even those not usually conscious of their architectural surroundings discover in Ghirardelli Square a place to learn about the potential pleasures of space and views.

The complex's two landmarks include the ornate 1916 clock tower on the southeast corner and the enormous electric sign that spells out "Ghirardelli" in beautiful lettering. The old electric sign was preserved and refurbished and ceremoniously relighted when the square opened in 1964. The clock-tower building housed the chocolate company's executive offices and was, as one would expect, specially treated. In the lower level of this building is the Ghirardelli ice-cream parlor, a perfect place to eat delicious ice cream and to inspect the antique chocolate-manufacturing equipment displayed in the back of the room. Built into the wall are three large cacao-bean roasters. There are also a series of belt-driven chocolate mills with granite millstones, conching machines, and giant mixers, *mélangeurs.* Of course, the chocolate made here is for demonstration only. The modern Ghirardelli chocolate factory is across the bay in San Leandro.

Leave the square through the metal-arched eastern gate, turn right, and walk up the hill to the corner. At the corner of Larkin and North Point is the elaborate clock tower designed by William Mooser, Sr., in 1916 and inspired by the chateau at Blois. In its vestibule is a mosaic of an eagle, the Ghirardelli chocolate trademark, and antique millstones set into the floor.

Cross Larkin Street to the heavily overscaled timber structure on the corner, Arthur Court Designs, 888 North Point. This complex timber construction of the late 1960s takes Northern California's traditional fascination with wood to mannerist extremes. It seems a combination Japanese pergola and timber pier.

5 872–80 North Point Street
· Garden and small galleries

Walk up North Point Street to the small cupola-topped doorway at Number 872–80. A tiny awning reads, "Antiques, Paintings, Decorative Arts." Hidden here, in what was originally only an alley and the backyard of a simple circa-1920 clapboard structure, is a landscaping jewel. Step through the Dutch door and descend the ivy-blanketed staircase to the right.

Here is a miniature Ghirardelli Square of art galleries and shops ensconced in some of the finest landscaping in San Francisco. The complex is open from Tuesday to Saturday during shopping hours. Like much of what is best about Northern California design, unpretentious materials and the love of plants have here been combined to produce an extraordinary environment. Decks, porches, and staircases are informally threaded across the backs of these ordinary buildings to create a venturesome system of circulation. The ground was paved with randomly set brick and stone. Potted plants are scattered about and vines were trained to grow along the walls and staircases. Savor the space—climb up and down its staircases, walk along the balconies, and peek into the painting and rug galleries tucked into the building. The sound of trickling water and the jungle of greenery transport you far away from the busy street outside.

6 Victorian Park
· Thomas D. Church, 1960

Leave this delightful and unpretentious San Franciscan oasis, return
to Larkin Street, turn right and walk downhill. Cross Beach Street at
Larkin and enter Victorian Park. Walk along the gravel mall toward
the small glass waiting pavilion at the end of the Hyde Street cable-
car line. The formal but open landscaping, comfortable iron and
wood benches, and elegant old-fashioned gas lamps belie the fact
that the park was built in 1960. It was designed by Thomas D.
Church with the advice of Karl Kortum. All of the one-time factory
and warehouse buildings across the street have been converted into
shops and restaurants.

Hyde Street Cable Rail Road Turntable

The glass and metal waiting station at the cable-car turntable is one
of the best modern park buildings in the city. It is simple and festive
and allows the old-fashioned cable cars to dominate the scene. Atop
the pavilion is a delightful weathervane of a mermaid looking into
a mirror and combing her hair. This fanciful weathervane is particularly appropriate in San Francisco—herself a sea creature much concerned with her appearance.

7 Buena Vista Café

Pass the cable-car turntable, leave the park, and turn right to the
corner of Hyde and Beach. On the corner is a curious pair of telephone booths, decked out to look like cable cars. The architectural
coherence of this intersection is truly remarkable. Across the street
is the famous Buena Vista Café—said to have introduced Irish coffee
to San Francisco—housed in the ground floor of a three-story bay-
windowed Edwardian building.

Hazlitt Warehouse
· Wharfside
· c. 1907

Diagonally across from the café is the old red-brick Hazlitt Warehouse built in 1907 by the California Fruit Canners Association. It
stands on the site of the Selby smelting works which operated here
in the 1860s. This smelter refined lead and much of the silver from
the Comstock Lode in Virginia City, Nevada. Old-fashioned black
cast-iron gas lamps line the sidewalk.

Fromm and Sichel Building
· Worley K. Wong, 1976

Opposite the Buena Vista and the Hazlitt Warehouse is the Fromm
and Sichel Building. This modern building combines the shape of the
Buena Vista with the red-brick material of the warehouse to produce
a bay-window-studded building that is both contemporary and re-
spectful of its two vintage neighbors. A pedestrian arcade was introduced along the Beach Street side of the building. Such careful stitch-
ing of a modern building into an old district is unfortunately all too
rare.
    Cross Beach Street at Hyde and enter the arcade of the Fromm and
Sichel Building. Notice from the arcade how the brick arches frame
the views of the red-brick warehouse across the street. The iron and
brass balustrades between the arches are especially luxurious
touches.

8 Wine Museum
· 633 Beach Street
· Gordon Ashby, 1976
· Open Tuesday–Saturday, 11–5; Sunday, 12–5; free; 673-6990

Walk down the arcade and turn right up the stairs to the Wine
Museum of San Francisco. This superb small museum houses the
Christian Brothers collection of historical and contemporary wine-
related artwork. Poetry, prose, painting, sculpture, glass, and silver-
ware devoted to wine or the grape fill this treasure house. It is among
the most civilized, literate, and artistic of museums. Wine, its charms,
its powers, have inspired artists since time immemorial. The museum
embraces all dimensions of wine: from the cultivation of the vine to
the consumption of wine in everything from Bacchic excess to sacra-
mental reverence. The collection is outstanding; particularly notable
are the rare drinking vessels and the glassware against the illuminated wall in the back of the gallery.
    Though the Franciscan missionaries introduced the Mission grape
to California in the eighteenth century, it was not until the arrival of
the Germans—and in particular one Hungarian, Ágoston Haraszthy
—in the second half of the nineteenth century that California's viticulture and winemaking achieved any sophistication. In 1861, a
state-appointed Viticultural Commission under Haraszthy scoured
Europe and sent back 200,000 cuttings and rooted vines of every
attainable variety to be found in Europe, Asia Minor, Persia, and
Egypt. These varietal grapes found congenial soils and climates in the
Golden State. In Napa and Sonoma counties north of San Francisco
Bay, dry red and white wines of the highest quality are produced. In
the Central Valley and in the south of the state, sweet bulk wines are
mass-manufactured.

The Bay Area probably has more sophisticated wine-drinkers per capita than any other part of the country. An ordinary corner grocery store in San Francisco will boast an impressive selection of local squeezings from decent jug wine to very good wines indeed. And the best wine shops, of which there are more every day, can satisfy the most discriminating palate and the deepest pocket. Try the wine shop in The Cannery if you try no other.

Almost every other kind of food and drink in the United States grows more homogenized and bland every day as processing destroys local specialties and traditions; in contrast, the Napa, Sonoma, and Mendocino wine-growing regions are continually sprouting small, new, and fiercely independent "boutique" wineries. Whereas wealthy Northeasterners buy fine sailboats, and well-heeled South-westerners run their own prime herds, the ultimate in prestige in San Francisco is to have one's own select winery and private label. Many of the very best California wines never leave the Bay Area and are enjoyed right here.

9 The Cannery
- California Fruit Canners Associations, 1909
- Remodeled Esherick Homsey Dodge and Davis, 1968

Leave the museum, cross the street, and enter the courtyard between the Hazlitt Warehouse and The Cannery. From the terrace at the top of the stairs is an unobstructed view down Columbus Avenue to the Transamerica Pyramid at the edge of the Financial District.

The olive-studded courtyard was originally the loading dock be-tween the world's largest fruit cannery on the right and the Hazlitt Warehouse on the left. The Cannery was built by the California Fruit Canners Association, about 1909. It was remodeled into shops and restaurants and is among the most sophisticated adaptive reuses in the country. It is essentially a modern steel-frame building built within the four concrete-reinforced walls of the old red-brick Can-nery.

Walk down the staircase, past the exterior elevator, and turn right into the white-pillared hallway. The illusion is quite successful: what appears to be the ground level of an old factory with massive mush-room-headed pillars holding up the floor above is, in reality, all new light construction made to look industrial. Indirect lighting hidden behind the vaulting turns what could have been an oppressive space into a light and airy one.

Walk down the hall to the small wooden kiosk. Around its base are six photographs showing the reconstruction of the building. The fifth picture shows The Cannery when only the exterior brick walls remained. Joseph Esherick is a gifted and witty designer who has quipped that the retention of the walls at least decided for him where the doors and windows would have to be!

Turn left and continue down the corridor to the courtyard at the heart of the building. The courtyard, too, looks like an adapted industrial space but is, in reality, a modern open space designed to look as if it had been randomly adapted over time. The giant metal star over the east entrance of The Cannery reproduces the design in the cast-iron plaques at the ends of the reinforcing rods that stud the exterior of the building.

Escalators carry the visitor to the top level of the complex, where shops are arranged along narrow pink-stucco-walled lanes reminiscent of a Mediterranean village. While an elevator and escalators hurry the shoppers upward, they must walk down. This makes people linger in the shops. The Cannery, like Ghirardelli Square, works with surprise and discovery in architecture.

Return to the courtyard and walk through to the Jefferson Street (Bay) side. A large movable glass wall protects the courtyard from the chilly northwest winds. Near this glass wall, to the right, is the Ben Jonson Restaurant. Beyond its lean-to-glass-and-canvas addition is the main dining room, paneled and furnished with some of William Randolph Hearst's European plunder. The dining room's interior was originally part of a 1609 Essex manor house, Albyns Hall. This 90-foot-long Elizabethan interior is the most interesting room in The Cannery.

Leave The Cannery, cross Jefferson Street, turn left, and walk half a block to the Hyde Street pier.

10 Hyde Street Pier Historic Ships
· Foot of Hyde Street
· Open daily, 10–5; summer, 10–6; free; 556-6435

The Hyde Street Pier was originally the terminus of ferry lines to Sausalito and Berkeley. In 1956 money from state tidelands oil royalties funded the beginnings of the Maritime State Historic Park and the restoration of a fleet of historic ships. The pier reopened in 1962 and is now part of the Golden Gate National Recreation Area. The entrance to the pier features large-scale nautical memorabilia such as anchors. The pier's sign once stood at India Dock. On the pier itself is a small ark, a cottage on a flat-bottomed barge, used as a summer retreat at the turn of the century. The ships include the black-hulled, three-masted lumber schooner *C.A. Thayer*, built in 1895, and the great white 1890 ferryboat, the *Eureka*. The small white scow is the *Alma*, built in 1891 at Hunters Point, and typical of the small, hard-working boats that carried California's agricultural abundance down the rivers and into San Francisco Bay to the city's piers and the hungry world beyond. Also in the collection is the gray-hulled 1915 steamer *Wampona*, and the 1907 tugboat *Hercules* with its red smokestack. Leave the pier and walk to Fish Alley north of Jefferson Street, between Leavenworth and Jones.

11 Fish Alley and Fishing Fleet

• North of Jefferson Street, between Leavenworth and Jones Streets
• Last piece of the real wharf

Though the restaurants and souvenir shops account for nearly all the activity along Taylor Street (the old fish wharf) and Jefferson Street, a tiny pocket of working fishing boats, timber wharfs, and simple galvanized metal sheds survives along the bayfront north of Jefferson, between Leavenworth and Jones.

Fishing boats with romantic names like the *Desirée* and the *Maria* tie up here for the night. There is the smell of the sea, the creaking of the moorings of the ships, and the cry of seagulls overhead. The warehouse of the Consolidated Fisheries is to the right, surrounded by enormous fishy-smelling packing crates. This short alley allows a brief glimpse of the last piece of San Francisco's real waterfront. Though the ships look modern, the industry is a living fossil. Large floating factory ships have made fishing fleets like San Francisco's industrial antiques. Highly profitable, high-volume restaurants and trinket shops would monopolize 100 percent of the wharf if public zoning powers did not preserve this small niche for the present-day fleet.

Architecturally, the split between the two fisherman's wharfs serves as a concise statement of the contrast between buildings as structures and buildings as images. As in an amusement park (which is what it is), the façades on Taylor and Jefferson Streets embody every "look" from red-tile-roof Mission, to stark stucco Modern, to decorated shed, to instant-antique pseudo-Victorian—everything, almost, except the corrugated gray galvanized-metal sheds which are the traditional California fisherman's wharf. Simple metal boxes (possible if the buildings don't need to be heated) are central to San Francisco's architectural and building history. Many of the earliest Gold Rush commercial and industrial buildings were prefabricated on the East Coast or in England and shipped to the boom town. Some of San Francisco's earliest buildings were high-technology, industrially produced structures.

The roster of family names proudly blazoned on Fisherman's Wharf's busy restaurants, names like Sabella, Tarantino, Scoma, Guardino, Alioto, Castagnola, and others, proclaim the virtual monopoly that Italian-Americans achieved in San Francisco's seafood industry. The hard and unpredictable work of fishing first drew northern Italians from Genoa, who comprised some 80 percent of the nienteenth-century fishing fleet. The Genoese captured the trade from the pioneer Chinese, developed the fleet, the operational structures of markets, and fish wholesaling. By the early 1900s, however, the northerners were superseded by Neapolitans, Calabrians, and most important, Sicilians, who continue as the most important group of fishermen, dealers, and now restauranteurs. The Italian-American fishermen cultivated a spirit of cooperation and camaraderie—*campagnismo*—which brought together fishermen from the same province against both the unpredictable elements and unpredictable competition. Specializations evolved, with the Genoese engaged in deep-sea tuna-fishing for the statewide California market while the Sicilians caught most of the freshwater and inshore fish for the San Francisco market.

Over some 120 years the progressive fishing-out of the bay, nearby rivers, and immediate coast has sent the fishermen farther and farther north. Today San Francisco's fishing fleet is only a pale, antiquated shadow of what it once was. Only the port of Eureka, far to the north near the Oregon border, harbors a substantial fishing fleet crowded around a genuine, working fisherman's wharf. The specialty landed there is the small north coast shrimp. San Francisco's fleet, tiny, old-fashioned, and still operated as small partnerships rather than large companies, is now only an atmospheric adornment to the restaurant district of modern Fisherman's Wharf. Long gone are the days when the colorful feluccas with their three-cornered red sails dotted the bay. No longer does the fleet return at sundown "like a flock of sea birds scudding on the wind to their roost." Today the Wharf is alive instead with visitors who migrate in seasonal shoals. Now automobiles are as plentiful as lateen-rigged feluccas once were. The business of the Wharf has changed from fishing to tourism.

Ever since the Gold Rush, San Franciscans and their guests have feasted on a gourmet catch of Dungeness crab, Olympia (Washington) oysters, king and silver salmon, bay shrimp (no longer fished for economic reasons), sea bass, rock cod, sand dabs, and rex and petrale sole. Such is the place of seafood in the city's culinary history that to this day the only proper, traditional, good-luck-inducing way for a San Franciscan to begin the new year on New Year's Day is with cracked crab and white wine. Visitors partake of San Francisco's favorite crustacean in walk-away cocktails first promoted by Fisherman's Wharf restauranteur Tomaso Castagnola in 1916. He apparently got the idea from the stand-up chowder stands that once served the fishermen and market workers, who had to eat on the run as they sold their perishable catch.

12 Restaurant Row
· Taylor and Jefferson Streets

From here to the east is an amusement park–like district devoted to wax museums, souvenir shops, and seafood restaurants that cater to San Francisco's twelve million visitors a year, who make this attraction second only to Disneyland in California.

13 The *Balclutha*
- Pier 43
- Square-rigged sailing ship, 1886
- Open daily, 9–11; $2; 982-1886

Walk down Jefferson Street past its shops, restaurants, and wax museums to Pier 43 and the black-hulled, square-rigged sailing ship *Balclutha,* built in Scotland in 1886 and restored in 1955. This 301-foot steel-hulled, three-masted sailing ship has had an eventful history. Her maiden voyage was around Cape Horn to San Francisco. Her first thirteen years were as a deepwater trader engaged in general trade between Auckland, Calcutta, New York, Rangoon, Capetown, and Callao. She carried wine and spirits from London, coal from Wales, and returning to Europe she carried California grain. In 1906 she was renamed *Star of Alaska* and spent a quarter of a century carrying workers to the Alaska canneries and salmon back to San Francisco. Scandinavian and Italian fishermen traveled under the poop, and Chinese cannery workers traveled 'tween decks. In 1930, when she made her final voyage north, she was the last square-rigger left in the salmon trade. After that the proud ship served as a carnival ship or showboat from 1933 to 1952. In 1954 the Maritime Museum Association bought the ship and, with a combination of private funds and labor donated by unions, restored its exterior and interior completely. A museum depicting the saga of the *Balclutha* has been installed 'tween decks.

14 Pier 39
- The Embarcadero, foot of Grant Avenue
- Walker Moody, 1978

This $54 million pier with its complex of restaurants, shops, and amusements brings to San Francisco Bay the tradition of amusement piers popular in California at the turn of the century. It is built in the contemporary wooden-shed style and works like an old-fashioned street in drawing the visitor down its length. There are interesting views of the bay and of the city from the marina-surrounded pier.

Alcatraz
- Pier 43
- Reservations necessary; $2; children $1; 546-2805/2815

The other side of the coin; a hell in the midst of paradise. A cold, clammy place of slow execution. First a harbor fort, later one of the cruelest of military prisons, then an infamous federal penitentiary of hardly less than medieval conditions. Its capacity was four hundred prisoners. Among those prisoners were Al Capone, Machine Gun Kelly, mail robbers Albert Bates, Gene Colson, and Limpy Clever, and the last great train robber, Roy Gardner.

Today Alcatraz is one of San Francisco's chief tourist attractions. Something stirs in the American psyche at the mention of Alcatraz: a memory of evil, of evil men evilly treated. The Devil's Island of the United States; an ineradicable blot of human crime and punishment facing a tolerant society; a grim machine of death. The silence once imposed on the inmates of the penitentiary has its eerie continuation in the automatic hush that comes over chatting sightseers as the visitors' launch approaches the landing dock of the uninhabited island.

Today Alcatraz, the wind- and fog-swept Island of the Pelicans of the Spanish explorers, is a bleak, peeling, stabilized ruin administered by the National Park Service and open to public tours. While the island is ugly architecturally, the views back to San Francisco are splendid. A visit to this shell of a human hell is deeply moving. As in a pilgrimage to the extermination camps of the Nazis, brutality overwhelms the thoughtful visitor. The sensation of having the windowless steel door of the solitary confinement cell closed while one stands inside is not an image of hell, it *is* hell. The tour includes the main cell block, solitary cells, and the recreation yard. "The Rock" was shut down by Attorney General Robert Kennedy in 1963. In 1972, Alcatraz was included in the Golden Gate National Recreation Area. The tour of the island takes two hours.

Index

Visitors Information Center, 15, 22

Walters, H. G., Warehouse, 79
Washington and Mason Cable Car Powerhouse and Museum, 227–28
Washington Square, 61, 62–64
Washington Square Inn, 9
Washington Street, 143, 208. *See also* Chinatown
Waverly Place, 206. *See also* Chinatown
Weather, 5–6
Wells Fargo Bank Headquarters, 109–10
Wells Fargo Dillingham Building, 106
Wells Fargo History Room, 20, 109–10

Whittier Mansion, 18, 143–45
Wine Museum, 21, 327–28
Wo Hop Building, 204
Woolen Mill, 324
Wurster Building, 324

Yee Fung Toy Building, 206
Yenching, 196
Yeon Building, 101
Yerba Buena Island, 73
Yet Wah, 196
York Hotel, 9

Zott's Restaurant, 107